BLACK An Introduction to
Electrical Instrumentation
and Measurement Systems

D1188780

Pl

An Introduction to
Electrical Instrumentation
and Measurement Systems

A guide to the use, selection, and limitations of electrical instruments and measurement systems

B.A. Gregory

Senior Lecturer Specialising in Electrical Instrumentation, Department of Electrical and Electronic Engineering, Brighton Polytechnic

Second Edition

MACMILLAN

© B. A. Gregory 1973, 1981

All rights reserved. No reproduction, copy or transmission of this publication may be made without written permission.

No paragraph of this publication may be reproduced, copied or transmitted save with written permission or in accordance with the provisions of the Copyright, Designs and Patents Act 1988, or under the terms of any licence permitting limited copying issued by the Copyright Licensing Agency, 90 Tottenham Court Road, London W1P 9HE.

Any person who does any unauthorised act in relation to this publication may be liable to criminal prosecution and civil claims for damages.

First published 1973 by
THE MACMILLAN PRESS LTD
Houndmills, Basingstoke, Hampshire RG21 2XS
and London
Companies and representatives
throughout the world

ISBN 0–333–29383–5 (hardcover)
ISBN 0–333–29384–3 (paperback)

Printed in Hong Kong

Reprinted 1975 (with corrections), 1977
Second edition 1981
Reprinted 1981, 1982 (twice), 1984 (with corrections), 1985, 1988, 1990, 1992

BLACKBURN COLLEGE
LIBRARY
Acc. No. BC 47314
Class No. ....
Date ....

Contents

Preface   ix

1. Introduction   1

   1.1   Methods of Measurement   4
   1.2   Display Methods   16
   1.3   Accuracy   22
   1.4   Input Characteristics   37
   1.5   Waveform   41
   1.6   Interference   49
   1.7   Selection   51

2. Analogue Instruments   53

   2.1   Moving Coil Instruments   53
   2.2   The Electrodynamic Instrument   97
   2.3   Other Pointer Instruments   103
   2.4   Energy Meters   113
   2.5   Solid State Indicators   114
   2.6   The Cathode Ray Oscilloscope   115
   2.7   Instrumentation Tape Recorders   134

3. Comparison Methods   146

   3.1   D.C. Potentiometer   146
   3.2   A.C. Potentiometer   155
   3.3   D.C. Bridges   156
   3.4   A.C. Bridges   166

4. Digital Instruments   186

    4.1   Counters   186
    4.2   Multi-function Digital Voltmeters   205
    4.3   'Intelligent' Instruments   215
    4.4   Hybrid Instruments   221

5. Transducers   234

    5.1   Resistance Change Transducers   238
    5.2   Reactance Change Transducers   255
    5.3   Semiconductor Devices   261
    5.4   Self-generating Transducers   264
    5.5   Ultrasonic Transducers   272
    5.6   Digital Transducers   272

6. Signal Conditioning   277

    6.1   Voltage Scaling   277
    6.2   Current Scaling   287
    6.3   Attenuators   294
    6.4   Filters   299
    6.5   Probes   308
    6.6   Modulation and Sampling   316
    6.7   Analogue Processing   319
    6.8   Digital–Analogue Conversion   329

7. Interference and Screening   331

    7.1   Environmental Effects   331
    7.2   Component Impurities   334
    7.3   Coupled Interference   341
    7.4   Noise Rejection Specifications   349

8. Instrument Selection and Specification Analysis   360

    8.1   Instrument Selection   360
    8.2   Specification Analysis   363

9. Instrumentation Systems   379

    9.1   System Design   379
    9.2   Analogue Systems   380
    9.3   Digital Systems   384

10. Problems and Exercises   398

    10.1 Principles   398
    10.2 Analogue Instruments   400
    10.3 Null or Comparison Measurements   404
    10.4 Digital Instruments   408
    10.5 Transducers   410
    10.6 Signal Conditioning   411
    10.7 Interference   413
    10.8 Selection   415
    10.9 Systems   421
    10.10 Answers   422

Appendix I: Units, Symbols and Conversion Factors   425

Appendix II: Dynamic Behaviour of Moving Coil Systems   430

Appendix III: Equations to Determine the components of a Resistive
   'T' Attenuator Pad   437

Index   439

Preface

Our ability to measure a quantity determines our knowledge of that quantity, and since the measuring of electrical quantities—or other parameters in terms of electrical quantities—is involved in an ever expanding circle of occupations of contemporary life, it is essential for the practising engineer to have a thorough knowledge of electrical instrumentation and measurement systems. This is especially so since in addition to his own requirements, he may be called upon to advise others who have no electrical knowledge at all.

This book is primarily intended to assist the student following an electrical or electronic engineering degree course to adopt a practical approach to his measurement problems. It will also be of use to the engineer or technician, who now finds himself involved with measurements in terms of volts, ampères, ohms, watts, etc., and faced with an ever increasing variety of instruments from a simple pointer instrument to a complex computer-controlled system. Thus, the object of this book is to help the engineer, or instrument user, to select the right form of instrument for an application, and then analyse the performance of the competitive instruments from the various manufacturers in order to obtain the optimum instrument performance for each measurement situation.

During that period of my career when I was employed in the research department of an industrial organisation I was, at times, appalled by the lack of ability exhibited by some graduates in selecting a suitable, let alone the best, instrument to perform quite basic measurements. Since entering the field of higher education to lecture in electrical measurements and instrumentation, my philosophy has been to instruct students to consider each measurement situation on its merits and then select the best instrument for that particular set of circumstances. Such an approach must of course include descriptions of types of instruments, and be presented so that the student understands the functioning and limitations of each instrument in order to be able to make the optimum selection.

There will undoubtedly be comments on and criticisms of this version and for those of the previous edition I am grateful. In this second edition, I have updated the material of the 1973 edition, taking into account the many changes that

have occurred in instrumentation during the past six years; I have also added
instructional problems (a deficiency of the first edition).

I have made appreciable rearrangements to the book, largely to accommodate
the changes in instrumentation that have resulted from the developments in
integrated circuits, such as the microprocessor, which has made possible programmable and calculating facilities within instruments. Hence, the general theme of
the book is to describe the techniques used to produce the various types of
instrument available and illustrate their description with examples of manufacturers' specifications. Unfortunately there is a limit to the amount that can be
included in a book of realistic size (and price). I have therefore omitted specialised topics such as medical instruments, chemical analysis, radio frequency
measurements, acoustic measurements and programming. The last of these topics
it might be argued should be included, for more and more instrumentation will
involve the use of programmable devices, be it the purpose-built microprocessor-
controlled instrumentation system, or the computer-operated system in which a
high level language is used. I would suggest that programming instruction is
better documented by the expert rather than by myself. To assist the reader
with difficulties of this and other kinds, there is a list of references for further
reading at the end of each chapter.

I would like to thank all the instrument manufacturers who have willingly
assisted me in producing this volume by providing application notes, specifications, reproductions of articles, and also their obliging field engineers. I have
endeavoured to acknowledge all sources of diagrams and other material, but I
hope that any oversights will be excused. I should also like to thank my
colleagues in the Department of Electrical and Electronic Engineering at Brighton
Polytechnic for their assistance and encouragement; in particular my thanks are
due to Doctors R. Miller, R. Thomas and K. Woodcock, for reading and comment-
ing on various parts of the manuscript, also to Brenda Foster for patience and
effort in typing the manuscript.

B. A. GREGORY

1

Introduction

Scientific and technical instruments have been defined as devices used in observing, measuring, controlling, computing or communicating. Additionally the same source* states that: 'Instruments and instrument systems refine, extend or supplement human facilities and abilities to sense, perceive, communicate, remember, calculate or reason'.

The principal concern of this book is to describe instruments and their attributes so that the magnitudes of, and variations in, electrical, mechanical, and other quantities may be monitored in an optimised manner for any measurement situation. Before describing any instruments in detail it is desirable to consider the questions that must be answered *before* making any measurement.

(a) What is the most suitable method of performing the measurement?
(b) How should the result be displayed?
(c) What tolerance on the measured value is acceptable?
(d) How will the presence of the instrument affect the signal?
(e) How will the signal waveshape affect the instrument's performance?
(f) Over what range of frequencies does the instrument perform correctly?
(g) Will the result obtained be affected by external influences?

These questions presuppose the possibility of being able to select an instrument without any restrictions—a situation unlikely to occur in practice where limitations of availability will be present, or if a new instrument is being purchased, financial restrictions are likely to apply. Thus, as in solving any engineering problem, a compromise between the ideal and the real will provide the solution.

However, so that the above questions can be honestly answered, the points they raise are discussed in the following sections.

Encyclopedia of Science and Technology (McGraw-Hill, London, 1971)

1.1 METHODS OF MEASUREMENT

When a measurement is to be made the procedures, instruments, inter-connections and conditions under which the measurement is to be made must be detailed or specified. On completion of the measurement a record of all the parameters relevant to these conditions must be carefully noted so that when it is necessary to repeat the measurement the original conditions can be faithfully reproduced.

Appreciation of the methods used in instrumentation and measurements can be assisted by categorising them into three broad groups under the headings of analogue, comparison and digital methods. It must, however, be realised that the developments in electronic engineering have resulted in an increasing mixture of these three basic groups to produce the most satisfactory instrument for a particular purpose.

1.1.1 Analogue techniques

Analogue measurements are those involved in continuously monitoring the magnitude of a signal or measurand (quantity to be measured).

The use of analogue instrumentation is very extensive, and while digital instruments are ever increasing in number, versatility and application, it is likely that analogue devices will remain in use for many years and for some applications seem unlikely to be replaced by digital devices; for example, it is possible for an operator to assimilate a far greater amount of information from a multi-analogue display (figure 1.1) than from a multi-digital display of the same information. However a gradual increase in the number of hybrid instruments does seem very likely.

A large number of analogue instruments are electromechanical in nature, making use of the fact that when an electric current flows along a conductor, the conductor becomes surrounded by a magnetic field. This property is used in electromechanical instruments to obtain the deflection of a pointer: (a) by the interaction of the magnetic field around a coil with a permanent magnet; (b) between ferromagnetic vanes in the coil's magnetic field; or (c) through the interaction of the magnetic fields produced by a number of coils.

Constraining these forces to form a turning movement produces a deflecting torque $= Gf(i)$ newton metres (N m), which is a function of the current in the instrument's coil and the geometry and type of coil system. To obtain a stable display it is necessary to equate the deflection torque with an opposing or control torque. The magnitude of this control torque must increase with the angular deflection of the pointer and this is arranged by using spiral springs or a ribbon suspension so that the control torque $= C\theta$ N m, where θ is the angular deflection in radians and C is the control constant in newton metres per radian and will depend on the material and geometry of the control device.[1]

The moving parts of the instrument will have a moment of inertia (J) and when a change in the magnitude of deflection takes place an acceleration torque

(a)

(b)

Figure 1.1. Multi-analogue display panels: (a) Mobil Aromatics Plant, Durban, South Africa; (b) panel being fabricated for Das Island LNG Plant (courtesy of Kent Process Control Ltd)

$(J\, d^2\theta/dt^2$ N m) will be present. Since the movable parts are attached to a control spring they combine to form a mass–spring system and in order to prevent
excessive oscillations when the magnitude of the electrical input is changed, a
damping torque $(D\, d\theta/dt$ N m) must be provided that will only act if the movable parts are in motion. The method by which this damping torque is applied
may be

(a) eddy current–where currents induced in a conducting sheet attached to the
    movement produce a magnetic field opposing any change in position.
(b) pneumatic–in this method a vane is attached to the instrument movement,
    and the resistance of the surrounding air to the motion of the vane provides
    the required damping. Fluid damping is an extension of this principle, a
    small vane then being constrained to move in a container filled with a
    suitably viscous fluid (see section 2.1.4).
(c) electromagnetic–movement of a coil in a magnetic field produces a current
    in the coil which opposes the deflecting current and slows the response of
    the instrument. The magnitude of the opposing current will be dependent
    on the resistance of the circuit to which the instrument is connected.

Combining the above torques, the equation of motion for a pointer instrument becomes

$$J\,\frac{d^2\theta}{dt^2} + D\,\frac{d\theta}{dt} + C\theta = Gf(i) \qquad (1.1)$$

which will have a steady state solution

$$C\theta = Gf(i) \qquad (1.2)$$

and a dynamic or transient solution of the form (see appendix II)

$$\theta = A\, e^{\lambda_1} + B\, e^{\lambda_2} \qquad (1.3)$$

where A and B are arbitrary constants and

$$\lambda_1 = \frac{-D}{2J} + \left(\frac{D^2}{4J^2} - \frac{C}{J}\right)^{\frac{1}{2}} \qquad (1.4)$$

and

$$\lambda_2 = \frac{-D}{2J} - \left(\frac{D^2}{4J^2} - \frac{C}{J}\right)^{\frac{1}{2}} \qquad (1.5)$$

For a particular instrument C and J are fixed in magnitude during manufacture,
but D (the amount of damping) may be varied. This results in three possible
modes of response to a transient

(a) when $D^2/4J^2 > C/J$–for which the roots λ_1 and λ_2 are real and unequal,
    and is known as the overdamped case, curve (a) in figure 1.2

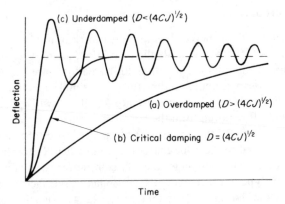

Figure 1.2. The effects of damping magnitude on the movement response

(b) when $D^2/4J^2 = C/J$—for which the root are real and equal, and D has a value termed the critical value, curve (b) in figure 1.2

(c) when $D^2/4J^2 < C/J$—which gives roots that are conjugate-complex quantities and the system is underdamped, curve (c) in figure 1.2. The frequency of the decaying oscillations being

$$\omega = \left(\frac{C}{J} - \frac{D^2}{4J^2} \right)^{\frac{1}{2}}$$ (1.6)

Thus it is apparent that the magnitude of the damping applied to a movement has an important effect on the dynamic performance or speed of response of an instrument, it being general practice to operate pointer instruments with slightly less than critical damping to ensure that the pointer changes rapidly from one position to another with the minimum chance of sticking.

1.1.2 Comparison Techniques

Comparison methods of measurement are capable of providing the result with the least uncertainty. However, they tend to require a greater amount of skill and experience from the operator, and in addition to this the time required to perform the measurement may be quite large. With the continual increases in operator costs these factors produce an incentive to replace the operator-manipulated comparison measurements by automatic or programmed instruments, the benefits being a reduction in the time taken to perform the measurement, and the possibility of performing consistent measurements with lower-grade staff, thereby releasing expensive highly skilled personnel to perform other duties.

It will become apparent that some of the contemporary instruments that fulfil this function use comparison techniques in their operation so an understanding of the principles involved is important.

Substitution Methods

As the name implies these methods require the substitution of the unknown by a known quantity, of such a magnitude that conditions are restored to a reference level. For example, consider the situation illustrated by figure 1.3. A constant voltage source causes a current I to flow through a simple circuit consisting of an ammeter in series with an unknown resistance R_x. If the switch, S, is changed so that the unknown is removed from the circuit and replaced by a good quality decade resistance box, R_s, the magnitudes of the decades can be adjusted until the current is restored to the value that was present when R_x was in circuit. The setting on the decade box will under these circumstances be equal to the magnitude of R_x. This type of process is only occasionally a satisfactory method of measuring resistance but in the Q meter (section 2.3.4) a substitution process is used for the measurement of small capacitance values—reference conditions being restored by reducing a known capacitor by an amount equal to the unknown capacitor.

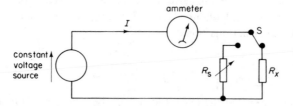

Figure 1.3. A possible circuit for the substitution method of resistance measurement

Null Methods

A logical progression from the substitution method of measurement is to arrange a circuit such that the difference between the unknown and the known is detected and reduced to zero by a balancing process, that is, a null detection method.

The potentiometer

The d.c. potentiometer was the first means of measuring voltage with a small uncertainty. For many years a good quality d.c. potentiometer was a necessary requirement for any electrical standards laboratory. However the developments in digital electronic voltmeters have meant that the potentiometer is being superseded in the standards laboratory and for other applications. Nevertheless, the principles involved in the operation of the d.c. potentiometer are of fundamental importance as they are commonly used in other instruments.

Consider the simple circuit in figure 1.4. The voltage source E drives a current I around the closed circuit ABCD. If the connection BC consists of a 1 m length

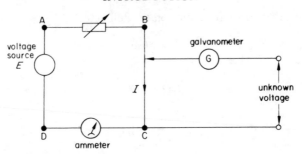

Figure 1.4. Slide wire potentiometer

of resistance wire having a resistivity and cross-section area such that its resistance is 20.0 Ω, and the value of I is 50 mA, the voltage drop along BC will be 1 V or 0.001 V/mm. Thus any d.c. voltage less than 1 V may be determined to three significant figures by adjusting the position of the slider to give zero deflection on the galvanometer G, and measuring the length of wire between the wiper and the end C.

The errors in the above will be largely dependent on the quality of the ammeter, and this limitation can be removed by comparing the slide wire voltage with a reference voltage such as that provided by a standard cell.

Bridges

Since voltages may be determined by a comparison process, a suitable circuit may be devised in which the voltage drops across known and unknown resistors can be compared and made equal.

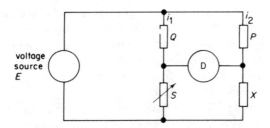

Figure 1.5. Basic bridge circuit

Consider the circuit in figure 1.5, which consists of a voltage source, a null detector and four resistors connected as shown. Let Q and P each have a fixed value; S be a variable decade resistor and X the unknown resistor.

The voltage source E will cause a current i_1 to flow through Q and S and a current i_2 to flow through P and X.

At balance, that is, a zero reading on the null detector

$$i_1 S = i_2 X$$

and

$$i_1 Q = i_2 P$$

Hence

$$\frac{i_2 X}{i_2 P} = \frac{i_1 S}{i_1 Q}$$

or

$$X = S \frac{P}{Q} \tag{1.7}$$

In the simplest case $P = Q$ and X the unknown is equal to the setting on the decade box. This type of arrangement is generally very much more satisfactory than the substitution method described earlier, for any variations in the magnitude of the voltage source will not affect the balance condition and the value found for the unknown—a situation that cannot be guaranteed when the substitution method is being used.

This basic form of bridge circuit is called a Wheatstone bridge, and it is of extreme importance in instrumentation. It is described in detail in section 3.3.

1.1.3 Digital Techniques

Most digital instruments display the measurand in discrete numerals thereby eliminating the parallax error, and reducing the human errors associated with analogue pointer instruments. In general digital instruments have superior accuracy to analogue pointer instruments, and many incorporate automatic polarity and range indication which reduces operator training, measurement error, and possible instrument damage through overload. In addition to these features many digital instruments have an output facility enabling permanent records of measurements to be made automatically.

Digital instruments are, however, usually more expensive than analogue instruments. They are also sampling devices, that is, the displayed quantity is a discrete measurement made, either at one instant in time, or over an interval of time, by using digital electronic techniques.

Sampling of data

Whenever a continuous signal is to be measured by a sampling process care must be exercised to ensure that the sampling rate is sufficiently fast for all the variations in the measurand to be reconstructed. If the sampling rate is too low, details of the fluctuation in the continuous wave will be lost whereas if the sampling rate is too high an unnecessary amount of data will be collected and processed. The limiting requirement for the frequency of sampling is that it must be at least twice the highest frequency component of the signal being sampled in order that the measured signal may be reconstructed in its original form.[2]

In a good many situations the amplitude of the measurand can be considered to be constant, for example the magnitude of a direct voltage, and then the sampling rate can be slowed down to one which simply confirms that the measurand does have a constant value.

Transmission of data

Having sampled the measurand it will be necessary to transmit the information from one part of the system to another. The transmission of digital data may be accomplished either in a *parallel* or a *serial* mode.

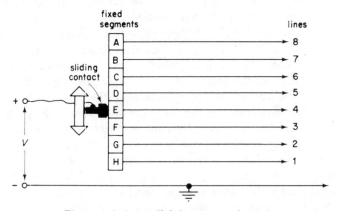

Figure 1.6. A parallel data transmitter

Consider the arrangement in figure 1.6, where a fixed-value direct voltage exists between the movable contact and an earth or zero potential line. As the contact is moved from one fixed segment to another a voltage will appear between the appropriate line and earth. Hence, by looking at the signal state of the lines it would be possible to determine which fixed segment the slider was in contact with and the position of the slider relative to one end.

The magnitude of the voltage, V, is relatively unimportant, (providing it is larger than any interference voltages) because to establish the position of the slider it is only necessary to detect the presence of the voltage, a situation which is normally denoted by the code '1', the absence of the voltage being denoted by the code '0', that is, the presence or absence of a binary bit. For the eight-segment system of figure 1.6; table 1.1 gives the states of the lines for the various positions of the slider. Each line of the table represents a 'binary word' of eight binary bits, that is, the condition of the signal level (0 or 1) on each line is contained within the word. Such an arrangement is referred to as parallel transmission.

Table 1.1. Relationship between the line conditions and the slider position

Slider in contact with segment	line 1	line 2	line 3	line 4	line 5	line 6	line 7	line 8
A	0	0	0	0	0	0	0	1
B	0	0	0	0	0	0	1	0
C	0	0	0	0	0	1	0	0
D	0	0	0	0	1	0	0	0
E	0	0	0	1	0	0	0	0
F	0	0	1	0	0	0	0	0
G	0	1	0	0	0	0	0	0
H	1	0	0	0	0	0	0	0

Consider figure 1.7 where the fixed segments have been connected to a motor-driven rotary switch. One revolution of the switch contact will sample the voltage condition of each of the fixed (lettered) contacts and transmit the information in sequence along the single-signal path, and thus produce serial transmission of data, the waveforms of the serial words corresponding to the position of the sliding contact on the lettered contacts (as shown in figure 1.8). It must be realised that the duration of the 'word' and the 'bits' will be dependent on the speed of rotation of the switch contact—the duration of each bit being one eighth of the word (in this case). The bit duration will directly affect the speed of transmission, which is the number of bits per second but more commonly referred to as the 'bit rate' or 'bit frequency'. In a complete serial system the receiver will be remote from the transmitter and for the receiver to make sense of the received signal it must be synchronised to the transmitter, that is, it must operate at the same bit rate as the transmitter. Because of this digital systems normally incorporate a clock, which is used to synchronise events throughout the system. The clock frequency and the bit frequency must therefore be equal.

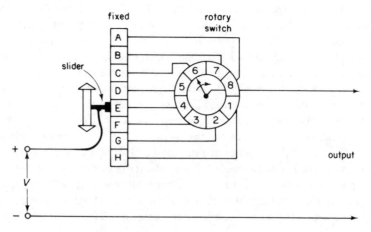

Figure 1.7. A serial data transmitter

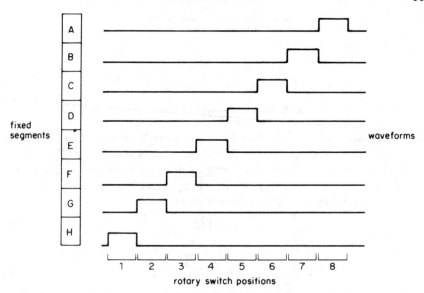

Figure 1.8. Waveforms of the 'words' generated when the sliding contact is on
particular fixed segments

Another point of importance in serial systems is that the receiver must know
in which order a word is being transmitted. For example if the sliding contact is
on segment A one direction of the rotary switch would produce the word

00000001

while the reverse direction of the rotary switch arm would produce

10000000

The speed of transmission of a digital system is slower than an analogue one
but a digital system is immune from many forms of electrical interference.

Logic

The manipulation of binary numbers is compatible with the operation of electrical circuits, that is, a binary bit can be represented by the presence or absence of
an electrical signal.

To design a logic system a form of mathematics known as Boolean algebra is
used. It results from the work of George Boole who described propositions such
that the results were either true or false, and can therefore be described by
signals that may take one of two values.

The basic rules can be expressed in terms of simple electrical circuits as follows.

Consider the circuit in figure 1.9. It requires both switches A and B to be
closed for the lamp to light. This condition can be written as

$$F = A \quad \text{AND} \quad B \qquad (1.8)$$

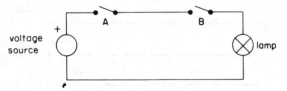

Figure 1.9. Simple equivalent circuit of AND gate

where the Boolean variable F takes the value 1 when the lamp is lit and 0 when it is unlit. Similarly A and B have the values 0 when open and 1 when closed.

The negations or compliments of these conditions are written as $\bar{A}$ and $\bar{B}$ and would indicate their having values of 1 when open and 0 when closed.

Equation 1.8 may alternatively be written as

$$F = A \cdot B \qquad (1.9)$$

or even

$$F = AB \qquad (1.10)$$

In every case the equations must be read as F equals A AND B.

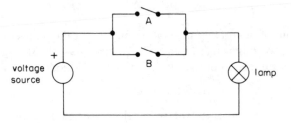

Figure 1.10. Simple equivalent circuit of OR gate

The circuit in figure 1.10 shows a situation in which the lamp is lit if either A OR B is closed.

This represents the logical OR function and is written as

$$F = A \text{ OR } B \qquad (1.11)$$

Alternatively this is written as

$$F = A + B \qquad (1.12)$$

Again this plus sign must not be confused with the arithmetic version and equation 1.12 must be read as

$$F = A \text{ OR } B$$

This analogy with simple circuits may be carried further to illustrate the operation of the basic logic functions.[3] It must be appreciated, however, that in digital electronics the switches are replaced by semi-conductor components[4] which in the simplest case are a diode and resistor arrangement, while in most instrumentation L.S.I. (large scale integrated) circuits will be incorporated to perform the logic functions.

In either case the components of digital electronics may be represented by a set of logic gates for which the BS and IEC symbols are shown in figure 1.11.

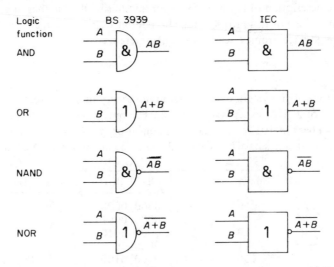

Figure 1.11. BS and IEC symbols for basic two input logic gates

The use of logic gates to realise a situation can be illustrated by considering the Boolean expression:

$$F = AB + CD \tag{1.13}$$

Using simple AND and OR gates, figure 1.12 can be drawn up where the AB and CD terms are each realised by using two input AND gates, the outputs from these being applied to a two input OR gate.

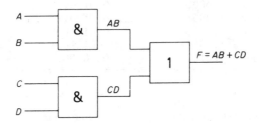

Figure 1.12. Realisation of the Boolean expression $F = AB + CD$

The NAND and NOR gates provide outputs which are the compliments of those produced by the basic AND and OR gates. This is shown in the symbols in figure 1.11.

Of importance in the realisation of a logic network is De Morgan's theorem, which states that to negate a logical expression of two or more variables, each variable should be negated and the logical operation changed (that is, an AND becomes an OR and vice versa).

Therefore any logic situation may be solved by using various combinations of gates. The description of the techniques for minimising the number of gates is beyond the scope of this introduction and reference should be made to specialised texts on digital electronics, see for example reference 4.

Codes

The electronic logic system operates with pure binary numbers, that is a system with a base of 2. The reader is no doubt used to operating with a decimal system which has a base of 10. To ease the communication problem between man and machine several codes have been evolved and some in common use are as follows.

Decimal	Binary	8421 BCD	Hexadecimal
0	0	0000 0000	0
1	1	0000 0001	1
2	10	0000 0010	2
3	11	0000 0011	3
4	100	0000 0100	4
5	101	0000 0101	5
6	110	0000 0110	6
7	111	0000 0111	7
8	1000	0000 1000	8
9	1001	0000 1001	9
10	1010	0001 0000	A
11	1011	0001 0001	B
12	1100	0001 0010	C
13	1101	0001 0011	D
14	1110	0001 0100	E
15	1111	0001 0101	F
16	10000	0001 0110	10
17	10001	0001 0111	11
18	10010	0001 1000	12
19	10011	0001 1001	13
20	10100	0010 0000	14

Memories

Sequential logic systems require the use of memory elements to record the state of the system at a particular instant in time. The basic component of a memory is the bistable or 'flip-flop' element. It is a component that has two stable states and changes from one state to the other on receiving a suitable input signal.

The various techniques used to provide a storage medium have created a specialist technology which aims at providing accessible data storage at low cost.[5,6]

In operating a logic system various styles of memory are used that are grouped as follows

RAM—random access memory—a bank or matrix of memory cells in which an individual element can be located by means of an address within the bank. Access to each memory element is obtained at random, and once gained data may be 'written in' or 'extracted from' the particular element.
ROM—read only memory—a bank of memory elements that permanently hold data, that is they cannot be altered by the user. A ROM could be used for example for storing the algorithms for performing scientific calculations in a calculator.
PROM—programmable read only memory—a ROM that may be programmed before insertion in the system by the user for a specific function.

In general RAMs are semiconductor devices and are 'volatile', that is, the user program will be lost if the power supply is removed, whereas ROMs and PROMs are 'nonvolatile' and will retain their data indefinitely.

Controllers

As computers became smaller and less expensive they became known as mini-computers and even as microcomputers. When such a computer ceases to be a general-purpose device and is dedicated instead to the control of a single piece of equipment such as an instrument in accordance with a fixed program, it is referred to as a controller, as is a computer when programmed to perform the control function.

The use of microcomputers as instrument controllers requires that the user must have at least an understanding of the terminology used in connection with such devices

I/O—input and output devices through which data may be fed into and out of the computer for example printers, keyboards, V.D.U.s, etc.
C.P.U.—Central processing unit or the central processor is the unit, which by following the instructions of the program, co-ordinates and controls the activities of the I/O and the memories. It is in the C.P.U. that the logic and arithmetic processes are performed on the data stored in the memory.
L.S.I.—large scale integration—the term applied to integrated circuits containing from 100 to 5000 logic gates or 1000 to 16 000 memory bits.
M.P.U.—microprocessor (unit)—an integrated circuit design that provides, on one or more silicon chips, the functions which were formally contained within the C.P.U. of a computer.

Hardware

In a system using a mixture of electronic circuit elements and programmed control for its operation the tangible items such as components, electromechanical I/O devices and so on are termed hardware. With the expansion of the programmable capabilities of L.S.I. many functions that were achieved by hardwired logic can now be performed by programmed instructions.

Software

This term is used to describe the program of instructions stored in the memory and used to direct the system so as to perform the desired sequence of operations. The development time for software is lengthy and in consequence in many installations the software is more expensive than the hardware. User's software (developed specifically for a user's application) is difficult to replace and so duplicate copies must be stored in safety.

Firmware

This is the software that has been embodied in the hardware, that is, programmed into ROM or PROM. This definition [7] may be an over-simplification, but the term firmware may certainly be used [8] to describe software in a ROM or PROM which is not essential to the function of a system and which the user may accept or reject depending on his requirements.

Programming

The writing of programs to perform specific functions or operations on the measurand will, in a 'computer' controlled system be in a high level language such as BASIC, ALGOL or FORTRAN. In a dedicated or purpose-built system, using a microprocessor as the controller, the programming will of necessity be in machine code. The writing of programs in machine code is expensive for it is a lengthy process requiring considerable skill and experience (see reference 15 and reference 19 of chapter 4).

System operation

The selection, by the user, of an operational or functional program (see section 4.3.2) from the controller's soft or firmware, simply requires the entry of coded instructions via a keyboard. In a dedicated system this is likely to be a simple entry of one or two digits, while in a 'computer' controlled system it may be necessary to first insert the appropriate cassette or floppy disc [5] into the container.

1.2 DISPLAY METHODS

In selecting a single instrument or a number of instruments to form a measurement system a decision that must be made at a fairly early stage is whether the visual presentation should be analogue or digital in form.

The major advantage of analogue displays is that an operator can assimilate a very much greater amount of information from an analogue display than from a digital display in the same period of time. A clear example of this is that a graph of the variation of one function relative to another is much quicker to interpret than the same data in tabular form.

1.2.1 Analogue Displays

The displays used in analogue instruments can be divided into those associated with pointer instruments and those providing some form of graphical display.

Pointer Instruments

Reading interpretation

One of the problems associated with pointer instruments is the misinterpretation of a reading due to parallax, that is, if the user is incorrectly positioned so that instead of looking vertically down onto the pointer and scale, an angled view is made. This will result in an incorrect observation as illustrated by figure 1.13. To assist the user in removing this source of reading error many better quality analogue instruments have a pointer in the form of a fine blade and a mirror adjacent to the scale, in which the reflection of pointer can be aligned (see figure 1.14).

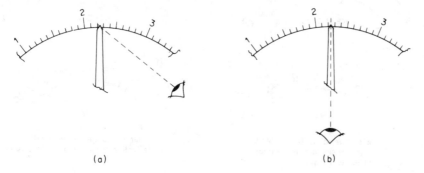

(a)   (b)

Figure 1.13. Illustration of parallax error: (a) angled view with error, (b) correct view of same reading

A further problem in the use of an analogue pointer instrument is the interpolation of pointer position between scale markings. In some instruments this problem is alleviated by an arrangement of the form illustrated in figure 1.14.

From the above it should be apparent that a certain amount of skill is required to correctly interpret the reading on a pointer instrument. It should also be appreciated that the limit of resolution on an analogue scale is approximately 0.4 mm and readings that imply greater resolution are really due to the imagination of the user.

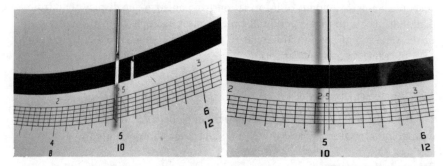

Figure 1.14 Scale arrangement of a class 0.1 instrument

Scales

The forms of scale in use are exampled by those in figure 1.15. The instruments with a linear scale are generally the most convenient to use particularly those with subdivisions in tenths.

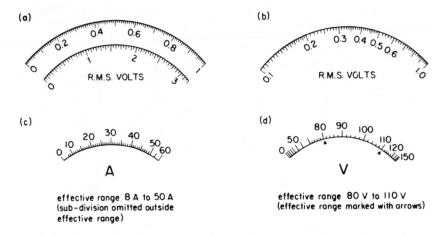

Figure 1.15. Examples of scales used on analogue pointer instruments

The effective range—that part of the scale over which measurements can be made with stated accuracy—should be recognisable without ambiguity. How this is accomplished is left to the manufacturer, figures 1.15c and d showing two possible methods. Unless stated otherwise the effective range of an instrument should be from the full scale value down to the value shown in table 1.2.

The term *fiducial* value is the quantity to which reference is made in order to specify the accuracy of an instrument. For most instruments the fiducial value corresponds to the full scale indication but there are exceptions notably instruments with off-set zeros. Table 1.3 gives examples of fiducial values for particular cases.

Table 1.2. Lower limit of effective range (extracted from BS 89: Part 1: 1970). (Reproduced by permission of the British Standards Institution)

Form of movement	Lower limit of effective range expressed as a fraction of the fiducial value
Permanent magnet moving coil	$\frac{1}{10}$
Electrodynamic and ferrodynamic wattmeter	$\frac{1}{10}$
Induction wattmeter	$\frac{1}{10}$
Rectifier instruments, except voltmeters below range 0 V to 15 V	$\frac{1}{10}$
Induction and moving-iron ammeter and voltmeter	$\frac{1}{5}$
Rectifier voltmeters, below range 0 V to 15 V	$\frac{1}{4}$
Electrostatic voltmeter*	$\frac{1}{3}$
Electrodynamic and ferrodynamic ammeter and voltmeter	$\frac{1}{3}$
Thermocouple ammeter and voltmeter	$\frac{1}{3}$

*Except that in an instrument having a scale length of less than 85 mm the effective range shall be from one-quarter to three-quarters of the full scale value.

Table 1.3. Examples giving the fiducial value for particular cases. (Reproduced by permission of the British Standards Institution)

Type of instrument	Limits of effective range		Fiducial value
Ammeter	10	100	100 A
Voltmeter	−60	+60	120 V
Millivoltmeter	−15	+35	50 mV
Frequency meter	375	425	425 Hz
Suppressed-zero voltmeter	180	260	260 V

Graphical Instruments

These devices provide a display that is a record of the variation of one quantity with respect to another.

Axes

The most widely used axes are some function and time (referred to as y–t). Hence, the display is the variation of the measurand with time, examples of this being the display of a voltage waveform on an oscilloscope (section 2.6) or the record of temperature variations in say a manufacturing process (section 3.1.2).

Instead of using time as one of the axes some other function can be used. Instruments with the capability of recording the variation in one quantity against another are referred to as x–y plotters (see figure 3.8).

One form of display that is particularly useful in waveform analysis is the presentation of the amplitude of the frequency components of a signal against frequency—an arrangement that is illustrated by the spectrum analyser (see figures 1.30 and 4.28).

Permanency of Display

If a graphical display is necessary as a function of the chosen instrumentation a factor that must be considered is if the record can be temporary or must be permanent.

If the latter is required either photographic techniques or some form of 'pen and paper' writing system (see section 2.1.3) must be used. The filing of quantities of recorded data can create reference and storage problems hence the use of temporary or 'nonpermanent' records is often desirable. The obvious example of this is the oscilloscope (section 2.6) where in a conventional instrument the path of the electron beam across the tube face only remains visible for a very brief time but by modifications to the tube and the use of certain phosphors a trace can be stored for a considerable time. A more recent development (section 4.4.3) is the use of a volatile digital store to record a waveform.

1.2.2 Digital

The principal advantage of a digital display is that it removes ambiguity, therefore eliminating a considerable amount of 'operator error' or misinterpretation. Unfortunately it often creates a false confidence—'I can see it, therefore it must be correct'; but this is not necessarily true (see section 1.3.2 and chapter 8). However, the concern here is to outline the methods currently in use [9] for displaying data in digital form—an area which is subject to considerable research effort and consequent change. One such area has been the need for an alphanumeric display rather than a simple numeric display. This requirement results from the incorporating of programming capability into instruments, thereby creating a need for a visual operator-instrument interface for communication.

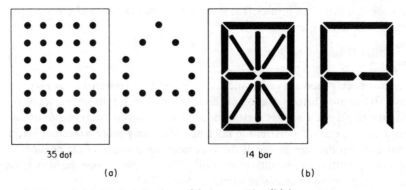

35 dot   14 bar

(a)   (b)

Figure 1.16. Digital displays: (a) dot matrix, (b) bar arrangement

The use of electronic devices for displays is generally based either on a dot matrix or on a segmented display. Figure 1.16 illustrates two types of array that are in use. The methods used to produce the display can be summarised as follows.

Light emitting diodes

These are bright, reliable, low cost devices, compatible with low voltage integrated circuitry. L.E.D.s operate by utilising electroluminescence—the emission of light from a solid by radiative recombination of electrons and holes. Gallium phosphide, gallium arsenide phosphide and gallium aluminium arsenide are all materials used to produce segmented displays with red emission. By substitution of the phosphorous by nitrogen in the materials L.E.D.s emitting yellow or green light have become commercially available.

Liquid-crystal displays

The main assets of liquid-crystal displays are their low power consumption and, since they are passive devices that can operate in a reflective manner, their good visibility in high ambient light conditions. Liquid crystals are organic materials, which at room temperatures are in the mesomorphic state (liquid but with the ordered structure of a solid). A character cell is made by trapping a thin layer of liquid crystal between the layers of transparent electrically conducting glass. Applying an electrical field to the transparent crystal causes it to become milky and reflecting. The shape of the characters is formed by etching the conducting coating on the glass into the required pattern, for example 7 bar shape for a numerical display (see reference 9).

Commercial liquid-crystal displays are normally limited to arrays of a few numerals, for their slow operating speed and threshold problems make them apparently unsuitable for use in larger arrays.

Gas-discharge display devices

This is one of the earliest electronic display technologies, which, in spite of its relatively high operating voltage, remains competitive for numerical displays, while for large alphanumeric applications it currently presents the main challenge to the cathode ray tube (c.r.t.).

Gas-discharge display devices utilise the light output of a cold-cathode discharge emanating from the excitation of gas atoms under electron bombardment. Thus a characteristic of the glow discharge is the bright glowing sheath, the so-called negative glow, that faithfully surrounds the cathode. This property was utilised in the original cold cathode numerical indicator 'Nixie' tubes, in which thin numeral (0 to 9) shaped cathodes were stacked one behind the other and surrounded by an anode structure the front of which was in the form of a gauze with good optical transmission.

The stacked array has a restricted viewing angle and the digits in a register are not in the same plane. These factors coupled with the fashionable use of seven-segment displays has led to the adaptation of this technology to produce gas discharge displays using seven cathode bars and a common anode per numeral. The electrical characteristics of the device make it particularly suitable for use in multiple units of up to 16 numerals in a single envelope.

The gas-discharge technology also lends itself to multi-segment and dot matrix arrays for alphanumeric displays. The ultimate, so far, being the so-called plasma panels for displaying up to 3000 characters.[10]

Cathode ray tube

The use of the c.r.t. for alphanumeric display is now becoming commonplace with its use in visual display units (V.D.U.s) as computer terminals. Variations on the basic c.r.t. specifically for alphanumeric applications have been devised,[9] and it should be appreciated that an increasing number of sophisticated oscillo-scopes (see section 2.6.1) include alphanumeric information with the displayed waveform on the tube face.

Other displays

As indicated at the start of this section this is an area of intense development and numerous techniques are under investigation as reviewed by Weston.[9] Perhaps the most promising at the present time are the electroluminescent, the electrochromic, the electrophoretic and the magneto-optic bubble displays.

Choice of display

In general the customer has no say in the type of display fitted to an instrument, it being an integral part of the instrument design. However, the properties of importance to the user must be the size of the display and its visibility under the operating conditions. Indirectly of consequence will be the power consumption of the display and the circuitry driving it.

1.3 ACCURACY

The appropriate British Standard[11] defines the accuracy of a measuring instrument as

> The quality which characterizes the ability of a measuring instrument to give indications equivalent to the true value of the quantity measured.

It then proceeds to note that

> The quantitive expression of this concept should be in terms of un-certainty.

1.3.1 Values and Uncertainty

True value

Various terms are used in connection with the value assigned to a quantity. Of greatest importance is its actual or true value. It must be realised that it is impossible to determine exactly the true value of any quantity: the value assigned to a quantity will always have a tolerance or uncertainty associated with it. In some instances this tolerance is very small, say 1 part in 10^9, and the true value is approached but it can never be determined exactly.

Nominal value

The nominal value, usually of a component, is the one given it by a manufacturer, for example, a 10 kΩ resistor. Such a value must be accompanied by a tolerance, say, $\pm$ 10 per cent and the interpretation of the complete statement is that the true value of the resistor is between 9.9 kΩ and 10.1 kΩ.

Measured value

This is the value indicated by an instrument or determined by a measurement process. It must be accompanied by a statement of the uncertainty or the possible limit of error associated with the measurement.

Tolerance and uncertainty

From the above definitions the accuracy of a measurement must be quoted as a tolerance or uncertainty in measurement. For example, if a measurement on a particular resistance gave the result

$$102.5 \ \Omega \pm 0.2 \ \Omega$$

the uncertainty in the measurement would be $\pm$ 0.2 Ω and the true value of the resistor will lie somewhere between 102.3 Ω and 102.7 Ω.

If the same resistor were measured by a different instrument and the value 102. 8 Ω $\pm$ 0.2 Ω were obtained, a narrowing of the band within which the true value must lie is possible. For from the second measurement it is apparent that the true value must be between 102.6 Ω and 103.0 Ω; hence by combining the two measurements the true value must lie between 102.6 Ω and 102.7 Ω. It is therefore possible to estimate or postulate that the value of the resistor is

$$102.65 \ \Omega \pm 0.05 \ \Omega$$

This type of situation can be represented by the 'band diagram' in figure 1.17.

In assigning a tolerance to a value, the two parts of the complete statement must be compatible, that is to say if a tolerance on a resistor is quoted as

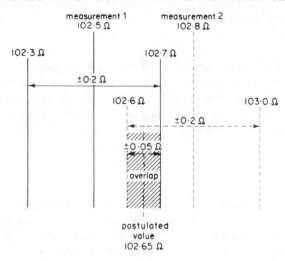

Figure 1.17. Band diagram for quoted resistance measurement

± 0.01 Ω the value of the resistor must be given to one-hundredth of an ohm otherwise ambiguities arise. Examples of acceptable and unacceptable statements are given in table 1.4.

The band diagram in figure 1.17 used two different measurements to obtain a value for the resistor closer to the true value than either of the individual measurements. Sometimes it is possible to use the nominal or manufacturer's value and a measured value to perform a similar exercise.

Table 1.4. Acceptability of values

Value	Tolerance	Acceptable
102.5 Ω	± 0.1 Ω	Yes
102.5 Ω	± 0.1 per cent	Yes
102.5 Ω	± 0.05 Ω	No
102.5 Ω	± 0.02 per cent	No
102.50 Ω	± 0.05 Ω	Yes
102.50 Ω	± 0.02 per cent	Yes
102.50147 Ω	± 5 per cent	No

Example

A capacitor has a nominal value of 220 pF ± 5 pF. If it was measured as 216 pF ± 1 per cent, postulate a value for the capacitor, together with a suitable tolerance.

From the nominal value, the true value is between 215 and 225 pF. From the measured value, the true value is between 213.8 and 218.2 pF. The true value must therefore be between 215 and 218.2 pF. Thus a postulated value could suitably be 216.6 pF with a tolerance of ± 1.6 pF.

Note Such a statement should be realistic in terms of values

(a) Anything less than the nearest tenth of a picofarad requires very carefully controlled measuring conditions (see section 7.2).
(b) Care must be taken to ensure that the tolerance includes all possible values for the true value of the component.

1.3.2 Errors

Error of measurement

The error in a measurement is defined as the algebraic difference between the indicated (or measured) value and the true value.[11]

It has been suggested in the previous section that the true value can never be found so in practice the 'true value' is replaced by 'the conventional true value' which is the value the measurand can be realistically accepted as having.

An alternative approach is that the error of indication of an instrument (A) can only be determined by its performance when compared with a reference instrument (B). Therefore the uncertainty of measurement associated with B must be very much less than that allowable on A.

Example

An ammeter under test indicates a reading of 0.87 A while the same current produces on a reference ammeter a reading of 0.900 A ± 0.001 A.

The error of measurement for the class 2 instrument is thus

$$0.87 - 0.900 \text{ A} = -0.030 \text{ A}$$

The tolerance on the reference value has been ignored and provided such a tolerance is less than one-tenth of the quoted tolerance on the instrument under test such a procedure is acceptable. Should one wish to be pedantic, however, the error of the instrument under investigation could be given as −0.030 A ± 0.001 A when indicating 0.87 A at $T\,°C$ on the date of measurement.

The details of the reference instrument and the method of measurement should also be given.

Arising from this example it is apparent that the '*correction*' that should be applied to the reading would, in this case, be +0.03 A and the percentage errror in reading (or indication) would be 100 × (−0.03/0.87) or −3.45 per cent.

Although, by using a calibration process, it is possible to establish the errors associated with a particular instrument, when an operator and a number of instruments are involved in a measurement, an assessment of the *total possible error* or *limit of uncertainty* must be made, for it must be established that the requirements of the measurement have been satisfied.

Sources of error

The possible causes of error, which may or may not be present can be summarised as follows.

(i) Construction effects This form of error is inherent within the manufacture of the instrument and will result from such causes as tolerances on dimensions and components, wear on bearing and contact surfaces, etc. It will almost certainly be unique to a particular instrument for it is unlikely that the same combination of all such factors will occur in any two instruments.

(ii) Detemination error This is the uncertainty in the indicated value due to the resolution of the instrument. The determination error will be dependent on the display method and in consequence will have, as a minimum, one of the following values

(a) ± 0.4 mm on an analogue scale or trace
(b) ± 1 count or least significant digit in a digital display
(c) $\pm$ half a unit of the least decade of a bridge arm (or decade box) assuming
        that a detector of sufficient sensitivity is in use.

(iii) Approximations of expressions In determining quantities by comparison methods the measurand is found by evaluating an expression. In deriving such expressions simplifications and approximations are often made. One such example is the balance equation for a Kelvin double bridge (equation 3.3) which is

$$R_x = \frac{QS}{M} + \left[\frac{mr}{m + r + q} \left(\frac{Q}{M} - \frac{q}{m} \right) \right]$$

In practice this equation is usually approximated to $R_x = QS/M$ which is very much easier to handle but provides an answer that has an error due to neglecting the result of the terms in the outer brackets.

(iv) Calculation error The effects of this form of error are likely in most cases to be negligible if sufficient calculating power is used, for example, an 8 or 10-digit calculator generally makes this form of error insignificant in comparison with other errors. However, such an assumption cannot be justified if very precise measurements are being made. Of greater consequence are likely to be the effects of rounding errors, for example, if 14.648 is rounded to 14.65 an error of 0.0137 per cent has been introduced. Should the 14.65 be further rounded to 14.7 a total rounding error of 0.355 per cent has occurred!

(v) Environmental effects All materials, and hence electrical components, are affected to some extent by changes in the environment in which they are operating. The effects of temperature changes are generally the ones of most concern and cause both a direct action on the component, for example, change in resistivity and an indirect effect due to such occurrences as dimensional changes, or the generation of thermoelectric voltages (see section 7.1.1). On the whole the effects due to humidity and pressure are of little consequence unless extremes of these conditions are encountered. One exception to this is the effect of atmospheric pressure variations on the measurement of high voltage using a spark gap. It is therefore important that for every measurement a careful record

is made of temperature, pressure and humidity so that if required a suitable allowance can be made when assessing the total uncertainty in the measurement.

(vi) Ageing effects   As equipment gets older slight changes may occur in some of the components and these may be such as to affect the performance of instruments. It is therefore necessary to ensure that instruments are checked or calibrated at regular intervals to ensure: (a) no faults in operation have occurred; (b) they are performing within their specification; and (c) that any changes occurring due to age are noted.

(vii) Strays and residuals   Among the possible effects of age is a build-up of deposits on surfaces. Such conditions can affect contact resistances, and surface leakage resistance. The first of these may be of consequence in the values of the lowest decade of a resistor box while the second is of importance between the terminals of an instrument with a high input resistance. While these forms of error may be monitored and allowed for by the calibration process, they may be reduced to negligible proportions by correct maintenance. Of a more random nature are the effects of the impedance (resistance, inductance and capacitance) of the connections between a measurand and an instrument. In general these effects are made small by using short connections of suitable conductor. This problem is particularly relevant at high frequencies when considerable skill must be exercised to overcome their effects.

(viii) Insertion errors   Almost any instrument when connected into a circuit will change the conditions that existed in the circuit prior to its inclusion. It is therefore important to ensure that this disturbance is insignificant otherwise incorrect readings will be produced, that is, an error in addition to those inherent in the instrument will be added to the measurement.

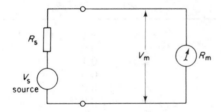

Figure 1.18. Equivalent circuit for evaluation of voltmeter insertion error

Consider the simple circuit in figure 1.18 (which may be the equivalent circuit of a more complex arrangement). Let V_m be the voltage indicated by the meter which has a resistance R_m, and is connected across the source V_s of internal resistance R_s. Then

$$V_m = V_s \left(\frac{R_m}{R_m + R_s} \right)$$ (1.14)

and the error in reading resulting from the voltage division effect will be

$$\text{Insertion error} = \frac{V_m - V_s}{V_s} \times 100\%$$ (1.15)

$$= \frac{V_s \left(\dfrac{R_m}{R_m + R_s} \right) - V_s}{V_s} \times 100$$

or

$$\text{Insertion error} = \frac{-R_s}{R_m + R_s} \times 100\%$$ (1.16)

By making R_m equal to nR_s, table 1.5 has been drawn up, from which it can be seen that R_m needs to be very much greater than the source resistance for the insertion error to be negligible, a point which must be borne in mind when, say, a digital voltmeter having an input resistance of 10 MΩ and a specified accuracy of ± 0.005 per cent is being used to measure the voltage from a source that has an output resistance of 10 kΩ. An analysis of the insertion effects of an ammeter in comparison with the resistance of a circuit will produce a table similar to 1.5 except in the case of an ammeter, the meter resistance will need to be $1/n$ of the circuit resistance.

Table 1.5. Magnitude of insertion error resulting from voltmeter resistance being 'n' times the source resistance

n	$\text{Insertion error} = \dfrac{R_s \times 100}{R_m + R_s}$ (%)
10	9.1
100	0.99
1000	0.1
10 000	0.01
100 000	0.001
1 000 000	0.0001

Summation of Errors

To establish the limit of uncertainty for a particular instrument all the above factors must be taken into account and a summation of the errors made. For example, consider that in the circuit in figure 1.19, the voltmeter has a full scale deflection (f.s.d.) of 10 V and an uncertainty in reading of ± 0.5 per cent of full scale, and that the ammeter has a f.s.d. of 1 A with an uncertainty in reading of ± 0.5 per cent of full scale. Then if the meter readings were 10.0 V and 1.0 A, respectively, the resistance would be 10.0 Ω ± 1.0 per cent since V could be 9.95

or 10.05 V and I, 0.995 or 1.005 A. Taking the worst possible cases the resistance $(R = V/I)$ is

$$\frac{10.05}{0.995} = 10.05\,(1 + 0.005) = 10.1, \text{ that is } + 1.0\,\%$$

or

$$\frac{9.95}{1.005} = 9.95\,(1 - 0.005) = 9.90, \text{ that is } - 1.0\,\%$$

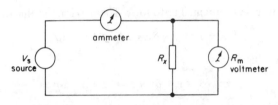

Figure 1.19. Measurement of resistance using an ammeter and a voltmeter

Thus it should be apparent that the more instruments involved in the performance of a measurement the greater the uncertainty that is likely to be in the value of the measured quantity and the totalising of construction/calibration errors is of considerable importance since, in most cases, these will account for the major part of the total error in a measurement. The above example indicates that when the result is derived from a quotient, the tolerance of the quantities involved is added. The determination of a quantity may, in general, be represented mathematically as a product or a sum of a number of quantities, which are illustrated by the following.

(a) As a product

$$X = \frac{ABC}{P^2 Q^3} \tag{1.17}$$

Taking natural logarithms of both sides gives

$$\log_e X = \log_e A + \log_e B + \log_e C - 2 \log_e P - 3 \log_e Q$$

Now

$$\frac{\delta(\log_e X)}{\delta X} = \frac{1}{X} \quad \text{or} \quad \delta(\log_e X) = \frac{\delta X}{X}$$

therefore by obtaining derivatives for both sides

$$\frac{\delta X}{X} = \frac{\delta A}{A} + \frac{\delta B}{B} + \frac{\delta C}{C} - \frac{2\delta P}{P} - \frac{3\delta Q}{Q} \tag{1.18}$$

But in practice the maximum possible error in X is the quantity it is desired to ascertain, and this will only be obtained if the moduli of the terms are used. Thus the maximum error in X would be

$$\frac{\delta X}{X} = \pm \left(\frac{\delta A}{A} + \frac{\delta B}{B} + \frac{\delta C}{C} + \frac{2\delta P}{P} + \frac{3\delta Q}{Q} \right) \times 100\,\% \qquad (1.19)$$

(b) As a sum

$$x = y + z + p$$

The error in this case is obtained as follows. The maximum value of x is

$$x + \delta x = y + \delta y + z + \delta z + p + \delta p$$

The minimum value of x is

$$x - \delta x = y - \delta y + z - \delta z + p - \delta p$$

Thus the error in x is

$$\pm \delta x = \pm (\delta y + \delta z + \delta p)$$

or

$$\frac{\delta x}{x} = \pm \frac{(\delta y + \delta z + \delta p)}{x} \times 100\,\% \qquad (1.20)$$

and if the errors of y, z and p had been given as percentages

$$\frac{\delta x}{x} = \pm \left(\frac{y}{x} \frac{\delta y}{y} + \frac{z}{x} \frac{\delta z}{z} + \frac{p}{x} \frac{\delta p}{p} \right)\,\% \qquad (1.21)$$

An example of this form of error analysis is in summing the errors for the decades of a resistance box. Consider a four decade resistor box having

decade 'a' of $10 \times 1000 \pm 1\ \Omega$ (0.1 %)
decade 'b' of $10 \times 100 \pm 0.1\ \Omega$ (0.1 %)
decade 'c' of $10 \times 10 \pm 0.05\ \Omega$ (0.5 %)
decade 'd' of $10 \times 1 \pm 0.01\ \Omega$ (1.0 %)

and set to 5643 Ω. The error of the set value is

$$\frac{\delta x}{x} = \pm \left(\frac{5 + 0.6 + 0.2 + 0.03}{5643} \right) \times 100\,\%$$

$$= \pm \frac{5.83}{5643} \times 100\,\%$$

$$= \pm 0.103\,\%$$

Alternatively

$$\frac{\delta x}{x} = \pm \left(\frac{5000}{5643} \times 0.1 + \frac{600}{5643} \times 0.1 + \frac{40}{5643} \times 0.5 + \frac{3 \times 1}{5643} \right) \%$$

$$= \pm \left(\frac{583}{5643} \right) \%$$

$$= \pm 0.103 \%$$

Thus

$$x = 5643 \ \Omega \pm 0.103 \text{ per cent} \quad \text{or} \quad x = 5643 \pm 6 \ \Omega$$

(c) As a combination of sum and product

$$Z = \frac{B}{A + C}$$

Treating the sum part first, from equation 1.20

$$\frac{\delta (A + C)}{A + C} = \pm \frac{(\delta A + \delta C)}{A + C} \times 100 \%$$

and from equation 1.19

$$\frac{\delta Z}{Z} = \pm \left[\frac{\delta B}{B} + \left(\frac{\delta A + \delta C}{A + C} \right) \right] \times 100 \%$$

Example

Determine the total uncertainty in the value found for a resistor measured using a bridge circuit for which the balance equation is $X = SP/Q$, given $P = 1000 \ \Omega \pm$ 0.05 per cent and $Q = 100 \ \Omega \pm 0.05$ per cent and S is a resistance box having four decades as follows

> decade 1 of 10 × 1000 Ω resistors, each ± 0.5 Ω
> decade 2 of 10 × 100 Ω resistors, each ± 0.1 Ω
> decade 3 of 10 × 10 Ω resistors, each ± 0.05 Ω
> decade 4 of 10 × 1 Ω resistors, each ± 0.05 Ω

At balance S was set to a value of 5436 Ω. Tolerance on S value from equation 1.20

$$\frac{\delta S}{S} = \pm \left(\frac{5 \times 0.5 + 4 \times 0.1 + 3 \times 0.05 + 6 \times 0.05}{5436} \right) \times 100 \%$$

$$= \pm \frac{3.35 \times 100}{5436} = 0.0616 \%$$

$$X \text{ value} = \frac{1000}{100} \times 5436 = 54.36 \text{ k}\Omega$$

Tolerance on X value is

$$\frac{\delta X}{X} = \pm \left(\frac{\delta P}{P} + \frac{\delta Q}{Q} + \frac{\delta S}{S} \right) \%$$

$$= \pm (0.05 + 0.05 + 0.062) \%$$

$$= \pm 0.162 \%$$

Therefore

$$X = 54.36 \text{ k}\Omega \pm 0.162 \%$$

or

$$X = 54.36 \text{ k}\Omega \pm 88 \ \Omega$$

Random Errors

The errors considered above may collectively be termed 'systematic errors' in that they may be systematically determined and allowed for. In any measurement processes errors may occur that are beyond the control of the operator. In most electrical measurements the occurrence of these is small, although present (for example, a transient or surge on the power supply, a mechanical shock or vibration, electrical (or acoustic) noise, etc.). These phenomena, which are unrelated to the measurement in progress, give rise to errors which are purely random in nature. While they cannot be eliminated, their effect can be reduced statistically by taking a large number of readings, and determining the mean or average value, which is likely to be nearer the conventional true value than any one individual reading.

The scatter of readings about the mean value gives a measure of the amount of random error involved in a measurement. Ideally this should be small, but the occasional reading, which is very different from the mean, occurs. This rogue value should not be ignored since it may be a true value at that instant in time and result from some hidden systematic error, which has changed during the course of the measurement. If the results of a measurement are subject to random errors, then as the number of readings increases they should approximate to a Gaussian or normal distribution which can be checked by plotting a histogram (see figure 1.20) that is a graph of the number of occurrences against the value of reading, and establishing that the median (centre line) of the curve coincides with the mean value.

To estimate the probable random error for a set of readings, it is necessary to deduce the magnitudes of the observation values within which half the readings lie. Let these values be $+ dx$ and $- dx$ for observations which have a mean value

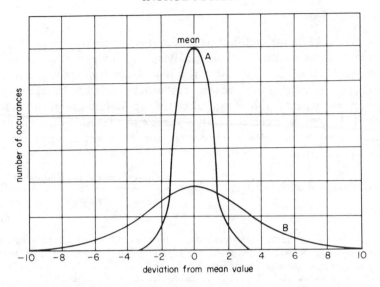

Figure 1.20. Histograms with normal distributions

of $\bar{x}$, then the probability of a reading lying within $\pm\,dx$ of $\bar{x}$ is 50 per cent and the probable random error may be quoted as $\pm\,dx$.

A more precise method of evaluating the randomness of a set of observations is to calculate the standard deviation for the distribution. Since the sum of the deviations for all the points in a distribution will be zero, the standard deviation for a set of observations is obtained by calculating the square root of the mean of the sum of the squared deviations that is

$$\sigma = \left[\frac{(x - \bar{x})^2}{N}\right]^{\frac{1}{2}}$$

where $\bar{x}$ is the mean value, x is an individual value, and N is the number of values.

For a normal distribution the chance of a valid point lying outside $\pm\,1.96\sigma$ is 5 per cent and outside $\pm\,3.09\sigma$ is 0.2 per cent. Also for a normal distribution the probable random error is 0.6745σ. The magnitude of σ is a clear indication of the quality of the distribution; in figure 1.20 the curve A would have a σ of 1 while for curve B $\sigma = 3$.

1.3.3 Specifications

To define limits of uncertainty in their operation all instruments are manufactured to a specification. This may be a national standard relating to a type of instrument, for example that relating to direct-acting electrical indicating instruments,[13] or a statement of performance issued by the manufacturer (see section 8.2).

Pointer instruments

BS 89: Part 1: 1970, the specification for direct-acting electrical indicating instruments, is the standard used for classifying single-purpose direct-acting instruments. In it an accuracy class system is used, which groups instruments according to the limits of intrinsic error as shown by table 1.6. The accuracy class of an instrument is also dependent on the type of instrument, and its scale length.[13] From the accuracy class it is possible to establish the limit of uncertainty in any reading within the effective range (section 1.2.1) by using the following expression

$$\text{Percentage. of uncertainty in reading} = \frac{\text{accuracy class} \times \text{fiducial value}}{\text{reading}} \cdot \%$$

(1.22)

Table 1.6. Limits of intrinsic error of instruments expressed as a percentage of the fiducial value (extracted from BS 89: Part 1: 1970). (Reproduced by permission of the British Standards Institution)

Class index	0.05	0.1	0.2	0.3	0.5	1.0	1.5	2.5	5.0
Limit of error	±0.05 per cent	±0.1 per cent	±0.2 per cent	±0.3 per cent	±0.5 per cent	±1.0 per cent	±1.5 per cent	±2.5 per cent	±5.0 per cent

Digital instruments

The accuracy specifications of digital instruments are normally written independently by the manufacturers of each instrument. The accepted method of presenting the specification is in two parts, namely

(a) a percentage of the input (or reading); and
(b) a resolution error equated to a number of digits in the least significant decade.

Typically for a three-digit (999) display

$$\pm (0.1\% \text{ of input} + 1 \text{ least significant digit (l.s.d)})$$

To convert this accuracy statement into a limit of error in reading requires a small amount of calculation.

Example

Determine, as a percentage of reading, the limit of error in a reading of 32.5 V on a digital voltmeter that has a full scale reading of 99.9 V and an accuracy specification of ± (0.1 per cent of input + 1 l.s.d.).

Contribution from first part of specification

$$0.1 \% \text{ of input} \equiv 0.1 \% \text{ of reading}$$

This may not be strictly correct but unless the instrument is well outside specification it is a realistic assumption.

Contribution from second part of specification, in a reading of 32.5 V

$$1 \text{ l.s.d.} = 0.1 \text{ V}$$

$$1 \text{ l.s.d.} \equiv \frac{0.1}{32.5} \times 100 = 0.307 \%$$

Thus the limit of error $= \pm (0.1 + 0.307) \%$

$$= \pm 0.407 \%$$

Undoubtedly this is an inconvenient process and when using a particular instrument a considerable saving in effort (and time) can be made by drawing up a curve of limit of error in reading against reading so that the uncertainty in a reading can be quickly established (see section 8.2).

It should be appreciated that the accuracy specification as stipulated above will only apply at a particular temperature or over a band of temperature and it may be necessary to add to the uncertainty in a reading a tolerance for temperature effects, a topic which is also covered in section 8.2.

1.3.4 Standards

So that it can be established that instruments are within their specification it is necessary to maintain a set of reference or standard quantities.

An instrument manufacturer will have a set of reference instruments and from time to time these will be sent to a calibration centre for checking. The calibration centres will in turn have instruments that are checked against the national standards.

Organisations such as the National Physical Laboratory (N.P.L.) of the United Kingdom, the National Bureaux of Standards (N.B.S.) of the United States and their equivalents in other countries have expended considerable effort in determining the absolute value of electrical quantities (see appendix I). That is to say quantities such as the ohm, the ampere and the farad have been determined in terms of the fundamental quantities of mass, length and time with the greatest possible precision although uncertainty still exists in their exact values, even if it is only a few parts in 1 000 000 000.

Such precise determinations of electrical quantities are necessary so that comparisons of the standards used in every country may be made, and engineers and scientists throughout the world may have a common set of references: for example, 1 Russian volt = 1 American volt = 1 U.K. volt = 1 Australian volt, and so on, hence performance of equipment and measurement of physical phenomena are made on a common basis.

In electrical measurements, the standards of greatest importance are those of current resistance, capacitance and frequency, it being possible to derive other quantities such as voltage and power from those listed. The absolute determination of electrical quantities is in itself a science and an appreciation of their necessity should be sufficient at this stage, where the absolute standards can be considered to be the reference by which derived or 'material' standards are calibrated.

1.3.5 Calibration Procedures

Environmental conditions will affect the performance of many electrical instruments; therefore calibrations must be conducted under known conditions of temperature, pressure and humidity. It is therefore important that a room in which temperature, and preferably humidity as well, are controlled, be set aside

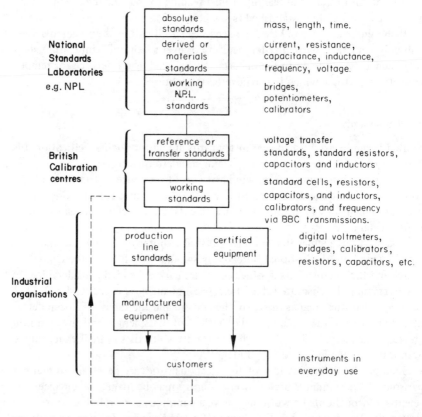

Figure 1.21. Relationship chain between instruments in everyday use and the absolute standards

solely for the calibration of instruments. The requirements for approval of a laboratory under the British Calibration Service (B.C.S.) scheme [14] are for the temperature to be maintained at $20\,^{\circ}C \pm 2\,^{\circ}C$ (or $23\,^{\circ}C \pm 2\,^{\circ}C$) and the relative humidity to be between the limits of 35 per cent and 70 per cent. The effects of variations in atmospheric pressure on the performance of electrical instruments are in general small, except in the measurement of high voltages by sphere-gap breakdown where they are of extreme importance and must be allowed for. However, the facility to measure atmospheric pressure in a calibration room for electrical instruments should not be overlooked as it may constitute an undetected systematic error in a particular measurement. For example, the dielectric constant of air is pressure dependent.

The hierarchy of reference between instruments in daily engineering use and the national or absolute standards can be summarised by diagram in figure 1.21.

Electrical instruments are usually calibrated either by comparing performance with a similar but superior instrument, or by using a source of selectable amplitude, this latter form generally being known as a calibrator. In either situation the uncertainty in the reference should be less than a quarter of the specified uncertainty in the instrument under calibration. [14]

1.4 INPUT CHARACTERISTICS

It has been shown (section 1.3.2) that the input resistance of an instrument is of extreme importance as the magnitude of that parameter will affect the disturbance the instrument causes when it is inserted in a circuit. Other input characteristics that must be considered when selecting an instrument are described in the following sections.

1.4.1 Sensitivity

The sensitivity of an instrument should either be quoted in terms of the number of units for full scale indication, or as a unit of deflection. Examples of these are 1 A full scale deflection, 10 mm/μA and 0.1 μA/mm. For digital instruments the sensitivity is usually quoted in terms of the resolution (1 l.s.d.) for the most sensitive range. For example, '10 μV on the 100 mV range', although on occasions the sensitivity is only deducible from the range and the display, for example, '2 V range and $3\frac{1}{2}$ digits (1999)'.

1.4.2 Scaling

Most instruments have an effective range that extends from 10 per cent to 100 per cent of the full scale value. However, many signals will be outside the effective range, those that are too large requiring scaling down by some division process while those that are too small will require amplification.

Current division

Since most direct-acting pointer instruments have a deflection that is proportional to some function of current, to increase the range of currents that can be measured, a current division circuit that shunts some of the current around the instrument is required. Figure 1.22 illustrates the situation and if the meter

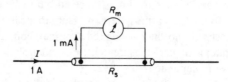

Figure 1.22. Current dividing or shunt circuit

movement has a full scale deflection of 1 mA and resistance 100 Ω, the shunt resistor R_s (to provide a full scale when $I = 1$ A) may be evaluated from the current division equation

$$\frac{I_m}{I} = \frac{R_s}{R_m + R_s} \tag{1.23}$$

therefore

$$R_s = \frac{I_m R_m}{I - I_m} \tag{1.24}$$

and substituting these particular values in equation 1.24 gives $R_s = 0.1001\ \Omega$.

Voltage division

The voltage across the meter, in the above section, corresponding to full scale deflection, is 1 mA $\times$ 100 Ω or 100 mV. To increase the voltages that may be measured by the meter simply requires a resistance in series with the meter so that the applied voltage is divided between R and R_m (figure 1.23). Hence for full scale indication to occur at an applied voltage V_a

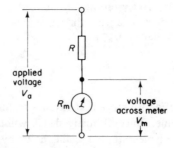

Figure 1.23. Simple voltage scaling circuit

$$\frac{V_m}{V_a} = \frac{R_m}{R + R_m} \tag{1.25}$$

or

$$R = R_m \frac{(V_a - V_m)}{V_m} \tag{1.26}$$

Hence for $V_a = 10$ V, $R_m = 9.9$ kΩ.

The methods of current and voltage division described above are to introduce the concepts of scaling. Other techniques, many of which are based on the above, are described in subsequent chapters.

1.4.3 Matching

In some instrumentation systems a factor of importance is the conveyance of the maximum amount of power contained in the output signal from a sensor into a display or recording instrument, for example to obtain the maximum deflection of a u.v. recorder galvanometer. Such a requirement necessitates the matching of the output impedance of the sensor to the input impedance of the measuring circuits. Consider a signal source, such as that shown in figure 1.24. Let V_s be

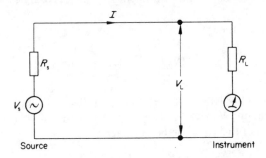

Figure 1.24. Source and instrument impedance mismatch

the source voltage, R_s be the source resistance and R_L be the load resistance. Then

$$I = \frac{V_s}{R_s + R_L}$$

and power transferred to the load $= I^2 R_L$

$$= \frac{V_s^2 R_L}{R_s^2 + 2R_sR_L + R_L^2} = \frac{V_s^2}{\dfrac{R_s^2}{R_L} + 2R_s + R_L} \tag{1.27}$$

To find the value of R_L that makes the load power a maximum, the denominator of equation 1.27 must be a minimum. This will occur when

$$\frac{d\left(\dfrac{R_s^2}{R_L} + 2R_s + R_L\right)}{dR_L} = 0$$

or

$$\frac{-R_s^2}{R_L^2} + 1 = 0$$

or

$$R_s = R_L \qquad (1.28)$$

In practice this desirable state may not exist. As an example consider the circuit in figure 1.24, where the source (V_s) has an impedance (R_s) of 600 Ω, and the instrument to which it is connected has an impedance of 1000 Ω; under these conditions the power transmitted to the load is 93 per cent of the maximum power that could have been transmitted, and for the d.c. case the optimum may only be attained by changing to an instrument that has an input impedance of 600 Ω. If the signal from the source is purely a.c. (no d.c. component) it is possible to match the source and instrument impedances using a matching transformer.

From transformer theory

$$R_{eqs} = \frac{N_p^2}{N_s^2} \times R_s$$

where R_{eqs} is the equivalent value of resistance in the secondary circuit referred to the primary circuit; N_p and N_s being respectively the number of primary and secondary turns. Let the equation be rewritten

$$\frac{R_1}{R_2} = \left(\frac{N_1}{N_2}\right)^2$$

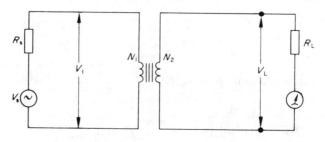

Figure 1.25. Use of a matching transformer

where R_1 is the resistance of the circuit on the side of the transformer which has N_1 turns; R_2 and N_2 being the resistance and turns on the other side of the transformer. Then if this transformer is added to the circuit of figure 1.24 it may be redrawn as in figure 1.25, and for matching of the source and instrument, the transformer should have a turns ratio of

$$\frac{N_2}{N_1} = \left(\frac{R_2}{R_1}\right)^{\frac{1}{2}} = \left(\frac{R_L}{R_s}\right)^{\frac{1}{2}} \tag{1.29}$$

which for the above example requires

$$\frac{N_2}{N_1} = \left(\frac{1000}{600}\right)^{\frac{1}{2}} = 1.291$$

that is, the matching transformer would have to have a turns ratio of 1.291 giving $V_L = 1.291V_1$ and

$$\text{power transferred to the instrument} = \frac{V_L{}^2}{R_L} = \frac{(1.291)^2 V_1{}^2}{1000}$$

$$= 0.001\,666 V_1{}^2 \text{ W}$$

Now

$$V_1 = \frac{V_s}{2} \text{ (for maximum power transfer)}$$

Therefore
power to the instrument $= 0.001\,666\,\dfrac{V_s{}^2}{4} = 0.416\,V_s{}^2 \text{ mW}$

$$\text{power available from the source} = \frac{V_s{}^2}{2R_s} = \frac{V_s{}^2}{2 \times 600} = 0.833\,V_s{}^2 \text{ mW}$$

The above shows that the maximum possible (that is 50 per cent) of the power available may be transferred to the instrument using a matching transformer. In practice, there are limitations to this principle. First, the practical transformer has losses and these must be supplied from the signal source; secondly, matching transformers are expensive and the increase in sensitivity obtained by matching may not be justifiable; thirdly, a matching transformer can only be used if the signal is alternating since d.c. signals will not pass through the transformer.

1.5 WAVEFORM

Signals that alternate or vary with time in a simple regular manner, result from many natural situations: for example, vibration, sound, sea waves, etc. They are also encountered when measurements are to be made on many electrical or electronic systems, examples being power supply networks and communication systems.

1.5.1 Definitions

Sinewave

The simplest form of alternating quantity is the single frequency sinewave (see figure 1.26), which for a voltage is usually expressed algebraically as

$$v = V_m \sin \omega t \tag{1.30}$$

where v is the instantaneous value of the voltage, V_m is the maximum value of the voltage, ω is the frequency in radians per second and t is time in seconds.

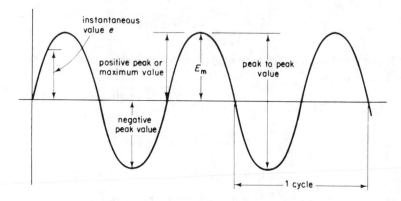

Figure 1.26. Single frequency sinewave

Since for direct quantities it may be accepted that $I = V/R$ the current at any instant in time will be

$$i = \frac{V_m}{R} \sin \omega t$$

or

$$i = I_m \sin \omega t \tag{1.31}$$

where I_m is the maximum current value.

Mean value

The true mean value of an unbiased sinewave will be zero. However, in measuring alternating signals the quantity referred to as the mean value is the *rectified mean value* which for half a cycle is by calculus (if $\omega t = \theta$)

$$I_{mean} = \frac{1}{\pi} \int_0^{\pi} [I_m \sin \theta] \, d\theta$$

$$= \frac{I_m}{\pi} [-\cos \theta]_0^{\pi}$$

$$= \frac{2I_m}{\pi} = 0.637I_m \tag{1.32}$$

Alternatively from figure 1.27

$$I_{mean} = \frac{i_1 + i_2 + i_3 + i_4 + i_5 + i_6 + i_7 + i_8}{8} \tag{1.33}$$

$$= I_m \left(\frac{0.195 + 0.556 + 0.831 + 0.981 + 0.981 + 0.831 + 0.556 + 0.195}{8} \right)$$

$$= 0.640I_m$$

This coarse method of taking eight samples in a half-wave would, by using a larger number of samples give a value nearer to that obtained by using calculus.

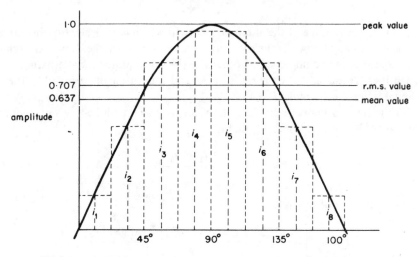

Figure 1.27. Evaluation of the mean value of a rectified sinewave

R.M.S. values

The power consumed by a resistor at any instant will be

$$p = v\,i = i^2 R \tag{1.34}$$

and since the current value is squared, p will be positive whether i is negative or positive. Thus the mean power supplied over a cycle will be

$$P = \frac{R}{2\pi} \int_0^{2\pi} [I_m^2 \sin^2 \theta]\, d\theta$$

$$= \frac{I_m^2 R}{2\pi} \int_0^{2\pi} \left[\frac{1 - \cos 2\theta}{2} \right] d\theta$$

$$= \frac{I_m{}^2 R}{4\pi} \left[0 - \frac{\sin 2\theta}{2} \right]_0^{2\pi}$$

$$= \frac{I_m{}^2 R}{2} \tag{1.35}$$

If the mean power is defined as the alternating power equivalent of that produced by direct voltage and current

$$P = I_{\text{direct}}{}^2 R = \frac{I_m{}^2}{2} R$$

Therefore

$$I_{\text{direct}} = \frac{I_m}{\sqrt{2}} \tag{1.36}$$

This effective value of the alternating current which is equivalent to the direct value is normally known as the *root-mean-square* or r.m.s. value. It is of considerable importance and unless stated otherwise the value quoted for alternating quantities is assumed to be the r.m.s. value, and conventionally denoted by the capital letter, for example, I or V.

If the signal is nonperiodic the r.m.s. value may be established by a procedure similar to that in equation 1.33, that is

$$I = \sqrt{\left(\frac{i_1{}^2 + i_2{}^2 + i_3{}^2 + i_4{}^2}{n} \right)} \tag{1.37}$$

Using the values of figure 1.27

$$I = \sqrt{\left[\left(\frac{(0.195^2 + 0.556^2 + 0.831^2 + 0.981^2)}{8} \right) 2 I_m{}^2 \right]}$$

$$= 0.7072 I_m$$

Similarly it may be shown that the r.m.s. value of a voltage wave is

$$V = \frac{V_m}{\sqrt{2}} = 0.707 V_m \tag{1.38}$$

Form factor and crest factor

These terms which are constantly used in connection with measurements of alternating quantities are defined using the expressions

$$\text{form factor} = \frac{\text{r.m.s. value}}{\text{mean value}} \tag{1.39}$$

$$\text{crest factor} = \frac{\text{peak value}}{\text{r.m.s. value}} \qquad (1.40)$$

For the single frequency sinewave the values of these quantities are 1.11 and 1.414 respectively.

Phase relationships

When alternating signals are present in a circuit containing a combination of resistive and reactive (inductive or capacitive) components, a time displacement will exist between the signals at various points in the circuit. If the signals are all of one frequency this time displacement is referred to as a phase angle, but this latter term cannot be used if more than a single frequency is present.

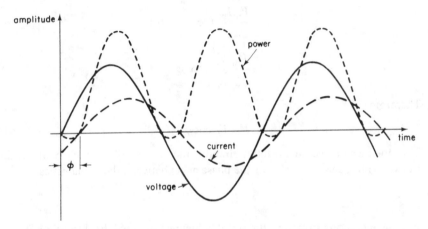

Figure 1.28. Voltage, current and power waveforms in a reactive circuit

Power

The power in a circuit at any instant in time is $p = vi$ (equation 1.34) for the conditions in figure 1.28

$$v = V_m \sin \theta$$

$$i = V_m \sin (\theta + \phi)$$

Thus

$$p = V_m \sin \theta \times I_m \sin (\theta + \phi)$$

$$= V_m I_m \sin \theta \sin (\theta + \phi)$$

$$= \frac{V_m I_m}{2} [\cos \theta - \cos (2\theta - \phi)]$$

Therefore the mean power over a cycle is the average power

$$P = \frac{1}{2\pi} \int_0^{2\pi} \frac{1}{2} V_m I_m \left[\cos \phi - \cos (2\theta - \phi)\right] d\theta$$

$$= \frac{I_m}{4\pi} \int_0^{2\pi} \left[\cos \phi - \cos (2\theta - \phi)\right] d\theta$$

Examining the terms to be integrated, $\cos \phi$ is a constant (ϕ does not change throughout a cycle), and $\cos (2\theta - \phi)$ will go through two complete cycles as θ goes from 0 to 2π, so its average value must be zero. Hence

$$P = \frac{V_m I_m}{4\pi} \int_0^{2\pi} \cos \phi \; d\theta$$

$$= \frac{V_m I_m}{4\pi} (\cos \phi \times 2\pi)$$

$$= \frac{V_m}{\sqrt{2}} \frac{I_m}{\sqrt{2}} \cos \phi$$

Therefore

$$P = VI \cos \phi \tag{1.41}$$

Thus the mean power in a reactive circuit is the product of the r.m.s. voltage, the r.m.s. current, and the cosine of the phase angle between these quantities.

Bias

In some measuring situations the signal being measured will be 'biased' or at a potential relative to the zero or earth line. Such a situation is illustrated by the waveform shown in figure 1.29 and it will readily be appreciated that the mean,

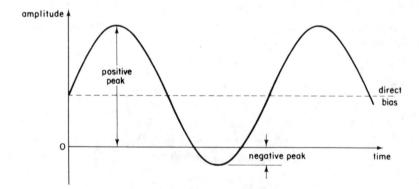

Figure 1.29. Sinewave signal with a direct bias

peak and other values characteristic of a signal referred to above will be affected
by the presence of a bias; a condition which can create considerable difficulties
in some measurement situations.

1.5.2 Harmonics

It is conveniently assumed that alternating signals are single frequency sinusoidal
waveforms. Although this is fortunately a satisfactory assumption for many
situations the presence of harmonics in signal waveforms cannot always be
ignored, and their magnitudes must be established, either by using Fourier
analysis or by a suitably designed electronic instrument that displays the unknown waveform as its frequency components.

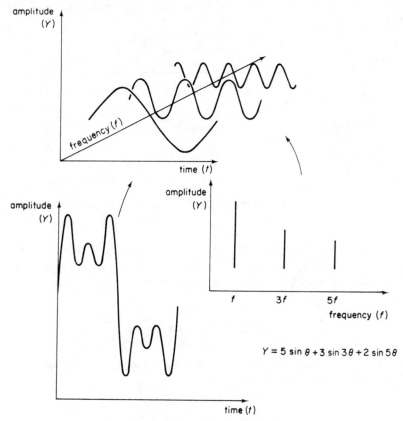

Figure 1.30. Presentation of a multi-frequency waveform on time and frequency
axes

Figure 1.30 presents a waveform that consists of a fundamental, a third and a
fifth harmonic both as a function of time and of frequency, the three-dimensional
arrangement attempting to link the two.

1.5.3 Frequency Effects

The frequency of the signals under investigation plays a very important part in deciding which measurement technique, and hence which type of instrument, should be used in a particular situation for some techniques are only suitable for direct signals while the presence of a series capacitor in the input of some instruments effectively blocks any direct or low frequency signal.

Bandwidth

The range of frequencies over which an instrument can be used is usually referred to as its bandwidth. This property is normally specified in terms of 3 dB points, that is, the frequencies, on the response curve (figure 1.31), at which the response has fallen by 3 dB or 30 per cent from the mid frequency response (see section 6.4.1).

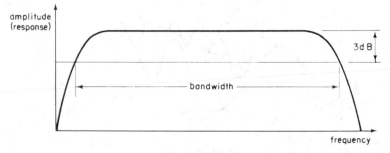

Figure 1.31. Response amplitude against frequency characteristic of an instrument

If two instruments are arranged in cascade, for example, recording the output of a transducer with an oscilloscope, the bandwidth (B) of the resulting system can be estimated using the empirical relationship

$$B_{system} = \frac{B_1 \times B_2}{\sqrt{(B_1{}^2 + B_2{}^2)}} \qquad (1.42)$$

A bandwidth should always be quoted with two frequency limits, examples being d.c. to 10 MHz, and 50 Hz to 10 kHz.

Rise time

The presence in electrical and electronic circuits of inductive and capacitive components means that the output of a circuit will not instantaneously follow changes in signal level. To evaluate this delaying property of an instrument, or circuit, it has become customary to specify the response of instruments, used for studying fast pulses, in terms of their rise time—the time interval measured from 10 to 90 per cent of a step change (see figure 2.61). This quantity should not be confused with the time constant of a circuit which is the value given to the time interval from the start to 63.2 per cent of the final value of a step change (see section 6.4.1).

1.6 INTERFERENCE

Measurements involving small electrical signals can be seriously affected by the presence of interference, that is, the displayed quantity will be the sum of the desired signal and unwanted or interference signals. It is therefore necessary to ensure that instruments and connections are adequately protected from, and capable of rejecting, interference signals.

1.6.1 Environmental Interference

The interference signals grouped under this heading are those related to effects dependent on such quantities as temperature, humidity, pressure, atmospheric pollutants, and so on.

The effects of temperature on the performance of an instrument are normally allowed for within the terms of the specification, that is, the quoted values are stated to hold over a range of temperatures, outside of which a further allowance to the measurement uncertainty must be made.

The effects of atmospheric pollutants require consideration of the environment in which the instrument is going to be used, for it must be realised that dust, moisture and fumes from some soldering fluxes can have unrealised effects on the signal measured (see section 7.1.2).

1.6.2 Coupled Interference

Electrostatic coupling

When a conductor A is maintained at a potential relative to zero (earth) potential, it will be enveloped in an electrostatic field (see figure 1.32a). If another conductor B, insulated from earth, is introduced into this electrostatic field it will attain a potential dependent on its size and its position in the field (see figure 1.32b), and should the potential of conductor A be alternating then the conductor B will 'pick up' an alternating voltage. This linking by means of an electrostatic field is termed capacitive coupling and may cause considerable interference problems in measurement circuits. To shield the conductor B from the electrostatic field of A simply requires the inserting of a conducting sheet, held at zero potential, between the two conductors as in figure 1.32c.

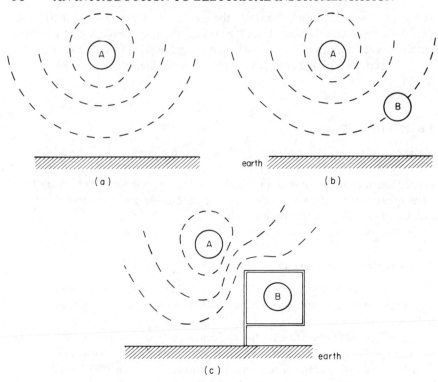

Figure 1.32. Conductor and shield in an electrostatic field

Electromagnetic coupling

Any current-carrying conductor is surrounded by a magnetic field, the strength of this field depending on the magnitude of the current, and should it be alternating, voltages will be induced in any conducting material that is positioned within this magnetic field. Thus any signal carrying connection passing near a current carrying conductor will be magnetically coupled to it, and an interference voltage will be induced in the signal carrying conductor. One of three forms of magnetic shielding may be used to reduce electromagnetic interference, these being

(a) Conducting shield. The positioning of a thick conducting sheet around the component or lead to be screened; then magnetic flux entering the conducting sheet induces currents which themselves produce a magnetic flux to oppose the applied field.

(b) Magnetic shield. The positioning of a high permeability path around the component to be screened so that the magnetic flux of the interference field is diverted into the shield and away from the component. (Note: the thickness of the shield required in both (a) and (b) will be a function of

(c) Lead twisting. By arranging equipment so that the coupling between the magnetic field source and the signal carrying connections is either cancelled out, or kept to a minimum. The former requirement may be met by ensuring that the two leads connecting a source to an instrument follow an identical path, and such an arrangement is greatly assisted by twisting the two leads together. The latter requirement can only be fulfilled by ensuring that the signal carrying conductors are remote from any source of magnetic flux.

In practice the most likely sources of electromagnetic interference are 50 Hz transformers and inductors, and all signal carrying conductors should be kept well clear of such items. If two, or more, inductors have to be used in a circuit they should be arranged for minimum coupling, that is their axes should be arranged at $90°$ to each other.

1.7 SELECTION

This introductory chapter began by posing a number of questions relating to the selection process that can be adopted to ensure the performance of a measurement in a satisfactory manner. Although the preceding pages cannot have answered these questions completely, hopefully they will have made the reader pause and wonder whether, in the past, he has always made measurements with sufficient forethought.

To reinforce the importance of those questions, they are restated here so that the reader may remember them when next making a measurement.

(a) What is the most suitable method of measurement?
(b) How should the result be displayed?
(c) What tolerance on the measured value is acceptable?
(d) How will the presence of the instrument affect the signal?
(e) How will the signal wave-shape affect the instrument's performance?
(f) Over what range of frequencies does the instrument perform correctly?
(g) What will the effects of interference be on the result obtained?

It should be realised that this set of questions is a starting point—a more detailed set of conditions and requirements are contained in chapter 8.

REFERENCES

1 C. T. Baldwin, *Fundamentals of Electrical Measurements* (Harrap, London, 1961)
2 S. Stein and J. Jay Jones, *Modern Communication Principles* (McGraw-Hill, New York, 1967)
3 E. C. Bell and R. W. Whitehead, *Basic Electrical Engineering and Instrumentation* (Crosby Lockwood Staples, London, 1977)
4 N. M. Morris, *Digital Electronic Circuits and Systems* (Macmillan, London and Basingstoke, 1974)

5 D. Moralee, Floppy discs, the storage medium for microprocessor systems, *Electronics Power*, **24** (1978) 637–41

6 K. Baker, Solid-state serial memories—the role of bubbles and c.c.d.s, *Electronics Power,* **24** (1978) 647–52

7 R. Squires, An introduction to microprocessors, *Kent tech. Rev., ***25** (1979) 20–4

8 E. Huggins, *Microprocessors and Microcomputers, their use and programming* (Macmillan, London and Basingstoke, 1979)

9 G. F. Weston, Alphanumeric display, *Proc. I.E.E.,* **125** (1978)

10 J. Smith, Experimental storage display panels using d.c. gas discharges without resistors, *I.E.E.E. Trans. electronic Devices,* **22** (1975) 642–9

11 BS 5233: 1975 Glossary of terms used in metrology

12 A. Simpson, *Testing Methods and Reliability, Electronics* (Macmillan, London and Basingstoke, 1976)

13 BS 89: Part 1: 1970 Single purpose direct acting electrical indicating instruments and their accessories

14 British Calibration Service, *General Criteria for Laboratory Approval* (London, 1967)

2

Analogue Instruments

An analogue device is one in which the operation and output are continuously variable and bear a fixed relationship to the input.

In section 1.1 the concepts of analogue instruments were outlined and for the purpose of this chapter analogue instruments have been divided into four groups

(a) those in which a 'moving coil movement' is used as the sensing element
(b) those in which some other form of electromechanical sensing element is used
(c) the instruments that use a cathode ray tube (c.r.t.) as the display medium
(d) the instruments that use magnetic tape as a storage medium.

2.1 MOVING COIL INSTRUMENTS

The principle used in the construction of this type of instrument is that current passing through a conductor generates a magnetic field around the conductor and if this field is arranged to interact with a permanent magnetic field, a force acts on the current carrying conductor. If the conductor (that is, the coil) is constrained to move in a rotary manner an angular deflection or movement proportional to the current may be obtained, resulting in an instrument that has a linear scale but which, due to its inertia, can only respond to steady state and slowly varying quantities. The linearity of scale is an extremely useful feature and accounts for the use of moving coil instruments as the display in many complex electronic instruments.

The general arrangement of the moving coil instrument is indicated in figure 2.1. The permanent magnet system has over the years been considerably reduced in size due to the improvements in magnet design as better materials have become available.

The coil may be air cored or mounted on a metal former; if the latter is present it will contribute to the damping of the instrument (eddy currents) but will add to the inertia of the movement.

If an air-cored coil offset from the axis of rotation (figure 2.2) is used, the

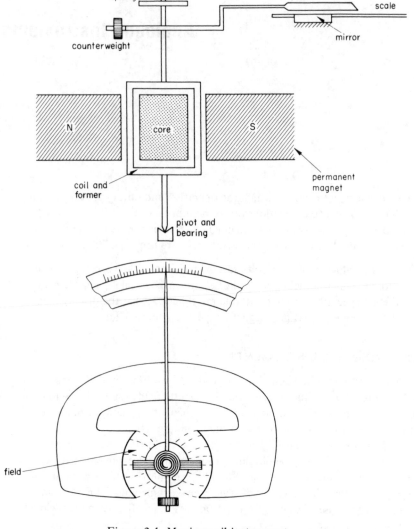

Figure 2.1. Moving coil instrument

scale length of the instrument can be increased from 120° to 240° or even 300° enabling a better resolution of reading to be obtained for the same measurement range.

The suspension may be either a variation on the jewelled bearing 'clock spring' arrangement (figure 2.1) or a ribbon suspension (figure 2.2) in which there are no bearings and where the control torque is derived from the twisting of the suspension ribbon. This latter method is claimed to be advantageous as it eliminates bearing friction.

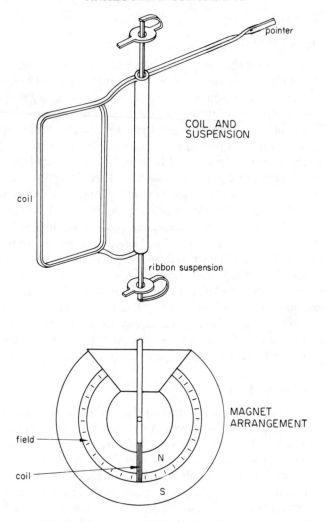

Figure 2.2. 'Long scale' moving coil instrument

Except in some inexpensive instruments, the pointer is normally of a light-weight construction being in the form of a fine blade. The section over the scale is vertical so that parallax errors are reduced (see section 1.2.1). The weight of the pointer is normally counterbalanced by weights situated diametrically oppo-site its centre of mass.

To damp the movement a combination of electrical eddy current effects, the passage of the movement plus vanes through the surrounding air, and friction in the bearings is used.

2.1.1 Null Detectors

Direct Acting Galvanometers

The normal use of a galvanometer is in the determination of a 'balance' condition, by detecting the absence of current flow between parts of a circuit. Since the moving coil movement is a current sensing device, giving a deflection dependent on the direction of the applied current and proportional to its magnitude, it is ideally suited for this purpose. Hence, by arranging for the zero current condition to occur when the pointer is positioned at the centre of the scale, and the pointer being free to move in a positive or negative direction depending on the direction of current in the coil, a satisfactory detector for use in d.c. bridge circuits (see section 3.3) is devised. The pointer versions are limited in sensitivity (typically -50 to $+50\ \mu A$). For the measurement of very small currents or for use as a sensitive null detector, galvanometers of high sensitivity (typically 430 mm/μA) are required, when the coil will have a large number of turns (bonded together for maximum strength and stability) and suspended by a high tensile alloy strip. This type of suspension provides the small control torque and also acts as connections to and from the coil (figure 2.3). A small amount of fluid damping may be included but the major part of the damping is electromagnetic (see section 2.1.4). To obtain a large deflection for a small movement of the coil the reflection of a light spot is used which by means of a mirror system within the galvanometer case (figure 2.3) results in a large magnification.

Vibration Galvanometer

The construction of a vibration galvanometer[1] is slightly different from the steady state galvanometer in that there is no iron core, the coil is very narrow and the control constant is large. The vibration galvanometer is used in a.c. circuits as a null detector, it being arranged that the natural frequency of vibration of the movement coincides with the frequency present in the a.c. circuit. The amplitude against frequency curve is sharply peaked (if the damping is small) so a vibration galvanometer tuned to the fundamental frequency of the a.c. circuit will have little or no response to harmonics in the electrical signal. Vibration galvanometers may be constructed to have resonant frequencies up to 1 kHz, but are now normally only used at power-line frequencies.

Electronic Galvanometer

The practical limitations on the sensitive light spot galvanometer are its susceptibility to vibration, it is relatively fragile (even allowing for the improvements in robustness obtained using taut band suspension), and the slow response exhibited as balance is approached. By replacing the optical magnification system with a low drift, high gain differential input amplifier (see p. 322) it is possible to revert to using a centre zero moving coil pointer instrument for the display and create a device known as an *electronic galvanometer* that has good overload protection,

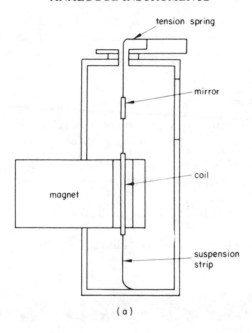

(a)

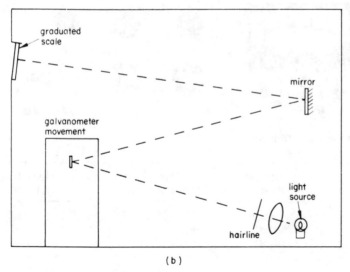

(b)

Figure 2.3. Light spot moving coil galvanometer: (a) galvanometer movement,
(b) optical system

is less susceptible to vibration, is easily read in a well-lit environment, is compact,
portable (if battery powered), may have a current sensitivity greater than traditional galvanometers, and have an output that is suitable for feeding to a chart
recorder.[2]

Although electronic galvanometers are less affected by the magnitude of the source resistance than the light spot equivalents, their response time will still be considerable if the source resistance is very much greater than the specified optimum value.[3]

Sample Specification

The following is an example of a specification for an electronic null detector that has a design optimised for use as a detector in bridge circuits.

Keithley Model 147 Null Detector and Nanovoltmeter

Range   30 nV full scale to 100 mV on a centre zero meter. 16 ranges in 1× and 3× steps

Accuracy   Meter: 2% of full scale on all ranges. Output: 1% of full scale on all ranges

Zero drift   Less than 25 nV per 24 h after 1 h warm-up. Long term drift is noncumulative

Input characteristics

Range	Input R greater than	Max. source resistance	Line freq. rejection
30 nV	10 kΩ	100 Ω	5000; 1
3 μV	1 MΩ	10 kΩ	300; 1
100 μV	1 MΩ	10 kΩ	50; 1

Common mode rejection   50 Hz greater than 10 dB

Isolation   (circuit ground to chassis ground) Greater than 10 GΩ shunted by 1 nF. Circuit ground may be floated up to ± 400 V with respect to chassis ground

Rise time   (10% to 90%) 30 nV range, less than 3 s when source resistance is less than 10% of maximum, 5 s when using max source resistance

The specification clearly shows the improved sensitivity possible with the use of electronic amplification. Drift, which in this type of instrument could be a problem, is specified as being less than full scale on the most sensitive range over a 24 hour period, and at 25 nV, is of the order of magnitude of variations due to external causes.

Tuned A.C. Detectors

In balancing an a.c. circuit it is not sufficient simply to use an a.c. microvolt-meter because as balance is approached the remaining fundamental or operating frequency signal becomes obscured in the residual harmonics and the balance point is ill defined. A very satisfactory way of overcoming this difficulty is to use a tuned amplifier detector.[4] In this type of instrument a frequency selective amplifier is used to magnify the fundamental of the input signal which is then rectified and fed to the moving coil meter. The adjustable frequency range of such a detector may be from 10 Hz to 100 kHz.

Phase-sensitive Rectifiers (Detectors)

In a number of cases it is the comparison between the in-phase components of two voltages which is required, so a detector which only compares these parts of two voltages will be at an advantage.

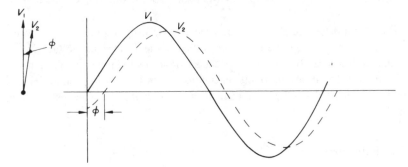

Figure 2.4. Voltages to be compared

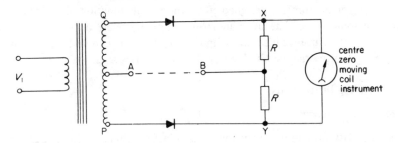

Figure 2.5. Principle of phase sensitive detector (rectifier) (see also figure 6.46)

Consider two voltages (figure 2.4) which are of different magnitudes and have a small phase angle between them, it being desired to compare only the component of V_2 in phase with V_1.

Let the voltage V_1 be applied to a transformer whose secondary winding is centre-tapped and connected to the circuit in figure 2.5. In the positive half-cycle of V_1 current will flow round the path XBAQ and the meter would deflect, say, to the right; in the negative half of the cycle current would flow round the path YBAP the meter deflecting to the left; but, providing the frequency of V_1 was greater than a few hertz, the resulting meter deflection would be zero, that is the true average over one cycle.

Suppose the link AB is now removed and the voltage V_2 is applied between these points. The total voltage driving current around path XBAQ in the positive half-cycle is then the sum of V_1 and V_2 and the meter needle will deflect further to the right. However, during the negative half-cycle when P is negative to A, B is also negative to A, and the resulting voltage driving current around YBAP is $(V_1 - V_2)$ and the meter deflection to the left will have been reduced. Thus the average deflection of the meter over a complete cycle will be to the right of the centre zero, the magnitude of this deflection depending on the relative magnitudes of V_1 and V_2.

If V_2 were antiphase ($180°$ out of phase) with V_1 the average deflection for one cycle would be to the left. Thus a detector is obtained which is sensitive to magnitude and capable of comparing the relative phase of a single voltage with a reference.

The circuit discussed above can be used satisfactorily in practice, an alternative being to interchange the reference voltage V_1 and the signal voltage V_2. A possible addition can be a smoothing capacitor across the moving coil meter.

To reduce the vibration effects on the pointer of the moving coil meter, circuits which yield a full wave rectification are advantageous (see also section 6.6).[5]

2.1.2 Multimeters

The properties of the moving coil movement, in particular its linear scale and good sensitivity (torque to weight ratio), have resulted in its use for the display in multi-range instruments designed either for a single function or for multi-function applications. The latter are more commonly referred to as multimeters. To provide the current ranges in such instruments, shunts could be used, while the voltage ranges may be obtained by the use of series resistors.

Direct Acting Instruments

Direct current ranges

The sensitivity of the movement that is used in a multimeter will be such that full scale deflection would be obtained when a current of (typically) 50 μA passes through the coil. To provide the current ranges a number of simple shunts could be used, but these are more suitably used in single-range instruments (where a manufacturer uses a standard movement in producing a 'range' of ammeters with various sensitivities) or alternatively as external shunts for use with high grade (accuracy class 0.1) instruments. The method used in most direct acting multimeters to obtain the current ranges is to employ a universal shunt. This form of current shunt consists of a number of resistors in series across which the movement is connected, the various current ranges are obtained by the current division resulting from applying the current to be measured to an appropriate tapping point in the resistor chain (see section 6.2.1).

Example

Consider the necessity to provide current ranges of 10 mA, 3 mA, 1 mA and 300 μA using a movement that has a full scale deflection of 100 μA, and a resistance of 2000 Ω. Consider the input current (I_i) applied to tapping point 'a' of figure 2.6. In this position, full scale deflection of the movement should correspond to an applied current of 300 μA. This means that 100 μA should pass

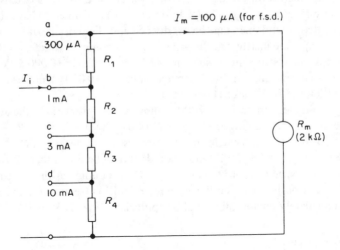

Figure 2.6. 'Universal' current shunt to obtain direct current ranges in a multimeter (see example)

through the movement and 200 μA through the shunt resistor. Thus to provide this current division $R_1 + R_2 + R_3 + R_4 = 0.5R_m$ or looked at in a different way $(I_i - I_m)(R_1 + R_2 + R_3 + R_4) = I_m R_m$. Hence in this case the total resistance of the universal shunt is $0.5R_m$ or 1000 Ω.

Considering now the input tapping 'b' for which full scale deflection of the movement should correspond to an input of 1 mA

$$900(R_2 + R_3 + R_4) = 100(R_m + R_1)$$

$$9(1000 - R_1) = 2000 + R_1$$

$$7000 = 10R_1$$

$$R_1 = 700 \; \Omega$$

and by similar calculations

$$R_2 = 200 \; \Omega$$

$$R_3 = \; 70 \; \Omega$$

$$R_4 = \; 30 \; \Omega$$

In a practical multimeter as many as seven or eight direct current ranges are provided by this kind of technique.

Direct voltage ranges

To obtain the multiplicity of voltage ranges required for the production of a versatile instrument, one of the two methods shown in figure 2.7 may be used. The chain arrangement shown in figure 2.7a may be claimed to save space, whereas the separate resistor arrangement (as in figure 2.7b) is claimed to have the advantage that should one range be overloaded and the series resistor damaged the other ranges are unaffected. In either case it is common to refer to the input resistance of the instrument as 'so many' Ω/V (for example 10 000 Ω/V) so that the total input resistance on the 1 V range would be 10 000 Ω, on the 3 V range 30 000 Ω, on the 10 V range 100 000 Ω and so on.

This would mean that for the 2000 Ω movement considered in the above example, in the chain arrangement $R_1 = 10\,000 - 2000 = 8000 \; \Omega$, $R_2 = 20\,000$ Ω, $R_3 = 70\,000 \; \Omega$, etc., while in the separate resistor arrangement $R_a = 8000 \; \Omega$, $R_b = 28\,000 \; \Omega$, $R_c = 98\,000 \; \Omega$, and so on. It should be noted that in some manufacturers' specifications the quantity (Ω/V) is quoted as the sensitivity and while the relationship between the accepted definition (section 1.4.1) and Ω/V is not immediately obvious, it should be appreciated that $\Omega/V \equiv V/I/V \equiv V^2/I$.

Resistance ranges

To utilise the moving coil movement for the measurement of resistance requires the provision of a source. In most multimeters this takes the form of one or more dry cells depending on the magnitude of resistances that can be measured, and the number of ranges provided. The methods used to perform this type of measurement are illustrated in figure 2.8, and are referred to as:

(a) the series arrangement in which the unknown is connected in series with the meter movement so that full scale deflection will correspond to an unknown resistance of 0 Ω and be on the right hand side of the scale; or

(b) the shunt arrangement in which the unknown is connected in parallel with

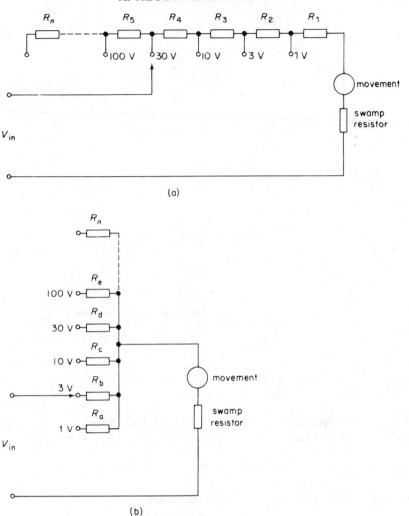

Figure 2.7. Resistor arrangements for multimeter voltage ranges: (a) chain, (b) separate

the meter movement so that short circuiting the meter terminals gives the zero on the left hand side of the scale and an open circuit or infinite resistance gives full scale deflection.

Example

Consider the adaptation of the 100 μA movement (used in the previous example) for the measurement of resistance, assuming the source to be a 1.5 V battery. For the series case the adjustment resistor that must be connected in circuit

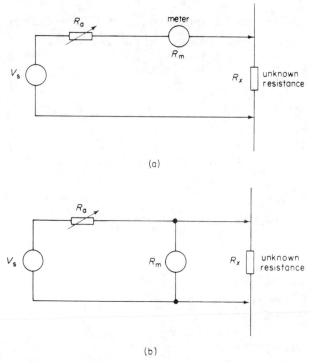

(a)

(b)

Figure 2.8. Arrangements used in multimeters for the measurement of resistance:
(a) series, (b) parallel circuit

should have a value such that when R_x is zero full scale deflection of the meter
is obtained. In other words, the current through the meter will be 100 μA.

$$(R_a + R_m) = \frac{1.5 \times 10^6}{100} = 15\,000\ \Omega$$

and since the movement had a resistance of 2000 Ω

$$R_a = 15\,000 - 2\,000 = 13\,000\ \Omega$$

In practice R_a must be adjustable to allow for the changes in the terminal voltage
of the battery as it ages, so this adjustment resistor could comprise of a fixed
10 kΩ and a variable 5 kΩ resistor, in series.

It is worth considering why for both the series and shunt arrangement the
adjustment resistor has the same value for a given movement sensitivity and
source voltage. To obtain more than one resistance range, a voltage divider may
be added as in figure 2.9.

In the specification relating to the resistance ranges of a multimeter the
accuracy of the resistance measurement is normally quoted as a percentage of
the mid scale value of the resistance range and not the full scale value as is
common on other ranges.

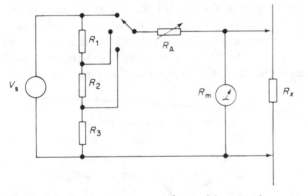

Figure 2.9. Shunt arrangement for multi-range ohm meter

Alternating current ranges

The deflection of the moving coil meter is dependent on the instantaneous value of the applied current and if the frequency of the applied signal is greater than a value determined by the mechanical properties of the movement it will remain stationary. Thus to facilitate the measurement of alternating quantities it is necessary to convert them to a direct current so that the signal applied to the meter movement is unidirectional. A copper oxide or silicon rectifier bridge circuit is commonly used to give full wave rectification of the applied waveform. However, the resulting instrument is an average or mean sensing device and although the scale will almost always be calibrated in r.m.s. values, on the assumption that the measurand is a single frequency sinewave, (that is, $V_{\text{r.m.s.}} = 1.11 V_{\text{mean}}$). Hence readings made of signals with distorted waveforms will be subject to considerable error.

The characteristics of the rectifier used for this alternating to direct conversion are of importance because the resistance of the rectifier changes with the

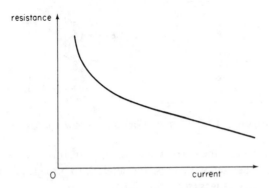

Figure 2.10. Rectifier resistance characteristic

current passing through it (figure 2.10). Hence a multi-range ammeter cannot be produced by the use of current shunts if the same linear scale is to be used for both a.c. and d.c. ranges. To overcome the problem an arrangement based on the circuit in figure 2.11 is used where the current transformer enables the various current ranges to be scaled to an appropriate magnitude for the rectifier characteristic.

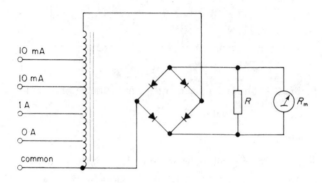

Figure 2.11. The use of a current transformer to obtain alternating current ranges

Alternating voltage ranges

In providing alternating voltage ranges the nonlinearity of the rectifier character-istic again creates a certain amount of difficulty. As before this may be overcome by resorting to the use of an instrument transformer. In this case a step-up voltage transformer must be used if it is desired to provide ranges that have a full scale value of less than 10 V or so, and the resulting arrangement could be as indicated by figure 2.12.

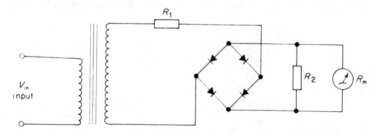

Figure 2.12. Multimeter circuit for low voltage range

In some multimeters the current and voltage transformers are combined into a single unit and operated with a resistor network to provide all the scaling for the alternating signal ranges (see figure 2.13).

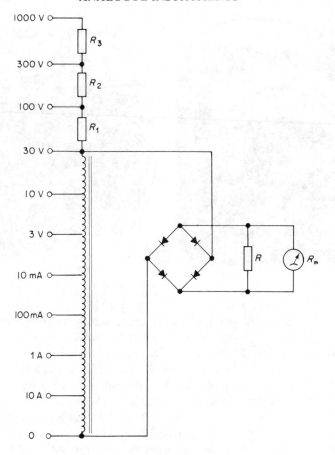

Figure 2.13. A circuit arrangement that uses a combined current and voltage transformer

Sample Specification

The specification example is for the instrument which, for many years, has been the name synonymous with multimeters. It is interesting to compare the input resistance of this instrument on the 1000 V ranges with the same quantity on the specifications of digital multimeters (see section 4.2.2).

Avo Model 8 mk5 and TS1 mk2

Ranges   d.c. volts: 100 mV, 3 V, 10 V, 30 V, 100 V, 300 V, 600 V, 1000 V, 3000 V
a.c. volts: 3 V, 10 V, 100 V, 300 V, 600 V, 1000 V, 3000 V
d.c. current: 50 μA, 300 μA, 1 mA, 10 mA, 100 mA, 1 A, 10 A
a.c. current: 10 mA, 100 mA, 1 A, 10 A

resistance: 0–2 kΩ, 0–200 kΩ, 0–20 MΩ

decibels: −10 to +55 using a.c. volts scale; range extension accessories are available; (select 50 μA d.c. range)

Accuracy at 20 °C   d.c.: ± 1% of full scale deflection

a.c.: ± 2% of full scale deflection at 50 Hz

resistance: ± 3% of reading at centre scale

Sensitivity (input resistance) d.c.: 20 000 Ω/V all ranges

a.c.: 100 Ω/V 3-V range; 1000 Ω/V 10-V range; 2000 Ω/V 30 V upwards

Voltage drop at terminals d.c.: from 100 mV at 50 μA to 700 mV at 10 A

a.c.: less than 450 mV at 10 A

Lead resistance   0.01 Ω per lead (approx) of standard Avo type

Temperature range   operation: −5 °C to +35 °C

storage: −40 °C to +50 °C

Temperature effect variation due to temperature change: ≯ 0.15% per °C

Flash test   7 kV a.c. r.m.s.

Overload protection   high speed electromechanical cut-out with fuse on two lower resistance ranges

Frequency response   for voltage ranges up to 300 V the change in reading due to a change in frequency is ≯ ± 3% over the range 15 Hz to 15 kHz. This is in addition to the accuracy figure specified for 50 Hz

Response time   typically 1 s to full scale

Magnetic field effect   variation due to external magnetic fields is within limits of BS 89: 1970

Dimensions   192 mm × 165 mm × 115 mm (excluding handle and lugs)

Weight   2.2 kg (approx.) with batteries and leads

Batteries   1.5 V cell SP2 or U2MJ, 212LP, IEC R20 and 15 V battery
B121 or 215G, 71, 411. IEC 10F20 or (using adaptor pt. no.
5210-064) 15 V battery B154 or Y10, GB15, 74, 504, IEC
10F15

Electronic Instruments

The usefulness of the direct acting multimeter as exemplified by the Avo 8
specified above cannot be doubted, and it is extensively used in many branches
of engineering. It does, as all instruments do, have its limitations, these being
predominantly those of accuracy, input impedance and sensitivity on a.c. ranges.
The first of these can only be improved by resorting to a digital instrument while
the latter limitations can be removed by using a stable amplifier between the input to the instrument and the meter movement so that the current to the
instrument on the voltage ranges is reduced from say 50 μA to 1 μA thus giving
an increase in the input resistance from 20 kΩ/V to 1 MΩ/V. This change in the
character of the instrument is particularly valuable if it is to be used for investi-
gating the operation of electronic circuits where the impedance of components
across which measurements are to be made is appreciable—for example, in
measuring the voltage across a 100 kΩ resistor, which is connected in series with
a 200 kΩ resistor to a 2 V source. On the 1 V range, the 20 kΩ/V instrument
will indicate 0.500 V and the 1 MΩ/V instrument 0.625 V: the true value would
be 0.667 V.

Direct current ranges

Another result of the use of an amplifier in the multimeter is that electronic
instruments are more appropriately considered as a voltage rather than a current
measuring device, hence measurement of current is performed by determining

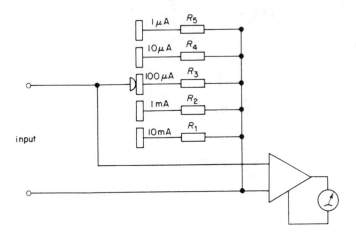

Figure 2.14. A current shunt arrangement used in some electronic multimeters

the voltage drop across a known resistor rather than using the unknown current to produce a deflection.

Hence the current ranges can be operated on an arrangement of the type illustrated by figure 2.14, which is a set of shunts rather than the universal shunt of the electromechanical instrument, a make-before-break switch being indicated to permit range change while the instrument remains in circuit.

Direct voltage ranges

To obtain the voltage ranges a chain of resistors arranged as in figure 2.15 may be used, the amplifier input being across the lowest unit of the chain. To overcome the problems of providing stable precise resistors of the large values which would be necessary for such ranges as the 300 and 1000 V ones, a complex switching arrangement could be included. Such a circuit allows the magnitude of the resistor across which the amplifier is connected to be changed for each of these ranges rather than adding further units to the chain. This results in the input resistance being limited to a maximum of, say, 100 MΩ.

For applications that require an instrument with a very high input resistance, voltmeters that utilise the 'electrometer' principle [6] (namely a voltage amplifier that originally made use of the grid to cathode resistance of a specially developed

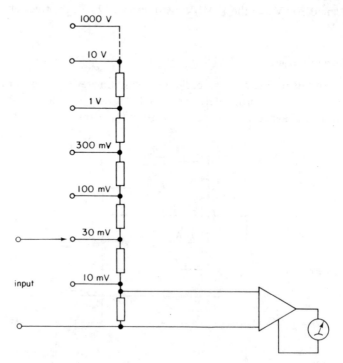

Figure 2.15. Voltage range circuit for an electronic multimeter

valve, to produce a sensitive instrument with a high input resistance of 10^{16} Ω) are used. The 1970s have seen these electrometer valves gradually being replaced by semiconductor devices such as the MOSFET. The resulting high input resistance d.c. multimeter is suitable for the measurement of such quantities as static charge, electrochemical e.m.f.s, high resistances, Hall effect, semiconductor resistivity, etc.

Resistance ranges

The use of electronic techniques facilitates an increase in the resistance measuring capabilities of a multimeter. If the output characteristic of the battery used as a power source in the instrument is converted to that of a constant current source, unknown resistors may be measured in terms of the voltage drop across them by making the current source of suitable magnitude. To increase the number of resistance ranges a voltage divider chain may be used, as shown in figure 2.16.

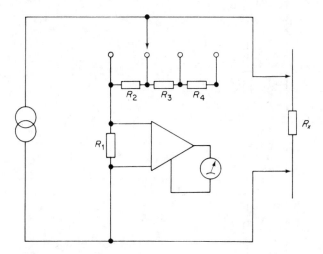

Figure 2.16. Circuit for resistance measurement ranges in an electronic multimeter

Alternating voltage ranges

In general the stability/drift requirements of a.c. amplifiers are not so stringent as those for d.c. because the low frequency changes (drift) can be prevented from having external effects by the use of 'blocking' capacitors. The design of the first stage of an a.c. amplifier is therefore less exacting than the equivalent stage of a d.c. unit. In addition to the advantage that is gained in sensitivity by using an amplifier, the use of electronic circuitry to improve the characteristics of the rectifier may be performed by what has become known as the 'ideal rectifier' circuit. This is shown in its basic form in figure 2.17, it being usual for the last stage of the a.c. amplifier to incorporate a circuit of this type.

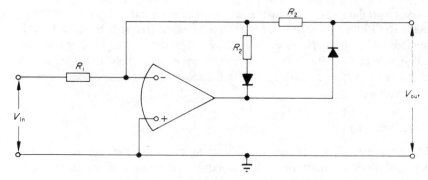

Figure 2.17. A circuit for an 'ideal' rectifier

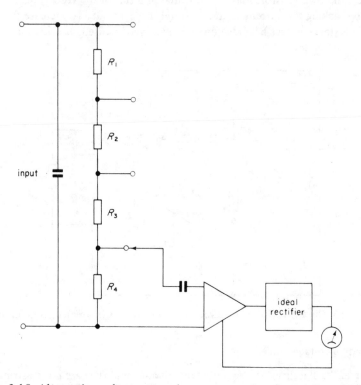

Figure 2.18. Alternating voltage ranges in a mean sensing electronic multimeter

The problems of producing high value nonreactive resistors may result in the use of a voltage divider of the type in figure 2.18 for alternating voltages, instead of using the direct voltage network.

The majority of electronic multimeters use some form of rectifier circuit for the a.c. to d.c. conversion, which will mean that they are mean or average sensing instruments although their scale will almost invariably be in r.m.s. values (that is,

1.11V_{av} for a single frequency sinewave). The upper frequency limit of such instruments is around 10 MHz, most having a bandwidth well below this, as exampled by the specification given at the end of this section.

To provide a meter that will operate at higher frequencies, some other form of conversion must be used and the method generally used is some form of peak detecting circuit in which the alternating input signal is half-wave rectified and then applied to a capacitor to charge it to the peak value of the applied voltage. This value of direct voltage may then be amplified and used to deflect a moving coil meter (figure 2.19a). This type of arrangement when used in a probe (figure 2.19b) can perform over a bandwidth extending to several hundred MHz and have a good linearity for input signals of 0.5 V and above. By using an arrangement of the type indicated by figure 2.19c, the peak-to-peak magnitude rather than the peak value can be determined thus removing the possibility of error due to the input waveform being asymmetric.

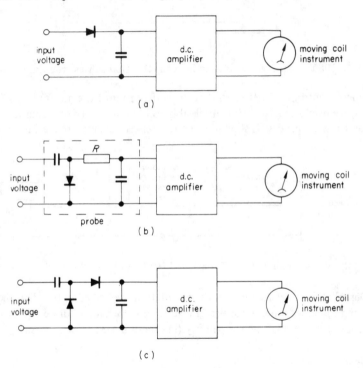

Figure 2.19. Some circuits used in peak responding voltmeters

For low voltages, special compensation techniques must be adopted to retain a linear meter scale. However, like the average responding meter, the peak responding instrument is usually calibrated in terms of r.m.s. values (r.m.s. = 0.707 peak for a sinewave), but they are more sensitive to harmonic distortion and care must be exercised in their use.

The final type of alternating to direct voltage conversion that is used in analogue instruments is one that tends to be used for measuring voltage only. It is the technique of sensing true r.m.s. values by using

(a) A thermocouple arrangement (see section 5.4.3) where to remove thermocouple nonlinearities and also to obtain a linear output or display, an arrangement of the form given in figure 2.20 may be used.

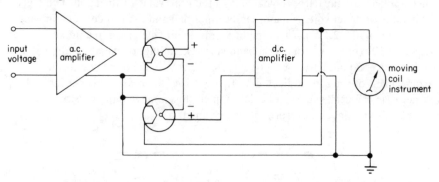

Figure 2.20. Thermocouple electronic voltmeter that senses true r.m.s. values

(b) Linear electronic circuitry so that the square root of the mean value of a voltage over a specified time interval is computed.[7] The schematic arrangement for the process is shown in figure 2.21 (see also reference 21, chapter 6).

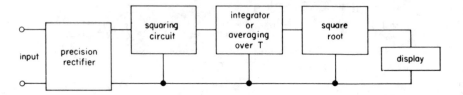

Figure 2.21. Schematic arrangement for computation of r.m.s. values

(c) Digital techniques to perform the calculations described in (b). This method being the most suitable for use in instruments that incorporate a microprocessor as part of their capability (see section 4.3).

Sample Specification

The following is an example of the capabilities and properties of an electronic multimeter as stated in the manufacturer's specification.

Avo Electronic Avometer Type EA 113
A solid state multi-range measuring instrument using silicon semiconductors throughout and having a sensitivity much higher than that of conventional multimeters. The instrument is designed for ease of operation and although

smaller and more compact than the traditional Avometer, a full five inch scale is provided. Range selection in general is accomplished by means of a single switch with simple push-button function selection. All controls are identified by graphical symbols.

Ranges a.c./d.c. voltage: 10 mV, 30 mV, 100 mV, 300 mV, 1 V, 3 V, 10 V, 30 V, 100 V, 300 V, 1000 V f.s.d.

a.c./d.c. current: 1 μA d.c. only (10 mV range), 10 μA, 100 μA, 1 mA, 10 mA, 100 mA, 1 A, 3 A f.s.d.

resistance:	min.	mid-scale	f.s.d.
	1 Ω	100 Ω	10 kΩ
	10 Ω	1 kΩ	100 kΩ
	100 Ω	10 kΩ	1 MΩ
	1 kΩ	100 kΩ	10 MΩ
	10 kΩ	1 MΩ	100 MΩ

Accuracy (f.s.d.) d.c. ranges: ± 1.25%

a.c. ranges: *10 mV to 100 V*

20 Hz–25 kHz: ± 1.25%   25 kHz–50 kHz:
± 2.5%

10 Hz–20 Hz: ± 2.5%   50 kHz–100 kHz:
± 5%

The above frequency response also applies to a.c. currents up to 10 mA range inclusive

300 V and 1000 V

20 Hz–5 kHz: ± 1.25%   5 kHz–10 kHz:
± 2.5%

10 Hz–20 Hz: ± 2.5%

resistance: ± 3% at mid-scale

Input resistance d.c. voltage ranges: 1 MΩ/V up to 100 V (constant 100 MΩ above)

a.c. voltage ranges: *Up to 300 mV:* 10 MΩ shunted by a
capacitance of less than 100 pF
All other ranges: 1 MΩ shunted by a
capacitance of less than 25 pF
a.c./d.c. current: Basically 30 mV drop
Power supply batteries 4 × ZM9 Mallory mercury cells (as supplied). The
battery life with the cells supplied is approximately
10 months continuous operation. This can be considerably increased with reasonable switch-off
time. Alternatives: 4 × HP7, 4 × V12/D14, 4 × AA
cells. Battery life using these alternative cells is
approximately 3 to 4 months

2.1.3 Pen Recorders

The instruments described so far, while giving a continuous indication of the
measurand, have required the presence of an operator to observe variations in
reading magnitude. This limitation is overcome in some of the graphical recording
instruments, in particular those designed to record permanently variations in the
level of a quantity, and with the ever-increasing emphasis on automation, continuously recording instruments are finding many applications, temperature
recorders being but one example.

Direct Acting Instruments

These are an adaptation of the moving coil instrument, the scale of the instrument being modified so that a chart may be driven at constant speed by an
electric or clockwork motor, under the modified pointer. The type of chart

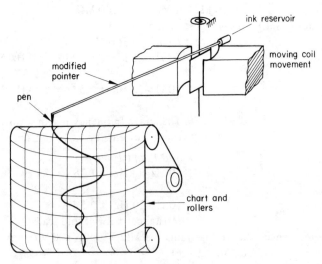

Figure 2.22. Components of a moving coil pen recorder

used in a moving coil recorder will depend on the form of movement and in the simplest form of instrument will have timing lines on a transverse axis that consist of a series of circular arcs (figure 2.22), which results in a distorted appearance of a regular waveform such as a sine or square wave. The longer the length of the pointer or pen the smaller this distortion in appearance will be, and whilst the errors in timing can be allowed for by the use of the curved scale, readings of deflection from the chart using the grid or longitudinal markings will be subject to geometric nonlinearity, that is, an error dependent on the length of the pen and the angle of deflection.

Consider the simple pen system as illustrated in figure 2.23a. The locus described by the pen tip as the coil rotates is an arc of a circle having a radius r, hence, y, the distance moved by the pen tip from the axis of symmetry due to an angle of deflection θ is $y = r \sin \theta$ or $\theta = \sin^{-1} y/r$.

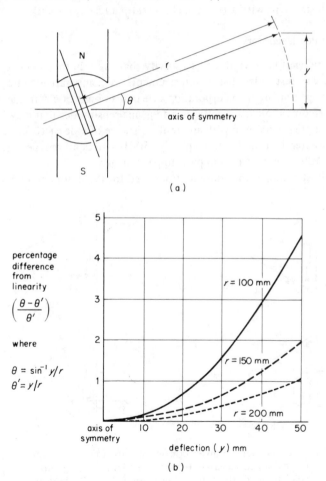

Figure 2.23. (a) Arrangement of simple deflection system. (b) Relationship between nonlinearity and deflection for the simple system

A perfectly linear writing system would have a pen deflection, y, that was directly proportional to the input current but since r has a fixed magnitude, r and y need to be related by some function of the angle of deflection to give a linear scale, that is $f(\theta) = \theta' = y/r$ and plotting a graph of the percentage difference between θ and θ' against the deflection or y value for various values of r results in a family of curves as presented in figure 2.23b. (An alternative approach is to compare y with the length of arc travelled by the pen.)

As would be expected the larger the value of r the smaller the percentage difference. The 1 per cent difference at a 50 mm deflection when a 200 mm pointer length is used corresponds to a θ value of 14.5° and indicates that to keep the linearity errors small θ should not exceed a quarter of a radian.[5,8]

The direct acting instrument is a comparatively inexpensive one having a narrow bandwidth (d.c. to 5 Hz) and a maximum sensitivity of about 4 mV/cm, or for an instrument with a 100 mm chart width a f.s.d. of 40 mV.

Electronic Pen Recorders

The limitations of bandwidth and sensitivity that occur in the direct acting recorder are so restrictive that such instruments are comparatively rare, the vast majority of pen recorders incorporating a certain amount of electronic amplification to overcome these disadvantages, and giving sensitivities that may be 1 mV/mm, or at a price 1 μV/mm with an input resistance of at least 10 kΩ, a bandwidth that extends from d.c. to (typically) 50 Hz with a 40 mm peak-to-peak display or 100 Hz with a 10 mm peak-to-peak display.

An understanding of the configurations used for the input amplifiers is

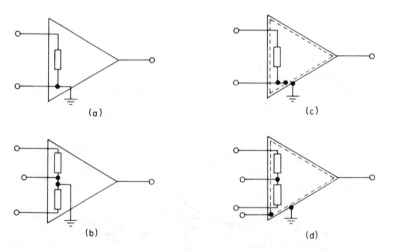

Figure 2.24. Pen recorder amplifier configurations: (a) single-ended and earthed, (b) balanced to earth, (c) single-ended, floating and shielded, (d) balanced, floating and guarded (after Whitlemore and Beswick [9])

necessary for it is essential to ensure that the signal it is required to record is not overshadowed by the presence of noise or other ambient signals (see chapter 7). There are four arrangements that are commonly used and these are shown diagrammatically in figure 2.24. Usually the more sophisticated the input arrangement the more widely it can be used. A recorder with a balanced, floating and guarded input (figure 2.24d) can be used for almost any form of signal source, but the cost is high—about four times that of a simple single-ended earthed input (figure 2.24a) and approximately double the cost of the other input configurations.[9]

To facilitate the display of more than one channel of information a number of channels are located side by side with a multi-track chart, each having its own signal processing. If the processing units are 'plug-in' modules, a versatile recorder capable of monitoring such quantities as temperature, voltage, current and the output from transducers can be recorded simultaneously on a chart having up to eight tracks.

Writing Systems[10]

The methods by which the actual trace of the signal is recorded on the chart are numerous, but can be summarised by the following categories.

Pen

This formed the basis of the earliest writing systems in that the modified pointer was required to support an ink reservoir and pen, or contain a capillary connection between the pen and a reservoir (figure 2.22). In general red ink is used but other colours are available and in an instrumentation display a colour code may be adopted. The frequency limit of recorders incorporating this method of writing is generally of the order of a few hertz, but by using a paper with a waxed surface and a pressurised ink system sophisticated recorders are marketed that have frequency responses up to 55 Hz.

Fibre pen

The correct diameter of the pen tip in a capillary pen is dependent on the required writing speed and can be critical. For this reason some manufacturers use a fibre tipped pen either at the end of a capillary or directly attached to an ink reservoir. In either case since the fibre tip is subject to wear such pens are manufactured as disposable items.

Pressure stylus

A number of recorders are marketed in which the ink pen is replaced by a metal stylus so arranged that the pressure it exerts on the surface of a special paper at the point of contact is sufficient to produce a trace. This writing system overcomes the clogging problems that are sometimes associated with the traditional capillary pen, but it produces a record on a paper that is inclined to be affected by careless handling.

Heated stylus

This form of writing system requires thermosensitive paper and a pointer modified to carry a heated stylus. It is slightly more complex than either of the above in that to obtain uniform density of trace over a d.c. to 50 Hz frequency range stylus temperature control circuits must be incorporated. The paper may have a temperature-sensitive outer layer, which is burnt away by contact with the stylus or be impregnated with a chemical that exhibits a marked colour change when heated.

Electrical stylus

A number of forms of electrically sensitive paper are used. These either utilise the heating of the passage of a current from the stylus to a backing of the paper to burn the paper surface or an electrostatic discharge between the stylus and the backing performs the same function.

Rectilinear Chart Systems

To overcome the curved transverse scale obtained with the basic direct acting movement (with or without incorporating electronic amplification), various manufacturers have evolved techniques that produce a trace on a rectilinear scale. The simplest of these is shown in figure 2.25a, in which an elongated heated stylus rests on a heat sensitive paper as it is passed over a fixed knife edge. This arrangement results in a relationship between the movement of the pen and the angle of deflection of $y = r \tan \theta$ so that although the visual distortion problem has been overcome, the nonlinearity between θ and the recorded deflection has not. Similarly for the linkage arrangements that are illustrated by figures 2.25b and c the geometric nonlinearity is governed by the relation $y = r' \sin \theta$ where r' is the effective radius resulting from the linkage arrangement. It should be noted that there are differences in the method used for specifying the non-linearity of recorder movements[11] and care must be exercised when comparisons of instrument specifications are being made.

A calculation of the percentage deviation from linearity for the tangent relationship will show a larger geometric nonlinearity than is shown for the sine case in figure 2.23b. This problem can, however, be overcome by using a servo-system so that the overall relationship between the signal and the display is a constant.

A further method of solving these problems is the use of a potentiometric system (see section 3.1.2).

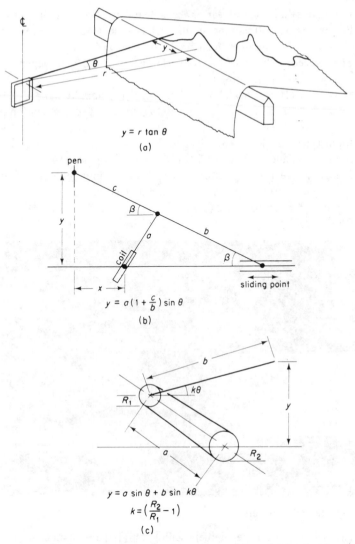

$$y = r \tan \theta$$

(a)

$$y = a\left(1 + \frac{c}{b}\right) \sin \theta$$

(b)

$$y = a \sin \theta + b \sin k\theta$$

$$k = \left(\frac{R_2}{R_1} - 1\right)$$

(c)

Figure 2.25. Rectilinear systems in moving coil recorders: (a) heated (or pressure) stylus on a knife edge, (b) linkage and sliding pivot, (c) linkage and pulleys

Sample Specification

The following data has been extracted from the complete specification of the *Washington 400 MD2 recorder*. It is a two channel instrument, primarily intended as a low cost unit for research and clinical applications. (*Note:* single and four channel versions of the recorder are also manufactured.)

Writing method   rectilinear or curvilinear (crossover or in-line pens)

Pen excursion   40 mm maximum each channel (rectilinear) 50 mm maximum each channel (curvilinear)

Chart speeds   choice of six from 60 mm/s to 1 mm/min (dependent on plug-in used)

Sensitivity (10 settings/plug in)   10 V–2.5 μV/mm alternating, or 10 V–50 μV/mm direct (dependent on plug-in used)

Input type   single ended or balanced

Input impedance   80 kΩ–2 MΩ (dependent on plug-in)

Linearity: rectilinear, better than 10% on ±15 mm deflection, curvilinear, better than 5% on ±15 mm deflection

Bandwidth   d.c. to 34 Hz (−3 dB)

Rise time   less than 16 ms

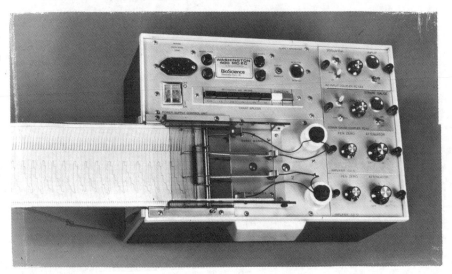

2.1.4 Light Spot Recorders

These have evolved from the Duddel oscillograph[12] the main changes resulting from: (a) the development of ultraviolet (u.v.) light sensitive recording paper that is relatively insensitive to ambient light; (b) the housing of the galvanometers in a common magnet block instead of individual magnets; and (c) a consequent reduction in size and weight.

Principle of Operation

Light from a mercury vapour or tungsten halogen source is directed on to mirrors attached to moving-coil galvanometers and then reflected via a lens and mirror system on to the special paper, which is driven past the moving light spot thereby forming a trace of current variations with time. In most recorders it is possible to select a paper speed, from the set values available or by adjusting a variable control. Additionally, in some light spot recorders the speed of the paper may be controlled by an externally applied voltage. An outline diagram of an instrument is given in figure 2.26. In addition to the traces of the input voltages, the following may be added to the record.

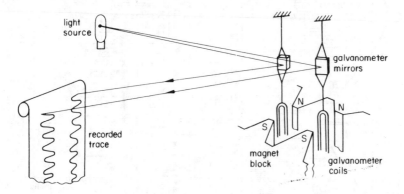

Figure 2.26. Outline of light spot recorder operation

(a) Grid lines. Lines along the length of the paper, obtained by shining the light through a 'comb' on to the paper.

(b) Timing lines. These may cross the full width of the paper, or merely project from the edge of the paper and are derived from a vapour tube energised from either an internal source of known frequency or from an external source.

(c) Trace identification. Since some recorders are manufactured with as many as 25 channels, each of which can produce a 100 mm peak-to-peak trace on a 300 mm width of paper, considerable overlapping of traces may result. To simplify the identification process, each trace is momentarily interrupted in turn; coinciding with this interruption a numeral is printed at the side of the record by directing u.v. light through cutouts of the numerals. Figure 2.27 shows a typical record from such an instrument.

The u.v. light sensitive paper may be processed in one of several ways.

(a) It may be photodeveloped, that is subjected to additional u.v. light, the traces appearing and giving a trace in 10 to 30 s (depending on the level of the u.v. light). Such a record will remain in a usable state for a considerable time providing it is not subject to excessive u.v. radiation. Some improved papers that are available have better contrast, and are less susceptible to the effects of additional u.v. radiation.

(b) It may be 'permanised', this being a developing process similar to the normal photographic one, that is, a chemical developing and fixing process. Some papers require photodeveloping before permanising to obtain the best

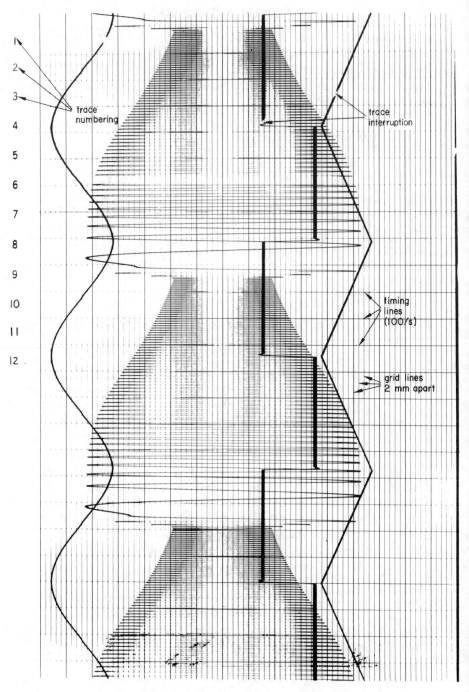

Figure 2.27. Trace from Bell & Howell 5–137 u.v. recorder fitted with 7-320 fluid damped galvanometers. Kodak paper was used at a speed of 1 m/s

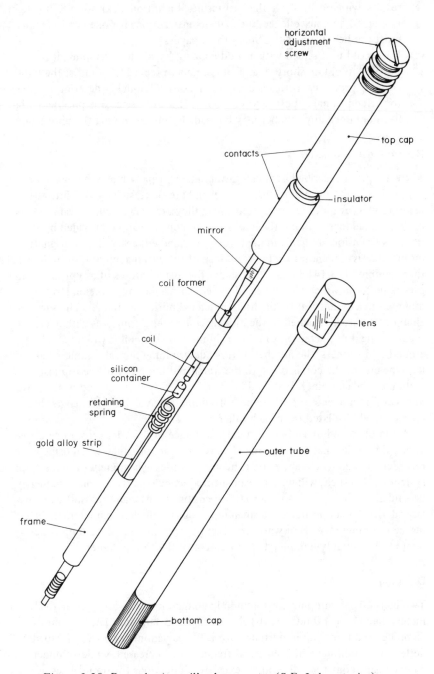

Figure 2.28. Recorder 'pencil' galvanometer (S.E. Laboratories)

results, whilst others give the best results if additional exposure to u.v. light is avoided; in consequence, the maker's instructions for one type of paper must not be considered to apply to all papers.

(c) If a record is obtained with a good contrast by photodeveloping, it is possible to obtain short lengths of permanent record by some of the photo-copying processes. If this is done, the record will quickly deteriorate (due to the additional exposure to u.v. light). However, once one photocopy has been obtained any number may be made by photocopying the photocopy.

Recorder galvanometers

These are often described as pencil galvanometers (many makes being about 75 mm long and 3 to 6 mm in diameter), and are fitted side by side into the recorder magnet block. As indicated above they are moving coil galvanometers, having a small mass and inertia, a restoring or control torque provided by the ribbon suspension, and a damping torque provided either by electromagnetic means, that is, depending on the resistance of the external circuit, or by internal fluid damping.[13,14] Figure 2.28 shows the main features of a typical recorder galvanometer in which a moving coil system suspended by a torsion strip is mounted in a cylindrical frame, housed in a cylindrical container. The surface-aluminised mirror attached to the moving coil system, coincides with a lens to focus the light projected on to it. The aluminium wire coil is wound as a loop around two formers, the number of turns determining the galvanometer sensitivity. One end of the coil is taken to the frame and the other to the top insulated section of the container. It should be noted that although one end of the galvano-meter coil is connected to its frame, galvanometers in a common magnet block are electrically isolated from each other.

A complete understanding of the performance of recorder galvanometers is essential in order that true records of waveforms are obtained when using a u.v. recorder. It is indicated above that the u.v. recorder galvanometer is a mass–spring system and, as such, will have a resonant frequency (that is, at some frequency dependent on its moment of inertia, suspension stiffness and mass, it will have a large deflection amplitude for a small input signal). Such a characteristic in a device to obtain records of waveform is extremely undesirable and must be removed by suitably damping the movement of the galvanometer.

Damping

Two methods of damping are common in connection with u.v. recorder galvano-meters, namely: (a) fluid; and (b) electromagnetic damping. The amount of damping used is of vital importance, for if the galvanometer is over-damped its deflection amplitude will decrease as frequency is increased, while an under-damped galvanometer will produce excessive deflections for frequencies near its natural or resonant frequency. Thus a compromise must be made, and curves of

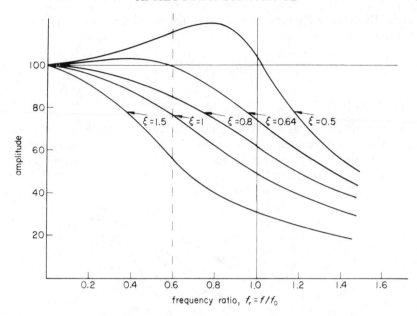

Figure 2.29. Trace amplitude/frequency ratio characteristics for a u.v. recorder galvanometer

deflection amplitude against frequency ratio (figure 2.29) show that if a fraction of critical damping $(\zeta) = 0.64$ is used, the deflection amplitude is within ± 5 per cent of the ideal signal amplitude for frequencies up to 60 per cent of galvanometer resonant frequency for a sinusoidal input signal. The expression used to obtain the curves in figure 2.29 is

$$\frac{A_a}{A_i} = \frac{1}{[(1 - f_r^2)^2 + (2f_r\zeta)^2]^{1/2}} \tag{2.1}$$

(For derivation see appendix IIc) where A_a is the actual amplitude of the trace deflection, A_i is the ideal (or d.c.) amplitude of the trace deflection, f_r is the ratio of signal frequency (f) to the galvanometer resonant frequency (f_0) and ζ is the fraction of critical damping used on the galvanometer.

In addition to the amplitude characteristics described above, some phase shift, equivalent to a time delay, must inevitably occur between the input of the electrical signal and the movement of the light spot on the photographic paper. This phase shift is unavoidable—due to the inertia and damping of the galvanometer a finite time will exist between the variation of the input signal level, and the movement of the light spot on the photographic paper—but it is of negligible importance provided it can be made directly proportional to frequency, that is, providing that all frequencies of input signal are delayed at the same time interval. The relationship between phase shift (ϕ) and frequency ratio (f_r) may be shown to be

$$\phi = \tan^{-1} \frac{2f_r\zeta}{1 - f_r^2} \qquad (2.2)$$

(see appendix IIc).

Curves plotted using this expression (figure 2.30) show that the desired linear relationship is approximately obtained with $\zeta = 0.64$, and this, fortunately, is the fraction of critical damping, which gives the optimum amplitude performance for a recorder galvanometer.

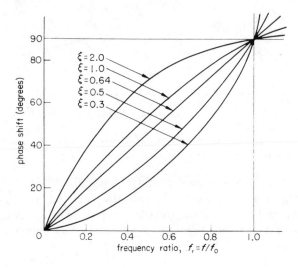

Figure 2.30. Phase shift/frequency ratio characteristics for a u.v. recorder galvanometer

To illustrate the effect of frequency and ζ value on the phase shift in a recording, first consider a 50 Hz signal applied to a galvanometer that has a resonant frequency of 500 Hz and is provided with fractional damping of 0.64. Then from equation 2.2

$$\phi_1 = \tan^{-1} \frac{2 \times 0.64 \times 0.1}{1 - 0.01}$$

$$= 7° \ 22'$$

or

$$\phi_1 = \frac{7.366 \times 1000}{360 \times 50} \text{ ms}$$

$$= 0.41 \text{ ms or } 410 \ \mu s$$

If now a 250 Hz signal were applied to the same galvanometer then the phase shift becomes

$$\phi_2 = \tan^{-1} \frac{1.28 \times 0.5}{1 - 0.25} = 40° \ 28'$$

or

$$\phi_2 = \frac{40.467 \times 1000}{360 \times 250}$$

$$= 0.45 \text{ ms or } 450 \ \mu s$$

Thus a time difference (or phase displacement) in a recording of these two frequencies with the suggested galvanometer would be 40 μs, and if a paper speed of 2.5 m/s were used in obtaining the record, a displacement of $(10 \times 250)/1\ 000\ 000 = 0.1$ mm or 0.2 per cent of the length of the waveform as recorded for the 50 Hz wave would result. Such an error is of the same order of magnitude as the resolution of measurement using a chart reader with vernier scales and in most cases may be neglected, although it must be included in an error analysis of the measurement (see p. 26).

Table 2.1 illustrates some important aspects of phase and amplitude errors in u.v. records.

Signal freq. (Hz)	Galvanometer resonant frequency (Hz)	Fraction of critical damping	Phase angle (θ)	Time lag (μs)	Time diff. (μs)	Amplitude difference from d.c.
50	500	0.5	5° 46'	320	54	+0.5%
250	500	0.5	33° 41'	374		+10.9%
50	500	0.64	7° 22'	410	40	+0.2%
250	500	0.64	40° 28'	450		+1.4%
50	500	0.8	9° 11'	510	11	−0.3%
250	500	0.8	46° 51'	521		−8.8%
50	1000	0.64	3° 40'	204	5	+0.04%
250	1000	0.64	18° 51'	209		+0.95%

From the above table it is clear that the 0.64 value for ζ is more important from consideration of amplitude error than from a phase difference viewpoint. However, one fact of considerable importance in relation to phase differences that does emerge is that if different galvanometers are used to measure the same or different frequencies on the same record considerable phase error may result. For example, if the 50 Hz signal were recorded using a galvanometer with a resonant frequency of 500 Hz, and the 250 Hz signal recorded using a 1 kHz galvanometer (both with 0.64 damping) then a time difference of 200 μs or 1 per cent of the 50 Hz waveform length would be obtained. This is an unfortunate shortcoming as it is often desirable that galvanometers of different sensitivities and hence different frequency ranges be used in the compiling of a record. The most satisfactory method of overcoming this problem is to use only one type of galvanometer and connect adjustable gain amplifiers between the signals and the galvanometers.

Transient response

The above description has been concerned with the performance of the galvanometers when supplied with a signal, which has a sinusoidal waveform. However, a number of very suitable applications for using the u.v. recorder are transient in nature. It is therefore important to be aware of the limitations of galvanometer performance under transient conditions. The simplest, yet most severe, form of transient is a step function of voltage. Applying such a transient to a u.v. recorder galvanometer will cause a deflection of the spot light to overshoot the steady state deflection x by an amount y and the magnitude of this overshoot will depend on the amount of galvanometer damping present as illustrated by table 2.2, in which the percentage overshoot = $y \times 100/x$ per cent, and ς is the fraction of the critical damping applied to the galvanometer.

Table 2.2

% overshoot	ς	% overshoot	ς
0.1	0.911	8.4	0.619
0.5	0.861	9.6	0.597
1.2	0.815	10.8	0.577
2.4	0.765	13.5	0.537
4.0	0.716	16.5	0.497
5.2	0.685	19.5	0.461
6.4	0.658	22.5	0.429
7.3	0.640	25.0	0.404

It is apparent from table 2.2 that to obtain a record without overshoot requires the galvanometers to be used with critical damping, but such a mode of operation is usually unacceptable because of the time delay between the change in signal level and the movement of the light spot on the record. Figure 2.31 shows the deflection/time characteristics for a galvanometer with a resonant frequency of 10 Hz and various values of damping when supplied with a step voltage. Also shown in this diagram are the characteristics for a galvanometer with a resonant frequency of 100 Hz with fractional damping values of 0.5 and 1.0. It should be observed that the time to steady deflection for this latter galvanometer is one tenth that for the 10 Hz galvanometer, indicating that for transient studies, galvanometers with high resonant frequencies must be used. Again it becomes apparent that 0.64 of critical damping results in an optimum of performance, being a compromise between excessive overshoot (with its associated oscillations) and no overshoot but excessive delay in attaining correct

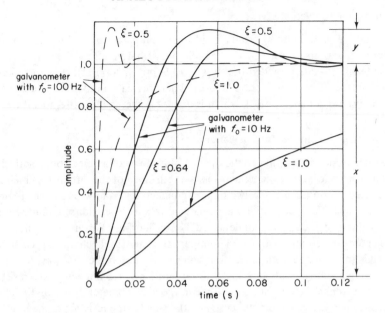

Figure 2.31. Galvanometer response to a step function

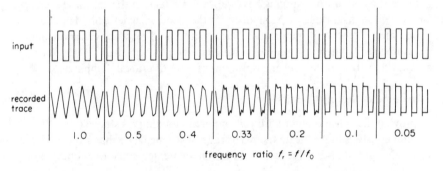

Figure 2.32. The effect of f_r on transient distortion in a recorded trace
(courtesy of Bell & Howell Ltd)

deflection. As a further illustration of the importance of using a galvanometer with a high resonance frequency when transient studies are being performed, figure 2.32 shows that only by using a galvanometer with a resonant frequency of at least 20 times that of the fundamental frequency of a square wave can a true record of the signal be approached.

From the above discussion it is apparent that the optimum in performance from a recorder galvanometer is obtained if a fraction of critical damping of 0.64 is used. It has also been stated that there are two types of galvanometer in common use in recorders, namely fluid damped, and electromagnetically damped.

Fluid damped galvanometers

These derive their damping from a fluid-filled compartment within the galvanometer casing, their performance being relatively unaffected by the impedance of the external circuit (provided that it is $> 20\ \Omega$ but $< 2000\ \Omega$). However, they may be affected by temperature, and fluid damped galvanometers should therefore be used in a magnet block which is maintained at constant temperature.

Electromagnetically damped galvanometer

The magnitude of damping applied to the movement of an electromagnetically damped galvanometer is dependent on the resistance of the circuit to which it is connected. For example, a galvanometer connected to a low resistance circuit will be heavily damped, while one connected to a high resistance circuit will be lightly damped. This is best understood by considering a galvanometer not connected to a circuit; if the galvanometer movement is mechanically twisted through an angle and then released, it will swing back to the zero position, generating a voltage at its terminals. If the terminals are connected to a resistance, a current will flow causing a force in the galvanometer opposing the change in position of the galvanometer coil, and the smaller the resistance, the larger the current will be, and so too the greater the damping force.

Since the amount of damping has a profound effect on the galvanometer performance, the magnitude of resistance that the electromagnetically damped galvanometer 'sees' is of importance. Manufacturers of recorder galvanometers therefore specify the magnitude of resistance (R_D) that a galvanometer must 'see' in order to operate with the optimum of 0.64 of critical damping.

Galvanometer Scaling Circuits

To provide the galvanometer with this required damping resistance (and simultaneously, suitably scale the magnitude of the signal so that a trace of sensible amplitude is produced), it will in general be necessary to adopt one of three procedures.

A source of large amplitude

There will be a peak voltage drop (v_g) across the galvanometer, which is equal to the product of the galvanometer's resistance and the peak of the signal current. When the source has a greater peak amplitude than the voltage across the galvanometer, then a circuit of the form in figure 2.33 can suitably be used for scaling the signal and damping the galvanometer.

The magnitudes of R_a and R_b are evaluated from

$$R_a = \frac{V_s}{v_g}\left(\frac{R_g R_D}{R_D + R_g}\right) - R_s \tag{2.3}$$

$$R_b = \frac{R_D}{1 - \frac{v_g}{V_s}\left(1 + \frac{R_D}{R_g}\right)} \tag{2.4}$$

These equations are derived from the expressions for the voltage ratio v_g/V_s and for the damping resistance R_D. It is worth noting that if $V_s \gg v_g$, R_b may be considered equal to R_D.

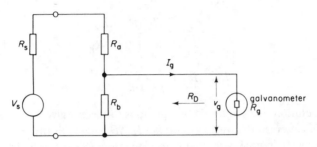

Figure 2.33. Galvanometer scaling and damping circuit

A source requiring a matched load

This is a more general condition than that described above, and arises when, for example, a galvanometer is supplied from an instrument transformer, (see sections 6.1.5 and 6.2.2).

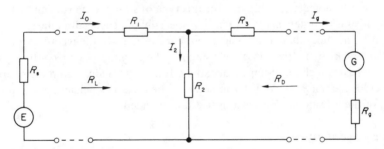

Figure 2.34. Attenuator to match both source and galvanometer impedances

The magnitudes of the resistors R_1, R_2, and R_3 in figure 2.34 are determined by evaluation of the equations

$$R_1 = R_L - \frac{R_2(k-1)}{k} \tag{2.5}$$

$$R_2 = \frac{k(R_L + R_s)(R_D + R_g)}{k^2(R_L + R_s) - (R_D + R_g)} \tag{2.6}$$

and

$$R_3 = R_2(k - 1) - R_g \tag{2.7}$$

The derivation of these equations is obtained by the solution of the network equations, that is

$$\frac{I_o}{I_g} = 1 + \frac{R_3 + R_g}{R_2} = k \tag{2.8}$$

$$R_L = R_1 + \frac{R_2(R_3 + R_g)}{R_2 + R_3 + R_g} \tag{2.9}$$

$$R_D = R_3 + \frac{R_2(R_1 + R_s)}{R_1 + R_2 + R_s} \tag{2.10}$$

Note: the solution to a similar set of equations to these is given in appendix III. It should be observed that the constant $k = I_o/SD$ where S is the sensitivity of the galvanometer (normally quoted in mA/mm) and D is the peak deflection desired on the record, that is $I_g = SD$ mA. The current I_o is the amplifier or source output current in mA.

Electronic signal conditioning circuits

Should the signal to be recorded have insufficient amplitude to give the required trace deflection it is necessary to position an amplifier between the signal source and the galvanometer. To provide for this type of situation most manufacturers of light spot recorders market a range of specially designed galvanometer driver amplifier modules that either plug into the main frame of the recorder or into a suitable rack. Such driver amplifiers simplify the operation of a recording system as they have a high input impedance, the galvanometer damping problems are removed, the same type of galvanometer can be used on all channels, and protection of the galvanometer against overload is provided.

Sample Specification

The following extract from the specification for the *Bryans Southern Instruments 4051 unit* shows the main characteristics of a typical driver amplifier.

Input   3 terminal balanced differential (Hi, Lo and guard). Floating with respect to ground—insulation rating 500 V
Common mode rejection > 100 dB
Sensitivity   1 mV/cm to 50 V/cm; 15 ranges in a 1, 2, 5 sequence
Input impedance   100 kΩ each side to guard on 1, 2, 5 and 10 mV/cm ranges; 500 kΩ each side to guard on other ranges
Source impedance   Maximum 10 kΩ for rated stability and noise
Linearity   0.1% f.s.d. for best straight line

Bandwidth   d.c. to 25 kHz ($<$ 3 dB at 15 kHz)
Galvanometer position control   ± full scale
Galvanometer sensitivity control   Front panel control of galvanometer
                                   current between 0.5 mA/cm and 23
                                   mA/cm

Operation

In operating a light spot recorder it is normally recommended that the peak
deflection should not exceed ± 50 mm. Table 2.3 gives examples of a manufacturer's specification data for two recorder galvanometers so the peak of
current for a type 7-349 would be ± 3.24 μA, and for the 7-362, ± 23.6 mA.
This gives an indication of the range of galvanometer sensitivities available. The
upper limit of flat frequency response of u.v. recorder galvanometers is approximately 8 kHz, and at a paper speed of 10 m/s this would produce a trace having
a distance between peaks of 1.25 mm which is insufficient for a sensible study of

Table 2.3

Type no.	External damping resist. $R_D(\Omega)$	Natural freq. f_0 (Hz)	Flat (5%) freq. range f(Hz)	Terminal resist. (± 10%) $R_g(\Omega)$	d.c. sensitivity S (mA/cm)	Maximum safe current (mA)	Damping
7-349	350	10	0–6	130	0.00065	15	electromagnetic
7-362	20–2000	4150	0–2500	69	4.72	100	fluid

(Reproduced by kind permission of Bell & Howell Ltd)

the waveform. These high frequency galvanometers are however vital in transient studies. The limit of frequency to which a u.v. recorder can be used will depend on the magnitude of the displayed trace, and the paper speed, but as a guide a trace with a peak-to-peak deflection of 5 cm is recognisable as a sinewave providing the length of one cycle is greater than 10 mm.

Galvanometer Selection Factors

In selecting a galvanometer it is important to choose one to comply with the following.

(a) A flat frequency range in excess of the frequency of the highest harmonic of importance in the a.c. signal (a low frequency galvanometer may be used as a low pass filter to remove unwanted 'noise' from a signal). Alternatively if transients are being studied, the galvanometer's resonant frequency should be at least 20 times that of the 'fundamental' frequency of the transient, thus demonstrating the necessity for the manufacture of galvanometers with high resonant frequencies, for example a galvanometer with an f_0 of at least 1000 Hz should be used when recording the effects of a step change in the load on a 50 Hz supply.

(b) A sufficiency of sensitivity so that a satisfactory magnitude of deflection on the record may be obtained, it being appreciated that the larger the trace the smaller the error due to the uncertainty in measuring deflections on the trace.

The final selection of a galvanometer will invariably be a compromise between the two requirements given above, and the limitations of the circuit to which the galvanometer is to be connected. From the specification data in table 2.3 it is apparent that the sensitivity of a galvanometer is inversely proportional to the flat frequency response, and a galvanometer with a sufficiency of sensitivity and frequency range may be unobtainable. The sensitivity problem is, of course, overcome by using galvanometer driver amplifiers which unfortunately add to the cost of the system.

Calibration

Having selected a suitable galvanometer and signal conditioning circuitry, it is sensible to calibrate the complete system before using it to take measurements. The most satisfactory method of performing such a calibration is to replace the measurand by a signal of known amplitude and monitor the resulting trace deflection. If several levels of known or calibrating signal are used to obtain short lengths of trace, a mean signal-to-deflection constant of calibration may be derived. This procedure must be followed for each galvanometer and its matching circuit, for each application of the recorder.

Applications

It has already been indicated that the range of frequencies over which the light spot recorder can generally be used is for alternating signals having a fundamental frequency from zero up to 400 or 500 Hz depending on the paper speeds available on the recorder being used. The recording of higher frequencies is possible on the few recorders with very high (10 m/s) paper speed. The application of the recorder is suitable in any situation where a trace of a waveform is required, and resolves to the problem of scaling the signal to be measured to a suitable magnitude, while ensuring that the matching requirements of a particular galvanometer are met.

The commonest method of scaling voltages is to use a resistance divider or to use a galvanometer driver amplifier with a suitable sensitivity selector.

Current waveforms are obtained by recording the voltage drop across a known resistance. Having recorded traces of voltage and/or current waveform it is possible to determine their frequency and any phase differences between traces (using the known time scale projected on to the record by the time markers), remembering that the resolution of reading is of the order of 0.3 to 0.5 mm and corrections for unequal galvanometer phase shift must be included.

Typical applications of the u.v. recorder are in recording regulation transients of generators, the performance of control systems, the outputs of transducers, and the magnitudes of low frequency signals which cannot be measured by pointer instruments. The development of PLZT electro-optic materials [30, 31] has led to the marketing (in 1980), by Bell and Howell Ltd, of a 'galvanomterless' light spot recorder, which is capable of simultaneously monitoring 28 sinewave signals of frequencies up to 5 kHz.

2.2 THE ELECTRODYNAMIC INSTRUMENT

2.2.1 Principle

This instrument, often termed a dynamometer, relies for its deflecting torque on the interaction of the magnetic fields produced by a pair of fixed air-cored coils and a third air-cored coil capable of angular movement and suspended within the fixed coils (figure 2.35). The deflecting torque produced within the instrument is proportional to the product of the current in the moving coil (I_m) and that in the fixed coil (I_f), that is, torque $\propto I_m I_f$.

Note: This is an approximation, since the torque is also dependent on the initial angle between the axes of the coils.[12] Also, in some instruments, known as ferrodynamic instruments, the electrodynamic effect is increased by the presence of ferromagnetic material.

This instrument is suitable for the measurement of direct and alternating current, voltage and power. If no iron is present within the coil system the magnetic fields are weak and to obtain sufficient deflecting torque requires coils of either a large number of turns or capable of carrying a moderate current. The control torque is derived from a helical spring and the movement damped by air resistance.

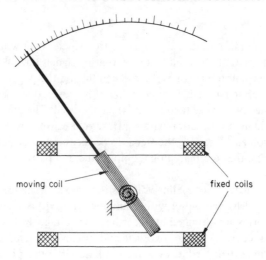

Figure 2.35. Coil arrangement of the electrodynamic instrument

The properties of electrodynamic instruments may be listed as follows

(a) Voltmeters and ammeters have approximately square law scales; wattmeters have approximately linear scales.[15]
(b) It is more expensive to manufacture than the moving coil instrument and has a higher power consumption.
(c) It measures true r.m.s. values of a.c. waveform irrespective of waveshape.
(d) It is an instrument suitable for use in either a.c. or d.c. circuits, being comparatively unaffected by frequency. Some models are available for use over the range d.c. to 2.5 kHz.[16]
(e) Stray magnetic fields can affect the operation of the dynamometer and therefore the coil system is enclosed in a magnetic shield.

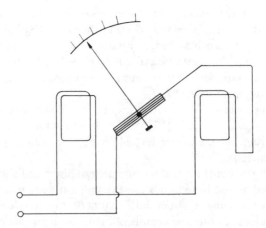

Figure 2.36. Coil connections for electrodynamic milliammeter

2.2.2 Application

Ammeter and Voltmeter

For the measurement of small currents (5 to 100 mA) the instrument would be arranged to have the fixed and moving coils connected in series (figure 2.36). To convert such an instrument to a voltmeter simply requires the addition of a suitable series resistance. For measuring larger currents (up to 20 A) it becomes impracticable to pass the full value of current through the moving coil, so this is then shunted by low resistance (figure 2.37). This arrangement could be used for still larger currents, but in most cases it is better to use a current transformer (see section 6.2.2) and an ammeter with a f.s.d. of 5 A.

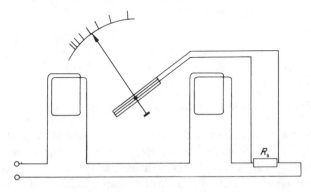

Figure 2.37. Coil connections for electrodynamic ammeter

Wattmeter

For many years the electrodynamometer has been the instrument normally used for measuring power in a.c. circuits. The digital wattmeter is beginning to supplant it but the cost of replacement means that for some years the electro-dynamometer will continue to be used at supply line frequencies for power measurement.

Since deflection in the dynamometer is proportional to the product of the two currents, it is usual to make the current in the moving coil proportional to the circuit voltage and to make the fixed coils carry the load current (figure 2.38). Depending on the relative magnitudes of the currents in the fixed and moving coils the wattmeter should be connected as in figure 2.39a or figure 2.39c so that the minimum error in the measurement of power in a load is made. In figure 2.39a the current coil will produce a force proportional to the load current only, but the voltage coil (moving) will produce a force proportional to the voltage across the load plus current coil. However, in figure 2.39c the current coil (fixed) produces a force proportional to the sum of the currents in the load and in the voltage coil, while the voltage coil produces a force proportional to the voltage across the load. In either case correction for the error may be made but the wattmeter should always be connected to indicate with minimum error.

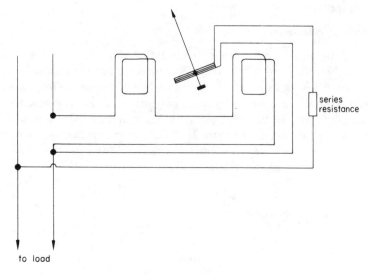

Figure 2.38. Electrodynamic wattmeter, internal connections

Let I_w be the current through the wattmeter current coil, I_L be the current in the load, V_w the voltage across the wattmeter voltage coil and V_L the voltage across the load. Let R_c and R_v be the resistances of the wattmeter current and voltage coils respectively, and R_L the load resistance. Additionally, let jX_c be the inductive reactance of the wattmeter current coil and jX_L the inductive reactance of the load. The inductive reactance of the voltage coil may generally be ignored since it will be 'swamped' by a series volt-dropping resistor. For the connection in figure 2.39a.

$$I_L = I_w = \frac{V_w}{R_c + R_L + j(X_c + X_L)}$$

therefore

$$I_w V_w = I_L{}^2 [R_c + R_L + j(X_c + X_L)]$$

$$\text{wattmeter reading} = I_w\, V_w \cos\theta$$

$$= I_L{}^2(R_c + R_L)$$

now

$$\text{watts in load} = I_L{}^2 R_L$$

$$= \text{wattmeter reading} - I_L{}^2 R_c$$

hence

$$\text{wattmeter correction} = I_L{}^2 R_c \qquad (2.11)$$

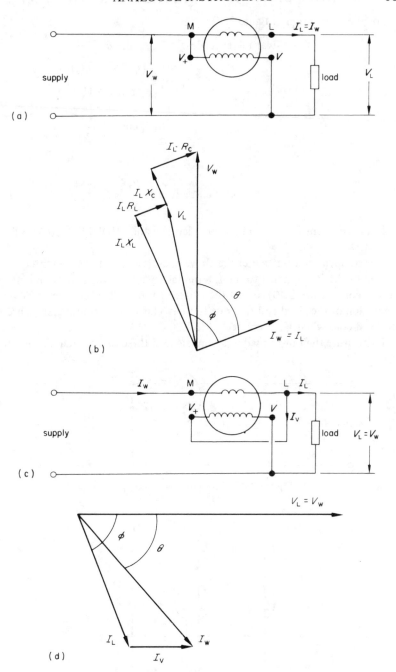

Figure 2.39. Wattmeter connection conventions and phasor diagrams: (a and b) high impedance load (c and d) low impedance load

For the connection in figure 2.39c

$$\text{wattmeter reading} = V_w I_w \cos \theta$$
$$= V_w (I_L \cos \phi + I_v)$$
$$= V_L I_L \cos \phi + V_L I_v$$
$$= V_L I_L \cos \phi + \frac{V_L^2}{R_v}$$

hence

$$\text{wattmeter correction} = \frac{V_L^2}{R_v} \tag{2.12}$$

The corrections for a.c. and d.c. are identical and SHOULD ALWAYS BE APPLIED.

In a compensated wattmeter the above error is eliminated by an internal connection of the V_+ terminal to the L terminal, by a lead which is wound into the current coils (figure 2.40) so that the current to the voltage coil cancels out the proportion of the fixed coil flux due to the voltage coil current passing through the fixed coils when V_+ is connected to L.

To measure the power used in an unbalanced three-phase circuit either three

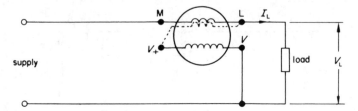

Figure 2.40. Compensated wattmeter

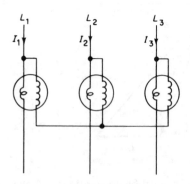

Figure 2.41. Measurement of three-phase power using three wattmeters

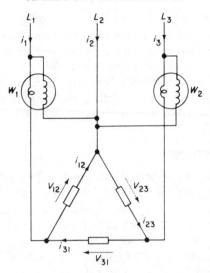

Figure 2.42. Measurement of three-phase power using two wattmeters

wattmeters can be used as shown in figure 2.41 or, to reduce the instrumentation cost, the measurement may be performed with two instruments connected as shown in figure 2.42. For this latter condition instantaneous power in load

$$p = v_{12}i_{12} + v_{23}i_{23} + v_{31}i_{31}$$
$$= v_{12}i_{12} + v_{23}i_{23} - i_{31}(v_{12} + v_{23})$$

since

$$v_{31} = -v_{13} = -(v_{12} + v_{23})$$

Thus

$$p = v_{12}(i_{12} - i_{31}) + v_{23}(i_{23} - i_{31})$$
$$= v_{12}i_1 + v_{23}i_3 \qquad (2.13)$$
$$= \text{reading on } W_1 + \text{reading on } W_2$$

Note: the power in the load is the *algebraic sum* of the wattmeter readings and at certain values of load power factor the connections to the voltage coil of one of the wattmeters will need to be reversed. This condition represents a negative reading.

2.3 OTHER POINTER INSTRUMENTS

There have been many methods used to produce the deflection of a pointer as a function of the voltage or current it is required to measure. Some of these instruments have fallen from normal use because of their fragility and small overload capacity, for example, the hot wire ammeter, while others were discarded because of their poor reliability or large power consumption. for example, the induction ammeter. Others have continued to be used for special applications or because they are inexpensive and robust, but are facing increasingly strong competition from electronic replacements. However, since the economics of the situation will not allow replacement of all pointer instruments overnight the more common ones in everyday use must be considered.

2.3.1 Moving Iron Instrument

The deflecting torque for this type of instrument is obtained either by attraction (figure 2.43a) of a soft iron vane into the field of the coil, or by magnetic repulsion between two bars or vanes positioned within a coil. The repulsion form of movement is the more widely used since, if shaped vanes are used (figure 2.43b), an instrument with 240° of deflection may be obtained. For either the attraction or the repulsion version of the moving iron instrument it may be shown for a simple vane geometry [1] that the deflecting torque is proportional to GI^2 (where G is the deflection constant) and it can therefore be used in either a.c. or d.c. circuits. In most instruments the control torque is derived from a helical spring and the damping torque pneumatically.

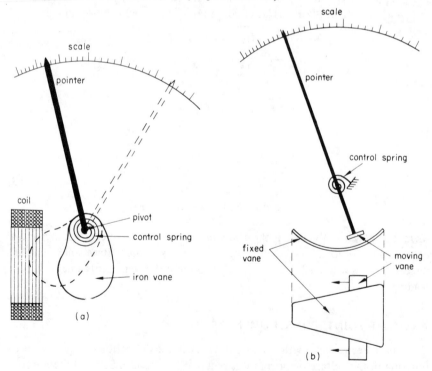

Figure 2.43. Types of moving iron instrument: (a) attraction, (b) repulsion

Properties

(a) Nonlinear scale, but a comparatively robust and inexpensive instrument to manufacture.
(b) Indication hysteresis. The moving iron instrument gives a low indication when measuring a direct current of slowly increasing magnitude, but yields a high reading when measuring a slowly decreasing direct current. This effect is due to the magnetic hysteresis curve of the iron used in the vanes.
(c) Frequency effects. If the range of a moving iron ammeter were increased by using a resistive current shunt, an error would result due to changes in the coil reactance with frequency, since this impedance variation will alter the current sharing between the shunt and the instrument coil. The effect can be reduced by using a 'swamp' resistor in series with the coil; by shunting the coil with a suitable capacitor; or by using a shunt with an inductance to resistance ratio equal to that of the coil.
(d) Waveform effects. Theoretically the moving iron instrument senses the r.m.s. value but due to nonlinearity in the *B–H* curve of the moving vane material, waveform errors result if a peaky waveform is applied to an instrument calibrated using d.c. or a sinusoidal waveform. The error may be large and is due to magnetic saturation effects in the iron vanes.
(e) It may be used from d.c. to around 100 Hz as an ammeter or as a voltmeter but when used as the latter it has a relatively low input impedance.

2.3.2 Thermocouple Instruments

These instruments also employ a technique which enables the moving coil instrument to be used for the measurement of a.c. quantitites. The conversion from a.c. to d.c. is in this case performed by using the alternating current to heat a small element, the temperature of which is converted to a direct current by a thermocouple attached to it. A thermocouple circuit is the term applied to two lengths of dissimilar electric conductor, joined at the ends to form a closed loop (see section 5.4.3). If the junctions of the dissimilar metals are maintained at

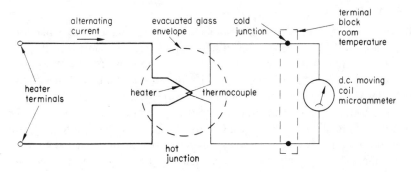

Figure 2.44. Principle of the thermocouple instrument (see also figure 5.39)

different temperatures a current which may be measured by a sensitive moving coil instrument flows in the loop. Since this current is approximately proportional to the temperature difference between the hot and cold junctions, and if the cold junction is maintained at a constant temperature, the current in the moving coil instrument will be proportional to the temperature of the heater, which in turn is dependent on the r.m.s. or heating effect of the current in the heater. In many instruments of this type the terminals of the moving coil instrument will form the cold junction as in figure 2.44, and will be subject to the variations in ambient temperature. However, these variations are generally insignificant (say 10 to 25 °C) compared with the temperatures of the heater which may be of the order of 1000 °C for the heater current corresponding to full scale deflection.

It should be noted that if a thermocouple is being used to measure the temperature of an object it is often more satisfactory to open circuit the dissimilar metal loop and measure, using an instrument with a high input impedance, the voltage that appears across the open circuit.

Properties

(a) Measures true r.m.s. value of an alternating current irrespective of its waveshape.
(b) Wide frequency range. May be used from d.c. up to the megahertz range, but pointer vibrations may be experienced at low frequencies (less than 10 Hz).
(c) Fragile, having a low overload capacity. Normally exceeding a 50 per cent overload will melt the heater element.
(d) May have a higher impedance than moving-iron or electrodynamic instruments.
(e) Nonlinear scale. The temperature of the heater will be proportional to current squared, also the temperature/voltage characteristic of a thermocouple is slightly nonlinear.

Applications

The main use is as an r.m.s. sensing milliammeter, and consequently when used with a series resistor it becomes a voltmeter. However, if it is intended that the instrument shall be used at high frequencies, it is important for the series resistance to be 'pure', that is, nonreactive, or its impedance, and hence the current in the heater will change with frequency (see section 7.2.2).

The thermocouple instrument is one of the few methods of determining the true r.m.s. value of an a.c. waveform (see p. 74). For precise measurement, the heater/hot junction and the cold junction are situated in an evacuated container and the d.c. output measured by a good quality digital voltmeter or potentiometer (see pp. 147 and 210). By this technique the a.c. to d.c. conversion may be performed with an error of less than 0.05 per cent over a range of frequencies from 20 Hz to 1 MHz; it also applies for higher frequencies (50 MHz), but with reduced accuracy. Reference 17 describes the construction of a thermal converter with a sensitivity of 1 part in 10^6.

2.3.3 Electrostatic Instruments

This type of instrument depends on the forces set up between charged plates to obtain a deflecting torque. The total force is proportional to the product of the charges on the plates and since the charge on a conducting plate is proportional to voltage the deflecting torque of an electrostatic instrument is proportional to V^2. The deflecting torque is derived from the force acting on a moving vane that is suspended in fixed quadrant-shaped boxes, as in figure 2.45. The control torque is derived from a spring system and damping is usually pneumatic.

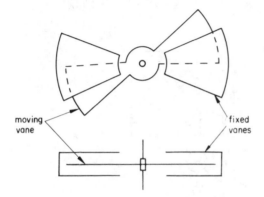

Figure 2.45. Electrostatic voltmeter vane arrangement

Properties

(a) Measures true r.m.s. values, because the deflecting torque is proportional to V^2 and can therefore be used as a transfer instrument.
(b) Used for d.c., and for a.c. where it constitutes a capacitive load, thus limiting its general application to frequencies below 100 Hz. However, it may be used to radio frequencies where it can be employed for aerial tuning, although its use for applications other than measuring power frequency high voltages is now comparatively rare.
(c) It is a comparatively fragile and expensive instrument.
(d) A high input impedance instrument, for direct voltages its input resistance being that of the leakage path through the insulation.
(e) Nonlinear scale, approximately square law, but this may be modified by the shape of the vanes.

2.3.4 The Q Meter

The 'Q' of a component is the term used for indicating its quality, and is defined as 2π times the ratio of energy stored to energy lost per cycle. Numerically this is the ratio of reactance to resistance at the frequency under consideration. The Q meter operates on the principle of creating a resonant condition between an inductor and a capacitor, so for a series circuit

$$Q = \frac{\omega_0 L}{R} = \frac{1}{\omega_0 CR} \qquad (2.14)$$

where L, C and R are respectively the apparent inductance, the apparent capacitance and the apparent resistance of the circuit at f_0 the resonant or measurement frequency. Consider the circuit in figure 2.46 in which the current

$$i = \frac{E_s}{R + R_s + j\omega L + 1/j\omega C} \qquad (2.15)$$

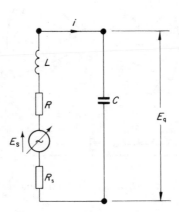

Figure 2.46. Equivalent circuit of a Q meter

The circuit may be made to resonate either by varying the supply frequency or the magnitude of the capacitor C and the current will have a maximum value of

$$i_{res} = \frac{E_s}{R + R_s} \approx \frac{E_s}{R} \text{ (since } R_s \text{ has been made small)}$$

occurring at the resonant frequency ω_0, that is

$$j\omega_0 L + \frac{1}{j\omega_0 C} = 0$$

or

$$\omega_0 = \frac{1}{(LC)^{1/2}} \qquad (2.16)$$

At this resonant frequency the voltage E_q across the tuned circuit is

$$E_q = i_{res} \times \frac{1}{j\omega_0 C} = \frac{E_s}{R} \times \frac{1}{j\omega_0 C} \qquad (2.17)$$

Thus

$$\frac{E_q}{E_s} = \frac{1}{\omega_0 CR} = \frac{\omega_0 L}{R} = Q \qquad (2.18)$$

The Q in equation 2.18 is the value for the circuit but the quantity really required is the Q of the component under test. Therefore the instrument must be designed either so that its operation has a negligible effect (when the Q of the circuit and of the component under test will be the same), or the effects of the operation of the instrument can be allowed for.

Thus, ideally, the capacitor should be pure (no leakage conductance), the input resistance of the voltmeter used to measure E_q should be infinite, and the output resistance of the source (R_s) should be zero.

The practical Q meter (figure 2.47) is an adaptation of the equivalent circuit in figure 2.46.

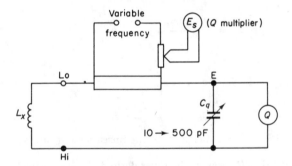

Figure 2.47. Practical Q meter circuit

The measurements of the voltage across the capacitor must be made using a very high impedance meter such as a vacuum tube voltmeter (v.t.vm.) (otherwise loading of the tuned circuit will result, and since the Q of the circuit is also the voltage magnification, the v.t.vm. may be calibrated in terms of Q provided E_s (Q multiplier) is adjusted to a predetermined value for all readings.

The measurement of E_s may be performed as a current measurement using a thermocouple ammeter since the effect of the resonant circuit on the current taken from the variable frequency oscillator will be insignificant. The unknown inductance (L_x) is connected between the Hi and Lo terminals, C_q being a variable air dielectric capacitor. Should it be desired to measure an unknown capacitance instead of an inductance, a known high Q inductor must be connected between the Hi and Lo terminals and the unknown C connected in parallel with C_q between the Hi and E terminals. One commercially available equipment is operable over a range of frequencies from 1 kHz to 300 MHz.

Applications

Determination of inductor properties

As indicated above the unknown inductor is connected in the tuned circuit and either the capacitor C_q or both it and the oscillator frequency are adjusted to obtain resonance, this being indicated by the maximum value of Q for the prescribed level of E_s, when

$$Q = \frac{\omega_0 L}{R} = \frac{1}{\omega_0 CR} \qquad (2.19)$$

These values for Q, L and C are those obtained from the instrument dials and may be used to give a value for R. All these quantities can be termed the indicated or apparent values and will be denoted as Q_1, L_1, C_1 and R_1. Since the purpose of the measurement is to determine the properties of an unknown inductor, it is necessary to consider the inductor as represented by its equivalent circuit (see section 7.2.3) and include the effects of its self capacitance, C_0, as shown in figure 2.48.

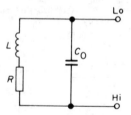

Figure 2.48. Equivalent circuit for the measurement of inductance

If it is assumed that R_s is as small as was desired, C_0 is effectively in parallel with C_q and the total capacitance in the circuit is $(C_0 + C_1)$ giving the effective inductance as

$$L_{eff} = \frac{1}{\omega_0{}^2 (C_1 + C_0)} = \frac{L_1 C_1}{(C_1 + C_0)} \qquad (2.20)$$

and the effective resistance as

$$R_{eff} = \frac{1}{\omega_0 Q_{true}(C_1 + C_0)}$$

where Q_{true} is|strictly the actual Q of the circuit but (since the leakage resistance of C_q is very large) it may be considered as the actual Q of the inductor and is obtained from the expression

$$Q_{true} = Q_1 \left(1 + \frac{C_0}{C_1}\right)$$

An explanation for this can be appreciated by remembering that in fact C_0 is distributed throughout the inductor so the apparent Q (or voltage across the inductor) will be less than the true value by an amount due to C_0. Hence

$$R_{eff} = -\frac{C_1}{\omega_0 Q_1 (C_1 + C_0)^2} \qquad (2.21)$$

Equations 2.20 and 2.21 both require the evaluation of C_0, the self capacitance of the inductor, and a Q meter may be used to determine this as follows.

(a) Setting C_q to the maximum value C_1 (typically 500 pF), a resonant frequency may be obtained. Let this be f_1. Then

$$f_1 = \frac{1}{2\pi L (C_1 + C_0)^{1/2}} \qquad (2.22)$$

(b) Doubling this frequency so that $f_2 = 2f_1$ and adjusting C_q for resonance gives

$$f_2 = \frac{1}{2\pi L (C_2 + C_0)^{1/2}}$$

Then

$$f_2 = \frac{2}{2\pi L (C_1 + C_0)^{1/2}}$$

Therefore

$$C_0 = \frac{C_1 - 4C_2}{3} \qquad (2.23)$$

and is the self-capacitance of the coil under test. *Note:* This assumes that L_{eff} is independent of frequency, an assumption that is not always valid (see section 7.2.3). Also, the true value of an inductor is the one to which L_{eff} tends at low frequencies.

Determination of capacitor properties

The properties of a capacitor that it may be desirable to determine are capacitance, loss angle and leakage resistance.

(a) Small values of capacitance (< 500 pF). The determination of capacitance is straightforward provided it is less than the maximum value of C_q. The measurement is performed by selecting a suitable, high Q, known inductor, connecting it between the Hi and Lo terminals and obtaining a resonance with

C_q set to a maximum. Let these values be C_1 (500 pF) and Q_1 occurring at a frequency f_1.

Connecting the unknown capacitor in parallel with C_q and adjusting its value to restore resonance will give values of Q_2 and C_2; also at frequency f_1. Then

$$C_x = C_1 - C_2 \text{ pF} \tag{2.24}$$

Treating this condition as one of a parallel circuit, that is, figure 2.49a

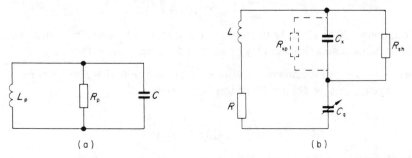

$$\text{(a)} \qquad\qquad\qquad\qquad \text{(b)}$$

Figure 2.49. Equivalent circuits for the evaluation of capacitor properties

$$Q_1 = \frac{\omega_0 L}{R_s} = \frac{R_p}{\omega_0 L_p} = \omega_0 C_p R_p$$

Now

$$Q_2 = \frac{R_p'}{\omega_0 L_p} = \omega_0 R_p' C_p$$

where

$$R_p' = \frac{R_x R_p}{R_x + R_p}$$

therefore

$$R_x = \frac{R_p R_p'}{R_p - R_p'} \tag{2.25}$$

$$= \left(\frac{Q_1 Q_2}{(Q_1 - Q_2)}\right) \frac{1}{\omega_0 C_p} \tag{2.26}$$

R_x being the leakage resistance of the capacitor C_x. Now

$$C_p = C_1 + C_0 = C_2 + C_x + C_0$$

$(C_0 = \text{stray capacitance of the standard inductor})$ therefore

$$R_x = \frac{Q_1 Q_2}{Q_1 - Q_2} \times \frac{1}{\omega_0 (C_1 + C_0)} \tag{2.27}$$

and the loss angle of the capacitor is

$$\delta = \tan^{-1} \frac{1}{\omega R_x C_x}$$

Therefore

$$\tan \delta = \frac{(Q_1 - Q_2)}{Q_1 Q_2} \times \frac{(C_1 + C_0)}{(C_1 - C_2)} \tag{2.28}$$

In addition to measuring the properties of a capacitor the above techniques may be used to determine the input impedance of a device or R-C network.

(b) Large values of capacitance (> 500 pF).   This is performed by connecting the unknown capacitance (shunted by a known resistance R_{sh}) in series with C_q, as in figure 2.49b. Again two 'balances' must be made. The first with C_x short circuited giving readings of C_1, f_1 and Q_1 for which

$$Q_1 = \frac{\omega_1 L}{R} = \frac{1}{\omega_1 C_1 R}$$

(C_q having been set to approximately midvalue for C_1). With C_x in circuit the meter is rebalanced by adjustment of C_q to give Q_2 and C_2 also at f_1 then

$$\frac{1}{C_2} - \frac{1}{C_1} = \frac{1}{C_x} \quad \text{or} \quad C_x = \frac{C_1 C_2}{C_1 - C_2} \tag{2.29}$$

and the leakage resistance of C_x is

$$R_x = \frac{Q R_{sh}}{\omega C_x R_{sh} - Q} \tag{2.30}$$

where

$$Q = \frac{Q_1 Q_2 (C_1 - C_2)}{C_1 Q_1 - C_2 Q_2} \tag{2.31}$$

and if $Q > 10$

$$\tan \delta = \frac{1}{\omega C_x R_{xp}} \tag{2.32}$$

2.4 ENERGY METERS

The amount of electricity used by a consumer must be metered and so energy meters are perhaps one of the most familiar electrical instruments.

The requirement here is for a display or integrated record of the electrical energy used over a period of time. This is performed by causing an aluminium disc to rotate (and hence drive a number of counting dials) at a speed proportional to the product of the voltage supplied to and the current in phase with the voltage taken by the consumer. That is, a given number of watts will have been consumed for each revolution of the disc, and by totalling the number of revolutions the energy consumed will be recorded.

To rotate the disc, eddy currents in it (induced by the combined action of a magnetic flux proportional to the supply voltage E_s and a magnetic flux proportional to the consumer's current I_s) produce a magnetic flux opposing the inducing flux, resulting in a torque on the disc proportional to $E_s I_s \cos \phi$ where $\cos \phi$ is the load power factor. It should be noted that although frequency is absent from this expression for the torque on the disc, it will affect the induced eddy currents and hence the torque. Thus the instrument is only suitable for use at its calibrated frequency.

A braking torque must be provided and this is obtained by using a permanent magnet to induce eddy currents of a frequency proportional to the speed of rotation of the disc. This form of instrument is shown diagrammatically in figure 2.50.

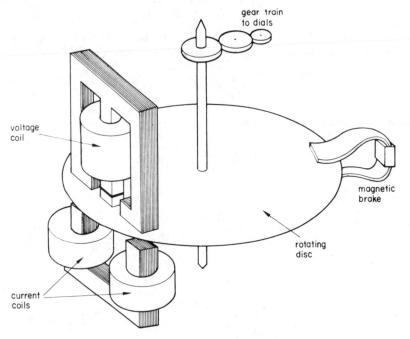

Figure 2.50. Energy meter components

2.5 SOLID STATE INDICATORS

For a number of years there has been an increasing use of strip indicators in process control application, where if a number of such indicators are placed side by side an operator can see at a glance if any part of the system is monitoring a malfunction. The development of low cost L.E.D.s and neon plasma displays has resulted in solid state analogue displays [18] of the type illustrated in figure 2.51.

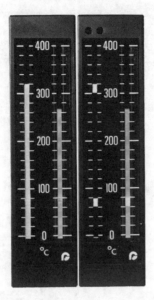

Figure 2.51. Solid state analogue display (Penny & Giles 'Striplite')

2.6 THE CATHODE RAY OSCILLOSCOPE (c.r.o.)

These are familiar pieces of measuring equipment, since no TV programme with a science content is complete without the display of instantaneous voltage values on an oscilloscope. It is an indispensible instrument in any laboratory where voltage waveforms have to be observed and it is manufactured in various degrees of complexity from a simple basic instrument to the sophisticated programmable instrument with digital readout (see figure 2.52). Since whole books are written on the oscilloscope,[19] only the principles and main features of these instruments are introduced here.

2.6.1 Conventional Oscilloscope

Principle of Operation

The simplest form of c.r.o. consists of a cathode ray tube (c.r.t.) and a deflection system (figure 2.53). Inside the c.r.t. is situated an electron gun which projects a fine stream of electrons between deflecting plates on to a phosphor coated screen, where a luminous spot is formed. The focusing of this spot is controlled by the application of a d.c. voltage level to biasing electrodes, while the quantity

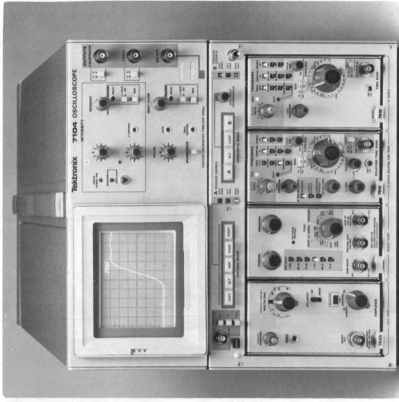

Figure 2.52. Cathode ray oscillospes: (a) simple, (b) complex (courtesy of Scopex Ltd and Tektronix (U.K.) Ltd)

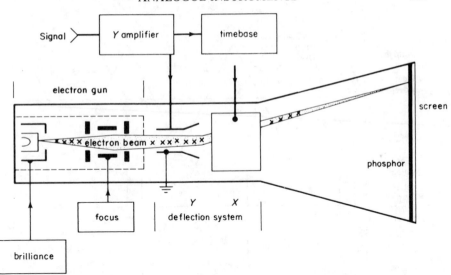

Figure 2.53. Schematic arrangement of cathode ray oscilloscope

of electrons projected, and hence the maximum writing speed of the oscilloscope, is dependent on the voltage difference between the cathode and accelerator electrodes of the electron gun.

Timebase

To move the spot across the tube face or screen at a time dependent speed a 'sawtooth' waveform (figure 2.54) is applied to the X deflection plates, the electron beam being bent towards the more positive plate. The sawtooth wave shape is used as the basis of the timebase so that the deflection of the luminous spot from left to right of the screen is at a constant velocity, whilst the return or 'fly back' is at a speed in excess of the maximum writing speed and hence invisible. Applying a difference in potential across the Y plates will cause the spot to move in a vertical direction, and if this voltage varies in a time dependent manner synchronised with the timebase, a display of the voltage variations with time will be obtained on the screen.

   In a practical oscilloscope[5,19] the timebase will be adjustable, so that signals having a wide range of frequencies may be displayed on a convenient time scale. A typical range of horizontal deflection sweeps being from 2 s/cm to 200 ns/cm, in 1, 2 and 5 unit steps. To synchronise the timebase and the Y deflecting signal, a triggering circuit is used. This is a circuit which is sensitive to the level of voltage applied to it, so that when a predetermined level of voltage is reached, a pulse is passed from the trigger circuit to initiate one sweep of the timebase. Thus on a timescale a series of events as shown in figure 2.54 are occurring within the oscilloscope. The trigger circuit of an oscilloscope will be adjustable so that a particular point on either the positive or negative half cycle

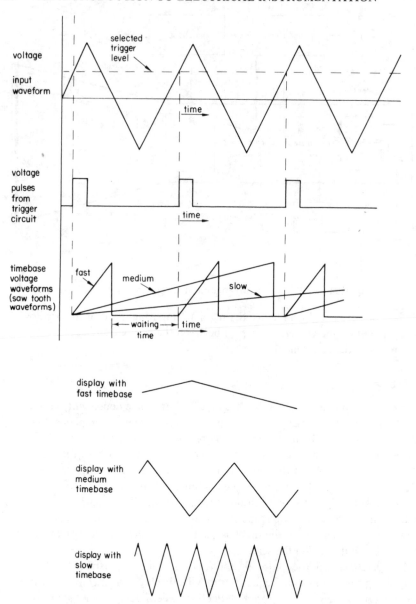

Figure 2.54. Effects of triggering and timebase selection on the c.r.o. display

may be selected, and used, to trigger the timebase. As an alternative to using the display signal to trigger the timebase internally it may in most oscilloscopes, be triggered by an independent external signal.

Some of the more sophisticated oscilloscopes[20] incorporate sweep magnification and sweep delay facilities, enabling the expansion and examination of

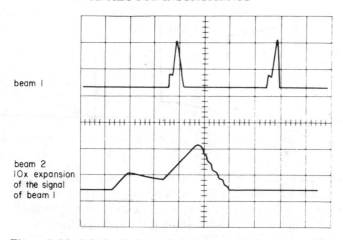

Figure 2.55. C.R.O. display using sweep magnification and delay

particular points in a waveform which occur some time after a suitable triggering point has occurred. Figure 2.55 illustrates the type of display that is possible with these facilities.

Vertical amplifiers

The direct application of the vertical or Y signal to the deflection plates would severely limit the versatility and sensitivity of the oscilloscope. To overcome both these difficulties a range 'attenuator' and amplifier arrangement is inserted between the incoming signal and the deflection plates. The steps of sensitivity are usually given in terms of mV or V/div. of deflection, and arranged in a 1-2-5 sequence. The range of sensitivities varies between oscilloscopes but in a general purpose instrument will probably be from 5 mV/div. to 20 V/div; a division is commonly 8 mm. As with the electrical pointer instruments the inclusion of an amplifier, while bringing the benefits of increased input impedance and sensitivity, introduces drift problems, limitations of bandwidth and accuracy. In general the most sensitive (50 μV/div) oscilloscope ranges have the narrowest bandwidth (for example, d.c. to 150 kHz) while the less sensitive ranges of some oscilloscopes extend into the region of hundreds of megahertz. To remove the effects on the display of d.c. drift in the circuit under investigation, most Y input amplifiers have an a.c. or d.c. mode of operation switch, which enables a blocking capacitor to be inserted in the input connection thus isolating the drift voltages from the input amplifier in the a.c. mode. Care must be exercised, however, when using this facility, for it is possible to introduce considerable distortion into the display of certain waveforms, for example low and medium frequency square waves (see figure 2.56).

The above assumes that all voltages are measured with respect to earth or ground potential. This is not always so, since it may be desirable to display the voltage waveform across a component in a line, that is, both ends of the com-

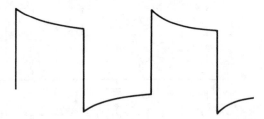

Figure 2.56. Distortion using a.c. input switch position when displaying square wave

ponent having a potential to earth. To overcome this problem some oscilloscopes' vertical amplifiers are manufactured with two inputs so that either input with respect to earth may be displayed or the difference between the two inputs may be displayed. This form of input amplifier is known as a differential input amplifier (see section 6.7.1).

X–Y display

As an alternative to the timebase circuits which may be connected to the X plates, most oscilloscopes have an uncalibrated X amplifier while some dual beam instruments have the facility for using one of the Y amplifiers as an X amplifier. This enables the display of loops or Lissajous' figures to be made (see figure 2.60 below).

'Z' modulator

The strength of the electron beam leaving the electron gun will depend on the voltage difference between its grid and the cathode. If a pulse of voltage were applied, via a blocking capacitor, to the grid it would be possible to blank out the display for the duration of the pulse. This is the purpose of the 'Z mod.' terminal available on many oscilloscopes, and enables part of a display to be either reduced or increased in luminosity.

Sampling oscilloscopes

The continuous display on an oscilloscope is, at present, limited to frequencies in the 50 to 300 MHz range, depending on the oscilloscope design. Above this order of frequency sampling techniques must be used to obtain a satisfactory display, which may be made up from as many as 1000 dots of luminescence. The vertical deflection for each dot is obtained from progressively later points in each successive cycle of the input waveform (figure 2.57). The horizontal deflection of the electron beam is obtained by the application of a staircase waveform to the X deflection plates.

Sampling techniques may not, of course, be used for the display of transient waveforms.

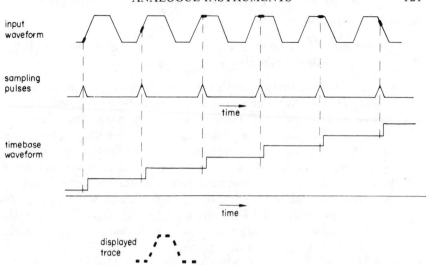

Figure 2.57. Simplified diagram of process waveforms in a sampling oscilloscope

Screen phosphors

The screen coating material absorbs the kinetic energy of the electron beam and gives off luminous energy. Several materials of different characteristics are available for this purpose,[21] examples in common use being as shown in table 2.4.

Table 2.4

Phosphor type	Trace type and use
P.1	Green trace of medium persistence, satisfactory for photographing, good for visual work. (Replaced by P.31 for most applications)
P.2	Bluish green trace with a long persistent yellow phosphorescence, very suitable for studying slowly varying signals. (Replaced by P.31 for most applications)
P.4	White trace, used in television displays
P.7	Blue-white trace, long persistence yellow-green phosphorescence
P.11	Blue trace of short persistence, good for photographic work, mainly used in high speed oscillography
P.31	Green trace, good general purpose phosphor. (Brightest available phosphor)
P.39	Yellowish green trace, for photographic applications

Thus the selection of a particular screen phosphor should be decided by the intended applications of the c.r.o. It should, however, be noted that while it is still possible to obtain c.r.t.s with phosphor types P.1 and P.2 their use has generally been superseded by the P.31 phosphors.

Multiple trace displays

In many instances it is necessary to compare one signal with another. To facilitate this, multiple trace displays are obtainable as follows.

(a) The use of two electron guns within the same cathode ray tube. This method produces an instrument known as a dual beam oscilloscope, in which the electron beams of the two channels are completely independent of each other. This effect may also be produced by a single electron gun, the output from it being split into two independently controllable electron beams.

(b) Using a single electron gun and producing a double trace by switching the Y deflection plates from one input signal to another for alternate sweeps of the screen. The eye interprets this as a continuous simultaneous display of the input signals although it is a sampled display. An oscilloscope using this technique, known as alternate mode, may only be used as a single channel instrument for recording transient phenomena.

(c) Switching the input to the Y deflection plates from one input signal amplifier to another at a rate not governed by the duration of the sweep; that is, the traces of each channel of input are built up from a series of dots as the electron beam receives a deflection derived from a particular input channel. This technique, known as chopped mode, may be used for multi-channel transient investigations.

Methods (b) and (c) reduce the cost of producing a multi-channel oscilloscope, it being possible to use either of these techniques to obtain a display of more than two channels.

Oscilloscope Accessories

To increase the versatility of an oscilloscope, various accessories are available for use with it, or built into it.

Calibrators

Many oscilloscopes have a built in reference source of voltage, which usually takes the form of a 1 kHz, square waveform of either a single magnitude or of selectable magnitudes. This facility enables the oscilloscope timebase and amplifiers to be checked for accuracy of calibration each time the oscilloscope is used. Should the calibration be found to be outside the specified limits for a particular instrument, the setting up procedures stipulated in the manufacturer's handbook should be performed by authorised personnel.

Probes

This topic is dealt with in chapter 6, but briefly the necessity for their use arises from the problem of ensuring that a circuit under investigation is unaffected by the presence of the measuring instrument. If the frequency in the said circuit is high then the capacitance of the cable conveying the signal to the oscilloscope will present the circuit under test with a low impedance. To reduce the errors that this would produce, a probe (having a high impedance) must be used at the measuring end of the connecting cable.

Cameras

The best method of obtaining permanent records of oscilloscope traces for analysis is to use photography. Special cameras are available for this purpose and are of the following two types.

(a) 35 mm, usually a prefocused unit bolted over the tube face. Some cameras have a fixed lens aperture, the exposure being simply controlled by hand operation of a flap shutter. More sophisticated units incorporate aperture and exposure control. The types of 35 mm film in common use are panchromatic and special blue sensitive films, which are faster and thus more suitable for the recording of high speed transients. Both of these give a 'negative' record, that is, a black trace on a transparent background, from which prints in the form of a white trace on a black background may be made. A third type of 35 mm photograph is obtainable by using recording paper, which results in a black trace on a white background. These are, however, difficult to enlarge.

(b) Polaroid film. This is almost 'instant' photography, a permanent record being obtained in 10 to 20 s. This process is considerably more expensive in materials than 35 mm photography, although the relative cost may be reduced by using the facility of some of these cameras to be moved relative to the screen, making it possible to place several traces (exposures) on one print. The camera is again prefocused, but normally provided with aperture and exposure controls. The record obtained on Polaroid film is a white trace on a black background—a print—and as such is difficult to reproduce.

Note: Time is money, and if only a few photographs are to be made, Polaroid photography is usually the most economical method.

Applications

The major and obvious use of the c.r.o. is that it enables the operator to 'see' what is happening to waveforms in a circuit—an extremely useful facility. In addition to this qualitative approach, by suitable use of the controls for the time base, vertical amplifiers and other facilities a considerable amount of quantitive information can also be obtained from the display. However, it must be remembered that the accuracy of direct measurements made using an oscilloscope is rarely better than $\pm$ 3 per cent on either the X or Y axes, and is therefore really a display instrument with facilities enabling the estimation of magnitudes of voltage and time.

Voltage measurement

The parameter of voltage that is most easily determined using an oscilloscope is, for a sinewave, the peak-to-peak value; and for a pulse its peak value. In either case the magnitude is determined using the engravings on the graticule, in conjunction with the calibrated ranges of the input amplifier.

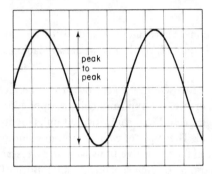

Figure 2.58. Measurement of voltage from a c.r.o. display

For example, for the waveform in figure 2.58, given that the amplifier sensitivity is set to 20 mV/div. the peak-to-peak amplitude is 20 × 6 = 120 mV. Should it be the r.m.s. value of voltage that is required then (assuming a distortionless sinewave) this peak-to-peak value must be divided by $2\sqrt{2}$; that is

$$V_{rms} = \frac{\text{peak-to-peak deflection} \times \text{amplifier sensitivity}}{2\sqrt{2}}$$

Current measurement

The oscilloscope is a high input impedance instrument, and therefore cannot be directly used for the measurement of current. Currents can of course be measured as voltage drops across resistors, but care must be exercised in connecting the oscilloscope leads to a resistor for this purpose because, unless a differential input amplifier is being used, one side of the voltage dropping resistor will have to be at earth potential.

Phase angle measurements

An approximate measurement of the phase angle between two voltages may be performed using the graticule of a dual trace oscilloscope to determine first the length of a complete cycle, and then the separation of the peaks of the two voltage waveforms on the two traces. A more accurate method of phase angle measurement is to form an elliptical display, by applying one voltage to the X input and the other to the Y input, as shown in figure 2.59.

For this situation consider the instant in time when the X input is zero. At that time the Y input will have an amplitude OA, where

$$OA = V_{y\,max}\,\sin\phi = OC\sin\phi$$

Therefore

$$\sin\phi = \frac{OA}{OC} = \frac{AB}{CD}$$

If the amplitudes of the X and Y deflections have the same amplitudes then it may be shown that

$$\tan\left(\frac{\phi}{2}\right) = \frac{b}{a}$$

where a and b are the axes of the ellipse as shown in figure 2.59.

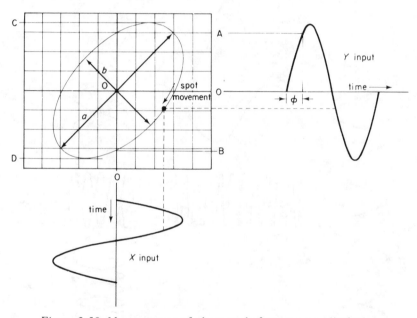

Figure 2.59. Measurement of phase angle from a c.r.o. display

Frequency measurements

The simplest method of measuring frequency with an oscilloscope is to determine (using the graticule) the distance between two identical points in a waveform and multiply this by the timebase setting to obtain the period and hence the frequency. This method, although quick, is subject to at least a ± 5 per cent error. More accurate methods of frequency measurement using an oscilloscope, use it as a display-detector in comparison techniques, using a stable known frequency from an external source, and the oscilloscope's X-Y display facility.

Consider first the problem of adjusting an oscillator's output frequency to be equal to that of a standard frequency signal. Applying one of these signals to the X plates of the oscilloscope and the other to the Y plates will result in an ellipse-type display, which will vary in shape at a rate dependent on the difference between the two signals. As the oscillator's frequency is adjusted to be equal to the standard frequency the rotations of the ellipse will become slower and when the two frequencies are equal will cease altogether. Thus it becomes apparent that the difference between two signals which have approximately equal frequency may be determined by counting the 'rotations' of the ellipse in a known time. In this manner extremely accurate frequency comparisons may be made using an oscilloscope. For example, if an oscillator's output frequency changes with

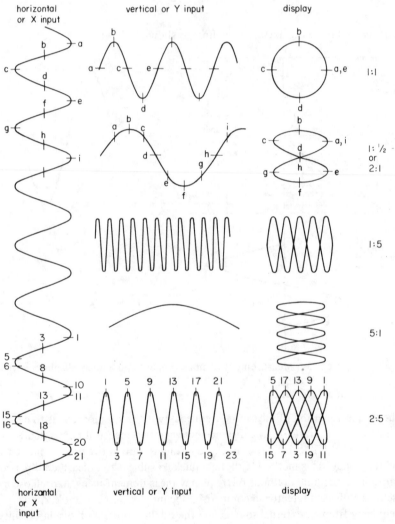

Figure 2.60. Lissajous' figures and the corresponding input signals on the X and Y axes

respect to a 1 kHz standard by one cycle (one rotation of the display) in 10 s then the difference in frequency between the two is one-tenth of a Hz or 0.01 per cent.

For multiples of a standard frequency, Lissajous' figures (figure 2.60) are used. The actual pattern of these displays will depend on the time displacement of the signals as well as their ratio, but at a particular time displacement for each ratio of frequencies a symmetrical pattern is obtainable, and under these conditions the ratio of peaks or loops on the left hand side to those on the top edge of the Lissajous' figure correspond to the frequency ratio of the signals applied to the X and Y inputs of the oscilloscope. Large ratios of frequency are difficult to interpret, apart from the complexity of the pattern, as any slight change in one of the frequencies will cause the pattern to roll. A method of overcoming the pattern complexity problem is to use 'roulette' patterns.

Another method of determining frequency ratios using an oscilloscope is to supply a common frequency signal to the X and Y inputs, these voltages having a 90° phase shift (to give a circular display), and applying a higher frequency signal to the Z modulator input. This higher frequency signal varies the intensity of the circular display, there being one bright and one dark section, for each multiple of X-Y input frequency. This method, although giving a display which is easy to interpret, is limited in application to exact multiples of input frequencies, with the additional requirement that the Z input frequency must be larger than the X-Y input.

Rise time measurements

When pulse waveforms are being studied, a property of considerable importance is the rise time of the pulse. The rise time of a step function is normally defined as the time interval for the change from 10 per cent to 90 per cent of the final

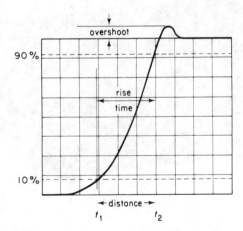

Figure 2.61. Rise time and overshoot measurements on the c.r.o. display of a step function

amplitude of the step change (see figure 2.61). The obvious method of measurement of this quantity is the straightforward use of the oscilloscope graticule and timebase as for voltage and frequency measurements. However, if the trace amplitude is adjusted using the variable gain control of the amplifier, and the timebase (in the calibrated position) operated with its calibrated multiplier a trace of the form shown in figure 2.61 can be produced, from which

$$\text{Rise time} = \frac{\text{timebase setting} \times \text{distance } (t_1 - t_2)}{\text{multiplier setting}}$$

Note: (a) Many c.r.t. graticules are 10×8 divisions and on such graticules the 90 per cent and 10 per cent amplitudes are shown by a dotted line. (b) If the pulse has a very fast rise time it must be established that the rise time of the step being measured is at least five times greater than that of the oscilloscope amplifier being used for the measurement. (c) There exists an empirical relationship between the rise time and bandwidth of an oscilloscope – their product has a value of approximately 0.35. Hence an oscilloscope with a 50 MHz bandwidth should have an amplifier rise time of approximately 7 ns and will therefore be suitable for measuring rise times greater than 35 ns.

Sample Specification

The following data on the *Telequipment D1016* is typical of that given in the specification sheet of a dual trace 15 MHz oscilloscope for use on mains power supply.

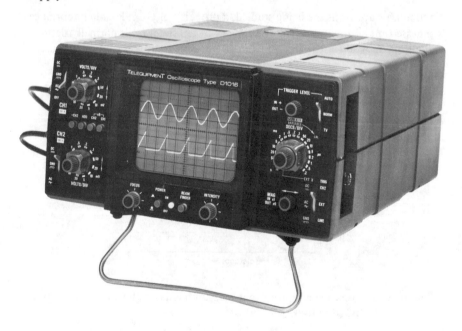

Vertical system   Two input channels

Bandwidth: d.c. coupled d.c. to 15 MHz (−3 dB); a.c. coupled 8 Hz to 15 MHz (−3 dB): rise time: 24 ns

Deflection factors: 5 mV/div. to 20 V/div. in 12 calibrated steps (1-2-5 sequence)

A × 5 gain switch extends each amplifier sensitivity to 1 mV/div. at a bandwidth of d.c. to 4 MHz (−3 dB)

Maximum scan: amplitude 8 div (6 div at 15 MHz); voltage measurement accuracy ± 5%

Input impedance: 1 MΩ + 45 pF (approx.) Input conditions: switched choice of d.c. a.c. or ground; the third position grounds the input of the attenuator but not the signal input

Maximum input voltage: 500 V d.c. or a.c. peak

Operating modes: channel 2 only; channels 1 and 2 chopped or alternated. The alternate/chop mode is selected by the secs/div switch (chop mode 0.2 s/div. to 2 ms/div. and alternate from 1 ms/div. to 0.2 μs/div. ADD CH1 and CH2 are algebraically added and an invert switch is available for CH2

X-Y CH2 is the vertical input and CH1 becomes the horizontal input. Bandwidth is d.c. to 2 MHz (−3 dB). Phase error less than 3° at 100 kHz

Horizontal System

Sweep speeds; 0.2 s/div. to 0.2 μs/div. in 19 calibrated steps (1-2-5 sequence)

A × 5 magnifier provides maximum sweep speeds of 40 ns/div.

A variable uncalibrated control provides continuous coverage between stepped ranges extending the slowest sweep range to 0.5 s/div.

Time measurement accuracy: normal ± 5%; × 5 ± 7% (approx)

Triggering

Bandwidth: 15 MHz on both auto and normal positions. TV triggers at field rate from 0.2 s/div. to 100 μs/div. and line rate from 50 μs/div. to 0.2 μs/div.

Sources: internal channel 2. External. Line.

Sensitivity: internal 0.5 div.; external 0.5 V (approx)

Polarity: Positive or negative

Trigger level: variable control selects virtually any point of the positive or negative slope of the input signal. This control is inoperative in the TV position

External X

Bandwidth: d.c. coupled d.c. to 2 MHz (−3 dB); a.c. coupled 10 Hz to 2 MHz (−3 dB)

Sensitivity: 1 V/div. (approx)

Input impedance: 280 kΩ + 30 pF (approx)

CRT

Display area: 8 div. × 10 div. (1 div. = 1 cm)

Phosphor: P31
Accelerating potential: 18 kV
Z modulation: 15 V amplitude, d.c. coupled
Calibrator
Output voltage: 250 mV peak-to-peak
Wave shape: a vertical step at the screen centre
Frequency: at sweep repetition rate
Accuracy: ± 2%
Power requirements
Mains voltages: 100–125 V or 200–250 V
Frequency: 48–440 Hz
Consumption: 50 VA (approx)
Dimensions and weight
Height 160 mm
Width 300 mm
Depth 420 mm
Weight 8.0 kg

2.6.2 Storage Oscilloscopes

The purpose of this form of c.r.o. is to provide the display of a waveform such
that it remains in existence after the signal has ceased. Depending on the properties of the particular instrument, the duration of the image retention is controllable from a few seconds to hours. The techniques used to achieve this are:
phosphor storage, mesh storage and digital storage (see section 4.4.3).

Phosphor storage

The phosphor or bistable storage oscilloscope [5,22] uses a c.r.t. which is similar
to a conventional one but with a phosphor doped so as to provide two stable
states which are sometimes referred to as written and unwritten. Other important
differences from the conventional c.r.t. are the presence of flood guns—which
are used to cover the viewing area with low-velocity electrons—to ensure that
the written trace remains visible, and a collector electrode which is a transparent
metal coating between the phosphor and the screen (see figure 2.62). Direct
view bistable storage is based on a secondary emission principle, it being
arranged that the two stable potentials (or states) of the storage target area are
such that one is approximately the flood gun potential and the other near the
collector potential. When the writing beam is scanned across the screen it dis-
lodges secondary electrons and the written area charges positively and changes
from the first stable state to the second. The electrons from the flood guns strike
the written area with sufficient velocity to dislodge enough secondary electrons
to keep the written area positively charged and visible. To erase a displayed waveform the collector is first raised to the positive potential so that the entire screen

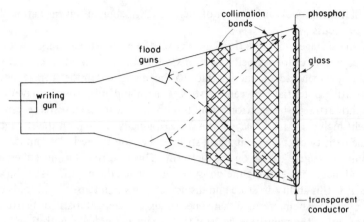

Figure 2.62. Diagrammatic presentation of a direct view bistable storage c.r.t. (after ref. 22)

is fully written, then it is dropped negatively before being slowly returned to the 'ready-to-write' level. In some oscilloscopes the storage target is split into two sections so that two signals may be stored, viewed and compared or erased independently.

Mesh storage

A mesh storage c.r.t.[22,23] functions by using two mesh-type elements adjacent to the phosphor (figure 2.63). The mesh nearest to the writing gun is fairly coarse and serves as the collector electrode to accelerate electrons towards the storage target, also to collect secondary electrons emitted by the storage target. The second mesh is very fine (approximately 200 lines/cm) and coated by using

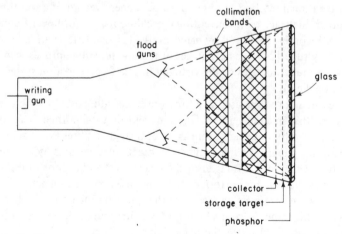

Figure 2.63. Diagrammatic presentation of mesh storage c.r.t. (after ref. 22)

thin film techniques with a layer of dielectric, it being on this insulation that the storage occurs.

In the storage mode the flood guns cover the entire storage target with a continuous stream of low-velocity electrons, which are prevented from reaching the phosphor screen except where a trace has been written on the storage mesh. An accelerating potential between the storage mesh and an aluminised layer on the phosphor attracts the electrons from the flood guns to the phosphor resulting in a bright high contrast display of the trace originally written on the storage mesh.

The density of the writing beam striking the storage mesh determines the amount of positive charge on the dielectric. This in turn determines the quantity of flood electrons reaching the phosphor and hence the brightness of the stored trace. It is this ability to store and display changes in intensity that leads to this type of storage being termed 'halftone storage'. A characteristic of halftone storage is that the unwritten parts of the storage mesh, begin with time to 'fade positive', that is to say the whole of the storage mesh will gradually become positively charged due to positive ion generation in the flood electron system, and when this has occurred the trace will be lost for the whole screen is then in a written state. To prevent this from occurring the entire screen may be slowly erased during operation by applying variable width pulses to the storage mesh, a process that is usually controlled by a front panel control normally labelled 'persistence'.

A further development of the mesh storage system is the introduction of a third mesh between the storage mesh and the screen. This third mesh has a bi-stable property and the resultant c.r.t., known as transfer storage, has a considerably longer store time and a much faster writing speed than the halftone tube.

2.6.3 Recording Oscilloscopes

The conventional method of obtaining a permanent record of a waveform is to photograph the trace on a conventional oscilloscope, or for lower frequencies to use a u.v. recorder. However, by using an oscilloscope fitted with a fibre-optic cathode ray tube,[24] the advantages of the u.v. recording process can be combined with the advantages of the virtually inertia-free deflection system of the conventional c.r.o.

The cathode ray tube used in a fibre-optic recording oscilloscope is essentially the same as that in a conventional c.r.o. except that the normal faceplate of the tube is replaced by one made from short optical glass fibres (see figure 2.64). The recording paper is held in intimate contact with the glass by a spring-loaded plate, so that the optical transfer of the image on the phosphor to the sensitive emulsion on the paper is performed with the maximum efficiency.

When a waveform is being recorded, the traces on the c.r.t. are obscured and because of his some instruments of this type have an additional monitor tube that simultaneously displays the signal being recorded.

In addition to being able to use this instrument as a conventional oscilloscope

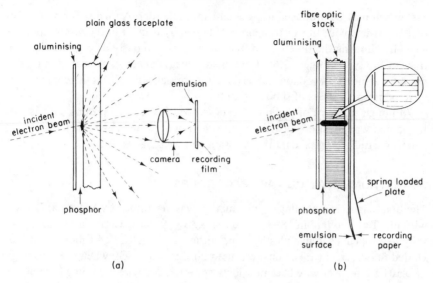

Figure 2.64. Recording using a c.r.t. with a fibre-optic faceplate: (a) conventional
c.r.t. and camera (luminous output only partially used), (b) fibre-
optic c.r.t. (film in direct contact with transmitted light) (courtesy
of Medelec Ltd)

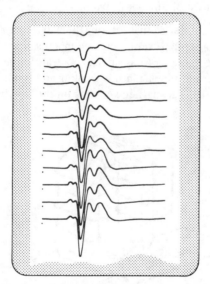

Figure 2.65. The raster mode achieves paper economy and simplifies comparison
between successive responses to a series of similar stimuli

and produce single-frame records of waveforms, continuous records of waveforms
may be obtained by driving the paper past the tube face while the electron beam
is deflected across it. This technique produces a multi-channel record similar to

that which may be produced using a light spot recorder. A further form of record that is possible with this instrument is obtained by using it in the *raster mode* when by allowing the timebase to free run and continuously driving the paper, a trace of the type in figure 2.65 is obtained. This is a method of operation that not only achieves an economical use of paper but also simplifies the comparison of responses to a series of similar stimuli.

Although this type of recorder was developed for medical purposes it has found many applications in areas as diverse as underwater sonar, noise and vibration studies, digital data transmission and welding research.

2.7 INSTRUMENTATION TAPE RECORDERS

The first magnetic recording of information was performed by Valdemar Poulsen with his 'Telegraphon' in 1893, in Denmark. By 1935 the Germans had successfully developed a suitable plastics 'tape' although in the United Kindom and the United States, steel wire or tape was used until around 1950 when the advantages of plastics tape over wire became widely accepted and wire recording became limited to particular applications such as flight recorders. Advances in materials technology have led to the tape recorders of today having a performance many times superior to that of the 'Telegraphon' but the magnetic principles remain the same.

Tape recorders consist of three basic parts.

(a) A recording head. A device that responds to an electrical signal in such a manner that a magnetic pattern is created in a magnetisable medium. Its construction (see figure 2.66), is similar to a transformer with a single winding, the signal current flowing in this winding and producing a magnetic flux in the core material. The magnetic coating on the tape bridges the non-

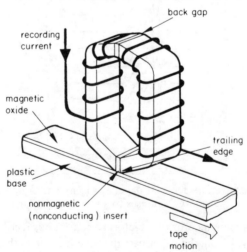

Figure 2.66. Simplified diagram of a record head

magnetic gap in the 'head' core and if the tape is moving past the gap the state of magnetisation of the oxide as it leaves the gap will be retained, thus the actual recording takes place at the trailing edge of the gap.

(b) The magnetisable medium. 'Magnetic tape' is composed of a coating of fine magnetic oxide particles on a plastics ribbon. The oxide particles conform to and retain the magnetic pattern induced in them by the recording head. Associated with the tape will be the tape transport system for precise control of tape movement.

(c) The reproduce head. This device detects the magnetic pattern stored on the tape and translates it back into the original electrical signal. The reproduce head, although similar in appearance to the record head, is fundamentally different in operation.

Consider the magnetised tape travelling across the gap of a head such as that shown in figure 2.66; to induce a voltage in the winding requires that there be a change in the level of magnetisation on the tape, that is $e_{rep} \propto N \, d\phi/dt$, N being the number of turns in the winding of the reproduce head. Since the voltage in the reproduce head is proportional to $d\phi/dt$, the reproduce head acts as a differentiator.

For example, if the signal to be recorded is $A \sin \omega t$, both the current in the record head and the flux in its core will be proportional to this voltage. Assuming that the tape retains this pattern and regenerates it in the reproduce head core, the voltage in the reproduce head winding will be

$$e_{rep} \propto \frac{d\phi}{dt}$$

and

$$\frac{d\phi}{dt} = \omega A \cos \omega t$$

so

$$e_{rep} \propto \omega A \cos \omega t$$

and the signal out of the reproduce head is the derivative of the input. In addition to this its magnitude is proportional to the frequency of the input. Thus to maintain amplitude fidelity these factors must be compensated for by the characteristics of the output electronics. This process is known as equalisation, the overall output characteristic being shown in figure 2.67.

In instrumentation recording, three techniques are in general use: direct, frequency modulated, and pulse duration modulation. Comparison of the three methods indicates that although the first method may have the greatest bandwidth, smaller errors are possible with the other methods, the frequency modulation recording process having the greatest number of applications in instrumentation.

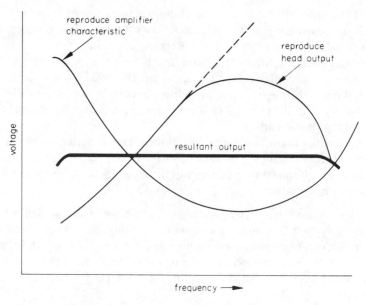

Figure 2.67. Characteristics of the components of the reproduce system to obtain amplitude fidelity (adapted from Hewlett-Packard data)

2.7.1 Direct Recording

While direct recording can be used for instrumentation purposes it is more usually used for the recording of speech and music. It is the simplest method of recording and usually requires one tape track for each channel.[25,26] The signal to be recorded is amplified, mixed with a high frequency bias, and fed directly to the recording head as a varying electric current. The bias is introduced in order to eliminate the nonlinear effects of the tape material's magnetisation curve. Both the amplitude and frequency of the bias are selected to be several times larger than the maximum amplitude and highest frequency contained in the input signal. The result of this is that the intensity of the magnetisation is proportional to the instantaneous amplitude of the input signal (see figure 2.68).

It should be noted that the combining of the bias and the input signal is accomplished by a linear mixing process that is not an amplitude modulation process.

The advantage of the direct record process is that it provides the greatest bandwidth obtainable from the recorder. It also requires only simple, moderately priced electronics. However, since a signal is induced in the reproduce head only when there are variations in the level of magnetisation on the tape as it passes this head, the low frequency response of a direct record system does not extend to d.c., the limit being around 50 Hz, the upper frequency limit being around 2 MHz at a tape speed of 3.05 m/s (120 in/s). The direct recording process is also characterised by some amplitude instability caused by random surface in-

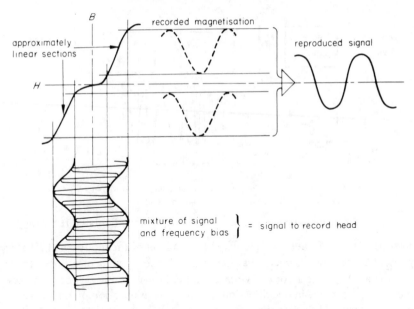

Figure 2.68. Classical representation of 'direct recording' (adapted from Hewlett-Packard data)

homogenities in the tape coating. At long wavelengths (low frequencies) the amplitude variations caused by this may only be a few per cent; however for frequencies near the upper bandwidth limit for a given tape speed, amplitude variations can exceed 10 per cent and momentary decreases of over 50 per cent (called 'dropouts') may occur. This also indicates one of the difficulties associated with magnetically recording digital data.

Direct recording should therefore only be used when maximum bandwidth is required and amplitude variations are not unacceptable. If maximum bandwidth with relative freedom from dropouts is required, a single input signal can be recorded on several channels simultaneously.

In sound recording the ear will average amplitude variation errors, and whilst the audio tape recorder utilises the direct recording process, it is seldom satisfactory to use an audio recorder for instrumentation purposes. The former is designed to take advantage of the rather peculiar spectral energy characteristics of speech and music, whereas an instrumentation recorder must have a uniform response over its entire range.

2.7.2 Frequency Modulated Recording

Frequency modulation overcomes some of the basic limitations of direct recording at the cost of reducing the high frequency response. The bandwidth of the recording may be extended down to d.c. and the reproduced signal is not significantly degraded by amplitude variation effects. In the f.m. recording system, a

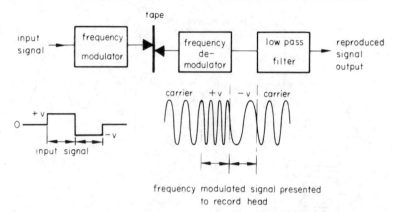

Figure 2.69. Schematic representation of 'frequency modulated recording'

carrier oscillator is frequency modulated by the level of the input signal. That is, a particular frequency is selected as the centre frequency and corresponds to zero input signal. Applying a positive voltage input will deviate the carrier frequency a specified percentage in one direction, whereas the application of a negative input voltage would deviate the frequency by an appropriate percentage in the opposite direction (see figure 2.69). Thus d.c. voltages are presented to the tape as frequency values, and a.c. voltages as continually changing frequencies, hence amplitude instabilities will have little or no effect on the recording.

On playback, the reproduce head output is demodulated and fed through a low pass filter which removes the carrier and other unwanted frequencies generated in the modulation process. In a typical f.m. recording system, ± 40 per cent deviation of the carrier frequency corresponds to plus and minus full scale of the input signal.

Although f.m. recording overcomes the d.c. and amplitude limitations of the direct recording process its own limitations are

(a) limited (20 to 50 kHz) high frequency response compared to the direct record process;
(b) dependence on the instantaneous tape velocity;
(c) associated electronics that are more complex and therefore more costly than those required for the direct process.

2.7.3 Pulse Duration Modulation Recording

Recording by pulse duration modulation (p.d.m.) is a process in which the input signal at the instant of sampling is converted to a pulse the duration of which is made proportional to the amplitude of the input signal at that instant. For example, in recording a sinewave, instead of recording every instantaneous value of the wave, the sinewave is sampled and recorded at uniformly spaced discrete intervals; the original sinewave being reconstructed on playback by passing the discontinuous readings through an appropriate filter.

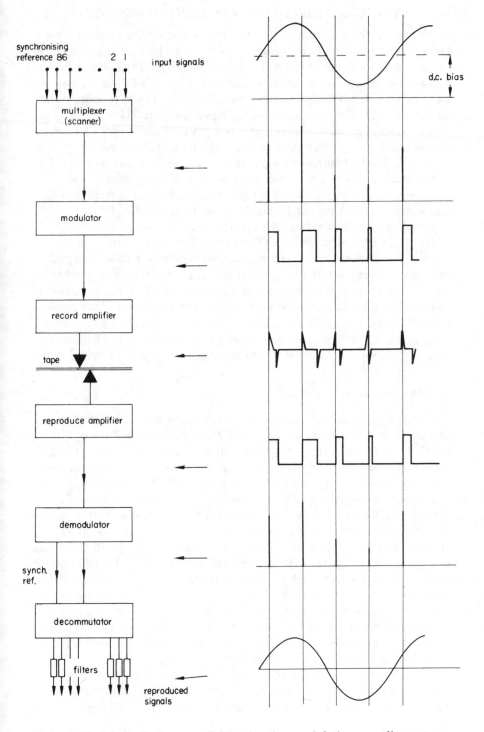

Figure 2.70. Schematic diagram of pulse duration modulation recording system

If a signal is being sampled at discrete intervals it is possible to use the time between them for sampling other signals (see p. 316). This may be accomplished by using some form of scanning switch or multiplexer.[27,28] A schematic diagram of such a system is shown in figure 2.70, where if a total of 900 samples are made via a 90 position scanner, 86 channels of input can be recorded per tape track, provided that the frequencies of the input signals are all less than 1.5 Hz, the four scanner positions not connected to input channels being used for zero and maximum voltage calibration levels and synchronising purposes.

Thus the chief advantage of the p.d.m. recording process is its ability to record 'simultaneously' a large number of channels of information. Other advantages are its high accuracy, due to the possibility of self-calibration, and a high signal-to-noise ratio. The disadvantages are the very limited frequency responses and the complexity of the auxiliary electronic equipment.

The direct and f.m. processes are those generally used in instrumentation, a number of commercial recorders being available with input modules designed so that the signal may be recorded by either direct or f.m. recording, depending on which is the more suitable for the particular signal. The p.d.m. process is normally only used for special applications such as flight recorders, where a large number of slowly changing variables are to be recorded. Digital tape recording is limited in use in instrumentation (apart from storing the output from data loggers), its major application being associated with digital computing and control.

2.7.4 Magnetic Recording Heads

The limitations of each recording process are closely related to the specific characteristics of the record and reproduce heads. Each head consists of two identical core halves built up of thin laminations of a material that has a high magnetic permeability, and good wear properties, to ensure high efficiency, low eddy current losses, and a long life. The two halves of the core are wound with an identical number of turns and assembled with nonmagnetic inserts to form the front and back gaps. Only the front gap contacts the tape and enters into the recording or reproducing process, the presence of the back gap is purely to maintain symmetry and minimise the effects of random pick-up in the windings. In a record head the gap must be large enough to achieve deep flux penetration into the tape and short enough to obtain sharp gradients of high frequency flux at the trailing edge, for a particle of magnetic oxide crossing the gap remains in a state of permanent magnetisation proportional to the flux that is flowing through the head at the instant that the particle passes out of the gap. The gap length (typically 5 to 15 μm) of a record head has little effect on the instrument's frequency response, but the accuracy of the trailing gap edges is of extreme importance and considerable care is taken in its manufacture to obtain a sharp well defined gap edge. In a reproduce head, the front gap size (0.5 to 5 μm) is a compromise between upper frequency limit, dynamic range, and head life.

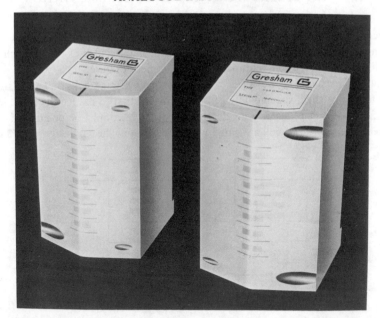

Figure 2.71. (a) A 14 track interlaced IRIG head set (courtesy of Gresham
Recording Heads Ltd); (b) dual head stack mounting in an Ana-log 7
recorder. The transparent tape is part of a 'lead in' system for automatic threading of the magnetic tape (courtesy of Pye–Unicam Ltd /
Philips)

In multi-track heads (see figure 2.71a and b) a compromise must be established between track widths (wide tracks giving a good signal-to-noise ratio), track spacing (large spacing preventing crosstalk), and overall width of the tape which it is desirable to keep to a minimum. Typical dimensions are: track width, 0.5 mm, and spacing between tracks 0.75 mm, giving four tracks on a 6.25 mm wide tape. The small spacing between tracks means that to reduce the noise level between the heads of a stack, an electromagnetic screen must be positioned between them,[29] as well as using two heads offset as shown in figure 2.72. In

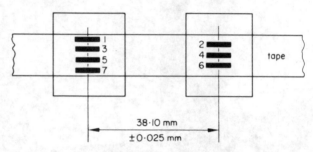

Figure 2.72. Offset of multi-track heads

a multi-track head it is essential that close tolerances are maintained on mechanical positioning and in electrical characteristics so that uniformity of response from track to track and from one recorder to another is maintained. It should be noted that for digital recorders the signal to noise requirements are less severe and as many as 16 tracks may be used on a 25 mm tape.

2.7.5 Tape Transport

To move the tape past the heads at a constant speed a 'tape transport' is used. This must also be capable of handling the tape during the various modes of operation without straining, distorting or wearing the tape. To accomplish this, a tape transport must guide the tape past the heads with extreme precision and maintain the proper tension within the head area to obtain adequate tape-to-head contact. Spooling or reeling of tape must be performed smoothly so that

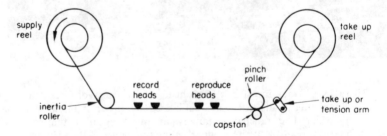

Figure 2.73. Simple tape transport system

a minimum of perturbations are reflected into the head area. Take-up torque must be controlled so that a good pack results on the take-up reel. It is also the job of the transport to move the tape from one reel to the other quickly when rewinding. Even with fast speeds, the tape must be handled gently and accurately so that a good tape pack is maintained on each reel. In going from a fast speed to stop (or vice versa) precise control of the tape must be maintained so that undue stress or slack is not incurred in the tape. A simplified arrangement of a tape transport is shown in figure 2.73 where a capstan and pinch roller are used to drive the tape.[26,27,28] Some manufacturers use a closed-loop drive, and others a two capstan arrangement. Considerable development work is in progress to establish even better tape transport systems.

2.7.6 Tape Motion Irregularities

Variations in the motion of the tape give rise to: *flutter*, which is caused by variations in the tape speed that have a frequency greater than 10 Hz; *wow*, which is caused by tape speed variations that are between 0.1 and 10 Hz; and *drift*, which denotes variations in the tape speed accuracy that are below 0.1 Hz. Common usage has broadened the definition of the term *flutter* to include all variations in the range 0.1 Hz to 10 kHz and in a recorder specification this should be quoted as either a r.m.s. or peak-to-peak value over a specific band of frequencies. The term *skew* is used to describe the fixed and variable time differences associated with a particular head stack. It implies that the tape is not moving in a longitudinal manner as it passes the heads. Fixed or static skew contributes a constant relative timing difference, and dynamic skew produces a variable timing difference between tracks.

Fixed skew is usually caused by the misalignment of a head to the tape, misalignment of individual heads in a stack, and bad guiding that produces differences in tension distribution as the tape crosses the heads. Dynamic skew is produced when there is a varying uneven tension distribution across the tape, which may be initiated by tape scrape, vibration, and tape irregularities. Fixed skew and some forms of dynamic skew produce relative timing errors between tracks proportional to the spacing between tracks. Thus tape transport specifications usually show skew (static and dynamic) or total interchannel displacement error as a time interval for a particular tape speed, for example ± 13 pm: 0.5 μs at 3.05 m/s.

Flutter and skew errors are imposed by both the recording and reproducing operations, and tapes reproduced on the same machine as they were recorded on will have less skew error than tapes reproduced on different machines.

Stretching of the tape causes a timing error between odd and even tracks of the tape. It was indicated in figure 2.72 there is a separation of 3.8 cm between the two head stacks,[29] and if the tape changes length between recording and reproducing due to stretching or environmental conditions, a timing error will be created between odd and even tracks.

Properties

The advantages of the tape recorder, compared with the data logger (section 9.3.1), are that it facilitates a continuous record of a number of signals, which may have a wide range of frequencies, to be made simultaneously. This has distinct advantages in the study of transient and 'once only' situations, for example, car crashing at road research establishments. When using a tape recorder it is possible to 'play back' a recording any number of times without deterioration of the record: it is also possible to change the time scale between recording and reproducing a signal, that is, a 'fast' occurrence may be recorded with a fast tape speed (1.52 or 3.05 m/s) but for analysis of the signals the tape could be played back at a slow speed 4.76 or 2.38 cm/s), enabling the recorded signal to be traced on an X-Y plotter (see p. 154). The reverse time scaling procedure is also possible, that is a slow process could be recorded with a tape speed of (say) 2.38 cm/s and reproduced from a tape speed of 1.52 m/s.

Some instrumentation tape recorders have 'level' sensing circuits on the input so that if the instrument is being used for data recording and a preset limit on the magnitude of the input signal is exceeded, an alarm indicator may be operated.

The main disadvantage of the instrumentation tape recorder is that the recorded signals on the tape are in no way visual, and must be reproduced before any analysis may be performed.

REFERENCES

1 E. W. Golding and F. C. Widdis, *Electrical Measurements and Measuring Instruments* (Pitman, London, 1963)
2 *J. J. Instruments—New Generation Measurements*, Vol II (J. J. Lloyd Instruments Ltd, Southampton, 1970)
3 *Measurement Notes 1977 Catalogue* (Keithley Instruments, Cleveland, Ohio)
4 S. D. Prenski, *Electronic Instrumentation*, 2nd Ed. (Prentice-Hall, Englewood Cliffs, N.J., 1971)
5 B. M. Oliver and J. M. Cage, *Electronic Measurements and Instrumentation* (McGraw-Hill, New York, 1971)
6 *Electrometer Measurements*, 2nd Ed. (Keithley Instruments, Cleveland, Ohio, 1977)
7 R. N. Reeder, Measuring true rms voltages, *Electron. Engng News,* **49** (1977) 61-3
8 T291: Unit 14 Instrumentation, Recording (Open University Press, 1974)
9 W. K. Whitlemore and R. Beswick, Direct writing chart recorders, *Electronics Power,* **23** (1977) 49-55
10 D. R. Davis and C. K. Michener, Graphic recorder writing systems, *HP Jl,* **20** (1968) 2-7
11 R. Beswick and A. R. Thompson, Linearity—finding a way through the specification maze, *Control Instrumn.,* **8** (1976) 34-7

12 H. Buckingham and E. M. Price, *Principles of Electrical Measurements* (English University Press, London, 1955)

13 P. J. S. Ashley, Buying electronic equipment 5: ultraviolet recorders, *Electl Electron. Techn Engr*, 6 (1972) 8–16

14 *The Galvanometer Users' Handbook* (Consolidated Electrodynamics Corporation/Bell & Howell, Basingstoke, 1971)

15 C. T. Baldwin, *Fundamentals of Electrical Measurements* (Harrap, London, 1961)

16 A. H. M. Arnold, Audio frequency power measurement by dynamometer wattmeters, *Proc. I.E.E.*, **102** (1955) 192–203

17 F. J. Wilkins, T. H. Deacon and R. S. Becker, Multi-junction thermal converter, an accurate a.c./d.c. transfer instrument, *Proc I.E.E.*, **112** (1965) 794–805

18 Design evaluation of the Penny & Giles Striplite indicator, *Engng Mater. Design*, **20** (1976) 29–31

19 R. Van Erk, *Oscilloscopes* (McGraw-Hill, New York, 1978)

20 *Understanding delaying sweep: Service scope No. 50* (Tektronix U.K. Ltd, 1968)

21 Phosphor data, *Tektronix Catalogue 1980* (Tektronix Inc., Beaverton, Oreg.)

22 Three new instruments, 3 kinds of storage, *Tekscope*, **4** (1972) 2–6

23 Storage expands your oscilloscope measuring capabilities, *Tekscope*, **7** (1975) 12–15

24 J. R. Huntingford, Fibre optic recording oscilloscopes, *Electron*, 37 (1973) 45–51

25 E. A. Read, Analogue recording, *Electron. Equip. News*, **12** (1970) 20–5

26 Magnetic Tape Recording Handbook, Hewlett-Packard Application Note 89 (1967)

27 C. B. Pears, Jr (ed.), *Magnetic Recording in Science and Industry* (Van Nostrand Reinhold, New York, 1967)

28 G. L. Davis, *Magnetic Tape Instrumentation* (McGraw-Hill, New York, 1961)

29 *IRIG Telemetry Standards, Document No. 106–69* (Defence Documentation Centre for Scientific and Technical Information, Ministry of Technology, Orpington, Kent)

30 A. S. Krause, HR-2000 A new state of the art in data recordings, *Measurements and Control* (October 1979) 87–9

31 N. E. Samek and W. R. Raymond, A PLZT electro-optic shutter array, *Instrument Society of America Instrumentation Symposium* (May 1979) 488–500

3

Comparison Methods

The methods described in this chapter could, as an alternative, have been termed 'null methods'—the purpose of the measurement process being to reduce the difference between a known and an unknown quantity to zero, that is so a null can be indicated. Inherently, such methods have a greater precision than direct measurements; for example, by using a detector that has a resolution of a microvolt it is possible to compare in terms of microvolts two voltages that have magnitudes of the order of, say, 1 V. The accuracy of such methods must, however, depend on the limits of error that apply to the 'known' or 'standard' quantity used.

3.1 D.C. POTENTIOMETER

3.1.1 Commercial Arrangements

The 1 m potentiometer used to describe the principle of operation in section 1.1.2 would be unwieldy in a practical situation but if two movable contacts are used, one on a shorter slide wire and the other on fixed lengths of resistance wire, a more compact instrument can be constructed. If the circuit in figure 1.4 is thus modified to that in figure 3.1, where the slide wire now has a length of 0.1 m and a resistance of 2 Ω connected in series with fifteen 2 Ω resistors, the total voltage drop (with a current of 50 mA) will be 1.6 V.

To standardise or calibrate such a potentiometer it is necessary to connect the divider voltage, via switch S, to the standard cell. Then, with the movable contact set at points such that the voltage appearing on the divider should be equal to the standard cell voltage, adjustment of the variable resistor R is made until the value of current in the potentiometer circuit causes these voltages to be equal, this being apparent when the galvanometer deflection (at maximum sensitivity) is zero.

The switch S can then be changed to connect the divider voltage, via the galvanometer, to the unknown and the divider contacts moved until balance is

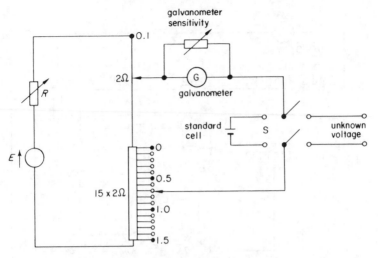

Figure 3.1. Simple d.c. potentiometer

obtained—this being the basis of single range potentiometers, which typically have a resolution of 1 mV and an accuracy of 0.1 per cent. They are, however, limited in application, and to increase the magnitude of the voltages which may be measured, it is necessary to use a voltage dividing resistor chain (see p. 277). To measure voltages less than say 0.1 V, the resolution may be improved by causing the current in the divider circuit to be decreased by a factor of 10 by adding a resistance in series with the divider and simultaneously shunting it with another resistor, as in figure 3.2 where, with the plug switch in position A the current flowing through the divider (of total resistance R) is $E/R = I$ and when the plug is in position B, the current in the divider becomes

$$i = \frac{I \times \dfrac{R}{9}}{R + \dfrac{R}{9}} = \frac{I}{10} \tag{3.1}$$

the current I through the standardisation resistance R_s remaining constant. This type is known as a double-range potentiometer.

Two other modifications are illustrated in figure 3.2.

(a) a fixed resistor R_s having a value adjusted so that with the correct value of current in the divider circuit, the voltage across R_s is equal to the standard cell voltage, and

(b) the small extension of the slide wire so that zero voltage on it does not coincide with the end stop.

The resolution, and hence order of accuracy, obtainable for a potentiometer will depend on the degree of subdivision and quality of the resistor units. In the

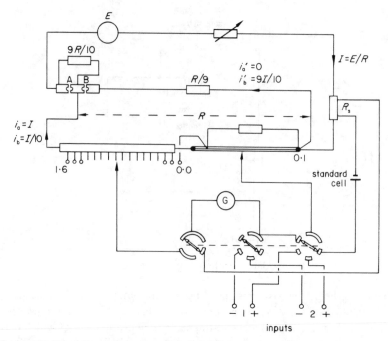

Figure 3.2. Double-range potentiometer, with switched standardising and input facility

potentiometers so far described the degree of subdivision is limited by the number of steps that it is practicable to construct. To obtain potentiometers with a higher degree of precision, it is necessary to modify further the basic circuit. One of the best methods of obtaining further subdivision of the divider is by means of the Varley vernier principle (originally devised for fault location in submarine cables), which is described in detail in chapter 6. By using such a technique the coarse adjustment could (for example) be calibrated in steps of 0.1 V, the vernier in steps of 0.01 V and the slide wire have a total drop of 0.01 V (10 mV) readable to 0.0001 V (100 μV).

Figure 3.3 outlines the main feaures of a three-dial potentiometer with a resolution of 1 in 180 000; an additional feature of such a circuit is the parallel arrangement which provides both a true zero and negative potential values on the lowest dial.

Properties

(a) Can only be used for direct voltage measurements.
(b) Extremely high input impedance at balance, for in the balance condition there is zero current flow between the source of voltage being measured and the potentiometer. Hence the latter appears to have an infinite input impedance. This situation will not apply if a voltage divider is used.

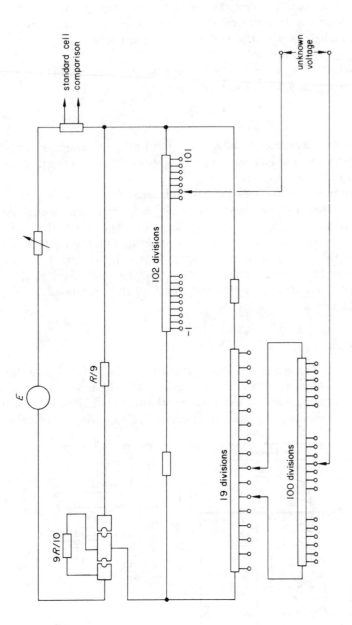

Figure 3.3. Simplified diagram of a three-dial potentiometer

(c) A small uncertainty in measurement is possible, the least expensive of potentiometers usually having an error limit of the order of 0.1 per cent of reading ± 1 unit of the least significant figure, while a good quality instrument would have an uncertainty of ± 0.001 per cent of reading ± 1 unit of the least significant figure.

(d) Operated by hand balance, requiring time, a moderate amount of experience and skill to obtain reliable, consistent readings.

Applications

The d.c. potentiometer is a small voltage (less than 1.8 V) measuring instrument. All other measurands must be scaled to that magnitude for measurement, either by using voltage dividers or current shunts.

To measure an unknown resistance a potentiometer may be used to firstly determine the voltage across a known resistor (R_s) and then across the unknown (R_x), when they are connected in series. Such a process requires that the current through them remains constant with time, a feature which may be established by making readings alternately across the resistors over a period of time. The process should be repeated for both directions of current and the results averaged to eliminate any thermo electric e.m.f.s, which can occur at the junctions of dissimilar metals.

3.1.2 Pen Recorders

The moving coil pen recorders described in chapter 2 are limited in chart width by the difficulties of providing a linear deflection system although by using complex linking arrangements and/or sophisticated electronic control, good linearity and a fairly high frequency response can be obtained. By applying the potentio-

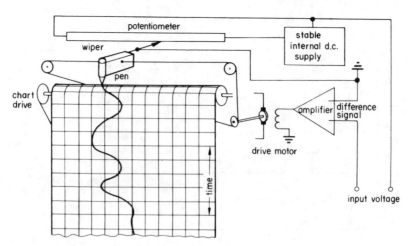

Figure 3.4. Potentiometric pen recorder

meter principle a better accuracy performance and greater chart width can be obtained but at a lower writing speed.

Consider the arrangement illustrated in figure 3.4. The unknown or input voltage is compared with the voltage between the wiper and one end of the potentiometer. The error signal, or difference between these voltages, is amplified and used to energise the field coils of a d.c. motor that is mechanically coupled to the wiper (movable contact) on the potentiometer. The energising of the motor field causes it to drive the wiper in the appropriate direction to reduce the magnitude of the error signal and attain balance. To improve the performance of the pen drive system some manufacturers[1,2] have developed linear motor arrangements for driving the pen. These techniques result in a number of forms of graphical recorder which characteristically have a high input impedance, a sensitivity maximum of 2.5 μV/mm, an intrinsic error of less than $\pm$ 0.25 per cent, and a bandwidth extending from d.c. to 2 or 3 Hz.

Process recorders

The original and one of the major uses of the potentiometric pen recorder is for the recording and control of process temperatures. In this type of application the output from a thermocouple (see p. 268) forms the input of the recorder. the scale and sensitivity of which is calibrated in a suitable range of temperature, for example 0 to 100 °C. The output from a thermocouple is nonlinear and if, as is usually the case, it is desired that the record is on a linear scale, linearisation of the thermocouple output must be performed within the circuitry of the recorder.

Figure 3.5. Circular potentiometric recorder (courtesy of Foster Cambridge Ltd)

The chart for such a recorder may be rectangular or circular, and driven (as a function of time) by a motor synchronised to the supply frequency. To change the chart speed alteration is made to the gear ratio in the chart drive gear train. In the case of the circular recorder (see figure 3.5) one revolution of the chart usually takes 24 hours or sometimes 7 days. It is this circular form of recorder that commonly incorporates level switches, which can be used to actuate an alarm if a preset level is exceeded; alternatively these switches can be used for off/on control purposes.

Rectangular strip chart recorders may also incorporate control features; additionally many models are available in which one movement may be used to log several inputs. This feature may be performed either by having several pens whose travel overlaps each other and can be used to monitor up to six inputs simultaneously (figure 3.6), or by replacing the pen with a print wheel geared to

Figure 3.6. A six-channel potentiometric recorder (courtesy of Chessel Ltd)

a selector switch so that when a particular input is connected to the balancing circuit, a point in an identifying colour, or character, is printed on the chart. This form of multi-point recorder may monitor as many as 24 inputs although 6 is a more usual number. A recent development[3] using digital storage and thermal printing has resulted in a multi-channel recorder with a built-in clock, so that, in response to a command, the continuous recording of three identifiable traces is interrupted and time, day and information on up to eight other channels may be printed on the chart.

Flat bed recorders

The demand for a pen recorder suitable for use as a bench instrument has resulted in the adaptation of the process recorder into what is generally termed a flat bed recorder. It is normally a one, two or four-pen instrument, fitted with a multi-range sensitivity control for each channel and a chart drive with selectable speeds. In a number of recorders an externally produced pulse may be used to control the stepper motor which drives the chart.

Sample Specification

The following has been extracted from the complete specification of the *Tekman T.E. 200/1 flat bed recorder* (figure 3.7).

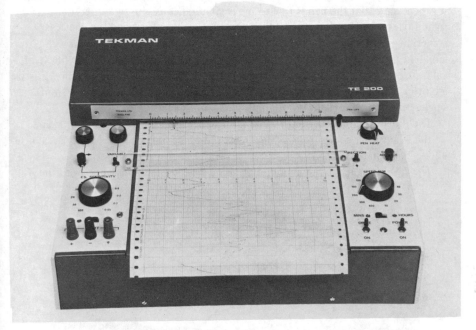

Figure 3.7. A two-pen flat bed recorder (courtesy of Tekman Ltd)

Ranges (20)   50 μV to 100 V full scale in 5–10–20 sequence
Chart width   200 mm
Accuracy   better than 0.3% f.s.d.
Dead band   0.1%
Input impedance   100 MΩ below 100 mV range; 2 MΩ above 100 mV
    range
Zero setting -100% to $+200\%$
Writing system   heated stylus or ink

Input   floating, asymmetrical

Chart drive   23 selectable speeds, from 10 mm/s to 10 mm/h or can be actuated by external pulse; chart may be driven in forward and reverse directions

The above indicates the scope of signal amplitudes that can be recorded with a typical flat bed recorder.

X-Y Plotters

The preceding forms of recorder have all had time as one of their axes, however, a number of applications exist where it is desirable that both axes should be capable of representing some function other than time. To devise such a recorder it is necessary that the pen is free to move simultaneously in two directions, at right angles to each other. (The other possibility, that of moving the chart, is sometimes used.) By using two potentiometric systems, one to move the pen along a carriage and the other to move the carriage along the recorder, a mechanical transport system fulfilling this requirement is produced. Figure 3.8 shows such a plotter which may be fitted with either a multi-range (5 μV/mm to 1 V/mm) or single-range (variable gain) input amplifier on both axes.

The illustrated recorder has a maximum velocity on the Y axis of 2 m/s, and on the X axis of 1.5 m/s giving a slewing speed of 2.5 m/s over a plotting area of 420 × 297 mm (A3).

The slewing speed is the maximum writing speed obtainable when both the X

Figure 3.8. The Bryans Southern X-Y recorder detailed in the text

and Y drives are operating at maximum velocity. It is therefore equal to $(U_x{}^2 + U_y{}^2)^{1/2}$, where U_x and U_y are the X and Y velocities respectively.

The writing speed when recording a sinewave signal will be dependent on the velocity and acceleration characteristics of the pen drive mechanism,[7] for below a frequency, ω' equal to the acceleration divided by velocity, the peak recording amplitude, A, is velocity limited $(A = v/\omega)$ and above ω' recording amplitude is acceleration limited $(A = a/\omega^2)$. Although this is a simplification of the true situation it does indicate that for the Bryans Southern 50 000 recorder, which has an acceleration from rest of 68 m/s^2, frequencies below 5.4 Hz are velocity limited while those above this frequency are acceleration limited.

Typical applications of the X-Y plotter are in drawing stress–strain curves, characteristics of semiconductors, frequency response curves, or the provision of any other information in graphical form. The presentation of such information has been enhanced by developments such as those described in references 4 and 5 where IEC BUS compatible instruments (see section 9.3.2) provide the possibilities of adding printed data and details to graphs or the use of colours for identification/clarification in the presentation of the graphical record.

3.1.3 Linear Indicators

The servo balancing potentiometric system may be used to provide an analogue bar or strip display by linking a colour change in an endless belt to the potentiometer's wiper. Such an indicator may be incorporated in a recorder as shown in figure 3.6 or it may be used alone as a linear indicator providing a display visible from a considerable distance. The characteristics of this type of device should be compared with the device described in section 2.5.

3.2 A.C. POTENTIOMETER

As the potentiometer proved to be such a powerful instrument for the precision measurement of direct voltages, its application to the measurement of alternating voltages was an obvious extension of its utility.[6] There were, however, difficulties to be overcome: first the measurement of phase, and second the standardisation of the potentiometer.

The measurement of phase was performed in one of two ways: either by rotating the measuring voltage until it was in phase with the unknown, or by using two components of voltage at right angles, their magnitudes being adjusted until the phasor sum of the two components balanced the unknown voltage. The former of these techniques produced the 'polar' potentiometer and the latter the 'co-ordinate' potentiometer. The problems of standardisation were overcome by standardising on d.c. and using a transfer instrument to reproduce the d.c. calibrated condition at the operating frequency.

A combination of the operational difficulties and the developments in devices such as phase sensitive detectors have resulted in the almost complete disappearance of the a.c. potentiometer from practical measurements. However the co-ordinate potentiometer has a useful function as an educational tool, for the measuring and computation technique used is remarkably similar to that used in some L.C.R. meters (see section 4.4.1).

Example

Consider the circuit in figure 3.9 where an a.c. potentiometer is used to determine an unknown impedance: V_1 being $0.5 + j0.36$ V and $V_2 = 0.7 - j0.43$ V, and the supply frequency being 50 Hz. The unknown $Z_x = V_1/I$.

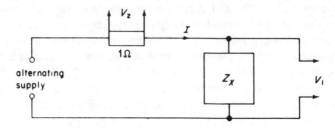

Figure 3.9. The circuit used in the example

It is satisfactory to assume that the input impedance of the a.c. potentiometer at balance is sufficiently large so that the current it takes can be neglected. The unknown Z_x is given by

$$Z_x = \frac{V_1}{I} = \frac{V_1}{V_2/R} = \frac{RV_1}{V_2}$$

$$= \frac{0.5 + j0.36}{0.7 - j0.43}$$

$$= 0.748 + j0.0548 \ \Omega$$

That is, the unknown impedance is a resistance of $0.748 \ \Omega$ in series with an inductance of $174 \ \mu H$.

The other functions of the a.c. potentiometer, primarily the measurement of small amplitudes of power and voltage, are more conveniently now performed by electronic instruments.

3.3 D.C. BRIDGES

3.3.1 Wheatstone Bridge

The d.c. potentiometer is used to measure voltage by a comparison process and resistance values may be determined by comparing voltage drops across known and unknown resistors. The restrictions on this technique are that variations in

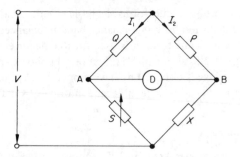

Figure 3.10. Wheatstone bridge (equivalent circuit)

the current in the resistors between measurements can cause a large random error (see section 1.3.2).

The basis of this bridge was described in section 1.1.2 where it was shown that for the circuit in figure 3.10 the balance equation is

$$X \text{ (the unknown)} = \frac{SP}{Q} \ \Omega \tag{3.2}$$

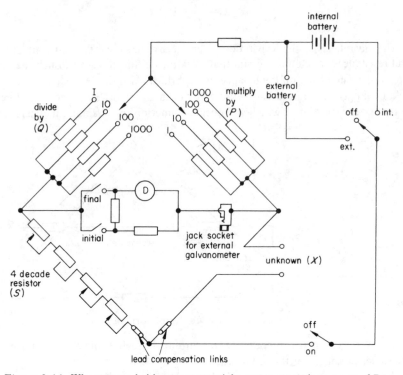

Figure 3.11. Wheatstone bridge, commercial arrangement (courtesy of Pye–Unicam Ltd)

The Wheatstone bridge circuit forms the basic circuit for a considerable amount of instrumentation both in a balanced and unbalanced mode of operation. In its commercially available form, it is used for the measurement of resistance values in the range 1 Ω to about 11 MΩ. Figure 3.11 shows one such circuit. The wide range of the bridge is obtained by having one arm (S) variable from 1 Ω to 10 kΩ and the ratio P/Q adjustable in decade multiples from 0.001 to 1000.

3.3.2 Low Resistance

To measure resistance values less than 1 Ω, a modification of the Wheatstone bridge by Kelvin is very satisfactory. The balance equation[7] for the Kelvin double bridge (figure 3.12) is

$$X = \frac{QS}{M} + \left[\frac{mr}{r+q+m} \left(\frac{Q}{M} - \frac{q}{m} \right) \right] \Omega \qquad (3.3)$$

In practice $m = M$, $q = Q$ and r (the resistance of the connection between X and S) is made very small and the expression for the value of the unknown becomes

$$X = \frac{QS}{M} \; \Omega \qquad (3.4)$$

The advantages of the Kelvin double bridge are that the effects of contact and lead resistances are eliminated and that variations in the current through the unknown have no effect on the balance of the bridge. Also the resistance of the unknown may be measured at its rated or working current. To reduce the effect of thermoelectric e.m.f.s which will occur at junctions of dissimilar metals, it is

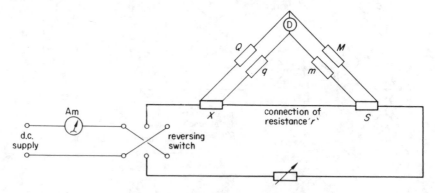

Figure 3.12. Kelvin double bridge

necessary to reverse the direction of the current through X and S and average the values obtained for the unknown.

The range of resistance values which may be determined with this bridge is normally from 1.000 Ω to 0.100 mΩ with an error of 0.1 to 0.01 per cent (depending on the quality of the instrument).

3.3.3 High Resistance

The measurement of high resistance is very prone to errors, because parallel leakage paths are difficult to eliminate,[8] and the values obtained are affected by the magnitude of the applied voltage, the temperature of measurement, the duration of the voltage application, and the humidity. The measuring techniques used for determining high resistances are various. Let us consider here those which are an extension of the Wheatstone bridge circuit (figure 3.13).

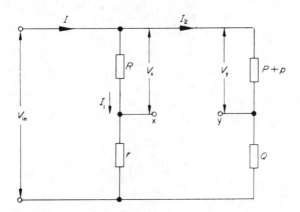

Figure 3.13. Modified Wheatstone bridge circuit

Let R be the resistance of the leakage path, and V_{in} be the applied voltage, P, Q, and r the remaining arms, having magnitudes such that: $R \gg r \gg P \gg Q$. Then with X-Y open circuit, and the bridge balanced

$$I_1 R = V_x, \quad I_2 P = V_y, \quad V_x = V_y \quad \text{and} \quad I_1 r = I_2 Q$$

Therefore

$$\frac{R}{r} = \frac{P}{Q} \quad \text{or} \quad R = \frac{rP}{Q}$$

Alternatively

$$RQ = rP$$

If the arm P is unbalanced by a small amount p, then

$$V_y' = I_2 (P + p)$$

and

$$V_{xy} = I_1 R - I_1 (P + p)$$

Now

$$I = I_1 + I_2$$

$$I_2 = \frac{(R + r)I}{R + P + Q + r + p}$$

and

$$I_1 = \frac{(P + p + Q)I}{P + Q + R + p + r}$$

Therefore

$$V_{xy} = I\left[\frac{QR - (P + p)r}{P + Q + R + r + p}\right]$$

$$= \frac{Ipr}{P + Q + R + r + p}$$

(since $QR = rP$). Now

$$I = \frac{V}{\dfrac{(R + r)(P + p + Q)}{P + Q + R + r + p}}$$

Thus

$$V_{xy} = V\left[\frac{QR - r(P + p)}{(R + r)(P + p + Q)}\right]$$

$$= \frac{Vpr}{PR + pR + pr + rQ}$$

The terms pR, pr and rQ will all be much smaller than PR and may therefore be neglected, giving

$$V_{xy} = \frac{Vrp}{RP} \text{ V} \tag{3.5}$$

Thus the voltage applied to a detector connected between X and Y will be proportional to a fractional change (p/P) in the arm P, and provides a method of measuring resistances up to 100 GΩ. For example, using a 1 kV supply, $r = 1$ MΩ, $P = 1$ kΩ, $Q = 1$ Ω, and $p = 10$ Ω, gives

$$V_x = \frac{1}{100} \text{ V/G } \Omega$$

The detector used in such a circuit may be a sensitive galvanometer (sensitivity 1 mm deflection per pA) or alternatively an electronic detector could be used, when the input current could be as low as 0.1 pA.

Such an instrument would have a very high input impedance (for example the input stage could contain an electrometer valve (see p. 71), and this provides another method of determining insulation resistance in which the sensitive detector is used to measure the voltage across a known resistor r which forms the low resistance part of a voltage divider consisting of r and the insulation resistance, for example, an arrangement similar to that shown in figure 3.14 from which

$$R = r\left(\frac{V_{in}}{V_r} - 1\right) \qquad (3.6)$$

Commercial instruments built using this principle have a scale calibrated in MΩ and may be used to measure resistances between 1 MΩ and 100 TΩ.

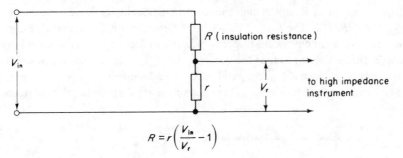

Figure 3.14. Potential divider method of measuring insulation resistance

3.3.4 Unbalanced Bridge

In many strain gauge and transducer applications (see section 5.1.2) it is necessary to measure variations in the value of a resistor. A widely used means for performing this task is to make the variable resistor one arm of a Wheatstone bridge instead of continually trying to keep the bridge balanced by changing the value of a variable arm; the current through the detector is then monitored, and this signal is normally termed the bridge output.

Principle of operation

Consider the basic Wheatstone bridge arrangement in figure 3.15 where three arms are fixed value resistors of resistance R Ω and the fourth arm variable by a small amount δR. The voltage

$$V_{AC} = I_1 R, \quad V_{BC} = I_2 (R + \delta R)$$

and

$$V_{BA} = V_{BC} - V_{AC}$$

Now

$$I_1 = \frac{V}{2R} \quad \text{and} \quad I_2 = \frac{V}{2R + \delta R}$$

Therefore

$$V_{BA} = V\left(\frac{R + \delta R}{2R + \delta R} - \frac{R}{2R}\right)$$

$$= V\frac{2R + 2\delta R - 2R - \delta R}{4R + 2\delta R}$$

$$= V\frac{\delta R}{4R + 2\delta R} \qquad (3.7)$$

This expression indicates that providing δR is small, $V_{AB} \propto \delta R$, and if δR is less than 7 per cent of R, this assumption of proportionality is justifiable, that is $V_{AB} = V(\delta R/4R)$. The current through the detector will depend on its impedance and the total equivalent impedance between the detector and the voltage source, that is the impedance the detector 'sees'. This impedance is known as the Thévenin impedance Z_{th} and is calculated by replacing the source by its internal impedance and computing the impedance of the resultant network (see figure 3.16).

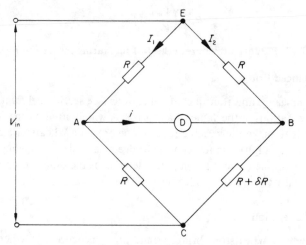

Figure 3.15. Unbalanced Wheatstone bridge

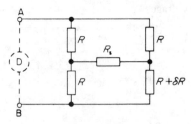

Figure 3.16. Rearrangement of unbalanced Wheatstone bridge (detector open circuit)

In general the impedance of the voltage source used in conjunction with such a circuit will be very small and R_s may be taken as zero. This simplifies the calculation of Z_{th} considerably for then

$$Z_{th} = \frac{R}{2} + \frac{R(R + \delta R)}{2R + \delta R} \tag{3.8}$$

and if $\delta R \ll R$

$$Z_{th} \approx \frac{R}{2} + \frac{R}{2} = R$$

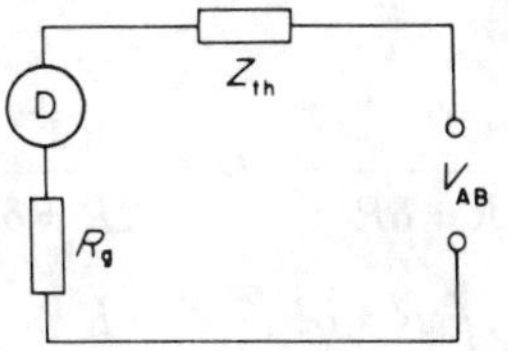

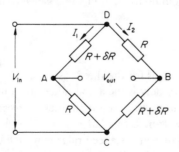

Figure 3.17. Equivalent circuit of figure 3.16

The circuit may be redrawn as figure 3.17, where R_g is the internal resistance of the detector, hence the detector current

$$i_g = \frac{V_{AB}}{Z_{th} + R_g} \tag{3.9}$$

(V_{AB} being the voltage which would occur at the terminals AB if the detector were open circuit). Such a circuit will produce only small output voltages which can be used to drive a sensitive pointer instrument or pen recorder movement. The output of such a system can be increased by using more than one variable arm, for example as shown in figure 3.18, from which

$$V_{AC} = I_1 R, \quad V_{BC} = I_2 (R + \delta R)$$

Figure 3.18. Unbalanced bridge with two variable arms

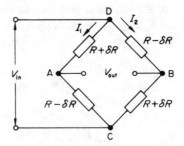

Figure 3.19. Unbalanced bridge circuit with four variable arms

$$I_1 = \frac{V}{2R + \delta R}, \quad I_2 = \frac{V}{2R + \delta R}$$

$$V_{AB} = V \left(\frac{R + \delta R}{2R + \delta R} - \frac{R}{2R + \delta R} \right)$$

$$= V \times \frac{\delta R}{2R + \delta R} \approx V \frac{\delta R}{2R} \qquad (3.10)$$

Finally figure 3.19, where the four arms are variable as shown giving

$$V_{AC} = I_1 (R - \delta R)$$

$$V_{BC} = I_2 (R + \delta R)$$

$$I_1 = \frac{V}{2R}, \quad I_2 = \frac{V}{2R}$$

Therefore

$$V_{AB} = V \left[\frac{R + \delta R}{2R} - \frac{(R - \delta R)}{2R} \right] = V \frac{\delta R}{R} \qquad (3.11)$$

This last circuit is one commonly used in strain gauge transducers (see section 5.1.2).

Output characteristics

The open circuit output voltages for the three cases are shown in figure 3.20 where it can be seen that not only is the amplitude of the output increased but the linearity of response is improved. To obtain these curves R was made 100 Ω, V, 10 V and δR given values from 0 to 12 Ω.

The transducer or unbalanced resistance bridge may well be connected to a u.v. recorder galvanometer and the effect on the galvanometer deflection of the variation in transducer output impedance is illustrated by the following example.

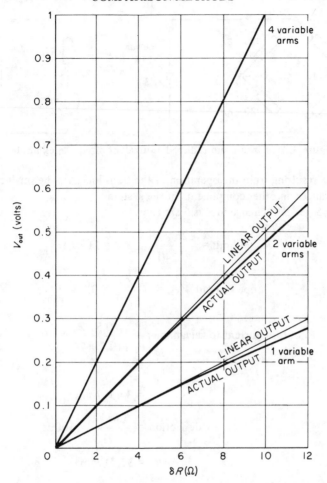

Figure 3.20. Curves showing the nonlinear output from one, two and four
variable arm unbalanced bridges

Example

Consider a transducer constructed using four 120 Ω strain gauges operating as in
figure 3.21, supplied from a 10 V direct voltage supply of negligible output
resistance, and connected to a fluid damped u.v. recorder galvanometer that has
the following specification.

Resonant frequency: 1 kHz
External damping resistance for 0.64 of critical damping: 50 to 2000 Ω
Terminal resistance: 26 Ω
Sensitivity: 91 μA/mm

If the operation of the transducer causes up to a 5 per cent change in the resistance of each strain gauge, show that the effect of the variations in output

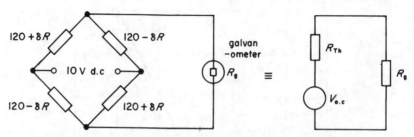

Figure 3.21. Circuit and reduced equivalent circuit in example

impedance resulting from the operation of the transducer will be small compared with tolerances on other components of the system.

δR for 5 per cent change in R is 6 Ω. Therefore

$$R_{th} \text{ at limit} = \frac{126 \times 114}{240} \times 2 = 119.7 \ \Omega$$

$$\text{open circuit } V_{AB} = \frac{10 \times 6}{120} = 0.5 \text{ V}$$

$$\text{output current to galvanomer} = \frac{0.5}{119.7 + 26} \times 1000$$

Hence

$$= 3.4317 \text{ mA}$$

$$\text{deflection} = \frac{3.4317}{91} \times 1000$$

$$= 37.71 \text{ mm}$$

If δR values ignored

$$R_{th} = 120 \ \Omega$$

$$I_g' = \frac{0.5}{146} = 3.4247 \text{ mA}$$

$$\text{theoretical deflection} = \frac{3.4247}{91} \times 1000 = 37.6341 \text{ mm}$$

Hence

$$\text{error in deflection} = 0.201\%$$

Since the tolerance on the galvanometer will be at least ± 5 per cent the effect of δR values on the transducer output resistance is negligible.

Note: Although the above statement is generally true, should δR be a relatively large percentage of R its effect on R_{th} cannot be neglected.

3.4 A.C. BRIDGES

3.4.1 Classical Bridge

The a.c. bridge circuit (figure 3.22) is similar in principle to the d.c. Wheatstone bridge, but is used to measure capacitance and inductance as well as resistance.

The general principle is the same, that is to obtain a balance so that the detector D gives a null reading when $V_{AE} = V_{AB}$, but with the a.c. bridge these voltages must be equal in magnitude and phase.

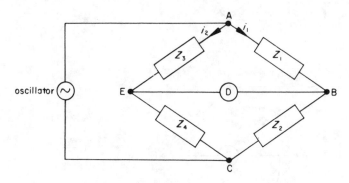

Figure 3.22. The basic a.c. bridge circuit

Detectors

The source of a.c. is usually an oscillator (see figure 3.22), the detector being one of the following types.

(a) Vibration galvanometer. A light spot galvanometer which may be tuned to mechanically resonate at the supply frequency—commonly 50 Hz—but may be designed for use up to 1 kHz.

(b) Earphones. Used from about 250 Hz up to 3 or 4 kHz, useful for variable frequency bridges.

(c) Tunable amplifier detector. These are the most versatile of the detectors and consist of a transistor amplifier which may be tuned (electrically) to respond to a narrow bandwidth at the bridge frequency, the amplifier out put driving a pointer instrument. This detector is usable over a frequency range of 10 Hz to 100 kHz (see section 2.1.1).

The variations of the a.c. bridge circuit are numerous and the details of each are published in many textbooks.[9] Common examples, such as figures 3.23 and 3.24, are attributed to Maxwell, Heaviside, Owen, De Sauty, Wien and Schering. The first three are suitable for measuring inductance, the last three for capacitance. Many commercial variations of these bridge circuits were devised, but the development of the transformer bridge (see next section) has tended to

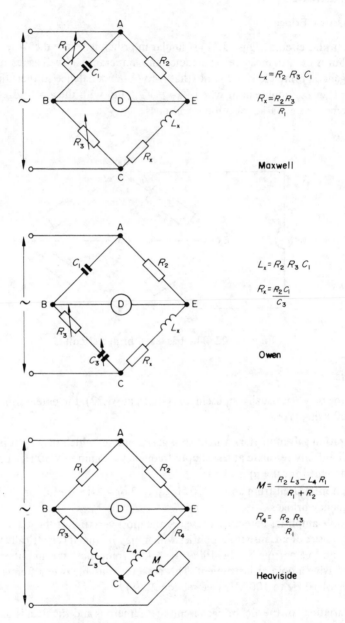

Figure 3.23. Some classic inductance bridges

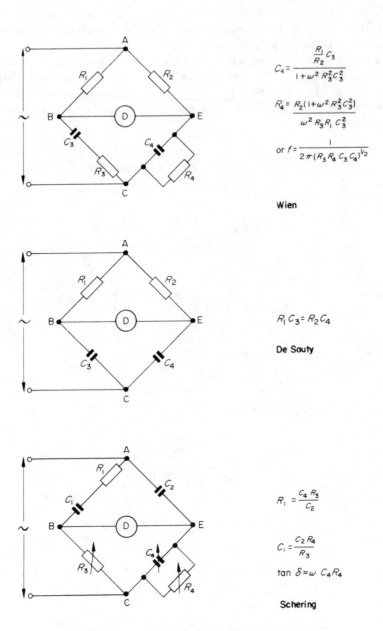

$$C_4 = \frac{\frac{R_1}{R_2} C_3}{1 + \omega^2 R_3^2 C_3^2}$$

$$R_4 = \frac{R_2(1 + \omega^2 R_3^2 C_3^2)}{\omega^2 R_3 R_1 C_3^2}$$

or $f = \dfrac{1}{2\pi(R_3 R_4 C_3 C_4)^{1/2}}$

Wien

$$R_1 C_3 = R_2 C_4$$

De Souty

$$R_1 = \frac{C_4 R_3}{C_2}$$

$$C_1 = \frac{C_2 R_4}{R_3}$$

$$\tan \delta = \omega C_4 R_4$$

Schering

Figure 3.24. Some classic capacitance bridges

supplant them. The current developments in component meters (see section 4.4.1) will undoubtedly continue the trend of replacing manually balanced bridges by automatic electronic equipment.

A bridge that is still used in high voltage work is the Schering bridge, and to demonstrate the principles of determining the balance conditions for a.c. bridges this will be considered in detail.

The balance conditions derived assume a series circuit for the unknown C_1, R_1. At balance

$$\left. \begin{array}{c} V_{AB} = V_{AE} \\ V_{BC} = V_{EC} \end{array} \right\} \text{ in magnitude and phase}$$

Therefore

$$i_1 \left(R_1 + \frac{1}{j\omega C_1} \right) = i_2 \frac{1}{j\omega C_2} \tag{3.12}$$

and

$$i_1 R_3 = i_2 \left[\frac{R_4(1/j\omega C_4)}{R_4 + (1/j\omega C_4)} \right]$$

giving

$$i_1 R_3 = i_2 \left(\frac{R_4}{1 + j\omega C_4 R_4} \right) \tag{3.13}$$

From equations 3.12 and 3.13

$$\frac{R_1 + \dfrac{1}{j\omega C_1}}{R_3} = \frac{\dfrac{1}{j\omega C_2}}{\dfrac{R_4}{1 + j\omega C_4 R_4}}$$

Therefore

$$\frac{1 + j\omega C_1 R_1}{j\omega R_3 C_1} = \frac{1 + j\omega C_4 R_4}{j\omega C_2 R_4}$$

$$j\omega C_2 R_4 - \omega^2 C_2 C_1 R_1 R_4 = j\omega R_3 C_1 - \omega^2 C_4 R_4 R_3 C_1$$

Equating real terms

$$C_2 C_1 R_1 R_4 = C_4 R_4 R_3 C_1$$

Therefore

$$R_1 = \frac{C_4 R_3}{C_2} \qquad (3.14)$$

Equating imaginary terms

$$C_2 R_4 = R_3 C_1$$

Therefore

$$C_1 = \frac{C_2 R_4}{R_3} \qquad (3.15)$$

Also tan δ, the loss angle of the unknown capacitor for the series case, $= \omega C_1 R_1$. Therefore

$$\tan \delta = \frac{\omega C_2 R_4}{R_3} \times \frac{C_4 R_3}{C_2}$$

$$= \omega C_4 R_4 \qquad (3.16)$$

For high voltage application, C_2 would be a standard high voltage capacitor (see figure 7.16).

3.4.2 Single-ratio Transformer Bridges

Due to the accuracy and versatility of ratio transformers (see section 6.1.4), a number of forms of a.c. bridge circuit incorporating these devices, as ratio arms, have been developed and have proved very satisfactory when making precise measurements. Examples of their application are as follows.

Resistance measurement

The arrangement of the ratio transformer into a simple bridge for comparison of resistance values is quite straightforward as shown by figure 3.25. The current through R_x (the unknown) is

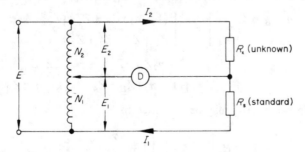

Figure 3.25. Resistance measurement using a ratio transformer

$$I_2 = \frac{E_2}{R_x} = \frac{K'N_2}{R_x}$$

($K' = 4K\Phi_m f$ from equation 6.4) and the current through R_s is

$$I_1 = \frac{E_1}{R_s} = \frac{K'N_1}{R_s}$$

At balance the difference between these currents will be zero, that is $I_1 = I_2$ and

$$\frac{K'N_2}{R_x} = \frac{N_1 K'}{R_s}$$

or

$$R_x = R_s \frac{N_2}{N_1} \tag{3.17}$$

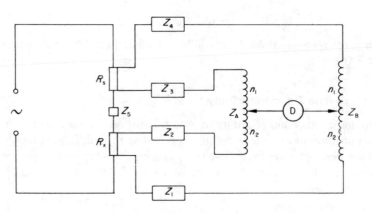

Figure 3.26. Measurement of a low resistance

By using two ratio transformers a form of Kelvin double bridge for measurements of low resistances may be devised (figure 3.26), where

$$R_x = R_s \left[\frac{n_2 Z_B + Z_1}{(1 - n_2) Z_B + Z_4} \right] + Z_5 \left[\frac{(1 - n_1) Z_A + Z_3}{Z_1 + Z_2 + Z_3 + Z_5} \right] \times$$

$$\left[\frac{n_2 Z_B + Z_1}{(1 - n_2) Z_B + Z_4} - \frac{n_1 Z_A + Z_2}{(1 - n_1) Z_A + Z_3} \right] \tag{3.18}$$

and this expression [10] may be simplified to

$$R_x = R_s \left[\frac{n_2}{1 - n_2} \right] \left[1 + \frac{Z_1}{n_2 Z_B} - \frac{Z_4}{n_1 Z_B} \right]$$

and provided the lead impedances are small, the input impedances of the trans-formers large and R_x and R_s of the same order of magnitude, the expression for R_x can be simplified still further to

$$R_x = R_s \frac{n_2}{n_1} \tag{3.19}$$

Such a bridge can, of course only be used with an alternating signal but by plotting the values of R_x against frequency, an extrapolation for the direct current value of R_x may be performed to determine R_x within a few parts per million.

Capacitance measurement

For the measurement of capacitance a circuit of the form in figure 3.27 can be used, when

$$C_x = \frac{C_s N_1}{N_2} \tag{3.20}$$

and the parallel leakage of the resistance of the capacitor

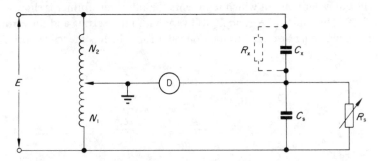

Figure 3.27. Capacitance measurement using a ratio transformer

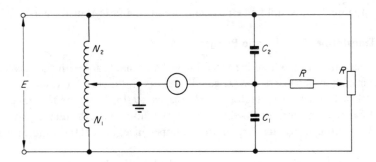

Figure 3.28. A circuit for the measurement of a 'good' capacitor

$$R_x = \frac{R_s N_2}{N_1} \tag{3.21}$$

An alternative arrangement of this circuit, sometimes used in connection with capacitance transducers (see section 5.2.1), is shown in figure 3.28 where provided the parallel leakage resistance of both capacitors is large, the resistance effects can be neglected and

$$C_2 = \frac{C_1 N_1}{N_2}$$

Other uses[11,12]

Other application examples of the auto or ratio transformer are in the measurement of small phase angles, the converting of a fixed standard into a variable one, the determination of amplifier gain and transformer ratios, and as a precision voltage divider.

However, in practice it must be appreciated that the ratio transformer is not ideal and in all its uses that involve drawing a load current through part of the winding, allowance should be made for the resistance and inductance of the windings. The equivalent circuit which represents the ratio transformer is shown in figure 3.29. The values of R_s and L_s will vary with ratio setting and the error they introduce must be added to the no-load error, which is the value normally quoted.

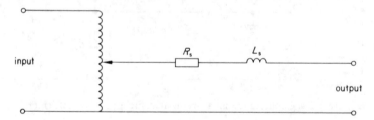

Figure 3.29. Simplified equivalent circuit of a ratio transformer

3.4.3 Transformer Double-ratio Bridges

The transformer bridges described so far have had a similarity with the classical bridges in that at balance, a voltage equality exists and there is no resultant current flow through the detector. An alternative to this would be to arrange that, at balance, the current flowing through the unknown was equal and opposite to that through the standard or known impedance, the detector indicating this equality.

Consider the circuit in figure 3.30 where the 'ideal' voltage transformer has a secondary winding of N_1 turns with a tapping at N_2 turns, so that voltages E_1 and E_2 are applied to impedances Z_x and Z_s respectively, resulting in currents

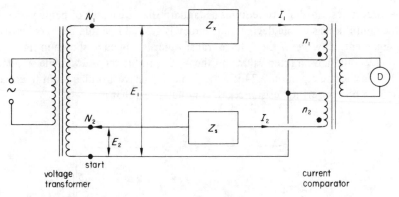

start

voltage
transformer

current
comparator

Figure 3.30. Basic circuit of a double-ratio transformer bridge

I_1 and I_2 flowing in the windings n_1 and n_2 of the current comparator.

The ampere turns $n_1 I_1$ and $n_2 I_2$ will produce fluxes in the core of the comparator that will oppose each other and a balance condition will be attained when the resultant flux is zero, this being indicated by the voltage in the winding connected to the detector also being zero. Thus, at balance

$$I_1 n_1 = I_2 n_2 \tag{3.22}$$

Now

$$I_1 = E_1/Z_x = kN_1/Z_x$$

and

$$I_2 = E_2/Z_s = kN_2/Z_s$$

Therefore

$$\frac{N_1 n_1}{Z_x} = \frac{N_2 n_2}{Z_s} \quad \text{or} \quad Z_x = Z_s \frac{N_1 n_1}{N_2 n_2} \tag{3.23}$$

If Z_x is resistive

$$R_x = R_s \frac{N_1 n_1}{N_2 n_2} \tag{3.24}$$

If Z_x is capacitive

$$\frac{1}{j\omega C_x} = \frac{1}{j\omega C_s} \frac{N_1 n_1}{N_2 n_2}$$

or

$$C_x = C_s \frac{N_2 n_2}{N_1 n_1} \tag{3.25}$$

The circuit described above requires a standard that is capable of being varied in value, and if a reasonable degree of accuracy is desired it would be an expensive arrangement. However if the voltage transformer is tapped as shown in figure 3.31, C_s could have a fixed value and the $N_2 C_s$ product be the variable standard.

Reconsidering equation 3.24 it may be made to have a similar form to equation 3.25 by converting resistances to conductances, that is

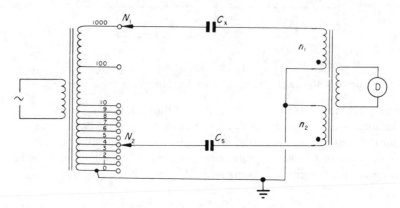

Figure 3.31. Double-ratio transformer bridge having a fixed value standard

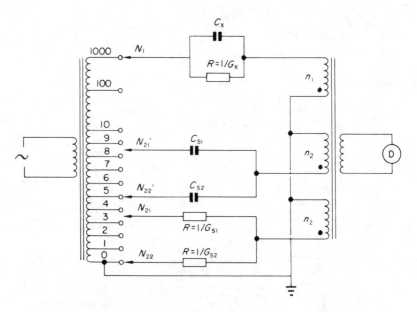

Figure 3.32. Double-ratio transformer bridge having fixed value capacitance and conductance standards

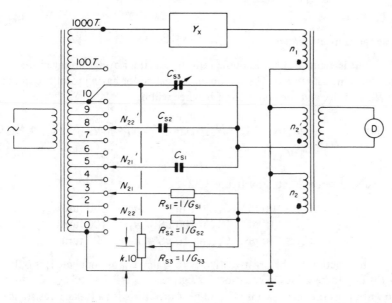

Figure 3.33. Double-ratio transformer bridge arranged for capacitance measurement

$$\frac{1}{R_x} = G_x = G_s \frac{N_2 n_2}{N_1 n_1}$$

Then if the unknown is a capacitor with a leakage resistance it may be represented as an admittance $Y_x = G_x + j\omega C_x$ that can be balanced against conductance and capacitance standards G_s and C_s as shown in figure 3.32 for which

$$G_x + j\omega C_x = \frac{n_2}{N_1 n_1} [G_{s1}N_{21} + G_{s2}N_{22} + j\omega (C_{s1}N_{21}' + C_{s2}N_{22}')] \qquad (3.26)$$

Only two decades of standard have been used for the bridge shown in figure 3.32; more could have been used although this tends to make the switching arrangements complicated. A compromise between a large number of switched standards and expensive variable standards is employed in most commercial bridges, resulting in a circuit of the form shown in figure 3.33 where in addition to the switched standards, a variable capacitance standard (C_{s3}) is permanently connected to the 10-turn tapping of the voltage transformer, while a variable conductance standard (G_{s3}), which theoretically may be required to have a value that can be varied from 0 to 10 μS (∞ to 100 kΩ), is in practice likely to be a 100 kΩ resistor connected to a continuously variable resistive divider that is connected across 10 turns of the voltage transformer; the travel of the wiper being calibrated as fractions of the 10 turns.

Applications

Capacitance measurement

The circuit in figure 3.33 is a double-ratio transformer bridge arranged for capacitance measurement. The unknown is a capacitor having parallel components R_x and C_x, and the equation of balance will be

$$\frac{1}{R_x} + j\omega C_x = \frac{1}{N_1 n_1} [n_2(N_{21}G_{31} + N_{22}G_{s2} + k10G_{s3}) + j\omega n_2'(N_{21}'C_{s1} + N_{22}'C_{s2} + 10C_{s3})] \tag{3.27}$$

If in the bridge represented by figure 3.33

$C_{s1} = 100\text{ nF}$	$G_{s1} = 1\text{ mS}$	$n_1 = 100$ turns
$C_{s2} = 10\text{ nF}$	$G_{s2} = 100\ \mu\text{S}$	$n_2 = 100$ turns
$C_{s3} = 630\text{ pF}$	$G_{s3} = 10\ \mu\text{S}$	$n_2' = 1000$ turns

and k (the fraction of the resistive divider to which G_{s3} is connected) is 0.35, substituting these values in equation 3.27 gives $1/R_x = 3.135\ \mu\text{S}$ and $C_x = 5.863\text{ nF}$; thus the unknown is a 5.863 nF capacitor with a leakage resistance of 319 kΩ.

In a commercially produced bridge (for example those marketed by Wayne Kerr) the turns values would be adjusted by the range selection switch, and the display at balance would be in the form of conductance and capacitance values, each with appropriate units. Thus in making measurements on a capacitor, the value of capacitance would be read directly from the display and the leakage resistance determined by computing the reciprocal of the displayed conductance value.

The standards of conductance and capacitance that are used in a transformer bridge may have impurities, that is, the capacitors have leakage resistance, and the conductances a reactive component. These impurities are balanced out during the manufacture of a bridge by circuit arrangements that permit the ampere turns due to the impurity component to be opposed for all conditions of bridge operation. A further refinement that is normally incorporated is a zero balance or trim control that enables the effects of lead capacitance to be balanced out for each application of the bridge.

The property of this type of bridge that allows the resistive and reactive components of an unknown to be adjusted independently of each other facilitates its use in a very wide range of applications, of which the following are a few examples.

Measurement of inductance

So that the independent balance of the resistive and reactive ampere turns can be achieved any inductive circuit must be considered as a two-terminal network, the components of which are in parallel. The ampere turns due to the resistive component of the unknown may then be opposed by those through the conductance standard, while those resulting from the inductive component of the unknown must be equated with the ampere turns due to the capacitive standard. To obtain a balance of these latter quantities it is necessary to reverse the current direction through the winding connected to the capacitance standard, this condition of bridge operation normally being indicated by the addition of a negative sign to the display of capacitance value (C_m).

Thus $1/R_p + 1/j\omega L_p = G_m - j\omega C_m$ and since it is usually the series components of an inductor that are required, these may be computed by a parallel to series conversion that results in

$$\text{series resistance } R = \frac{G_m}{G_m{}^2 + \omega^2 C_m{}^2} \tag{3.28}$$

and

$$\text{series inductance } L = \frac{C_m}{G_m{}^2 + \omega^2 C_m{}^2} \tag{3.29}$$

Measurement of low impedance

The range of a double-ratio transformer bridge may be extended [13,14] to measure low value impedances by the use of a pair of known noninductive resistors each having a value R and connected with the unknown (z) to form a T network as shown in figure 3.34. Then provided $R \gg z$

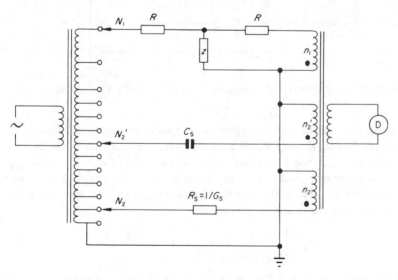

Figure 3.34. Double-ratio transformer bridge adapted for low impedance measurement

$$z = \frac{R^2}{N_1 n_1} \left[N_2 n_2 G_s + j\omega C_s N_2' n_2' \right]$$

or for a calibrated bridge

$$z = R^2 (G_m + j\omega C_m) \tag{3.30}$$

Measurements of components 'in situ'

One of the greatest advantages of double-ratio transformer bridges is the ability to use them for the measurement of components whilst these remain connected in a circuit. To appreciate how this is possible it is necessary to consider the transformers that are used in the construction of the double-ratio bridge. If these transformers were 'ideal', that is if they had zero leakage reactance, zero winding resistance, and zero magnetisation loss, the impedances Z_e and Z_i in figure 3.35

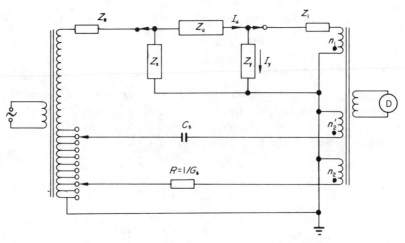

Figure 3.35. Measurement of components 'in situ' using a double-ratio transformer bridge

would be zero, and the voltage applied to Z_u (the unknown) would be unaffected by current flowing through Z_x. In addition to this all the current flowing through Z_u would flow into the n_1 winding, since $I_y = (Z_i I_u)/(Z_i + Z_y)$. In practice Z_e and Z_i will have small finite values and a correction must be applied to the values read from the balanced bridge. It may be shown that to a close approximation the true value of the unknown impedance

$$Z_u = \left[\frac{1}{G_m + j\omega C_m} \right] \left[1 - \left(\frac{Z_e}{Z_x} + \frac{Z_i}{Z_y} \right) \right] \tag{3.31}$$

The impedances Z_e and Z_i must be determined (for a particular range of the bridge) by measurements on a separate delta network that contains known values for Z_x and Z_y.

Network characteristics

As the conductance and capacitance standards may be made effectively positive or negative merely by reversing the current direction in part of the current comparator, the double-ratio bridge is extremely useful for measuring network characteristics.[15] An example of this is illustrated by figure 3.36 which shows an arrangement that may be used to determine the gain and phase shift of an amplifier that requires a terminating resistor R_t. When the bridge is balanced

$$\text{gain} = R_t (G_m{}^2 + \omega^2 C_m{}^2)^{1/2}$$

and

$$\text{phase shift} = \tan^{-1} (\omega C_m)/(G_m)$$

This technique may be used for a number of applications, examples being the determination of: (a) the ratio and phase shift of a transformer, and (b) the parameters of a transistor.[16]

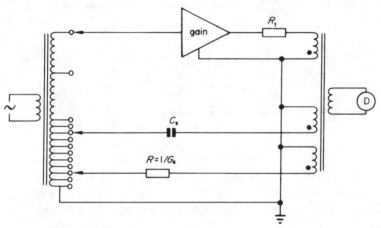

Figure 3.36. Circuit arrangement for the measurement of network characteristics by a double-ratio transformer bridge

Sample Specification

The following extract from the specification of the *Wayne Kerr B224 transformer ratio bridge* clearly shows the capabilities of such instruments.

Measurement ranges	As parallel compts	As series compts
Capacitance	0.1 pF–10 μF	10 μF–10 mF*
Conductance	1 nS–100 mS	100 mS–1 kS
Inductance	1 mH–10 kH*	100 nH–1 mH
Resistance	10 Ω–1 GΩ	1 mΩ–10 Ω
Accuracy* (200 Hz to 10 kHz)	± 0.1%	± 0.3%

*Accuracy frequency dependent on ranges marked.

3.4.4 Twin 'T' Networks

These can have zero transmission (with all components finite) and can thus be used in a similar manner to a bridge, that is, the balance conditions may be calculated, an impedance to be measured introduced into one of the network arms and the other arms adjusted for balance.

Principle of operation

Consider an a.c. voltage (V_{in}) applied to the input in figure 3.37. Zero output will occur when the currents due to each of the Ts are equal in magnitude but opposite in phase, that is, $I + I_1 = 0$. Under this condition the impedance of the

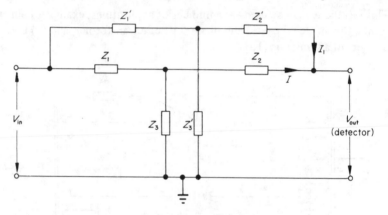

Figure 3.37. Twin 'T' network

detector does not matter, providing it is not infinite. This fact can be utilised in obtaining a solution for the balance condition, for the network containing $Z_1 Z_2 Z_3$ may be considered in isolation, having an input impedance of

$$Z = Z_1 + \frac{Z_2 Z_3}{Z_2 + Z_3} \tag{3.32}$$

and drawing a current from the source of

$$\frac{V_{in} (Z_2 + Z_3)}{Z_1 Z_2 + Z_2 Z_3 + Z_1 Z_3} \tag{3.33}$$

and I, the current flowing from the $Z_1 \, Z_2 \, Z_3$ network to the detector will be

$$\frac{Z_3}{(Z_2 + Z_3)} \frac{V_{in} (Z_2 + Z_3)}{(Z_1 Z_2 + Z_2 Z_3 + Z_3 Z_1)}$$

which for balance must be equal and opposite to the current I_1, that is

$$\frac{Z_3 V_{in}}{Z_1 Z_2 + Z_2 Z_3 + Z_3 Z_1} + \frac{Z_3' V_{in}}{Z_1' Z_2' + Z_2' Z_3' + Z_3' Z_1'} \tag{3.34}$$

and since $V_{in} \neq 0$

$$\frac{Z_1'Z_2'}{Z_3'} + Z_2' + Z_1' + \frac{Z_1 Z_2}{Z_3} + Z_2 + Z_1 = 0 \qquad (3.35)$$

and is the condition for balance.

The advantage of a twin T arrangement over the conventional bridge circuit is that it may be used at higher frequencies. This is due to its arrangement which makes it possible to operate with one side of both the source and the detector earthed—a feature which makes shielding much easier than in operating a bridge.

The twin T is also used as a rejection filter and as the feedback network on a tuned amplifier in a frequency selective detector.

3.5 Self-balancing Bridges

The principle of comparison methods is that an operator is required to perform manual operations to reduce the detected signal to a minimum. In some instances this can be a lengthy procedure, requiring experience of a particular type of bridge to obtain rapid operation. Thus in circumstances that dictate a bridge measurement as the only satisfactory method and many measurements are to be made, automatic or self-balancing bridges have been devised.

Principle of operation

As stated above the operation of balancing a bridge is to reduce the error signal presented to the detector to a minimum. Thus in a bridge using a resistance ratio the automatic operation is fairly simple, being basically similar to that used in a potentiometric recorder (see section 3.1.2), that is the error signal is amplified and used to energise the field windings of a motor coupled to the movable contact on a resistance divider, for example figure 3.38 where $R_x = R_s(R_2/R_1)$.

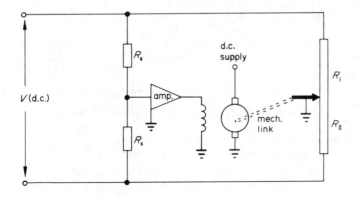

Figure 3.38. Self-balancing d.c. Wheatstone bridge

If R_s has a value of (say) 1000.0 Ω and the movable contact is connected via gearing to a numerical indicator covering a range of 0.0–999.9, the value of R_x may be automatically displayed using the mechanical position of the contact as a multiplication ratio on the value of R_s.

The above is a simple example in which the energising voltage is d.c. As with a potentiometric pen recorder if the error signals are small the problems of amplifier drift are overcome by using a chopper amplifier of either the electro-magnetic type or photoresistive type. If, however, the energising voltage were a.c. and R_x had a reactive component, the bridge would lose sensitivity, but

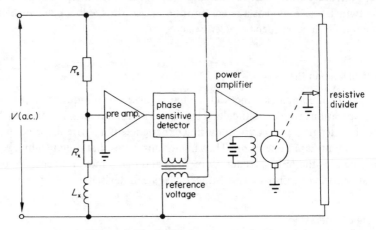

Figure 3.39. Self-balancing a.c. bridge

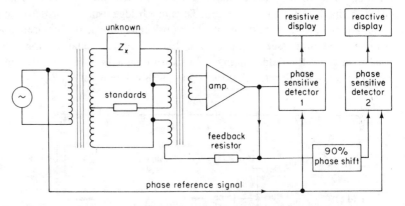

Figure 3.40. An 'electronic' self-balancing bridge

this could be restored by inserting a phase sensitive detector (see section 2.1.1) between the preamplifier and power amplifier stages, as in figure 3.39.

Another form of self-balancing bridge[15] is shown in figure 3.40 where a stable oscillator provides the signal for the bridge and also a phase reference volt-age that is fed to two phase sensitive detectors.

The output of the amplifier provides a bridge balancing voltage, which is applied through a resistor to a winding on the right hand transformer. The initial out of balance current flowing in the transformer is opposed by the 'feedback' current which can be made very nearly equal to the initial current. The approach to the ideal condition of equality is limited only by the gain of the amplifier, which can be made as large as necessary.

The amplifier output is also connected to the phase-sensitive detectors, one of which incorporates a unity gain, 90° phase shift network. The analogue voltage outputs from the two phase sensitive detectors independently show the difference of the resistance and reactive components set on the standards.

REFERENCES

1 B. Lazenby, The now and then in recorders, *Kent tech. Rev.*, **19** (1977) 9-12

2 L. W. Tsai and R. L. Ciardella, Linear step motor design provides high plotter performance at low cost, *HP Jl*, **30** (1979) 2-14

3 Technical data Models 304 and 306, Chessell Ltd, Worthing, Sussex (1980)

4 M. Azmoon, J. H. Bohorquez and R. A. Warp, Desk top plotter/printer does both vector graphic plotting and fast text printing, *HP Jl*, **29** (1978) 24-5, 27-32

5 L. G. Brunetti, A new family of intelligent multi-colour *X–Y* plotters, *HP Jl*, **29** (1977) 2-4

6 D. C. Gall, *Direct and Alternating Current Potentiometer Measurements* (Chapman & Hall, London, 1938)

7 C. R. Crooke, Dynamic accuracy of analogue X-Y recorders, *Electron. Engng*, **51** (1979) 41-8

8 W. P. Baker, *Electrical Insulation Measurements* (Newnes, London, 1965)

9 B. Hauge and T. R. Foord, *A.C. Bridge Methods*, 6th Ed. (Pitman, London, 1971)

10 J. J. Hill and A. P. Miller, An a.c. double bridge with inductively coupled ratio arms for precision platinum resistance thermometry, *Proc. I.E.E.*, **110** (1963)

11 A. H. Silcocks, Revolution in calibration, *Camb. tech. Rev.*, **1** (1968) 7-9

12 A. H. Silcocks, Measurement techniques, *Kent tech. Rev.*, (1971)

13 K. Fletcher, Use of Transformer Ratio Arm Bridges in Component Measurements, *Radio electron. Compon.*, (1962) 117-23

14 R. Calvert, The Transformer Ratio Arm Bridge, Wayne Kerr Monograph No. 1.

15 Some Notes on Bridge Measurement (Wayne Kerr Co., Ltd, Bognor Regis, Sussex)

16 B. Rogal, Semiconductor parameter measurements using transformer ratio-arm bridges. *Proc. Instn Electron.*, **4**

4

Digital Instruments

Digital instruments sample the measurand, perform a valuation using digital electronics and normally display the measurand in discrete numerals. In general, contemporary instruments use either L.E.D. or liquid crystal seven-segment displays (see section 1.2.2), although research into, and development of, other techniques continues[1] and the use of other forms of display must not be discounted nor must the possibility of instruments without a visual output. The major advantage of a digital display is that it eliminates parallax errors and reduces the human errors associated with interpreting the position of a pointer on an analogue scale.

Most digital instruments have superior accuracy and input characteristics to analogue instruments. They may also incorporate automatic polarity indication, range selection and provide a digitally coded output, properties that reduce operator training, the possibility of instrument damage through overload and improve measurement reliability.

The developments in microelectronics that have occurred in recent years have resulted in greater capabilities,[2] and/or an improvement in performance without an increase in cost. These attributes ensure that digital instruments will increase their proportion of the market, although they are unlikely to absorb all the market, for in some applications the true analogue instrument is unlikely to be outsted, while in others hybrid instruments (digital processing with an analogue display) are gaining acceptance.

The various forms of digital instrument use, with increasing sophistication, the principles of digital electronics that were described in chapter 1, although the hardware is increasingly more likely to be in the form of purpose made integrated circuits as opposed to hard wiring logic components.

4.1 COUNTERS

Electronic counters are digital instruments that can be used to measure the number of pulses in a controlled time interval, or alternatively the time interval between pulses. The accuracy of measurements made using counters is largely dependent on an internal oscillator. Electronic counters are marketed with various frequency ranges and measurement capabilities.

4.1.1 Principle of Operation

A digital counter may be considered to consist of a number of operational blocks which may be interconnected in different ways to perform the various time dependent measurements. The 'core' of this type of instrument will, of course, be the digital circuits that perform the count, and these are based on the following.

When a group of bistables (see section 1.1.3) are connected together so that they store related information, they are collectively termed a register. Registers of certain forms can be arranged to count pulses either synchronously or asynchronously.

Asynchronous counters

In these the pulses to be counted are applied to the input end of the array, and the process of adding each pulse to the count has to be completed before the 'carry bit' is propagated from the first to the second stage. This second stage has carry bits added to it until it produces a carry bit which is passed to the third stage, and so on. In counting a pulse train the carry bits will appear to 'ripple' through the counter, and for this reason an asynchronous counter is sometimes referred to as a 'ripple-through' counter. A three-stage asynchronous counter using $J-K$ bistables (flip–flops) is illustrated in figure 4.1a, and for such an arrangement the count proceeds as prescribed in table 4.1. Starting from an initial condition in which all the stages are set to zero, when a total of seven pulses have been applied to the counter all the outputs are in the '1' state, and the application of an eighth pulse will cause them all to fall to zero. Since the time taken for each change to propagate to the following stage is t_x (figures 4.1a and b) it will take nt_x s for the pulse causing this fall to zero to 'ripple through' an n stage counter, thus creating a restriction on the speed or maximum counting rate of a counter of this form.

Synchronous counters

In this form of counter the counting sequence is controlled by means of a clock pulse and all the changes in output from the bistables occur in synchronism. This effectively eliminates the propagation delay associated with ripple-through counters. To avoid the possibility (when feedback connections are made) of instability in the completed counter, 'master–slave' bistables are invariably used in synchronous counters. In operation the appropriate input signals are simultaneously gated into the master stages of all the bistables in the counter and when

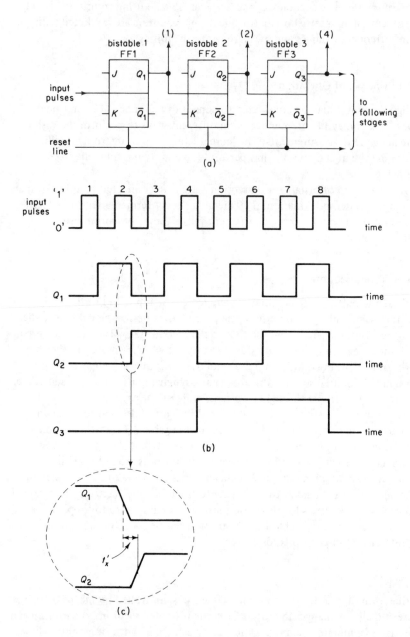

Figure 4.1. A ripple-through pure binary counter

Table 4.1

Pulse	Q_1 (4)	Q_2 (2)	Q_3 (1)	
Initial condition	0	0	0	
1	0	0	1	
2	0	1	0	
3	0	1	1	repeat
4	1	0	0	
5	1	0	1	
6	1	1	0	
7	1	1	1	
8	0	0	0	

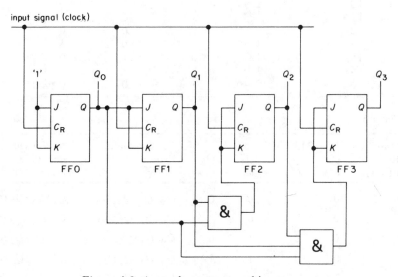

Figure 4.2. A synchronous pure binary counter

the input pulse falls to the '0' level, the new values of the count are transmitted synchronously to the outputs of the bistables. A form of synchronous binary counter is shown in figure 4.2, table 4.2 giving the sequence of events taking place in the counter. By adding a further AND gate and suitable connections,[3] a synchronous binary coded decimal (BCD) counter is produced. In practice such a counter will be a single integrated circuit, or part of an integrated circuit.

BCD to decimal converters

Since the desired display of the count will be in numeric form, it is necessary to convert the binary count to a form suitable for actuating a digital display (figure 4.3). The code sequence and appropriate decoding logic for such a converter are

Table 4.2.

Pulse	Q_0 (8)	Q_1 (4)	Q_2 (2)	Q_3 (1)	
Initial condition	0	0	0	0	
1	0	0	0	1	
2	0	0	1	0	
3	0	0	1	1	
4	0	1	0	0	
5	0	1	0	1	
6	0	1	1	0	
7	0	1	1	1	repeat
8	1	0	0	0	
9	1	0	0	1	
10	1	0	1	0	
11	1	0	1	1	
12	1	1	0	0	
13	1	1	0	1	
14	1	1	1	0	
15	1	1	1	1	
16	0	0	0	0	

Table 4.3.

Decimal value (output)	8421 BCD code				Basic decoding logic	Minimised decoding logic
	Q_0 (8)	Q_1 (4)	Q_2 (2)	Q_3 (1)		
Zero	0	0	0	0	$\bar{Q}_0 \cdot \bar{Q}_1 \cdot \bar{Q}_2 \cdot \bar{Q}_3$	$\bar{Q}_0 \cdot \bar{Q}_1 \cdot \bar{Q}_2 \cdot \bar{Q}_3$
unity	0	0	0	1	$\bar{Q}_0 \cdot \bar{Q}_1 \cdot \bar{Q}_2 \cdot Q_3$	$\bar{Q}_0 \cdot \bar{Q}_1 \cdot \bar{Q}_2 \cdot Q_3$
2	0	0	1	0	$\bar{Q}_0 \cdot \bar{Q}_1 \cdot Q_2 \cdot \bar{Q}_3$	$\bar{Q}_1 \cdot Q_2 \cdot \bar{Q}_3$
3	0	0	1	1	$\bar{Q}_0 \cdot \bar{Q}_1 \cdot Q_2 \cdot Q_3$	$\bar{Q}_1 \cdot Q_2 \cdot Q_3$
4	0	1	0	0	$\bar{Q}_0 \cdot Q_1 \cdot \bar{Q}_2 \cdot \bar{Q}_3$	$Q_1 \cdot \bar{Q}_2 \cdot \bar{Q}_3$
5	0	1	0	1	$\bar{Q}_0 \cdot Q_1 \cdot \bar{Q}_2 \cdot Q_3$	$Q_1 \cdot \bar{Q}_2 \cdot Q_3$
6	0	1	1	0	$\bar{Q}_0 \cdot Q_1 \cdot Q_2 \cdot \bar{Q}_3$	$Q_1 \cdot Q_2 \cdot \bar{Q}_3$
7	0	1	1	1	$\bar{Q}_0 \cdot Q_1 \cdot Q_2 \cdot Q_3$	$Q_1 \cdot Q_2 \cdot Q_3$
8	1	0	0	0	$Q_0 \cdot \bar{Q}_1 \cdot \bar{Q}_2 \cdot \bar{Q}_3$	$Q_0 \cdot \bar{Q}_3$
9	1	0	0	1	$Q_0 \cdot \bar{Q}_1 \cdot \bar{Q}_2 \cdot Q_3$	$Q_0 \cdot Q_3$
	1	0	1	0		
	1	0	1	1		
	1	1	0	0	'can't happen' conditions	
	1	1	0	1		
	1	1	1	0		
	1	1	1	1		

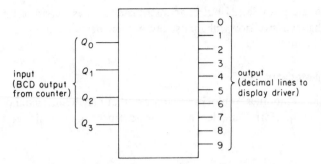

Figure 4.3. An 8421 BCD-to-decimal code converter

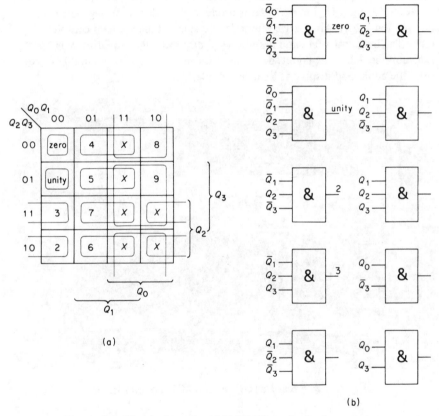

(a)

(b)

Figure 4.4. The design of an 8421 BCD-to-decimal converter

given in table 4.3. The basic logic would require 10 four-input AND gates, but by mapping these basic combinations on a Karnaugh map (figure 4.4a) the minimal expressions representing suitable groupings can be deduced, and these have been listed as part of table 4.3. The AND network corresponding to the minimal logic statements is shown in figure 4.4b. Alternative arrangements using NOR or

NAND gates are possible,[3] but in an instrument such as a counter timer, the binary to digital conversion will almost certainly be part of a composite integrated circuit.

Operational Modules

The operational modules or blocks of circuitry that may be interconnected in various ways to perform time dependent measurements may be described as follows.

Count and display

The majority of digital counters marketed at present use an 'in-line' display of 6, 8 or even 11 digits (figure 4.5) that is produced by using seven segment L.E.D.s (see section 1.2.2). Alternative methods of display in use are cold cathode numerical indicator tubes and liquid crystal displays. Since the display is inseparably linked to the count, decoding and drive circuitry, it is suitable to consider the count and display as a single module.

Figure 3.5. Racal-Dana 9906 200 MHz counter-timer

Internal oscillator

To provide a reference of frequency and time interval, a stable internal oscillator is used. This is normally a quartz oscillator operating at a frequency of (typically) 5 or 10 MHz, by dividing this frequency a reference time interval of, say, 1 μs is derived and used in the various measuring modes of the counter. The stability of the oscillator is sometimes enhanced by mounting it in a constant temperature 'oven' within the instrument, when stabilities of 1 part in 10^8 or better are obtainable, a necessary precaution if frequencies of 500 MHz to the nearest hertz are to be measured.[4]

The accuracy of the reference oscillator is commonly quoted in terms of its stability between calibration checks. An example of a typical specification is as follows.

Frequency Standard
Frequency: 5 MHz
Temperature stability: ± 8 parts in 10^6 over the temperature range 0 to
  + 55 °C. ± 3 parts in 10^6 over the temperature
  range +20 to 40 °C
Averaging ageing rate: ± 1 part in 10^6 per month, three months after
  delivery but less than ± 1 part in 10^5 in the first
  year
Frequency standard output: 1 MHz T.T.L. compatible rectangular wave

To this some manufacturers add an allowance for the effects on the frequency standard due to line voltage variations, but as these effects are small many manufacturers omit them.

From the above specification it can be estimated that the limit of error (or uncertainty) in the accuracy of the frequency standard for such a counter when six months old is < ± 6 parts in 10^6 if operated between 20 and 40 °C (3 parts from temperature and 3 parts from ageing).

Decade dividers

To provide a suitable range of operation for a counter timer a number (six or seven) of cascaded decade dividers are used to divide either the incoming signal or the frequency from the internal oscillator. The number of decades of division being used in a particular application is decided either by the operation of a front panel switch or by the instrument's control logic in the 'auto' mode of operation.

By way of an example seven decades of division would permit the production, from a 1 MHz reference, of time intervals of 1 μs, 10 μs, 100 μs, 1 ms, 10 ms, 100 ms, 1 s and 10 s.

Main gate

To control the interval over which pulses are applied to the display unit, a gate is incorporated. It is arranged as a pulse operated switch so that one command pulse opens the gate (start) thereby allowing the passage of pulses to be counted. The next command pulse closes the gate and thus stops the flow of pulses to be counted.

Input circuitry

The purpose of this is to convert the incoming or unknown signal into logic levels compatible with the logic circuitry within the instrument. Because of the variations in the magnitude (say 20 mV–200 V) of the signals that are likely to be measured in a laboratory environment, a sensitivity control is commonly provided thus preventing false triggering by superimposed noise to be avoided as shown in figure 4.6.

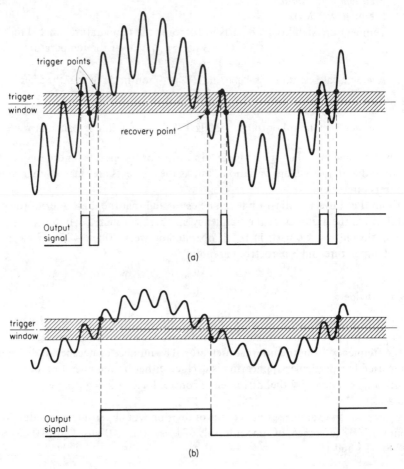

Figure 4.6. False triggering: (a) caused by large signal, (b) removed by reducing sensitivity

Selector switches and control logic

The front panel of a counter timer (for example, figure 4.5) has an array of switches, some of which are used to select the mode of operation (for example, frequency, count, period, ratio, etc.) and others which are used to control the duration of the measurement sample,[5] by selecting the magnitude of decade divider used. The switches that are used to select the mode of operation can, in some instruments, be used to activate the control logic so that either the counter continuously samples and displays the incoming signal, or a single sample is made on demand and 'held' on display. A number of instruments have an 'auto' or automatic ranging capability in their frequency mode of operation and in this condition their control circuits adjust the duration of the sample so that the display contains the maximum number of digits.

The above modules can be interconnected to perform the various time dependent measurements, although it must be mentioned that not every counter timer can perform all the following functions.

4.1.2 Totalise or Count

This is the simplest count function consisting of routing the pulses to be counted through the main gate which may be started and stopped either manually (by push button switches) or by some externally derived pulses (see figure 4.7), the display thus recording the total number of pulses received during the interval between the start and stop signals. The decade dividers have been included in the diagram for in some instruments it is possible to use them to divide the incoming signal so that instead of every pulse being counted only one in 10, or power of 10 is counted.

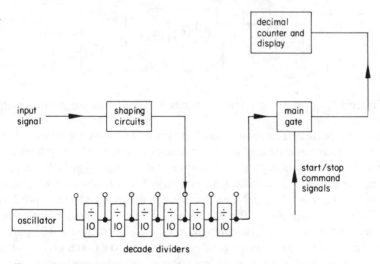

Figure 4.7. Schematic diagram for totalising or count measurement

The uncertainty in a measurement of a count will be the determination error in the count (normally ± 1 least significant digit) plus the uncertainty in the time interval over which the count is made, this latter quantity being a function of how the time interval is measured and how the command signals are produced.

4.1.3 Frequency Measurement

The logical step from the above section is to supply command signals to the gate at known time intervals (for example 1 s) derived from the internal oscillator, when the totalised number of incoming pulses will be a direct measurement of frequency (see figure 4.8). To measure frequencies above 1 MHz on a 6 digit counter a shorter time interval than 1 second must be used or an 'overflow' condition is created. The link between the decade dividers and the display ensures that correct positioning of the decimal point is maintained when the duration of the count is changed.

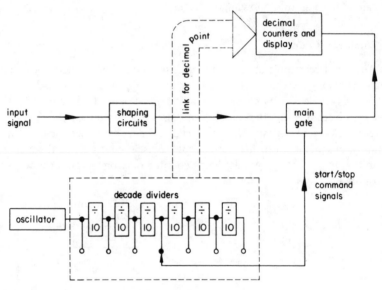

Figure 4.8. Schematic diagram of connections for frequency measurement

To measure frequencies above 500 MHz the direct gating techniques used at low frequencies could be used but this becomes very expensive.[4] A more economical solution is to divide, or prescale, the incoming signal down to a value that can be handled by standard logic circuitry. The prescaling can be by a suitable factor, say 2, 4 or 10 and then the counted pulses must be multiplied by the same factor in the display so that the correct value of frequency is displayed, for example a frequency of 1 GHz could, by prescaling be counted as 10^5 pulses in 1 ms and then displayed on an eight-digit counter as 1000000.0 kHz by offsetting the decimal point. The uncertainty in a frequency measurement will be the determination error in the display (usually ± 1 ℓ.s.d.) plus the tolerance on the frequency standard. For example, using the frequency standard details given in section 4.1.1, and assuming that 6 months have passed since the instrument was purchased, the total uncertainty in a reading of 1.01 kHz on a 10 s timebase would be 1 ℓ.s.d. in the display plus 6 parts in 10^6.

Now actual display would be 01.0100 kHz therefore

$$\text{limit of uncertainty} = \pm \left(\frac{1 \times 100}{10100} + \frac{6 \times 100}{10^6} \right) \%$$

$$= \pm (0.009901 + 0.0006) \%$$

$$= \pm 0.0105 \%$$

To calculate the uncertainty in measurement for each reading is a laborious process and so an accuracy curve of the form shown in figure 4.9 can be drawn, by using the information given in the manufacturer's specification. For example, for the *Racal-Dana 9901* in the frequency measurement mode:

Frequency range: d.c. to 50 MHz (direct)
Coupling: a.c. 10 Hz to 50 MHz; d.c. to 10 MHz
Gate times: Manual—1 ms to 100 s in decade steps. Automatic—gate times
           up to 1 s are selected automatically to avoid overspill.
           Hysteresis avoids undesirable range changing for small
           frequency changes

The curves in figure 4.9 are for the 9901 six months after purchase when operated in an ambient temperature between 20 and 40 °C. It is apparent that to obtain the minimum uncertainty in a frequency value the gate times having an unbroken line should be used. For example 20 kHz measured with a 10 s gate, 200 kHz with a 1 s gate and so on, the steps in the unbroken line corresponding to changes in gate time. *Note:* When operated outside these temperatures or more than three months after recalibration, appropriate additions should be made to the limit of uncertainty in a reading. Also, Racal-Dana Instruments market an alternative version of this instrument (identified as the 9905), which has an eight digit display and a specified frequency range of 10 Hz to 200 MHz; 10 Hz to 30 MHz direct, and 10 MHz to 200 MHz prescaled by 4.

4.1.4 Period and Multiple-period Measurement

The period of a waveform may be defined as the time interval between identical points in successive cycles, for example positive going zero crossings. It is also the reciprocal of frequency. Since the internal oscillator of a counter produces pulses with a known time interval between them referred to as a 'clock unit', period measurements are made by counting the number of clock units which occur during one cycle of the unknown frequency, the unknown frequency being used to open and close the main gate. Period measurements enable more accurate determination of low frequency signals to be made than would be obtained using a direct frequency measurement due to the increased resolution possible, although an allowance for the trigger error must be made.

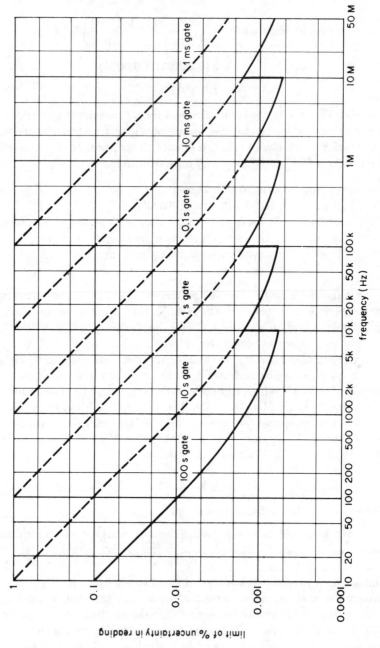

Figure 4.9. Accuracy curve for 6-month-old counter-timer (20 to 40 °C)

The resolution for medium frequency signals can be increased and the trigger error decreased by routing the input signal via the decade dividing assemblies (see figure 4.10), the number of cycles (*n*) of input over which the clock units are counted then being increased by powers of 10. To facilitate the display of the *average period* of the number of cycles, the energisation of decimal point L.E.D.s in the display is linked to the switches used to select the value of *n*. Hence, if the clock unit is 1 *μ*s, and an *n* value of 10 is selected, a decimal point L.E.D. between the least significant decade and the least decade but one will be illuminated.

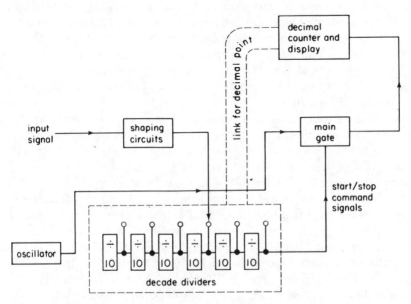

Figure 4.10. Arrangement for multiple period averaging

Sample Specification

The specification for single and multiple period measurements for the *Racal-Dana 9901* is as follows.

Input: channel A
Range: 1 *μ*s to 1 s
Clock unit: 1 *μ*s (a.c. or d.c. coupling)

Periods averaged: 1 to 10^5 in decade multiples

Accuracy: $\dfrac{\pm 0.3\%}{\text{Number of periods averaged}} \pm$ Frequency standard stability

$\pm$ determination error (1 ℓ.s.d.)

Bandwidth: automatically reduced to 10 MHz (3 dB) when period selected

Thus in measuring a frequency of, say, 20 Hz which has a period of 0.05 s or 50000 μs, the limit of uncertainty in measurement would on the six-month-old counter be

$$\pm \left(\frac{1}{50000} \times 100\% + 0.0006\% + \frac{0.3}{1} \right)\%$$

or $\pm$ 0.3026 per cent. If the measurement were made over 10 cycles, a display of 50000.0 μs would have been obtained and the tolerance on the measurement $\pm$ 0.0308 per cent. As with the frequency measurement method it is inconvenient to have to calculate the tolerance on each reading; an accuracy curve as shown in figure 4.11 gives a rapid evaluation of the uncertainty in measurement. As before this has been drawn for the six-month-old counter when operated at temperatures between 20 and 40 $^\circ$C.

Inspection of these curves shows marked differences to those of direct frequency measurement (figure 4.9). First, they slope in the opposite direction, and second at low frequencies there is a marked step increase in the uncertainty in measurement when n is decreased from 100 to 10 to 1. This is due to the effect of the trigger error on the total uncertainty in measurement.

The curves for n = 1, 10 and 100 have been extended with a broken line to show the extension of frequency range possible by using the overflow indication. Such a mode of operation may, for example, be used when measuring a frequency of 2.1 Hz. Using n = 1 would give a reading of 476190 μs $\pm$ 0.3 per cent but switching to the n = 10 condition, a reading of 761905 μs $\pm$ 0.031 per cent is given together with an overflow indication. The total value for the latter reading would be 4761905 $\pm$ 0.03 per cent effectively obtaining a seven-decade reading from a six-digit display. With care this technique can be extended to obtain an eight-decade reading, on a six-digit instrument.

If the families of curves in figures 4.9 and 4.11 are superimposed as in 4.12 it becomes apparent which frequencies can be measured with the smallest uncertainties by the two methods. It should, however, be remembered that if a frequency is measured by the multi-period method the determination of the tolerance on the value of the frequency must include an allowance for calculation error and unless a 10 or more digit calculator is used this may be significant.

The performance of this reciprocal calculation is inconvenient and for the measurement of low frequencies counters incorporating arithmetic processors,[6] and termed reciprocal computing frequency meters, have been developed. These instruments have the advantages over the conventional instrument when measuring low frequencies of greater resolution, shorter measuring time and a display of frequency value as opposed to a period. The Feedback FM610 is an example of such an instrument and has a frequency range from 0.0011 Hz to 10 MHz.

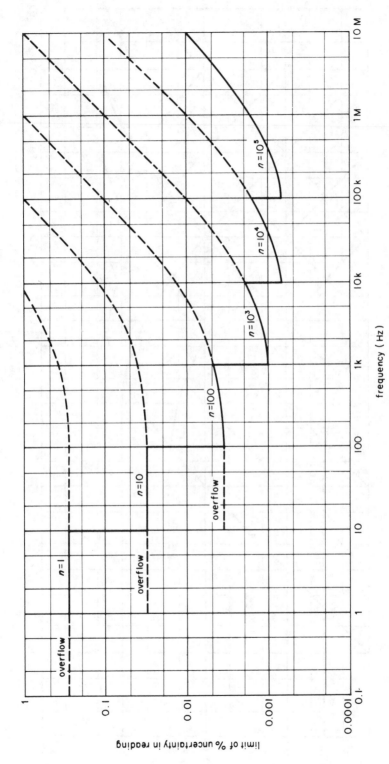

Figure 4.11. Curves of limit of uncertainty in single and multiple period measurements against frequency

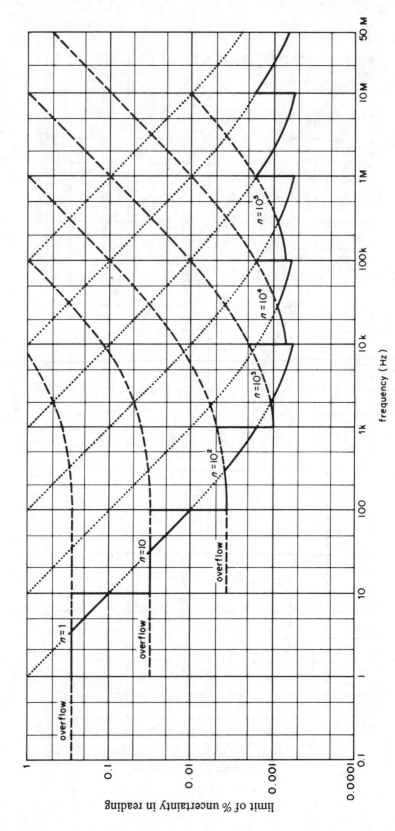

Figure 4.12. Combination of the curves in figures 4.9 and 4.11

4.1.5 Frequency Ratio Measurements

The ratio of two frequencies may be determined by using the lower frequency signal to operate the gate while the higher frequency signal is counted (see figure 4.13). If necessary the lower frequency may be routed through the decade dividers so that the resolution of the measurement may be increased, when the reading will be nA/B. Since the A and B inputs normally have different sensitivities a variation on this procedure may be necessary, for if the low frequency signal has a small amplitude it may be more satisfactory to apply it to the A input and use a large value of n to obtain a satisfactory display.

An example of the use of the ratio technique is for the conversion of transducer output signals from pulses to practical units. A number of commercially available counters incorporate selectable divider ratios to assist in this application.

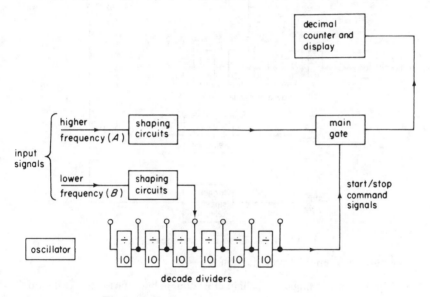

Figure 4.13. Frequency ratio measurements

Sample Specification

The specification for the *Racal-Dana 9901* for the ratio facility is

Higher frequency input: channel A
Higher frequency range: d.c. to 50 MHz
Lower frequency input: channel B
Lower frequency range: d.c. to 10 MHz
Display: frequency $A \times n$/frequency B
Multiplier, n: 1 to 10^5 in decade multiples

The limit of uncertainty in reading for the ratio of two sinewaves is the determination error in reading plus the trigger error. The latter quantity is usually taken as ± 0.3 per cent divided by n.

4.1.6 Time Interval Measurements

In this mode of operation (figure 4.14) a clock unit of suitable duration, say, 1 μs, or 1 ms can be selected to measure the time interval between positive or negative going zero crossings of a single input wave or of two separate input signals.

Such a facility is suitable for measuring the positive or negative parts of a square wave, or a repetitive pulse wave.

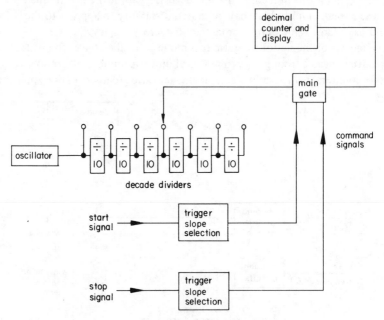

Figure 4.14. Time interval measurements

The 9901 time interval specification is

Input channel: single line, channel B; double line, start channel B stop channel A

Time range: 100 ns to 10^4 s (2.8 h approx.)

Clock units: 100 ns to 10 ms

Coupling: d.c.

Start/stop signals: electrical or contact

Trigger slope selection: electrical—positive or negative slopes can be selected on both start and stop signals; contact— opening or closure can be selected on both start and stop signals

A variation is time interval averaging in which a fixed clock unit (for example 100 ns) can be used to average the time interval over a number of cycles. This is arranged by connecting the oscillator to the main gate and routeing the stop command pulse through the decade dividers.

4.2 MULTI-FUNCTION DIGITAL VOLTMETERS

The multi-function digital meter is very much a product of the developments in solid state electronics that have resulted in cost savings and improved reliability. These instruments have evolved from the basic digital voltmeters that appeared in the 1960s and have since improved in scope and accuracy of measurement. Apart from digital panel meters there are few instruments now manufactured that only measure direct voltages, most having many alternating and direct, voltage and current ranges as well as resistance measuring ranges. However, since the multi-function meter is based on the digital voltmeter an appreciation of the techniques commonly used to convert a direct (analogue) voltage to a digital display is desirable.

4.2.1 Analogue to Digital Conversion [7,9]

There are four main methods used in the construction of digital voltmeters for the conversion of an analogue signal to its digital equivalent. These are

(a) successive approximation method
(b) ramp or voltage to time conversion technique
(c) voltage to frequency method
(d) dual slope technique.

The first and last of these are the methods perhaps of greatest importance, although the middle two are used by some manufacturers as indeed are some specially developed conversion techniques.[9]

Successive approximation method

This is the fastest and one of the most stable of the basic analogue to digital conversion techniques. Instruments using this method work automatically in a similar manner to the operator of a laboratory d.c. potentiometer. In the successive approximation d.v.m. (see figure 4.15) a voltage divider network, with coarse and fine steps, is connected via switches to a voltage comparator (analogous to the potentiometer operator's galvanometer), which compares the internal voltage with the unknown. The output of the comparator feeds the logic circuits which control the steps on the voltage divider network. A measurement sequence usually selects the largest steps of the internal voltage first, the magnitude of the steps decreasing until the null point is reached.

The high speed of measurement possible with this technique only applies if the unknown voltage is noise free. If it is not, filters must be fitted and the speed of operation is very much reduced.

The errors associated with a d.v.m. using this method of conversion will depend on

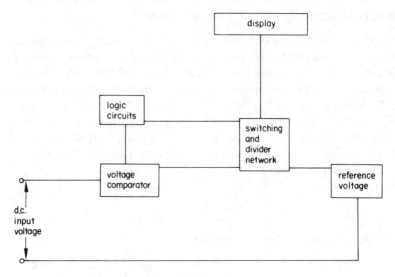

Figure 4.15. Simplified schematic diagram of a successive approximation digital voltmeter

(a) the resolution of the comparator
(b) the precision of the voltage divider network which is normally resistive but in some good quality instruments may be an inductive divider, and
(c) the stability of the reference voltage.

The overall performance of this type of converter may also be limited by the divider switch characteristics.

The successive approximation conversion is now less commonly used in d.v.m.s but finds application in high speed data-acquisition, waveform sampling, automatic test and process control systems.

Ramp method

This method of conversion utilises a digital counter technique. A carefully defined, internally generated, voltage ramp is fed to two voltage compai tors (see figure 4.16). When the ramp voltage, which may have either a positive or negative slope and a polarity in opposition to the input, is equal to one level of the input voltage (say earth) the ground comparator emits a command (start) signal to a gate which opens and permits the passage of pulses from a crystal oscillator to a digital counter. When the level of the input voltage is equal to the ramp voltage the second comparator produces a command signal to close the gate and prevent further counting. With suitable scaling the count may be made of equal magnitude to the difference in the two levels of the input voltage. The factors affecting the errors of a d.v.m. using this conversion technique are

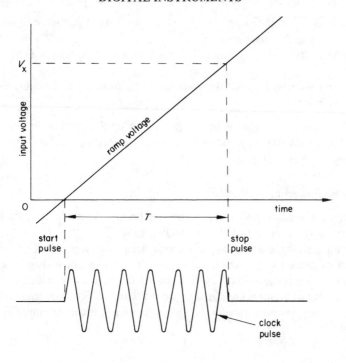

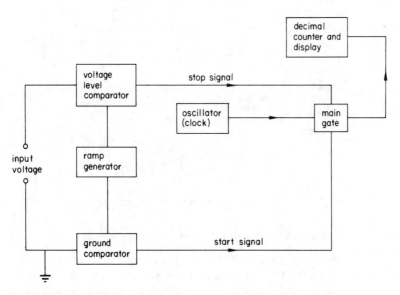

Figure 4.16. Basis of ramp conversion technique d.v.m.

(a) the linearity of the ramp voltage, which is normally generated by using an amplifier with capacitive feedback
(b) the stability of the crystal oscillator, which commonly operates at 1 MHz, and
(c) the precision with which the voltage comparators can make coincidence measurements.

As with instruments using the successive approximation method of conversion the measurement rate for input voltages having a noise content is reduced by the inclusion of filter circuits.

Voltage to frequency method[8]

Although this method also uses a counter technique the mode of operation is fundamentally different to the ramp technique. In the voltage to frequency conversion a signal is generated such that its frequency is precisely related to the differences in the levels of the input voltage. This frequency is then counted over a fixed time interval, usually 1 cycle of power line frequency, which results in a high rejection of mains noise signal without the use of filters. A schematic diagram of the components of a voltage to frequency d.v.m. is shown in figure 4.17.

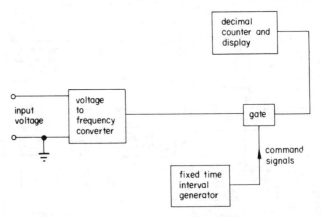

Figure 4.17. Schematic diagram for a voltage to frequency d.v.m.

The errors of a d.v.m. using this technique are dependent on

(a) the accuracy and linearity of the voltage to frequency conversion, which is not as inherently stable or accurate as the successive approximation method
(b) the precision of the time interval over which the frequency measurement is made, which may be made small by using crystal control, and
(c) the internal reference or calibration voltage.

Dual slope technique[10]

In this method of analogue to digital conversion an attempt is made to combine the advantages and remove the disadvantages of the two preceding methods, for although the actual measurement is a voltage to time conversion, the sample time is constant and can be arranged to reject power line noise. Thus the unknown voltage is determined by a two-stage operation, the first stage of which occurs in a fixed time T = 1/mains frequency, during which a capacitor (operational

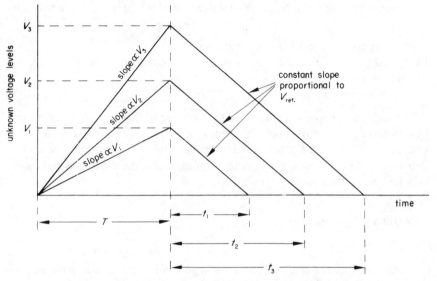

Figure 4.18. Voltage–time relationships in a dual slope d.v.m.

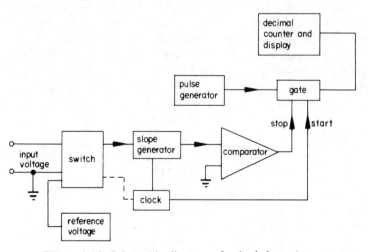

Figure 4.19. Schematic diagram of a dual slope d.v.m.

amplifier) is charged at a rate proportional to the input voltage (see figure 4.18). At the end of time T the input to the operational amplifier is switched to a reference voltage, of opposite polarity to the input voltage, and the capacitor discharged at a constant rate giving time intervals, for pulses to flow to the clock, proportional to the magnitude of the input voltages, for example, $t_1 \propto V_1$; $t_2 \propto V_2$, etc. Figure 4.19 shows a simplified schematic diagram for a dual slope d.v.m.; the clock and pulse generator signals would be derived from a common crystal oscillator operating at, say, 60 MHz for an instrument with five-figure resolution. The error of reading is not however dependent on this frequency but is affected by

(a) the 'input or reference' switch characteristics
(b) the voltage and leakage characteristics of the operation amplifier
(c) the comparator characteristics; and
(d) the reference voltage.

The major advantage and reason for the wide use of the dual slope technique is its inherent rejection of supply frequency interference (see section 7.4.1). Additionally good accuracy and stability are possible but the reading rate is limited to half the power line frequency thus excluding the use of this technique from high speed data acquisition systems.

4.2.2 Voltage Measurement

Direct Voltage

The measuring circuits of a multi-function digital voltmeter have a high input resistance, and are connected to the ouput of a voltage divider network of the type shown in figure 2.18. The input resistance is thus approximately constant on the direct voltage ranges, a common value being 10 MΩ, although an increasing number of models have higher input resistance (100 MΩ and even 1 GΩ). The upper limit of voltage is usually 1000 V and the smallest measurable value (the resolution on the most sensitive range) 10 μV. However, developments are reducing this to 1 μV and even 0.1 μV—a value which is viewed with scepticism by many as interference voltages (see p. 332) may be much larger than such values.

Sample Specification

Range	Maximum reading	Accuracy (12 months) 18–28 °C ±(% rdg + digits)	Maximum Allowable input
200 mV	199.99	0.04% + 3 l.s.d.	
2 V	1.9999	0.04% + 1 l.s.d.	
20 V	19.999	0.04% + 1 l.s.d.	1200 V
200 V	199.99	0.04% + 1 l.s.d.	
1200 V	1200.0	0.04% + 1 l.s.d.	

Temperature coefficient: (0–18 °C and 28–55 °C);

200 mV range: ± (0.006% + 0.4 l.s.d.) per °C;

all other ranges: ± (0.006% + 0.2 l.s.d.) per °C

Input resistance: 10 MΩ ± 0.1%

Normal mode rejection ratio: > 60 dB at 50 Hz and 60 Hz

Common mode rejection ratio (1 kΩ unbalance): > 120 dB at d.c., 50 Hz and 60 Hz

Settling time: 1 s to within one digit of final reading

This extract from the specification of the *Keithley Model 179 digital multimeter* contains the required information. Some manufacturers are a little reluctant to commit themselves, and may be vague over such details as temperature limitations. As with any digital instrument the accuracy specification makes it inconvenient to evaluate the uncertainty in every reading. Consequently it is useful, for an instrument in constant use, to draw up an accuracy curve. For example, for the 200 mV range

Reading mV	Accuracy (% reading + digits)	Total
199.99	$0.04\% + \dfrac{3}{19999} \times 100\%$	0.055%
100.00	$0.04\% + \dfrac{3}{10000} \times 100\%$	0.07%
50.00	0.04% + 0.06%	0.10%
20.00	0.04% + 0.15%	0.19%
10.00	0.04% + 0.30%	0.34%
5.00	0.04% + 0.60%	0.64%
2.00	0.04% + 1.5%	1.54%

By similar calculations the values for each range may be established and a curve as shown in figure 4.20 drawn.

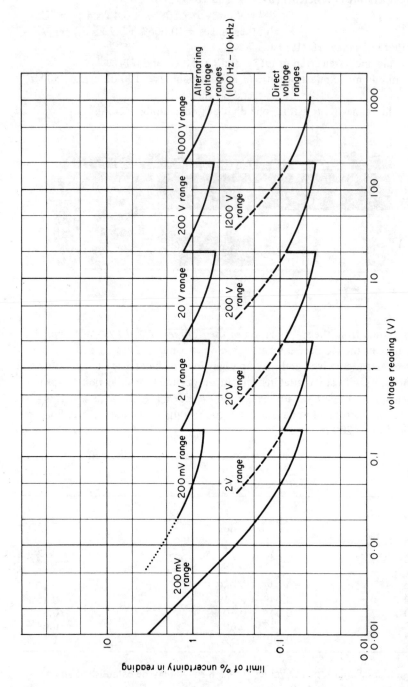

Figure 4.20. Accuracy curve for the voltage ranges of a Keithley 179 digital multimeter

Alternating Voltage

As in the analogue electronic multimeter, an arrangement to convert the alternating voltage to direct voltage must be used before the signal proportional to the unknown can be applied to the digitising circuits. In general mean sensing (ideal rectifier) or r.m.s. sensing circuits are used, the latter generally being some form of multiplier circuit (see reference 7 of chapter 2). The input impedance for the alternating voltage ranges is lower than that for the direct voltage ranges. Additionally, the uncertainty in reading is very much greater than that on the direct ranges, and may be given different values for particular bands of frequency.

Sample Specification

These points are all illustrated in the following specification extract for the alternating voltage ranges of the *Keithley 179 multimeter*.

Range	Maximum Reading	Accuracy (above 2000 counts) 18–28 °C; 100 Hz–10 kHz ±(% rdg + digits)	Temperature coefficient 45 Hz–10 kHz 0–18 °C and 28–55 °C ±(% read and digits/ °C)
200 mV	199.99	0.7% + 15 ℓ.s.d.	0.07% + 2 ℓ.s.d.
2 V	1.9999	0.6% + 15 ℓ.s.d.	0.07% + 2 ℓ.s.d.
20 V	19.999	0.5% + 15 ℓ.s.d.	0.05% + 2 ℓ.s.d.
200 V	199.99	0.5% + 15 ℓ.s.d.	0.05% + 2 ℓ.s.d.
1000 V	1000.0	0.5% + 15 ℓ.s.d.	0.05% + 2 ℓ.s.d.

Extended frequency accuracy: 45–100 Hz ± (0.7% + 15 ℓ.s.d.)
20 V and higher ranges: 10–20 kHz ± (0.8% + 15 ℓ.s.d.)
Response: true root mean square, crest factor, 3
Input impedance: 1 MΩ ± 1% shunted by less than 75 pF
Maximum input voltage: 1000 V r.m.s. 1400 V peak
Common mode rejection ratio (1 kΩ unbalance): 60 dB at d.c. 50 Hz and 60 Hz
Settling time: 2.5 s to within 10 digits of final reading

The accuracy curve for the 100 Hz to 10 kHz frequency band is also shown in figure 4.20.

4.2.3 Current Measurement

Since the multi-function meter is essentially a high input impedance voltage measuring device, all currents must be measured as the voltage drop across known resistors. This is adequately shown by the following extract from the specification for the current ranges of the 179 multimeter.

Sample Specification

Range	Maximum Reading (mA)	Accuracy (12 months) 18–28 °C ± (% rdg + ℓ.s.d.)		Shunt Resistance
		d.c.	a.c. 45 Hz–10 kHz	
200 μA	199.99	0.2% + 2 ℓ.s.d.	1% + 15 ℓ.s.d.	1 kΩ
2 mA	1.9999	0.2% + 2 ℓ.s.d.	1% + 15 ℓ.s.d.	100 Ω
20 mA	19.999	0.2% + 2 ℓ.s.d.	1% + 15 ℓ.s.d.	10 Ω
200 mA	199.99	0.2% + 2 ℓ.s.d.	1% + 15 ℓ.s.d.	1 Ω
2 A	1999.9	0.2% + 2 ℓ.s.d.	1% + 15 ℓ.s.d.	0.1 Ω

True r.m.s. sensing, crest factor: 3

As on the voltage ranges the tolerance in readings on the a.c. ranges is considerably larger than that on the d.c. ranges.

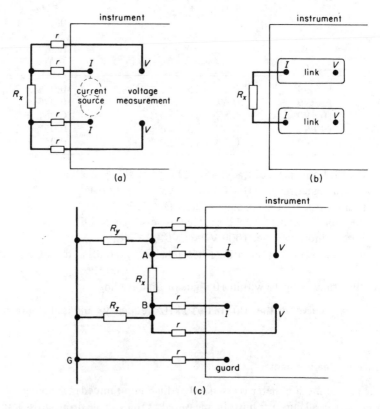

Figure 4.21. Arrangements for resistance measurement: (a) four terminal, (b) two terminal, (c) five terminal

4.2.4 Resistance Ranges

To measure resistance with a digital instrument it is necessary to provide, within the instrument, one or more constant current sources, the magnitude of the unknown resistance being derived from the voltage drop across it. If the instrument on its lowest resistance range has a resolution that is better than 0.1 Ω, four-terminal resistance measurement should be provided (figure 4.21a) as the resistance of the connecting leads, which may well be in excess of 10 mΩ, will add to the reading. On instruments that have this four-terminal facility it is customary for sliding links to be provided so that for measurements of large value resistances on the less sensitive ranges a two-terminal resistance measurement can be adequate if lead lengths are made reasonably short.

In some instruments a five-wire system is available.[11,12] The fifth wire provides a means of 'guarding out' unwanted current paths by maintaining G in figure 4.21c at the same potential as A, thus allowing in-circuit testing.

Sample Specification

The specification for the resistance ranges of the *Keithley 179* is as follows, there being a choice between a high (Hi) or low (Lo) current through the unknown resistance.

	Range	Maximum Reading	Accuracy (12 months) 18–28 °C ± (% rdg + ℓ.s.d.)	Temp. coefficient 0–18 °C and 28–55 °C ± (% rdg + ℓ.s.d.)
High count:	2 kΩ	–	–	–
max. voltage	20 kΩ	19.999	0.04% + 1 ℓ.s.d.	0.003% + 0.2 ℓ.s.d.
across un-	200 kΩ	199.99	0.04% + 1 ℓ.s.d.	0.003% + 0.2 ℓ.s.d.
known 2 V	2000 kΩ	1999.9	0.04% + 1 ℓ.s.d.	0.003% + 0.2 ℓ.s.d.
	20 MΩ	19.999	0.10% + 1 ℓ.s.d.	0.02% + 0.2 ℓ.s.d.
Low count:	2 kΩ	1.9999	0.15% + 15 ℓ.s.d.	0.02% + 2 ℓ.s.d.
max. voltage	20 kΩ	19.999	0.15% + 15 ℓ.s.d.	0.02% + 2 ℓ.s.d.
across un-	200 kΩ	199.99	0.15% + 15 ℓ.s.d.	0.02% + 2 ℓ.s.d.
known 0.2 V	2000 kΩ	1999.9	0.15% + 15 ℓ.s.d.	0.03% + 2 ℓ.s.d.
	20 MΩ	–	–	–

The 'low' condition of operation has obviously a poorer accuracy specification but can be a very useful facility when making measurements on semiconductor components, such as switching diodes.

4.3 'INTELLIGENT' INSTRUMENTS

As inferred at the beginning of this chapter the developments that are occurring in micro-electronics are influencing the design and capabilities of digital instruments at a faster rate than any others. This growth of ability has led to the use of the term 'intelligent' being applied to instruments that can make decisions based on previous readings, manipulate information, process values and initiate action based on the results of these abilities.[13]

4.3.1 Concepts

A view of the trends in instrument design is given in figure 4.22. Initially the whole operation of an instrument was based on precision analogue circuits controlled on the instrument's front panel (figure 4.22a), an arrangement that

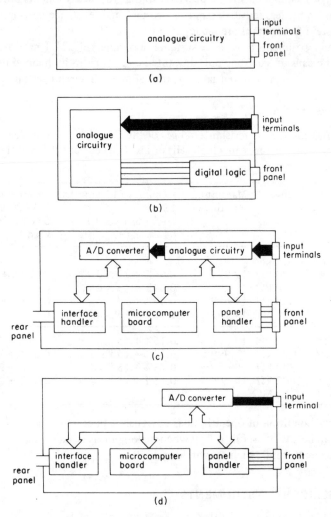

Figure 4.22. Diagrammatic representation of trends in instrumentation (after Moralee[2])

required the operator to directly control all aspects of the measuring process. Particularly in more complex instruments, it led to problems in the design of the front panel controls, which were required to handle complex multi-way switching and sequencing introducing additional sources of measurement error.

To solve some of these front panel control problems, instrument designers began to incorporate control circuits inside the instrument, initially by using relays, and then T.T.L. (figure 4.22b). Some of these controllers developed into complete hard-wired processor systems; thereby freeing the operator from the detailed operation of the measuring circuits, and simplifying the design of the instruments front panel, for example, digital voltmeters that are completely auto ranging.

The shift towards the use of digital controllers was therefore under way before the introduction of the microprocessor and the associated L.S.I. components. The availability of these powerful, low-cost programmable devices completed the trend towards the controller based system or 'architecture', which characterises the generation of instruments represented by figure 4.22c.

In such an approach to instrument design, the microprocessor is the centre of the instrument's operation, controlling all the other circuitry by means of a central data bus. Hence analogue inputs may be switched through various analogue circuits, under control of the microprocessor, to a final analogue-to-digital converter, which in turn produces an output that can be read by the microprocessor for further manipulation, storage or display. It may be argued that the only function of the analogue circuitry in such a situation is to condition the inputs for the A/D converter, and as the range of inputs acceptable to A/D converters increases the need for 'front end' analogue circuitry will decrease, and ultimately disappear (figure 4.22d).

The use of a microprocessor in the design of an instrument results in a number of benefits. It allows the use of very simple front panels, commonly based on a standard numeric keyboard. This makes the instrument easier to use, allowing the operator to set up complex measuring sequences with a few key strokes by calling up of coded measuring processes. The microprocessor can also change the measuring sequence in response either to the measurand or to external signals if the instrument is interfaced to other devices (see section 9.3.2).

Internally, the most important result of including a microprocessor in the instrument is the capability of performing calculations on the readings of the measurand and relating the readings to stored reference values.

4.3.2 Voltage Facilities

Since the greatest number of measurands are, or can be, presented as voltages, an examination of the more common functions that can be performed on voltages is worth considering.

Automatic Calibration

The regular recalibration of a high-grade digital voltmeter is a lengthy, expensive and skilled operation, which can be disruptive to a production situation. With the inclusion of the calculating microprocessor and the associated memory media into a digital multimeter, it has become realistic to make calibration corrections by a purely digital operation.

The technique involved,[14,15] requires appropriate external calibration standards to be accessed for each range of each measurement function in turn. A 'calibration-error' constant for each condition is internally calculated and then stored in nonvolatile memory. During a measurement operation, the appropriate 'calibration-error' constant is recalled for the selected range and used to correct the reading. While such a process is a great improvement on the 'take away for calibration' situation, it cannot cover all eventualities. For example, the effects of an input bias current, or frequency response are not catered for although techniques have been evolved to overcome such problems.[14]

Functional Programs

The programmable facilities that are available on a particular instrument will vary slightly from one manufacturer to another and may also depend on the options selected at the time of purchase. Figure 4.23 shows the front panel of a typical microprocessor-controlled digital multimeter, which in addition to the normal range buttons has a numeric keyboard. Examples of functional programs that may be available on such an instrument and selected by a coded instruction are as follows.

Figure 4.23. 'Intelligent' digital voltmeter (courtesy of Datron Ltd)

Uncertainty read out

The rapid interpretation of a digital multimeter specification is difficult, and a way around the problem is to utilise the computational ability of the micro-processor to calculate the uncertainty in a reading and call up the display of this quantity by depressing a suitably inscribed key (for example, error).

Percentage deviation

By using the numerical keyboard a particular value, V, is entered. Each reading, x, is compared with the entered value and then displayed as a percentage deviation so that

$$\text{displayed value} = 100\frac{(x - V)}{V}$$

Multiplication

Each measurement is multiplied by a constant that has been entered using the keyboard. Such a constant may be greater or less than unity and if there is a linear relationship between, say, the voltage output from a transducer and the measurand in engineering units this facility may be used to provide a display in the appropriate units.

Offset

In many situations it is desirable to know the variations in a quantity above a fixed or reference level. By keying-in the appropriate offset level the display can be made the difference between the measured value and the offset. If this facility and the multiply program are used in conjunction with each other the output from a transducer in a current transmission system (see section 6.7.3) can be displayed in engineering units.

Ratios

Various ratio facilities are possible, the simplest being the division of the measurement by a preset constant. Some instruments, by using additional rear input sockets, can be programmed to sample two inputs in turn and compute either the direct ratio of these, or compute the logarithm of the ratio and display the result in decibels. This is a useful facility for measurements of gain, attenuation, noise levels, etc.

Maximum and minimum

The level of voltage may vary for a number of reasons. It may therefore be desirable to store the maximum and minimum of such excursions, replacing existing recorded values when these are exceeded and to determine the magnitude of the peak-to-peak excursions. It must be possible to display each of these quantities and the magnitude of the most recent sample. The display of each of these quantities will be initiated by appropriately coded keystrokes.

Limits

A limits program would compare the sample with set levels, compute the number of samples exceeding high limits, low limits and within the set limits.

Statistics

The facility to calculate and display the number of measurements in a given time, their average, standard deviation, and the r.m.s. of their values are all possible useful statistical manipulations.

Linearisation

The relationship between the output voltage and temperature for a thermocouple (see section 5.4.3) is nonlinear. By suitable programming, the sensed voltage can be converted to degrees Kelvin, or Celsius, for any one of the commonly used types of thermocouple.

Time

Since a clock needs to be built into the instrument it is sensible to be able to programme for readings to be made at and/or during defined time intervals, which are, of course, limited by the measuring speed of the instrument.

Combination of programmes

The details of operation for these intelligent instruments will vary between manufacturers and the capabilities will largely depend on the decisions made at the time of purchase although many instruments can have their capabilities extended by the addition of circuit boards for specific functions.

4.3.3 Resistance Measurement

The programmable instruments described in the preceding section will usually have a resistance measuring capability and can therefore be used in an inspection situation for (say) verifying that resistors are within acceptance levels. Other applications are the determination of resistance ratios, variations in magnitude, etc. These programmable instruments may therefore be useful in quality control applications.

The existence of a microprocessor within a multi-function meter provides the possibility of a ratiometer technique for resistance measurement. Figure 4.24 shows the principle involved where by measuring V_1, V_2, V_3 and V_4, R_x may be calculated from

$$IR_x = V_3 - V_4$$

and

$$IR_s = V_1 - V_2$$

which combine to give

$$R_x = R_s \left(\frac{V_3 - V_4}{V_1 - V_2} \right)$$

(4.1)

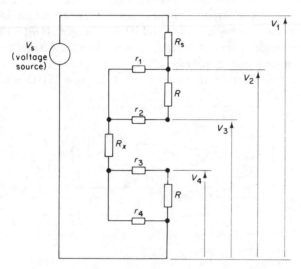

Figure 4.24. Equivalent circuit used in some microprocessor voltmeters for the determination of an unknown resistance by calculation

This expression is valid irrespective of the lead resistances (r_1, r_2, r_3 and r_4), so to simplify the measuring process r_2 and r_3 can be made infinite (that is open circuit) and the precision of a four-terminal measurement is possible with a two-terminal connection.

4.4 HYBRID INSTRUMENTS

As indicated at the beginning of this chapter the range of application of digital instruments is expanding continually. This results from the extension of digital techniques into areas of application which at one time would have been considered solely the province of analogue or comparison methods of measurement. The last sections of this chapter are concerned with instruments that are a mixture of digital and other techniques, thus illustrating the type of innovations which are taking place.

4.4.1 Component Measurements

The measurement of resistance has been a feature of the digital multimeter for a considerable time but the measurement of reactance is a more complicated process involving alternating excitation and the resolving of the unknown into quadrature components. The use of comparison or bridge methods for this (chapter 3) is a relatively skilled operation, particularly when the resistive and reactive components have magnitudes such that balance must be obtained by the alternate adjustment of two variable bridge arms.

Self-balancing bridges tend to be expensive and relatively slow in operation; an alternative solution to this problem has been the development of instruments incorporating phase sensitive detection and ratio techniques.[16,17,18]

In such impedance meters a technique is used, when the parallel components of the unknown are required (for example, C_p and G_p), whereby feedback is used to hold the voltage across the unknown constant (figure 4.25). However, should

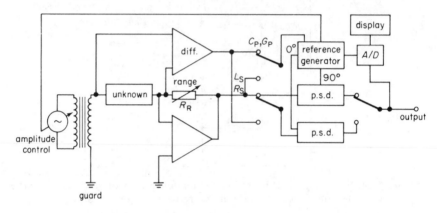

Figure 4.25. Simplified circuit diagram of impedance meter

the series components be desired (for example, L_s and R_s) the voltage across the range resistor is the quantity held constant. Under such conditions the evaluation of the unknown simplifies to determining the magnitudes of the in-phase and quadrature components of the appropriate signal, which for the parallel case is the voltage across the range resistor

$$E_R = IR_R = R_R E_X (G_p + j\omega C_p) \tag{4.2}$$

and since R_R and E_X are constants, the outputs from the in-phase and quadrature phase sensitive detectors (p.s.d.s) will be directly proportional to the components of the unknown.

When the series components are required E_R is held constant and E_X connected to the p.s.d.s so that

$$E_X = \frac{E_R}{R_R} (R_s + j\omega L_s) \tag{4.3}$$

and the magnitudes of the components of the unknown will be proportional to $(E_R R_s/R_R)$ and $j\omega(E_R L_s/R_R)$.

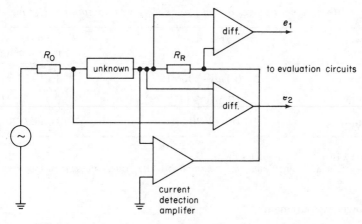

Figure 4.26. An alternative arrangement used in impedance (L.C.R.) meters

An alternative arrangement[18] is to use the phasor ratio of the voltage e_1 and e_2 in figure 4.26, and then for the parallel case

$$\frac{e_1}{e_2} = - (G_p + j\omega C_p)R_R \qquad (4.4)$$

and for the series case

$$\frac{e_2}{e_1} = - \frac{(R_s + j\omega L_s)}{R_R} \qquad (4.5)$$

The use of meters of this type is extremely simple, since in general all that is required is the connection of the component in a jig and the selection of the correct function. This makes them ideally suited for use in quality checks by 'goods inwards', stores or nontechnical personnel.

The capabilities of meters based on the techniques described above have been considerably extended by the inclusion of further developments in electronic devices and circuit techniques,[19,20] which facilitate the fast automatic or controlled measurement of components at, or close to, the actual working conditions of frequency, level and direct voltage bias. Alternatively, characteristics such as capacitance variation with voltage can be established for evaluation of semiconductor wafers and chips.

Sample Specification

Table 4.4 shows the specification of the *Wayne Kerr B424 component test meter* which has a $3\frac{1}{2}$ digit liquid crystal display with 24 ranges and can be used for measuring resistance, inductance and capacitance. An interesting comparison can be made between this specification and that of the B224 given in section 3.4.3.

Table 4.4. Measurement ranges of the Wayne Kerr 424 component test meter

Unknown	As parallel components	As series components
Capacitance	0.1 pF–200 nF	1 nF–20 mF
Inductance	10 mH–2 kH	0.1 μH–2 H
Resistance	100 Ω–20 MΩ	10 mΩ–20 kΩ

Accuracy: ± (0.25% of reading + 1 digit); (Q > 10).
Frequency: The underlined values are measured at 1 kHz, other values are measured at 100 Hz.

4.4.2 Power Measurement

The measurement of the power consumed by a load requires the determination of the product of the instantaneous values of the appropriate voltage and current. This can be performed by analogue techniques using a multiplier, [17] by patented techniques,[21] or if the current and voltage are suitably sampled and stored the average power may be computed. In most commercially available instruments an analogue technique is used to determine the power, the output from the multiplying circuits being connected to an A/D converter so that a digital display of the power is provided.

The input impedance of the voltage circuits for an instrument of this type is very much greater than for an electrodynamometer while the input resistance of the current ranges may be much less than for a direct acting instrument. Additionally, the range of power that the electronic instrument can measure will in general be greater than that of the conventional instrument, although the uncertainty in measurement may be greater.

4.4.3 Recorders

The development of high speed A/D converters, together with the availability of low cost memory circuits, has led to the production of digital storage oscilloscopes. One instrument of this type, shown schematically in figure 4.27, uses a 1024 × 8 bit memory; the general operation of the oscilloscope is described below.

The incoming signal waveform is fed into an A/D converter, which works at a speed determined by the timebase speed control up to a maximum of 1.8 MHz. The digital output of the converter is fed into the memory, the eight vertical bits giving a resolution of 1 part in 256 (0.4 per cent) and the 1024 points giving a horizontal resolution of approximately 0.1 per cent on a single trace or 0.2 per cent when two traces are stored each as 512 points.

To view the waveform, the information is read from the memory, passed through a D/A converter and the resultant signal displayed on the c.r.t. screen. A 'refresh' or 'roll' mode of operation is also available and in that condition the in-

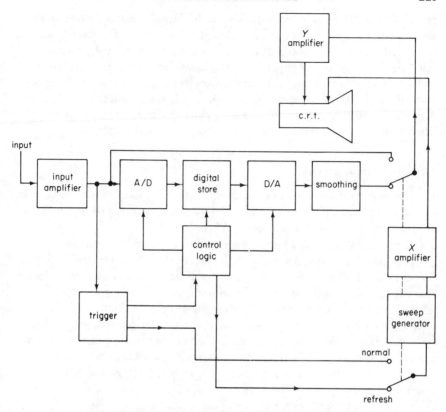

Figure 4.27. Schematic arrangement of the operation of a digital oscilloscope

formation is read continuously from the store, updated information being entered until a store instruction is given to hold the information in the store. The contents of the store are then cycled continuously, to display a stored wave on the c.r.t. screen. A further facility exists so half of the store may be held, so that a real time trace may be viewed simultaneously with a stored trace.

Other developments of this digital storage technique are numerous, one example being 'the visual trend display'[22] where four or eight channels of information are continuously updated, stored and displayed on a c.r.t. simultaneously as bar charts and as 'pen recorder' type traces. Perhaps the ultimate in this form of instrumentation is the digital processing oscilloscope[23] developed by Tektronix in which analogue data is digitised, processed and then displayed in a format required by the operator.

Programmable recorders

The use of digital storage and microcomputing capabilities have been combined to provide a potentiometric recorder,[24] having eight differential input channels, each with 12 ranges and a multi-channel sample rate variable from 1 sample every 999 s to 250 samples per second when in the eight-channel mode or 2000 samples per second in the single-channel mode of operation. The stored data can be plotted against time, or one channel against another with a 0.1 per cent of full scale resolution on A4 paper. The calculating functions are add, subtract, multiply, divide, average any two curves point by point, differentiate, integrate, normalise and determine logarithms or reciprocals. In addition to these functions the data for plotting may be offset, scaled, expanded or compressed, and if fitted with a magnetic disc can be used to store up to 300 graphs.

4.4.4 Spectrum Analysers

The conventional c.r.o. has a horizontal scale which is a simple function of time. In many measurement situations the analysis and display of signals in the frequency domain is an important and useful concept.

The spectrum analyser, which was originally developed for the analysis of the components of radio frequency signals, is a swept frequency receiver which provides a visual display of amplitude against frequency. It shows on a single display how energy is distributed as a function of frequency, displaying the absolute value of the Fourier components of a given waveform, like figure 1.30. The contemporary instrument (figure 4.28) incorporating microprocessor technology makes it possible to perform an immediate Fourier analysis on a waveform, [25,26] an analysis which a few years ago was only possible in theory, or by a laborious process involving manual measurement on a graph and computer analysis.

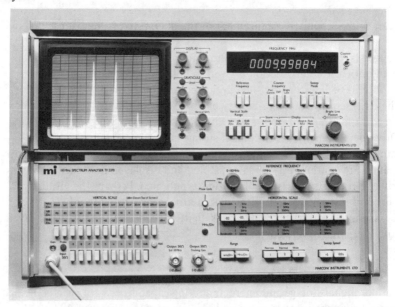

Figure 4.28. Spectrum analyser (courtesy of Marconi Instruments Ltd)

The applications of this powerful instrument are many, for example, acoustic noise and vibration levels are of major concern to manufacturers and users of mechanical vehicles, and by using appropriate transducers (see section 5.4) electrical signals derived from the vibrations can be examined to assist in locating the source. In the field of communications, spectrum analysers may be used to provide performance information on carrier wave purity, modulation, frequency response and electrical noise. Furthermore in the area of general electronics analysers can be used for:

(a) identifying signals resulting from non-linear amplification, filtering or mixing
(b) determining the purity of signals
(c) measuring and displaying frequency and modulation characteristics, and
(d) for determining the frequency response of a network.

4.4.5 Logic Analysers

The increasing complexity and use of digital integrated circuits, together with the limitations of conventional instruments has resulted in the need for specialised instruments[27,28] designed to ease the solving of the complex software and hardware problems encountered in the development of digital systems. These instruments have become known as logic or microprocessor analysers and since different design philosophies are involved, instruments are normally associated either with hardware (timing analysis) or software (state analysis). Some manufacturers, however, produce instruments capable of both modes of operation.

Timing Analysers

This form of logic analyser samples all data channels simultaneously on an internal reference clock. The recorded data indicates whether the input lines are high or low relative to a defined threshold voltage at the active clock transition. Data from all channels is subsequently displayed on a c.r.t. with any changes appearing as ideal transitions. The timing resolution (or uncertainty) is determined by the sampling clock period. The major use of the timing analyser is in functional timing measurements, for example, in displaying sequences on control buses, I/O data transfers, or examining 'handshakes' on interface buses (see section 9.3.2). It is the sequence in which the lines 'toggle' that is the timing analyser's strength, not the precision resolution of these transitions, and sampling rates of five times the data will normally provide more than adequate resolution for functional displays.

One essential feature of a timing analyser is the ability to capture and display 'glitches' (narrow spikes that occur within a sample period). Some analysers with this facility can capture and store for later display a random glitch (such as a noise spike that may occur once every few hours), thereby drastically reducing the troubleshooting time. Another very useful feature is the ability to pretrigger on an event, in effect to provide a time display of events prior to the trigger point.

State Analysers

These instruments are designed primarily for software analysis by displaying in truth table format the logic 1s and 0s of the input. They can also be used for analysis of hardware synchronisation faults.

The state analyser uses a clock from the system under test to sample the system data synchronously. It monitors the word (state) parameters and the word (state) sequence of the system under test in exactly the same way as the system hardware.

A typical application for a state analyser would be in trouble-shooting a microprocessor system when, for example, it would be necessary to monitor a 16-bit address field, an 8-bit data bus, together with some control and I/O activity. To monitor this amount of data the state analyser must be multi-nodal and for an easily interpreted presentation the data must be condensed to an appropriately coded display such as hexadecimal. So that a desired portion of activity may be selected, extensive qualification and triggering capabilities should be provided, either by clock qualification (when data is strobed into the analyser only if additional inputs occur at the clock edge) or by the analyser being programmed to trace only specified states. Ideally, of course, a state analyser should be capable of both modes of operation.

4.4.6 Data Analysers

Automatic data logging and recording result in large quantities of data that must be analysed. This may be accomplished by feeding the data into a digital computer that has been suitably programmed, or by using an instrument that has been specifically designed for coping with the analysis of a particular type of data.

Pulse Height Analysers

For large quantities of data to have a meaningful form it is usually necessary to adopt a graphical presentation; for example, a histogram of a large quantity of data is easier to assess than columns of figures. To perform this type of analysis, instruments have been manufactured that can sense the magnitude of a pulse and classify it as belonging to one of a number of predetermined bands of pulse height, it then being possible to display the histogram on a c.r.t. or, in a slow speed statistical analyser, as a count of pulses within the preset bands of pulse height.[29]

Such a device is suitable for the analysis of statistical data, for example, the weight of potatoes, the radiation levels from an isotope, etc., but much of the time spent in analysing data is consumed in trying to form relationships between the occurrence of events, and to locate the source of a phenomena; in other words to correlate the effect with a cause, when the signals from both may be partially or completely obscured by noise.

Correlator

The development of the signal correlator has reduced the correlation of signals from an extremely time-consuming two-stage process (data recording and computer analysis) to a 'real time' process. The simplest method of obtaining a factor which describes the correlation between two waveforms is to multiply sampled amplitudes of the two waveforms at regular intervals throughout the duration of the waveform. If the waveforms to be compared (see figure 4.29) are identical and in phase (no time displacement) then the summation of the products obtained will result in a large positive number. However, should the waveforms have been different the final number would have been smaller, due to some products having a negative value. If the waveforms to be compared are identical but with a time displacement (see figure 4.30), then a direct comparison would yield a low correlation, but by varying the time shift (τ) between the two waveforms it is possible to obtain a curve of average correlation product against time shift.

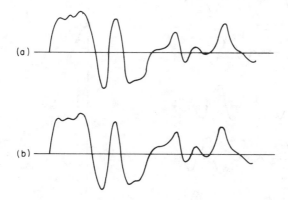

Figure 4.29. Waveforms with good correlation

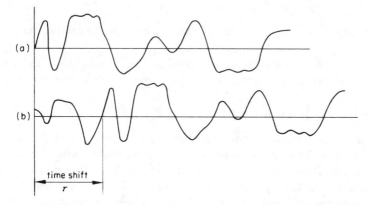

Figure 4.30. Waveforms that have good correlation when one is time shifted by τ

Autocorrelation function

The above results in a curve known as the autocorrelation function (see figure 4.31). The average correlation product for each value of τ is determined by dividing the total of the correlation products for each value of τ by the number of products contributing towards it. Thus the autocorrelation function of a waveform is a graph of the similarity between a waveform and a time shifted version of itself, as a function of the time shift. The autocorrelation function of any signal, random or periodic, depends not on the actual waveform but on its frequency content. This means that the autocorrelation function of any periodic wave is periodic and of the same period as the waveform, while the autocorrelation function of a wide band nonperiodic waveform will be nonperiodic (see figure 4.32). Autocorrelation is uniquely successful in the determination of the

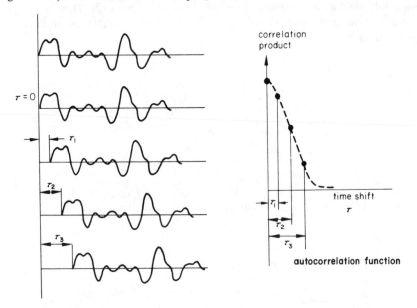

Figure 4.31. Autocorrelation or variation of correlation with time

periodic content of an unknown noisy signal, a striking example of this being the detection of periodic signals from outer space, for example emissions from pulsars.

Cross-correlation function

To compare the similarity of two nonidentical waveforms a technique similar to that which gave the autocorrelation function may be used to obtain a cross- . correlation function. An example of this is in correlating a signal with a reflection that has been modified by noise. Now in general there will be no correlation between the original signal and the noise (giving a high signal-to-noise ratio), and

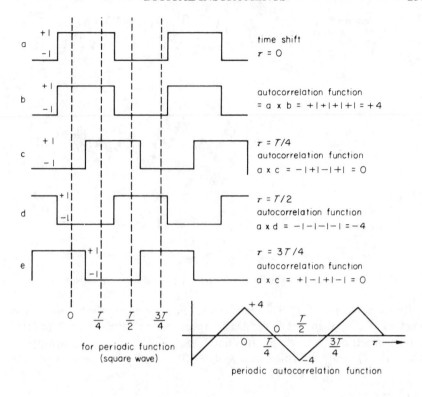

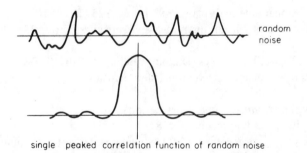

single peaked correlation function of random noise

Figure 4.32. Autocorrelation functions of periodic and nonperiodic waveforms

the cross-correlation function between the original signal and the reflection plus noise will take the form of an autocorrelation function having a delay that is proportional to the transmission time between sending the signal and receiving the reflection. Figure 4.33 shows (a) a swept frequency transmitted signal, (b) a received signal that has a noise content, and (c) the cross-correlation function of the two signals, which is a delayed version of the autocorrelation function of the transmitted waveform.

'transmitted' signal
swept frequency
sine wave

'received' signal
swept frequency
plus noise

cross—correlation
of transmitted
and received
signals

Figure 4.33. Detection of a known signal 'buried' in noise

It may be shown[30,31,32] that the relationship between the autocorrelation function of a signal and its power density spectrum is a Fourier transform pair. This enables the autocorrelation function to be related to the power density (spectrum) as measured with a wave analyser fitted with a true square law meter.

REFERENCES

1   G. F. Weston, Alphanumeric display, *Proc. I.E.E.*, **125** (1978) 1077–99
2   D. Moralee, Towards intelligent instruments, *Electronics Power*, **25** (1979) 16–21
3   J. D. Kershaw, Digital Electronics (Duxbury, Belmont, Calif., 1976)
4   Fundamentals of the electronic counters, Hewlett-Packard Application Note 200 (1978)
5   B. A. Gregory, *The Counter Timer* (Instructional video tape, Learning Resources, Brighton Polytechnic, 1978)
6   R. D. Ely, Frequency measurements by frequency meter or timer counter *Electronics Power*, **24** (1978) 45–6
7   J. R. Pearce, An introduction to digital voltmeters, D.V.M. Monograph No. 1 (Solartron Ltd, Farnborough, Hants)
8   E. Zuch, Consider v/f converters, *Electron. Des.*, **24** (1976) 160–6
9   R. Mewett, Conversion techniques for D.V.M.'s, *Electron. Equip. News*, **13** (1971) 52–3
10 J. R. Pearce, Dual ramp voltmeters—basic theory, D.V.M. Monograph No. 7 (Solartron Ltd, Farnborough, Hants)
11 J. Pickering, Multifunction digital voltmeters, *Electronics Power*, **23** (1977) 30–1

12   D. T. Crook, Analog in-circuit component measurements: problems and
     solutions, *HP Jl,* **30** (1979) 19-22
13   S. Runyon, Brainy instruments take top honours with computer power that
     boggles the mind, *Electron. Des.,* **24** (1976) 160-6
14   D. Jessop, Simplifying the calibration of digital voltmeters, *Electronics
     Power,* **25** (1979) 22-5
15   A. Goskin, A fast-reading high-resolution voltmeter that calibrates itself
     automatically, *HP Jl,* **28** (1977) 2-10
16   H. P. Hall, An AC-DC ratiometer and its use in a CRL meter, *I.E.E.E. Trans.
     Instrumn Measmt,* **IM-22** (1973) 387-90
17   D. H. Sheingold (ed.), *Multiplier Application Guide* (Analog Devices,
     Boston, Mass., 1978)
18   S. Hashimoto and T. Tamamura, An automatic wide-range digital LCR
     meter, *HP Jl,* **28** (1976) 9-15
19   K. Maeda and Y. Narimatsu, Multi-frequency LCR meters test components
     under realistic conditions, *HP Jl,* **30** (1979) 24-31
20   D. F. Bond, Microprocessors for high accuracy component measurement,
     Microelectronic Reliability, **18** (1978) 53-63
21   Technical Information Catalogue No. YEW 2800H (Yokogawa Electric
     Works Ltd, Tokyo, 1979)
22   A. B. Gardiner, The visual trend display, *New Electronics,* **9** (1976) 73, 76
23   Digital processing oscilloscope (Tektronix Inc., Beaverton, Oreg., 1974)
24   Analogue signal processor—series BS8000. Technical data, Bryans Southern
     Instruments Ltd., Mitcham, Surrey, Oct. 1978
25   R. Ganderton, Spectrum analysers today, *Electronics Power,* **24** (1978)
     42-4
26   S. N. Holdaway and M. Dee Humpherys, The next generation R.F. spectrum
     analyser, *HP Jl,* **29** (1978) 2-7
27   R. Allan, Logic analysers, *I.E.E.E. Spectrum,* **14** (1977) 34-9
28   Logic analysers, product notes, *Hewlett-Packard Electronic Instruments and
     Systems Catalogue* (1979)
29   Statistical analysis of waveforms and digital time-waveform measurements,
     Hewlett-Packard Application Note 93 (1969)
30   R. L. Rex and G. T. Roberts, Correlation, signal averaging and probability
     analysis, *HP Jl,* **21** (1969) 2-8
31   F. H. Lange, *Correlation Techniques* (Illiffe, London, 1967)
32   Jens Trampe Broch, On the measurement and interpolation of cross-power
     spectra, *Brüel Kjaer tech. Rev.* (1968) 3-20

5

Transducers

Definitions

Transducers

These devices have been defined as components that may be used to interconnect like or unlike systems and transmit energy between them. Although such a definition can be justified, a more generally acceptable definition to electrical engineers is that a transducer is a device used to convert a physical phenomenon into an electrical signal.

In many cases the conversion may be via an intermediate stage, that is, the measurand (for example, pressure) is first converted to a mechanical displacement which in turn is converted to an electrical signal. The mechanical conversion is accomplished by one of two fundamentally different methods, as follows.

Fixed reference devices

In these devices one part of the transducer is attached to a reference surface, and the other part connected, either directly or via a linking mechanism, to the variable as in figure 5.1. Should the displacement be small, some means of mechanical magnification or electrical amplification must be used to obtain a satisfactory sensitivity.

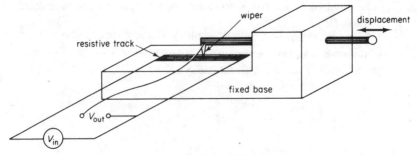

Figure 5.1. Fixed reference transducer

Mass–spring or seismic device

In these transducers there is only one contact or anchor point, this being the attachment of the transducer base to the point where the variation is to be measured. The motion of the measurand is inferred from the relative motion (δ) of the mass (m) to that of the case (figure 5.2), and will depend on the size of the mass and the stiffness of the spring (k), the magnitude of the damping being

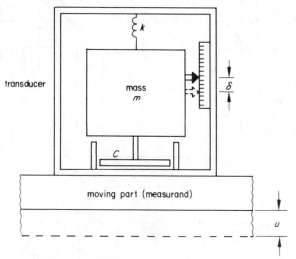

Figure 5.2. Seismic or mass–spring transducer

determined by the damper (C). The seismic type of transducer is indispensable in the study of movements and vibrations in any form of vehicle, it has a sensitivity–frequency characteristic similar to a recorder galvanometer (see figure 2.29), and it may be shown that to avoid amplitude distortion when using a seismic displacement transducer ω (the frequency of sinusoidal movement) must be greater than 2 ω_0 (where ω_0 is the internal resonant frequency of the transducer), while for an accelerometer undergoing sinusoidal acceleration, the ratio ω/ω_0 must be less than 0.2. In figure 5.3 the effects of damping magnitude on both of these characteristics are shown.

The relationships between sinusoidal displacements, velocities, and accelerations are shown in figure 5.4 from which

$$\text{peak acceleration} = \omega^2 S_{max} \text{ m/s}^2$$

$$= \frac{\omega^2 S_{max}}{g} \text{ in } gs \text{ of acceleration} \qquad (5.1)$$

An accelerometer's output performance is usually specified in terms of peak mV/g.

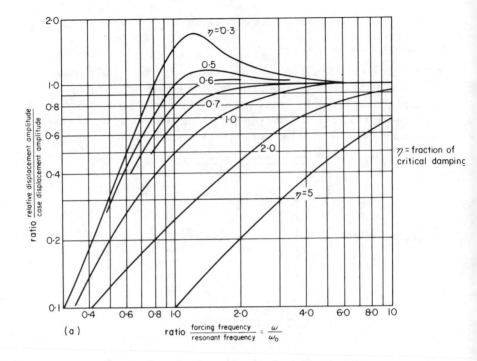

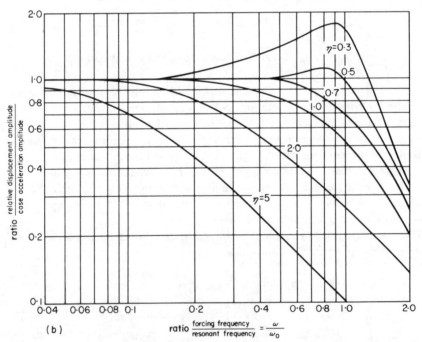

Figure 5.3. Characteristic curves for seismic transducers showing the effect of damping magnitude on displacement amplitude of internal mass: (a) response to sinusoidal displacement of transducer case, (b) response to sinusoidal acceleration of transducer case

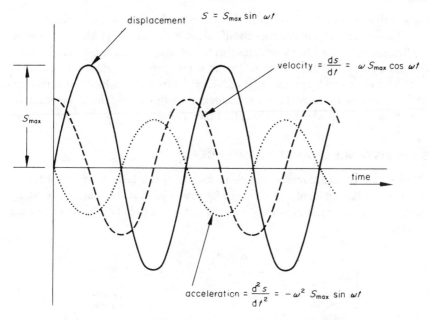

displacement $S = S_{max} \sin \omega t$

velocity $= \dfrac{ds}{dt} = \omega S_{max} \cos \omega t$

S_{max}

time

acceleration $= \dfrac{d^2 s}{dt^2} = -\omega^2 S_{max} \sin \omega t$

Figure 5.4. Relationships of oscillatory motions

Transducer classification

A detailed study of transducers is more suited to specialised books[1,2,3] rather than this introductory text on instrumentation. However, because they form such an important part of any instrumentation system it is desirable to examine the transduction methods used to convert physical phenomena into electrical signals. Transducers may be classified either by the transduction method used, or by the function they are capable of measuring, for example acceleration, displacement, etc. In table 5.1 are tabulated the more common measurands and the possible methods of transduction. The method of classification adopted in this

Table 5.1. Table of measurands against transduction methods

	Resistance change	Reactance change	Electro-magnetic	Semi-conductor	Digital	Thermo-electric
Acceleration	*	*	*	*	*	
Displacement	*	*	*	*	*	
Flow	*	*	*			
Force	*	*		*		
Humidity	*					
Level	*	*			*	
Pressure	*	*	*	*		
Temperature	*			*	*	*
Thickness	*				*	
Velocity	*	*	*	*	*	

book is that of transduction method, it being considered that in a teaching/ introductory text this method of classification is the more logical, whereas in an application-orientated book on transducers, classification by use would be more appropriate.[1] It should be noted that in many cases the various transduction methods have equal merit, and that each of the various transducer manufacturers, having specialised on a particular transduction method, will tend to incorporate it in the majority of the transducers that they make.

5.1 RESISTANCE CHANGE TRANSDUCERS

The methods of transduction involving a change of resistance are perhaps the easiest to understand and will therefore be described first. The variable resistance method of transduction is not widely used but serves to illustrate the underlying principles.

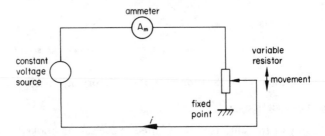

Figure 5.5. Variable resistance position transducer

Consider figure 5.5 where the operation of this circuit as a position measuring system simply requires that the sliding contact on the resistor be linked to the motion or displacement under observation. A change in the measurand will cause a change in the resistance in the circuit and a consequent change in the current. If the ammeter were calibrated in suitable units a continuous display of the measurand would thus have been obtained. For such a transducer to operate satisfactorily the voltage must have a constant magnitude irrespective of circuit resistance, so that the current in the circuit is only dependent on the variations in the resistance R. Another drawback of this type of transducer is that if a plus and minus variation is to be observed, current will be flowing in the circuit when the measurand is in the zero or reference position.

5.1.1 Potentiometric Transducers

The variable resistance transducer results in a current variation which is a function of the magnitude of the measurand. In a potentiometric transducer the output is a voltage variation, that is, the resistive divider is used as a potentiometer or

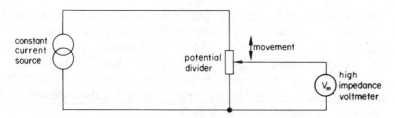

Figure 5.6. Principle of the potentiometric position transducer

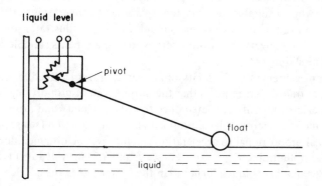

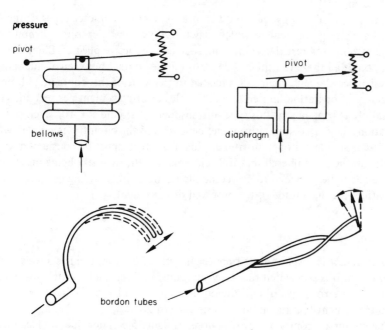

Figure 5.7. Some transducer actuating mechanisms

potential divider (figure 5.6) and is in general a more satisfactory arrangement. A potentiometric transducer should be supplied from a constant current source, the ransducer output being monitored by a high impedance instrument so that the loading effects across the potentiometer are negligible. It will be seen that mechanically coupling the measurand to the sliding contact of the potentiometer will result in an output voltage that will be proportional to the displacement of the wiper from one end of the resistive path.

Since the resistance potentiometer may be used to convert a displacement into a proportional electrical signal, the measurement of quantities such as flow, force, pressure, humidity, etc., can be performed by a fixed reference potentiometric sensor when a suitable quantity to displacement converter is positioned between the sliding contact and the measurand. Figure 5.7 illustrates some of the techniques used to convert physical properties to displacements suitable for applying to the sliding contact.

To obtain measurements of velocity or acceleration from a fixed reference potentiometric transducer, requires that the output voltage proportional to displacement is electrically differentiated once to obtain velocity and differentiated twice to produce an electrical signal proportional to acceleration (see section 6.7.2). A signal proportional to acceleration can however be obtained directly from a seismic potentiometric transducer (see figure 5.2) provided its mechanical resonant frequency ω_0 is much higher than the frequency of the acceleration (ω), that is $\omega/\omega_0 < 0.2$.

Both the variable resistance and the resistance potentiometer types of transducer have a resistive element which may be wire wound, deposited carbon film, platinum film, or a resistive compound such as conductive plastics. Since the operation of all these transducers depends on the contact between a slider and the resistance element, their life is related to the wear of this contact, and the frequency of operation limited to a few cycles of displacement per second. The typical life expectancy of this type of transducer is around 3×10^6 cycles of operation; they are comparatively inexpensive, and the circuitry associated with their use is simple although instrument loading effects must be considered. It should also be remembered that if displacement is the quantity being measured, a force has to be provided to overcome the friction of the sliding contact and this may affect the magnitude of the observed displacement.

Example

A potentiometric displacement transducer with a 20 mm travel has a resistance of 10 kΩ. If it is connected to a 10 V d.c. source of negligible output resistance, calculate the error in position if the output is measured as 5 V (that is, $\equiv 10$ mm) on an instrument that has an input resistance of 20 kΩ.

The circuit appropriate to this example is figure 5.6. The wiper divides the potentiometer resistance into R and $(10\ k\Omega - R)$, then

$$\frac{V_{out}}{V_{in}} = \frac{5}{10} = \frac{\dfrac{20(10-R)}{(30-R)}}{R + \dfrac{20(10-R)}{30-R}}$$

or

$$\frac{5}{10} = \frac{20(10-R)}{200 - 20R + 30R - R^2}$$

Hence

$$R^2 - 50R + 200 = 0$$

or

$$R = 4.385 \text{ k}\Omega$$

This is 615 Ω from the mid position and means an error of $(615 \times 100/5000)$ or 12.3 per cent.

5.1.2 Resistance Strain Gauges

An important series of transducers is derived from the use of resistance strain gauges, and before considering such transducers the principles and applications of resistance strain gauges should be understood.

If a length of electrical wire is subjected to a tensile force it will stretch, its length being increased by an amount of δL (say), and provided that the elastic limit of the material is not exceeded, the change in length is proportional to the load and the wire will revert to its original length when the load is removed. Corresponding to this increase in length there will be a slight decrease in the cross-sectional area of the wire (the increased length has to come from some-where), and since resistance of a conductor = $\rho L/A$, where ρ = resistivity of the material, L = length and A = cross-sectional area, the increase in length and the decrease in area will both contribute to an increase in the resistance of the stretched wire. In addition to the dimensional changes the resistivity of the material changes, this effect (termed piezoresistivity) is small for metals but does make a contribution to the change in resistance. Obviously, it is inconvenient to have long lengths of resistance wire attached to a test object so the general arrangement of a strain gauge is one in which the resistance wire (which typically has a 0.025 mm diameter) is folded into a grid and mounted on a backing of paper or Bakelite. A development from this is the foil gauge (see figure 5.8), which is manufactured by techniques similar to those used in the production of printed circuits. Such a process readily lends itself to the production of shaped, special purpose, strain gauges. The size of a strain gauge will depend on the

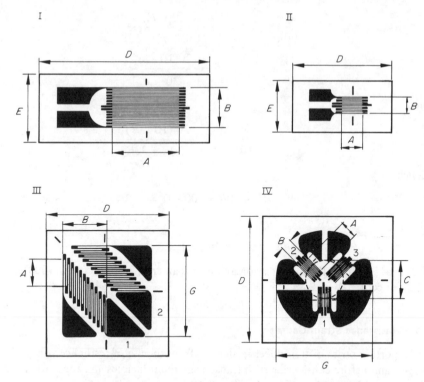

Figure 5.8. Resistance foil gauges (courtesy of Philips)

intended application but resistance gauges are available in a variety of lengths from around 3 mm to 150 mm, there being a range of nominal resistance values, preferred magnitudes of which are 120 Ω and 600 Ω.

It was stated above that the electrical resistance (R) of a straight wire will change when it is stretched; let this change in resistance be δR. The definition of mechanical strain is the ratio 'change in length/the original length' or $\delta L/L$ and is denoted by the symbol ϵ. To relate these two quantities, a factor known as the strain sensitivity is used such that

$$\text{strain sensitivity} = \frac{\delta R \text{ per } R}{\delta L \text{ per } L} = \frac{\delta R/R}{\epsilon} \tag{5.2}$$

and has a characteristic value dependent on the type of resistance wire. *Note:* ϵ is often quoted as microstrain ($\mu\epsilon$), for example, micrometres per metre.

When the wire is bent into a grid to form a strain gauge there are small lengths of the wire at each bend that are no longer acted on by the strain parallel to the axis of the gauge. This part of the gauge resistance is termed 'dead resistance' and the ratio of dead resistance to total gauge resistance will depend on the type of fold and length of the gauge.

When a gauge is attached to an object that is stressed parallel to the axis of the strain gauge it may sense two strains: (a) the principal or longitudinal strain which is in line with the gauge axis, and (b) the transverse or Poisson strain which is at right angles to the gauge axis. If the gauge has appreciable dead resistance it will exhibit a transverse strain sensitivity, which is typically 1-2 per cent of the longitudinal sensitivity; this effect may be reduced in foil gauges by increasing the width of material at the bend (see figure 5.8). The output resulting from this Poisson strain acts to oppose that from the principal strain, thus reducing the overall gauge sensitivity.

The advantages of foil gauges over the wire gauges may be summarised as follows.

(a) The foil is thinner and therefore more flexible.
(b) The cross-sensitivity of the foil gauge is much lower due to the large cross-sectional area of the ends.
(c) The surface area of the conductor is much greater; it is therefore easier to dissipate the power loss in the strain gauge.
(d) A better adhesion of the conductor to the backing is obtained.
(e) Large area terminal connections are easily provided.
(f) The photographic production techniques provide consistency in manufacture.
(g) The dimensions of the gauge may be made very small, enabling the measurement of localised strains and strains on curved surfaces.

Gauge factor

The strain sensitivity of a manufactured strain gauge is termed the *gauge factor*, and is less than that of the resistance wire used in its construction, as it will include the effects of the dead resistance, the Poisson ratio of the surface to which the gauge is attached, and the transverse sensitivity. The majority of resistance gauges have a gauge factor of around 2, copper–nickel wires giving values between 1.9 and 2.1; however, iron–chromium–aluminium and iron–nickel–chromium alloys may be used to give a gauge factor of 2.8 to 3.5.

Vibratory movement

When a strain gauge is used in a dynamic situation, for example, for the determination of strains caused by vibrations or movement, the frequency response of the gauge must be considered. Since a gauge will average the strain over its active length, if the wavelength of the strain variations are of the same order of magnitude as the gauge length, considerable errors will be introduced. In the worst case, if the gauge length is equal to the vibratory wavelength, the effective average strain and hence the output, will be zero (see figure 5.9). If the frequency were increased above this point, output would again be obtained but its amplitude could not be easily related to the measurand.

To determine the frequency of vibration at which zero output would occur requires the application of the expression relating frequency and wavelength to

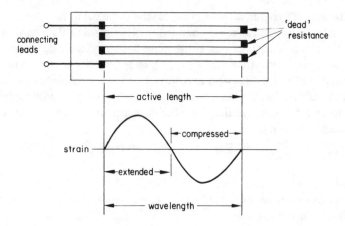

Figure 5.9. 'Worst case' of vibration frequency, occurring when the vibration
wavelength equals the active length of the strain gauge

the velocity of sound, that is $fL = u$, where f is the frequency of vibration in the
test object, L is the active length of the strain gauge and u is the velocity of
sound in the medium to which the strain gauge is bonded. If, as is commonly
the case, the gauge is attached to a steel member, in which u is 5×10^3 m/s
(approximately), the frequency for zero output is $f = (5 \times 10^3)/L$ Hz and if
$L = 5$ mm, $f = 1$ MHz. Alternatively if $L = 150$ mm, $f = 33$ kHz.

These values of frequency are theoretical values, and in practice (due to the
effects of bonding) the frequency at which zero output occurs will be considerably less. To obtain an error of 1 per cent or less in the output, the theoretical
values should be divided by a factor of 20, giving practical upper frequency
limits of 50 kHz and 1.6 kHz for the 5 mm and 150 mm gauges respectively.
Since instrument specifications normally quote frequency limits as 3 dB points
(where response is 30 per cent down) (see p. 303), these may be determined for
the strain gauge by $f \approx u/4L$, giving bandwidths B for the above gauges of
250 kHz and 8 kHz respectively. To obtain the bandwidth of the measurement
system—when the gauge is joined to a display instrument—the empirical expression for the system bandwidth (as shown in equation 1.42) is used, remembering
that the resulting system bandwidth should be divided by 5 to obtain a system
frequency range over which the measurement errors should be of the order of
1 per cent.

Temperature effects

Another factor which may affect the performance of the resistance strain gauge
is that of temperature, and its effects are threefold. First, the gauge filament will
have a temperature coefficient of resistance, and since this may be as large as
50 p.p.m. per $^\circ$C for some of the copper–nickel alloys (constantan $\pm$ 20 p.p.m.
per $^\circ$C), it cannot be lightly ignored. The second temperature effect results from

the presence of dissimilar metals in the construction of the gauge, it being common practice to form the leads from nickel clad copper, and the thermal e.m.f. generated by various resistance wire materials at their junctions with copper varies from about 2 μV/°C for manganin to about 47 μV/°C for constantan. The third temperature effect results from the difference in the temperature coefficients of expansion of the materials of the test object and the resistance wire of the gauge. For example, should the test object expand (thermally) at a greater rate than the gauge wire, the latter will be stretched and to the measuring instrument it will appear as if the test object is being stressed, this phenomenon being known as apparent strain.

To compensate for these temperature effects a 'dummy' or nonactive gauge is often incorporated in the measuring circuit. A dummy gauge is one which is nominally identical to the active gauge, but is attached to a nonstressed piece of the test material in the same environment as the active gauge. The resistance changes due to the temperature effects can then be made to counterbalance each other in the measuring circuit.

5.1.3 Measuring Circuits

The circuit commonly used in strain gauge work is some form of d.c. Wheatstone bridge circuit. Since the variations in strain are dynamic the bridge circuit is operated in the 'unbalanced condition' (see section 3.3.4), that is, an output proportional to the variation in the resistance of the active gauge is obtained. To increase the sensitivity, two or four active gauges may be used, in which case the need to use dummy gauges is removed.

Example

An unbalanced Wheatstone bridge arrangement incorporating two active gauges is to be used to monitor the strain in a cantilever. If the unstrained resistance of each gauge is 120 Ω, the bridge is completed with two further 120 Ω resistors, and the gauges (which have a gauge factor of 2) are subject to a strain of 100 microstrain; calculate the output voltage from the bridge when it is supplied from a 10 V d.c. source.

Now the gauge factor is $(\delta R/R\epsilon)$ or $\delta R = 2 \times 100 \times 120/10^6$. Hence $\delta R = 0.024\ \Omega$. For an equal arm bridge with two active arms (increments of opposite sign)

$$V_{out} = V_{in} \left[\frac{R + \delta R}{(R + \delta R) + (R - \delta R)} - \frac{R}{2R} \right]$$

$$= V_{in} \frac{\delta R}{2R}$$

$$= \frac{10 \times 0.024}{240} = 1\ \text{mV}$$

This output signal of 1 mV is fairly typical of the signal levels encountered in operating strain gauges, and shows a possible amplification requirement.

Bridge Balancing

When strain gauges are used to form a bridge circuit it is unlikely that the bridge will be balanced in the zero or no-load condition. The unstrained gauges are unlikely to have exactly the same resistance; additionally, unequal strains are likely to occur when the gauges are mounted. It thus becomes necessary to add a

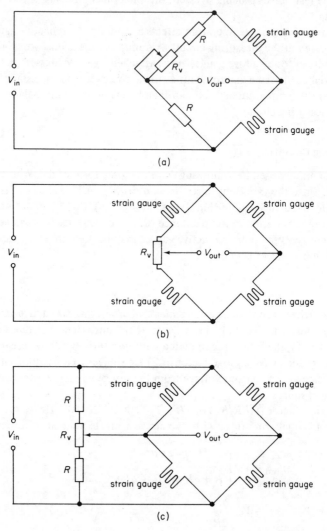

Figure 5.10. Strain gauge bridge balancing arrangements: (a) series balancing resistor, (b) apex balancing resistor, (c) parallel arm balancing

variable component to the bridge circuit so as to provide for this initial balance. Figure 5.10 illustrates some of the methods used for this purpose. The series resistance arrangement is only satisfactory if one or two strain gauges are being used, whereas the apex and parallel balancing arrangements are both suitable for use with two or four active gauge circuits. For the apex circuit R_v should be small, perhaps 10 to 25 per cent of the strain gauge resistance. However, for the parallel circuit if $2R + R_v$ is made too small a reduction in the sensitivity of the bridge results. Combining the parallel balancing network with an operational amplifier as shown in figure 5.11 produces a practical solution to the small signal and initial unbalance problems.

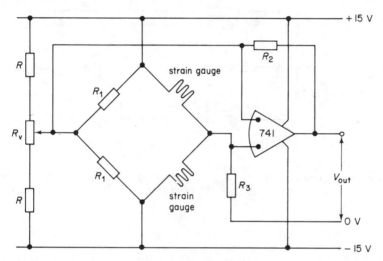

Figure 5.11. Two active arm strain gauge bridge with initial balance and amplification

Lead resistance

In many applications the measuring/display instruments will be remote from the active gauges, and the effect of the wires connecting the active gauges to the remainder of the circuit is equivalent to inserting a small resistance in series with it. This resistance will vary due to temperature effects and to reduce its influence additional connections as given in figure 5.12a and b are required and then, the lead resistances are approximately self-cancelling.

The above discussion of strain gauge measuring techniques has assumed that all methods use a d.c. supply. While the tendency is towards such methods due to the development of sensitive, drift free d.c. amplifiers, digital voltmeters and data logging system, the a.c. carrier system has not completely disappeared from use. The a.c. system had a considerable advantage in its stability of amplification, but stray capacitance and the need to balance its effect from the measuring circuits are a considerable disadvantage. Figure 5.13 illustrates the general principles involved in an a.c. carrier system of measurement.

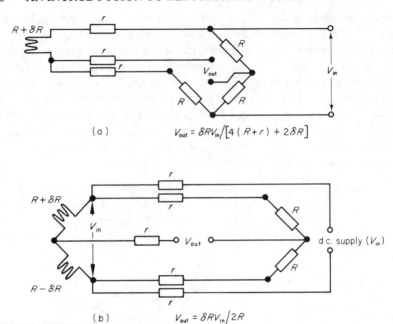

$$V_{out} = \delta R V_{in} / \left[4 \left(R + r \right) + 2 \delta R \right]$$

$$V_{out} = \delta R V_{in} / 2R$$

Figure 5.12. Arrangements for self-compensation of lead resistance: (a) single active gauge, (b) two active gauges

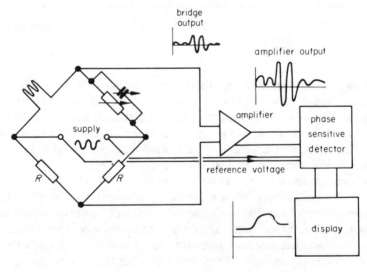

Figure 5.13. A.C. carrier system

Strain Gauge Attachment

In the majority of strain gauge applications it is necessary to attach the gauge to the test object by means of an adhesive. The thickness of the adhesive layer should be made small to avoid errors in transmitting the size changes in the test object to the strain gauge. This is best performed by using a clamp, curved metal plate, rubber pad and nonadhesive foil film as indicated in figure 5.14, the excess adhesive being squeezed out from under the centre of the gauge. An alternative

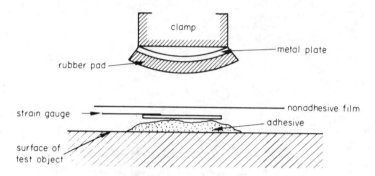

Figure 5.14. Clamping method of attaching strain gauges

method is to stick the gauge upside down to a piece of adhesive tape, then having aligned the gauge with its desired position, start at one end and press it firmly on to the test object. While satisfactory results are obtainable by using this method it is not as reliable as using a clamp. Having attached the gauge to the test object it may be desirable that the guage is covered with a waterproofing agent to prevent it from the effects of a moist environment. Waterproofing compounds are available for this purpose but many do not adhere to the PVC insulation of leads commonly used to connect the gauge to the measuring instrument. To overcome this difficulty clamps or crimped-on sleeves may be used over the connection leads.

Applications

The uses of resistance strain gauges are almost limitless but their direct uses may be summarised as applications involving the measurement of stress and strain in existing structures such as aircraft, railway wagons, bridges, cranes, reinforced concrete, automobiles, buildings, etc. It is usually necessary to investigate a large number of points and ease of attachment and connection is often a very important factor. This type of application of the resistance strain gauge is usually in connection with research or development investigations. They are also extensively used in sensors for monitoring, and in control systems, where they form the active part of a transducer.

5.1.4 Resistance Strain Gauge Transducers

To operate, a strain gauge transducer requires that the phenomenon under investigation shall first be converted into mechanical strain, that is, the gauge is attached to an elastic member within the transducer, which is subjected to a force proportional to the measurand. If the force is small, for example, as in the measurement of small pressure differences, an unbonded strain gauge system may be adopted where the strain gauge wire itself acts as the elastic member.

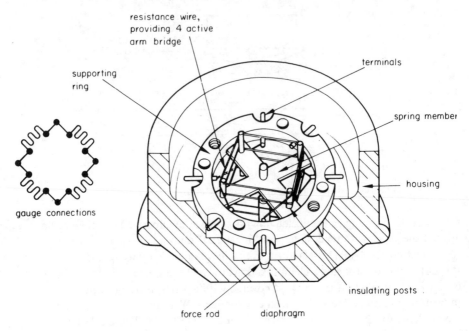

Figure 5.15. Unbonded strain gauge pressure transducer (courtesy of Bell & Howell Ltd)

Figure 5.15 shows such a sensing element, which may be incorporated in a wide range of pressure transducers simply by varying the area or thickness of the diaphragm that operates the force rod. This type of assembly contains four resistance strain gauges, two being relaxed and two stretched when a force is applied to the spring element. The four gauges are connected to form a Wheatstone bridge, unbalance in the bridge arms in the unloaded condition being compensated for during construction by the addition of small resistances in the appropriate arms. In a good quality unbonded strain gauge transducer, consistency of operation is ensured by temperature and pressure cycling during manufacture, the sensing unit being sealed in a container of dry helium, quality checks being conducted at each stage of manufacture of the transducer. The use of unbonded strain gauge transducers is not limited to pressure gauges—figure 5.16 illustrates its application in the construction of a seismic accelerometer. Since many physical

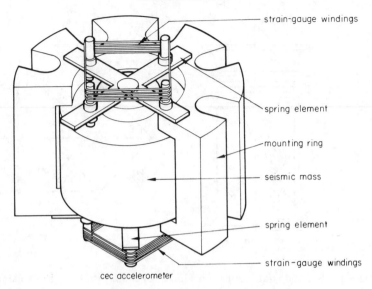

Figure 5.16. Unbonded strain gauge seismic accelerometer (courtesy of Bell & Howell Ltd)

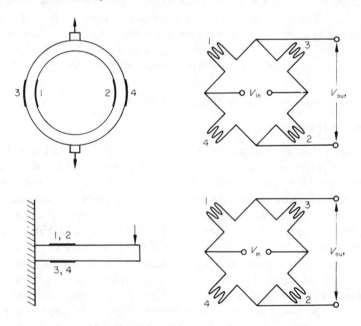

Figure 5.17. Some bonded strain gauge force transducers (load cells)

phenomena may be converted to a variation of force, a strain gauge element of the type shown in figure 5.15 could be incorporated into transducers to measure such properties as weight, temperature, humidity, flow and viscosity.

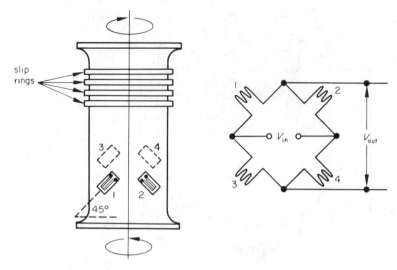

Figure 5.18. Bonded strain gauge transducer for the measurement of torsion in a shaft

The use of strain gauges in the construction of transducers is by no means limited to unbonded gauges;[4] common examples of the use of bonded gauges in transducer construction are in the measurement of force (load cells) figure 5.17 and torsion, figure 5.18. A more recent development has been the application of thin film techniques to the manufacture of transducers.[5]

5.1.5 Other Resistance Change Transducers

Resistance Thermometer

Some materials have a high temperature coefficient of resistance (α), and since the resistance (R_T) of such a material at a temperature T may be related to its resistance at $0\,^{\circ}$C by the expression $R_T \approx R_0 (1 + \alpha T)$ Ω, this property may be made use of in the measurement of temperature. Platinum resistance wire is normally used in the manufacture of resistance thermometers, which may be formed in a manner similar to a resistance strain gauge. Alternatively the resistance element may be housed in some form of sheath as shown in figure 5.19.

Resistance thermometers have high intrinsic accuracies, and they are used as an International Standard for comparing temperatures in the range 150–1100 K, and thus their major use is in laboratories where precise temperature measurements are important. However, in some industrial applications, for example, where high accuracy may be required or if signal amplification is undesirable, a platinum resistance thermometer may be used since these transducers exhibit approximately a 39 per cent change in resistance between 0 and 100 $^{\circ}$C. However, they are fragile, expensive, error producing when mishandled and have a long (0.5–10 s) response time (compared with thermocouples).

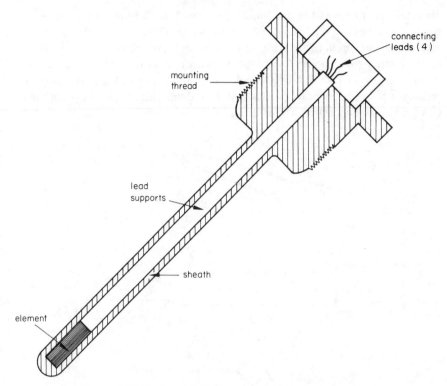

Figure 5.19. Industrial platinum resistance thermometer

The variations in thermometer resistance may be measured by

(a) some form of Wheatstone bridge circuit which may operated in a balanced or
     unbalanced mode
(b) using a specially developed resistance bridge,[6] or
(c) an inductively coupled ratio bridge of the type shown in figure 3.26.

The arrangements covered by (b) and (c) are all precision devices capable of
resolving temperatures to 0.0001 °C and their use is thus normally limited to the
standards laboratory.

Hot Wire Anemometers

For measuring air flow rate, a resistance change transducer consisting of a tungsten or platinum alloy wire through which a current is passed (see figure 5.20)
may be used. The magnitude of the current is sufficient to heat the wire, and
any movement of air over the wire will cool it and cause a change in resistance,
and a consequent change in the voltage drop across the wire. If this volt drop is
applied to an oscilloscope or u.v. recorder, a display or record of the air flow
variations is obtained. The hot wire is small (typically 1 mm long and 0.1 mm

diameter) and capable of responding to quite rapid fluctuations in flow. The greatest speed of response is obtained by using the constant temperature arrangement shown in figure 5.20c where a control unit incorporating a feed-back amplifier compensates for changes in the resistance of the hot wire (caused by the fluid flow), by varying the input level to the bridge and thus restoring the resistance of the hot wire to its initial value. In doing this the output voltage will be varied in a manner proportional to the air flow.

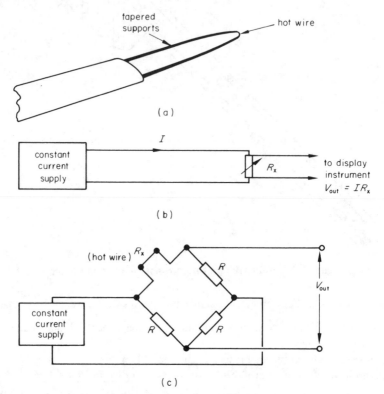

Figure 5.20. Hot wire anemometer and measuring circuits: (a) anemometer probe, (b) simple measuring circuit, (c) constant temperature operation

Humidity Gauges

Humidity is a measure of the amount of water vapour present in a gas. It may be described in a number of different ways, but the most widely used expression is in terms of *relative humidity* which is the ratio of water vapour pressure present in a gas-to-water vapour pressure required for saturation of that gas at the temperature of measurement. The ratio is usually expressed as a percentage (% r.h.), and is temperature dependent.

Resistive humidity gauges may be classified as belonging to one of two types.

One type is those having a resistive sensing element, that is, a variation in the ambient humidity causes a variation in the resistance of the element that is usually a mixture of a hygroscopic salt, for example, lithium chloride and carbon on an insulating substrate between metal electrodes as shown in figure 5.21. The other form of resistance change humidity gauge is one in which the length change with humidity of a human hair or strip of animal gut is used to operate a displacement sensor which could be either potentiometric or strain gauge.[7]

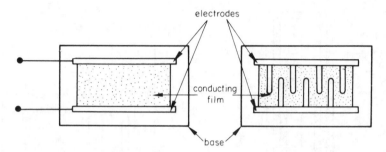

Figure 5.21. Resistive sensing element humidity transducers

5.2 REACTANCE CHANGE TRANSDUCERS

This is a group of transducers in which a displacement is used to modulate either a capacitive or inductive reactance. Since variations in reactance may only be measured when the supply is an alternating voltage (or current) the excitation source for reactance change transducers must be alternating. This may, however, make the transducer incompatible with the remainder of the measuring system, and to overcome this a number of reactance change transducers are manufactured with an internal d.c. to a.c. converter and an output demodulator so that both the transducer input and output are d.c. while the internal excitation is a.c.[1]

5.2.1 Capacitance Variation

It has been indicated that a change in almost any physical phenomenon may be converted to a displacement and as the capacitance between two parallel conducting plates is approximately proportional to $\epsilon A/d$, (where ϵ is the dielectric constant of the material between the plates of area A, separated by a distance d) varying any of these quantities will result in a change in the capacitance between the plates.

Variable dielectric

Figure 5.22 shows diagrammatically two types of dielectric variation transducer, one in which a dielectric sleeve is slid between coaxial electrodes to vary capacitance, the other being a device for measuring the height of a liquid in a container.

In both cases it is important that the dielectric constant of the material between the electrodes is substantially different from that of air so that an appreciable change in capacitance is obtained.

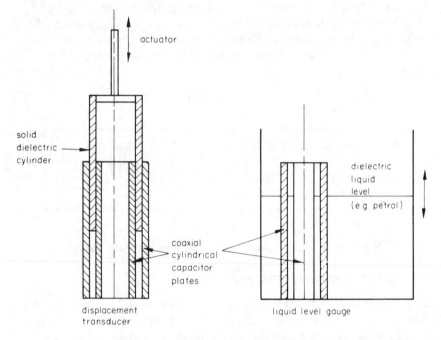

Figure 5.22. Variable capacitance transducers

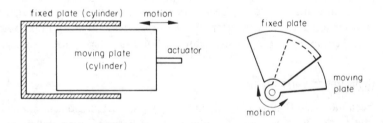

Figure 5.23. Capacitance transducers using plate area variation

Variable plate area

Transduction by variation of plate area may be performed by arrangements similar to those shown in figure 5.23, where linear or angular movement of the actuator causes one plate, or a set of plates, to vary the capacitance of the transducer.

Variable plate separation

The third form of variation, namely that involving a change in the electrode separation (see figure 5.24) is perhaps the most widely used for the construction of such devices and is comparatively simple, as the forces required to move one plate in relation to another may be made exceedingly small, and the alignment of

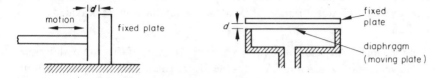

Figure 5.24. Capacitance transducers using plate separation

the fixed and moving parts may not be as critical as it is when some other forms of transducer are used. Figure 5.25 illustrates the use of this technique to produce a capacitance strain gauge, a major advantage of this being its potential use at elevated temperatures.[8,9]

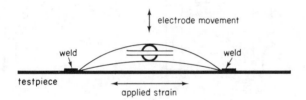

Figure 5.25. Capacitance strain gauge

Measuring techniques

The measuring circuitry associated with capacitance change transducers usually involves some form of bridge. The simplest form would have two resistive and two capacitive arms. A slightly more sophisticated form of bridge is shown in figure 3.28, where a ratio transformer is incorporated together with a resistance circuit to compensate for any leakage resistance effects associated with the capacitance of the transducer. Either circuit may be used in the balanced or un-balanced condition provided that for the latter mode of operation the unbalance is less than 10 per cent.

Some capacitance change transducers are produced with internal signal conditioning equipment which uses a d.c. input to supply an oscillator, for operation of the capacitance bridge, and conversion of the bridge output to d.c. Alternatively an oscillator circuit may be used so that a change in capacitance causes a change in output frequency.

5.2.2 Inductance Variation

The inductance of a coil depends on the manner in which magnetic flux links its turns, thus by using suitable 'measurand to displacement' converters to cause a change in the magnetic flux linkages in a coil, a series of transducers exhibiting a change in inductance proportional to the measurand may be obtained. This change in inductance can be measured either as an amplitude change in a bridge balance, or as a change of resonant frequency in an oscillatory circuit. The methods by which this variation of inductance (flux linkages) is obtained are as follows.

(a) By changing the reluctance (or magnetic resistance) of the flux path by the movement of an armature, so that the displacement may be either linear or angular (see figure 5.26) this being incorporated in transducers to measure such quantities as pressure, acceleration, force, and displacement or position.

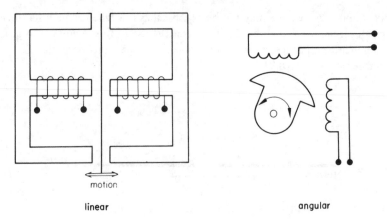

linear   angular

Figure 5.26. Variable reluctance transducers

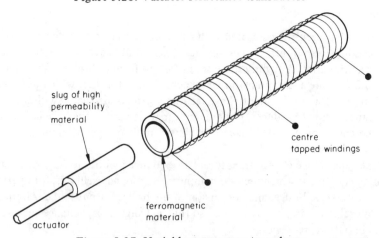

slug of high
permeability
material

centre
tapped windings

ferromagnetic
material

actuator

Figure 5.27. Variable permeance transducer

(b) By the displacement of a slug of material having a high magnetic permeance that is constrained to move inside a centre-tapped coil which is wound on a ferromagnetic core (see figure 5.27). When the slug is positioned centrally the inductance of the two halves will be equal; on movement to one side the inductance of one half will increase while that of the other decreases.

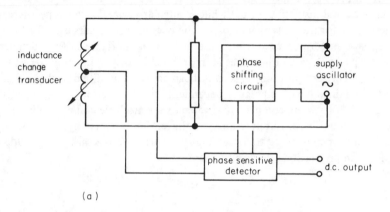

(a)

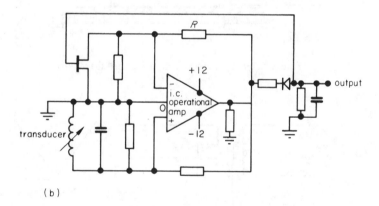

(b)

Figure 5.28. Inductive change transducer measuring circuits—arrangements for: (a) d.c. output, (b) frequency output

The inductor may form the arms of a bridge circuit, or be incorporated in an oscillator circuit (see figure 5.28a and b). The phase sensitive detector (see section 2.1.1) is included so that the d.c. output has a sign corresponding to the direction of the displacement. The phase shift circuit between the oscillator and the p.s.d. is necessary because at zero displacement there will be a phase angle between the reference voltage and the centre tap on the inductor (see also p. 316).

5.2.3 Linear Variable Differential Transformer (L.V.D.T.)

In this type of transducer, the change of inductance is a variation of mutal coupling between windings rather than a variation of self inductance. This variation of mutual inductance is obtained by the movement of a ferromagnetic core within a coil arrangement of the type shown in figure 5.29. There is usually one primary and two secondary coils. For a linear device the coils are wound on a nonmagnetic and insulating former while in angular devices of this type a ferromagnetic core for the coils may be used. The operational circuits used for the differential transformer range from those such as that in figure 5.30a which has an a.c. output voltage that increases in magnitude for displacement either side of the centre or zero position. This circuit can easily be modified so that a d.c. output is obtained having a polarity dependent on the direction of displacement (see figure 5.30b). More complex arrangements are available commercially, in which a d.c. input is converted to an a.c. voltage, that is, varied by the transducer operation and then restored to d.c. so that the output voltage has a magnitude and direction proportional to displacement.

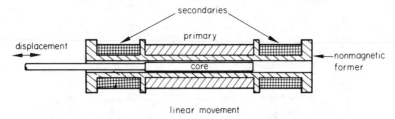

Figure 5.29. Linear variable differential transformer

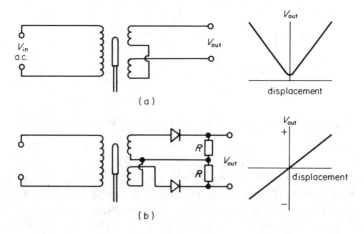

Figure 5.30. Operational circuits for use with differential transformer transducers

The differential transformer transducer is a durable, low impedance device, having little or no friction, and capable of measuring total, steady state, and dynamic displacements from 100 μm to 25 mm. It has become extensively used for measuring a wide range of quantities by positioning a suitable 'measurand to displacement' converter between the quantity and the differential transformer.

'Synchro'

A type of transducer used for the measurement and display of angular position or movement is the 'Synchro', in which two similar units are used, one termed the transmitter and the other the receiver. Each is constructed with a two-pole rotor and a stator having three windings distributed 120° apart (see figure 5.31).

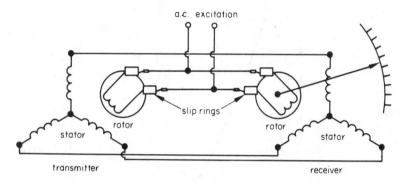

Figure 5.31. 'Synchro' measuring system

In operation the rotors of both units are fed, via slip rings, with an alternating current (usually 50 or 400 Hz) and if the rotors of the two units are in the same relative position to the stator windings no currents will flow between them. However, should the rotor of the transmitter be moved relative to its stator winding, the voltages induced in the two stators will be different and currents will flow in the connecting leads. These currents will produce a torque on the rotor of the receiver and cause it to move in sympathy with the rotor of the transmitter. The positioning accuracy of such a system is limited by the friction of the bearings in the receiver, and the calibration of the dial face attached to it.

5.3 SEMICONDUCTOR DEVICES

The electrical properties of semiconducting materials are affected by variations in temperature, illumination and force. The sensitivity of these semiconducting materials is very much greater than that of other materials, but this may introduce its own problems: for a semiconductor which, for example, is used in the measurement of strain may also be very temperature sensitive, and considerable additional circuitry will be required to compensate for such effects.

5.3.1 Thermistors

A very sensitive temperature transducer termed a thermistor may be manufactured by sintering oxides of such materials as manganese, nickel, cobalt, copper, iron, or uranium into tiny beads (0.1–2.5 mm diameter), then for protection, coated in epoxy resin or glass. Alternatively it may be mounted in an evacuated or gas filled bulb. Thermistors with resistance values of 10 Ω to over 100 MΩ may be obtained, and a typical thermistor will exhibit a *decrease* in resistivity of the order of 50 to 1 over a temperature range of 0 to 100 °C, and for the smallest versions can have a time constant of the order of 1 ms (see figure 5.32). The resistance variation is, however, exponential as opposed to the almost linear characteristics of a metallic resistance element.

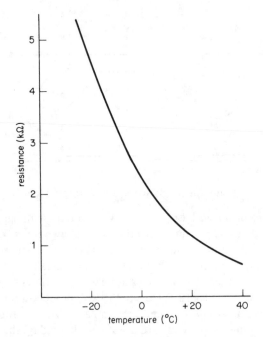

Figure 5.32. Resistance/temperature relationship for a thermistor with a negative temperature characteristic

A simple circuit would consist of a thermistor, a battery, and a microammeter calibrated in terms of temperature (see figure 5.33a) while a more sensitive arrangement would consist of a Wheatstone bridge arrangement (see figure 5.33b).

This latter type of circuit is capable of determining temperature differentials as small as 0.001 °C. For some applications the thermistor is superior to other temperature transducers, making possible measurements that were not practicable prior to their discovery. They are comparatively low cost devices.

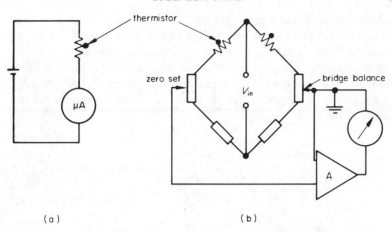

(a)   (b)

Figure 5.33. Circuits for measurement of temperature using thermistors

5.3.2 Semiconductor Strain Gauges

The materials used in the production of these devices are often termed piezo-resistive, meaning that when the gauge is subjected to a force there is alteration in the crystalline structure and a subsequent change in the electrical resistance. This variation in resistance is usually very much greater in a semiconductor than that obtained in a wire or foil strain gauge, and results in gauge factors of between 50 and 250 (+ or −) as opposed to the value of 2–3 for the resistance gauge. Typical semiconductor gauge arrangements are shown in figure 5.34, the gauge material normally being silicon, while the leads may be made from gold, silver, or nickel ribbon. Effective gauge lengths are typically between 2 and 7 mm.

Although the semiconductor strain gauge at first appears very attractive it does have severe drawbacks. First it is a nonlinear device: this effect may be reduced either by using heavily doped semiconductors, prestressing the strain gauge so that it operates over a linear portion of its characteristic, or by using compensation in the measurement circuit. The second major drawback is the effect of temperature variations on the semiconductor, for the temperature co-efficient of resistance materials used for these strain gauges is in the region of 60–100 times that of the materials used for resistance strain gauges. Therefore

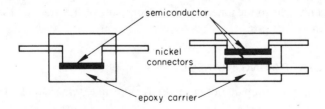

Figure 5.34. Semiconductor strain gauges

when semiconductor strain gauges are used, temperature compensation must be incorporated in the measuring circuit. This may take the form of a 'dummy' gauge (see section 3.3.4) or be obtained by connecting a thermistor with the appropriate temperature/resistance characteristics in series or parallel with the semi-conductor gauge, in each active arm of the bridge circuit (see figure 5.35) or by using a pair of gauges so that one is subject to a positive strain and the other a negative strain.

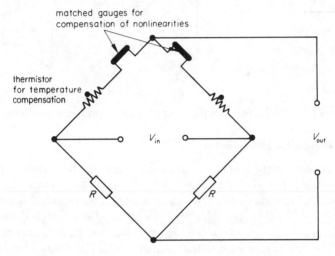

Figure 5.35. Semiconductor strain gauge bridge

5.3.3 Photodiodes and Phototransistors

The electrical characteristics of most diodes and transistors are affected by light, hence it is normal to prevent light from acting on the semiconductor junction of these devices, by enclosing it in a screening can or other opaque container. If this container is removed from a transistor (or diode) incident light falling on the junction will affect the output of the device. Photodiodes and phototransistors are constructed so that this normally undesirable property is enhanced.[3] The majority of light sensing semiconductors are silicon, but when optimum response in the infrared region is required germanium devices may be used. Both diodes and transistor are usually sealed in a metal can, there being a lens or window fitted to admit light to the junctions. Time constants of the order of 1 μs or less are common.

5.4 SELF-GENERATING TRANSDUCERS

Transducers in this group do not in theory require an external supply, for the electrical signal is produced either by the movement of a magnetic flux field in relation to a coil system, or by the application of force, heat or light to particular materials.

5.4.1 Electromagnetic Transducers

To provide self-generation the magnetic flux in electromagnetic transducers is usually derived from a permanent magnet, while the coil system may be air cored or wound on a core of ferrous material.

Linear velocity transducer

The simplest form of electromagnetic transducer is one in which a permanent magnet attached to an actuating shaft is free to move in a cylindrical coil, movement of the object/actuating shaft/magnet causing a voltage to be generated at the coil terminals; the magnitude of the voltage will be proportional to the velocity of the movement. A variation on this arrangement is shown in figure 5.36 where the permanent magnet is supported between springs, and fitted with low friction bearing rings. If such a transducer is attached to an object that is vibrating at a frequency in excess of the low natural resonant frequency of the transducer, the magnet would appear to an observer to be remaining stationary in space while the case and coil oscillate around it, resulting in an output volt-

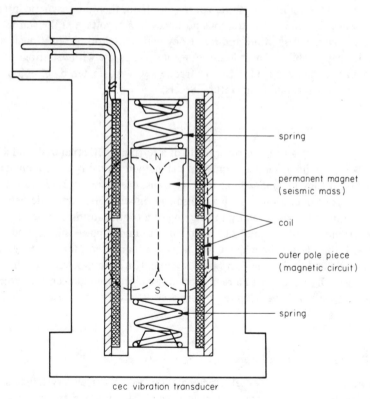

cec vibration transducer

Figure 5.36. Electromagnetic vibration transducer (courtesy of Bell & Howell Ltd)

age whose magnitude would be proportional to the amplitude of the vibration, with a frequency equal to that of the vibration. The relationships between sinusoidal displacement, vibration, and acceleration are shown in figure 5.4.

Instead of the magnet being the moving member it is possible for the coil to be moved, common examples being (a) some loudspeakers in which the coil has a linear movement, and (b) a moving coil instrument where the motion is rotary.

Angular devices

The use of transducers to determine angular motion has been widespread for many years, for it includes devices such as the d.c. tachometer or tachogenerator, in which the stator's magnetic field is derived either from a permanent magnet or from a separately excited field coil, while the rotor winding (armature) is of the form normally used in a d.c. generator fitted with a commutator. The output voltage of a tachogenerator is proportional to rotary speed (or angular velocity) it being about 5 V per 1000 rev/min for the permanent magnet tachometer, and around three times this value for the separately excited transducer. In both forms the polarity of the voltage is dependent on the direction of rotation.

If the rotor contains the permanent magnet field, then the magnetic interaction between it and the stator coils produces an a.c. voltage at the stator terminals having a magnitude and frequency which are both proportional to rotor speed. In many applications it is advantageous to operate with variations of frequency rather than voltage level, since frequency is unaffected by circuit impedance, loading, and temperature effects.

Toothed rotor tachometer

Tachometers using a toothed rotor made of a ferromagnetic material, and a transduction coil wound around a permanent magnet are probably the commonest form of frequency output angular velocity transducers. Figure 5.37 illustrates the principle of operation of such a transducer, in which the magnetic field surrounding the coil is distorted by the passing of a tooth causing a pulse of output voltage from the coil. If a multi-toothed rotor is used, a pulse is generated for each tooth that passes the magnet, and if six teeth are used the frequency of the output in Hz will be 6 x rev/min/60 or rev/min/10. The r.m.s. value of the output voltage will increase with a reduction in the clearance between the rotor and the pickup, with an increase in the rotor speed, and with an increase in tooth size.

5.4.2 Piezoelectric Transducers

These devices utilise the piezoelectric characteristics of certain crystalline and ceramic materials to generate an electrical signal. The piezoelectric effect was discovered by Pierre and Jacques Curie in 1880 when they found that by placing

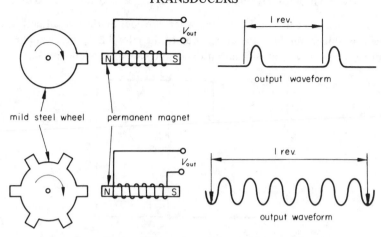

Figure 5.37. Operation of a toothed wheel tachometer

weights on to a quartz crystal an electrical charge could be generated. Subsequent researchers have shown that there are about 40 crystalline materials which when subjected to a 'squeeze' (the Greek word 'piezein' means to squeeze) generate an electrical charge. The Curie brothers also discovered the reverse effect, that is, a dimension change is obtained when an electric stress is applied to a quartz crystal.

The crystal materials are of two basic types, natural crystals and synthetic crystals, the latter type being mainly ceramic 'crystals' of which barium titanate was the first to be commercially used. The addition of controlled impurities such as calcium titanate was found to improve some of the 'crystal's' characteristics. Research on this and other synthetic 'crystals' has led to them being used more frequently than natural crystals in the production of piezoelectric transducers.

The force applied to the crystal may be that of shear, compression, or bending, depending on the particular application for which the transducer has been designed. The merits of operating the crystal with the various force modes will not be discussed here—they are described in detail in reference 1. It must, however, be remembered that since piezoelectric transducers belong to the self-generating category their use is predominantly in dynamic applications, a common form being as seismic accelerometers, although the piezoelectric principle may be effectively used in any situation where the measurand can be converted to a force that results in the stressing of a suitable crystal.

All piezoelectric crystals have a high output impedance, and for this reason the instrumentation to which the piezoelectric transducer is connected must have a high input impedance, or for most applications a charge amplifier (see section 6.7.1) must be connected between the transducer and the display instrument. A disadvantage is the additional expense involved. The equivalent circuit of a piezoelectric transducer is shown in figure 5.38, and this in practice may for simplicity be considered as a voltage source whose series impedance is a capacitor having a value of a few picofarads. The internal resistance (R_i) will normally exceed 20 GΩ and can thus be ignored when considering the overall performance of the transducer; similarly the effects due to the lateral inductance are beyond the upper frequency limit of the transducer and can also be ignored.

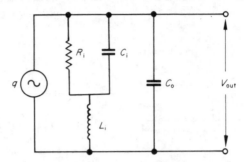

Figure 5.38. Equivalent circuit of a piezoelectric transducer

5.4.3 Thermoelectric Transducers

In 1822 John Seebeck reported that if a magnetic needle was held near a circuit made from conductors of two different materials, the magnetic needle was deflected when heat was applied to part of the circuit, thus implying the presence of an electric current. In 1834, a French watchmaker, Jean Charles Peltier, found that when a current was passed through a junction of two different conductors it changed temperature. In 1854 William Thompson (Lord Kelvin) discovered that if a current carrying conductor is heated at one point along its length, points at equal distances on either side of the heat source along the length of the conductor will be maintained at different temperatures, points on the negative potential side of the heat source being lower in temperature than those on the positive potential side.

Thermocouple

The Seebeck effect, which is a combination of the Peltier and Thompson effects, is utilised in what is probably the most widely used method of thermometry, namely the thermocouple.

These transducers consist of a pair of bars or wires of dissimilar metal joined at both ends: one end is used as the hot (sensing) junction, while the other end is used as a cold or reference junction, as shown in figure 5.39. The term thermo

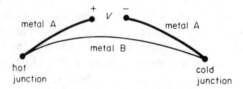

Figure 5.39. Basic thermocouple circuit (see also figure 2.44)

couple has through usage come to mean a single thermojunction, consisting of two lengths of dissimilar wire, insulated from each other but joined at one end. In conforming with this usage it becomes necessary to describe the combination of a 'hot' and 'cold' junction as a thermocouple circuit.

A suitable cold junction may be obtained by the use of melting ice, but such a reference is not always convenient or for that matter necessary; for example if a thermocouple is being used to measure a temperature that is of the order of 1000 K, variations of 5 °C or so in the temperature of the reference junction will have only a small effect on the accuracy of the measurement. Thus ambient air temperature may satisfactorily be used as a reference for some applications.

Output measurement

A thermocouple may be used as a voltage source, when its output should be measured by a high impedance instrument, for example, a digital voltmeter or a d.c. potentiometer, the displayed millivolts being dependent on the unknown temperature. Alternatively a low impedance instrument may be used to complete the circuit as in figure 5.40 when the magnitude of the current in the circuit will be dependent on the magnitude of the unknown temperature. When near ambient temperatures are to be measured with a thermocouple and it is inconvenient to use a fixed temperature reference junction, compensating circuits must be incorporated in the measuring system. One method of arranging auto-

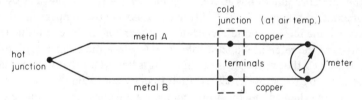

Figure 5.40. Commonly used thermocouple circuit

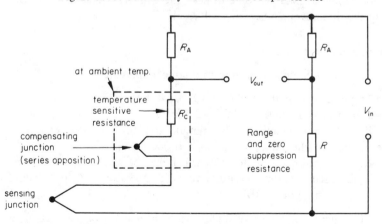

Figure 5.41. Thermocouple with bridge type compensation

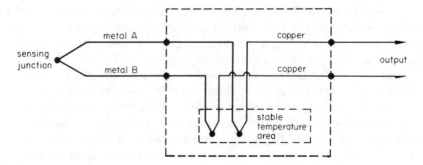

Figure 5.42. Thermocouple reference junction

matic compensation is shown in figure 5.41 where a temperature-sensitive bridge is included in the thermocouple circuit, such that variations in the ambient temperature level are compensated for by the changes in the resistance R_c and the compensating junction. Multi-channel thermocouple systems sometimes use a heated, thermostatically controlled reference junction (see figure 5.42) where by the use of regulated temperature control of the reference junction, a system accuracy of $\pm 0.3\,^{\circ}\text{C}$ may be maintained. When the reference junction is not held at $0\,^{\circ}\text{C}$, the observed value must be corrected by adding to it a voltage that would have resulted from a temperature difference equal to the amount by which the reference junction is above $0\,^{\circ}\text{C}$, that is $E_T = (E_t + E_r)$ where E_T is the total e.m.f. at temperature T, E_t is the e.m.f. due to the temperature differ-. ence between the sensing and reference junctions, and E_r is the e.m.f. due to the temperature of the reference junction above $0\,^{\circ}\text{C}$. Since the temperature–voltage characteristic of a thermocouple is nonlinear, it is important that temperatures are determined by the above process (rather than by converting an e.m.f. to a temperature and then adding this to the ambient temperature), also the reference junction should be maintained at, or near, the temperature used during calibration of the thermocouple or errors will result.

Thermocouple materials

The materials commonly used to form thermocouples are

Type T: copper–constantan 0–370 °C (270–640 K)
Type J: iron–constantan 0–760 °C (270–1030 K)
Type K: nickel/chromium–nickel/aluminium, 0–1260 °C (270–1500 K)
Type—: tungsten–rhenium, up to 2760 °C (3000 K) and
Type R: platinum–rhodium alloy 13% which may be used up to 1750 K, but is
        also used to define the International Temperature scale from 800–1340 K
        (see also reference 10)

The conductors of a thermocouple must be insulated from each other, and except at low temperatures, it has become the practice to use mineral insulation

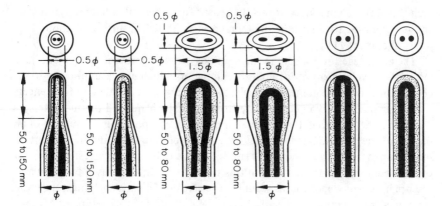

Figure 5.43. Hot junction shapes—mineral insulated metallic sheathed thermocouples (courtesy of Pye–Unicam Ltd)

and sheath the conductors and insulator with stainless steel. It is possible to
purchase thermocouples in a variety of sizes, from 0.25 mm to 3.0 mm dia., and
shape of sensing junction (see figure 5.43). In addition to this the locating of
the measuring junction is important, considerable care being necessary to ensure
that the temperature recorded is the unaffected temperature of the measuring
point.

When several thermocouples made from the same materials are connected in
series the hot junctions all being at one temperature and the cold junctions at
another, they are said to form a thermopile. The output voltage from a thermopile is equal to the output voltage from a single thermocouple multiplied by the
number of thermocouples in the thermopile assembly, provided that the materials
are connected in the correct sequence and the reference junctions are all kept at
the same temperature. If the thermopile is arranged in the configuration shown
in figure 5.44 so that the hot junctions are at the focal point of an optical system,

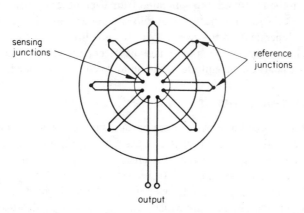

Figure 5.44. Thermopile formed into a radiation pyrometer

then the device so produced forms the sensor for a thermal radiation pyrometer, and may be used to determine the temperatures of heated surfaces without physical contact.[11]

The advantages of noncontacting methods of temperature measurement have led to the development of infrared thermometers which use vacuum thermocouples, metal film bolometers, or photodiodes as the detector of radiant energy. Such instruments vary in complexity from portable, hand held thermometers, which may be used to determine the temperature at a point on the surface of an object, to the sophisticated thermal imaging systems in which the focal point of measurement is scanned across the surface of the object under investigation. The output from the pyrometer head in this type of instrument is used to modulate the brightness of a spot that is scanning the screen of a c.r.t. enabling a 'television type' picture of temperature variations to be built up.[12] This type of equipment can be used to detect temperature differences as small as 0.1 °C and has many applications both in the industrial and medical fields.

5.5 ULTRASONIC TRANSDUCERS

These devices were originally developed using the magnetostrictive properties of ferromagnetic materials. This characteristic relates to the changes in shape of a ferromagnetic material caused by the variation in alignment of the domains when such a material is subjected to an alternating magnetic field. The phenomenon is reversible, that is, if a ferromagnetic material is extended and compressed in a regular manner an alternating voltage will appear at the terminals of a coil wound around it. This property is used in the construction of ultrasonic transducers[13] in, for example, underwater (sonar) detection.

The development of piezoelectric materials has resulted in a considerable extension of the use of the ultrasonic principle for many applications such as flow, thickness, fault detection and intruder detection systems. In general an ultrasonic transducer consists of two piezoelectric crystals, both in contact with the medium to be measured, but separated from each other by a short distance. One crystal acts as the transmitter of an ultrasonic pulse and the other receives it after a delay dependent on the geometry of the conditions in which the transducer is operating. By detecting the phase displacement between the transmitted and received signals the magnitude of measurand can be established.

5.6 DIGITAL TRANSDUCERS

True digital transducers are those whose output is represented by a number of discrete increments. The term is generally used, however, to include those devices which have a pulse output that can be applied to a digital counter. Examples of this latter type are the toothed rotor tachometer, and a similar effect obtained by using photoelectric transduction, for example, figure 5.45 where light shines through a segmented disc or plate which, when in motion, modulates the light falling on to the light sensor. The devices that generate a single pulse train can-

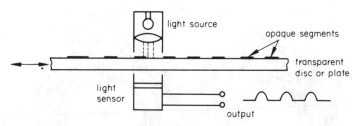

Figure 5.45. Photoelectric transducer for measurement of motion

not, in general, give an indication of direction, but this difficulty may be overcome for the toothed rotor tachometer by using two sensing heads positioned relative to each other so that their electrical outputs have a phase displacement that will be lagging or leading depending on the direction of movement of the rotor. In the case of the photoelectric transducer, determination of direction may be performed by the addition of a second track of opaque segments with its own illuminating sensor. A higher degree of resolution in photoelectric transducers may be obtained by using interference pattern techniques derived from the use of optical gratings.[3,14] A number of different pattern types exist, but the most widely known is the 'moiré' pattern. To obtain this a strip with alternate parallel opaque and transparent segments is moved past a similarly striped plate that is set at an angle to the moving plate. Positioning a line of light sensors on one side of the stripes and shining light through the stripes on to them results in a variation in the particular sensors illuminated, or obtains considerable variations in the sensor's output level with the movement of the striped strip. The outputs from such arrangements will approximate to a sinewave, the frequency of which will be dependent on the number of segments on the strips.

Digital encoder

The above transducers are all pulse producing devices, capable of detecting a change in the measurand rather than describing its absolute or unique state. In addition to this latter requirement a true digital transducer should have an output that is in a form suitable for direct entry into a digital computer or data handling system. This latter type of transducer is known as a digital encoder and may read continuously or be momentarily stopped to obtain a readout (depending on the design and code used). Encoders are generally an integral part of a more complex transducer, for example, a wind direction indicator.

While digital encoders may be made for linear applications, one of the commonest is the shaft position encoder. It consists of a disc or drum with a digitally coded scale which may be formed either from a combination of translucent and opaque segments, or a combination of conducting and insulating surfaces, which are coded so that there exists a unique form for each discrete position on the disc as shown in figure 5.46. Such discs are manufactured with diameters from 50 to 250 mm and give unique codes for between 100 and 50 000 positions per

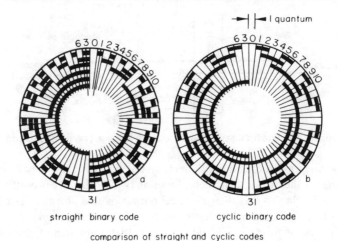

comparison of straight and cyclic codes

Figure 5.46. Shaft encoders (courtesy of Vactric Control Equipment Ltd)

360°. These coded positions are read either by a series of brushes or by a light source and sensor arrangement, and fed into an appropriate number of channels. The sequence and order of indications represent the shaft in the coded form. A special code known as the Gray code is commonly used in the operation of these devices.

REFERENCES

1 H. N. Norton, *Handbook of Transducers for Electronic Measuring Systems* (Prentice-Hall, Englewood Cliffs, N.J., 1970)

2 P. H. Mansfield, *Electrical Transducers for Industrial Measurement* (Butterworths, London, 1973)

3 G. A. Woolvet, *Transducers in Digital Systems* (Peter Peregrinus Ltd, Stevenage, Herts, 1977)

4 J. Vaughan, *Strain Measurement* (Brüel & Kjaer, Denmark, 1975)

5 A. L. Knight, The integrated strain gauge pressure transducer, *Transducer Technology*, **1**, 8 (1979) 14–16

6 J. L. Thomas, Precision resistors and their measurement, in *Precision Measurements and Calibration*, ed. F. L. Hermac and R. F. Dzruba, U.S. National Bureau of Standards Special Publication 300, Vol. 3, (1968) pp. 152–83

7 C. Watchorn, Relative humidity, *Cambridge tech. Rev.*, **2** (1968) 10–13

8 L. S. Phillips, A capacitance strain transducer for high temperature applications, 4th Transducer Conference, Wembley, 1978

9 H. Walton, Capacitance transducer applications, *Transducer Technol.*, **1**, 5 (1979) 14–19

10 BS 4937: 1973 International Thermocouple Reference Tables

11 H. D. Baker, E. A. Ryder and N. H. Baker, *Temperature Measurement in Engineering*, Vol. II (Wiley, New York, 1961)

12 D. F. Cassidy, Age of temperature monitoring by non-contacting methods, *Control Instrumn,* **4** (1972) 26-7

13 M. L. Gayford, *Electroacoustics* (Butterworth, London, 1970)

14 D. K. Ewing, Measurement of speed transients using optical gratings, N.E.L. Report No. 247 (1966)

6

Signal Conditioning

In many instances the values of electrical quantities (voltage, current and power) are too large or too small to be connected directly to the available instrument. It therefore becomes necessary to suitably reduce, or amplify, the magnitude of the measurand so that it has a value compatible with the measuring instrument to be used. In addition to these requirements, the effects of the instrument's impedance must always be considered for this may affect the value indicated for the measurand, (see p. 27). The disturbance resulting from the insertion of a measuring instrument should be minimal, that is to say the device used in measuring a current should have as low an impedance as possible, while for voltage measurement the requirement is a high impedance. In both cases the ideal instrument's performance will be independent of frequency.

The simple current and voltage situations do not, however, apply in every case. For example, sometimes it is necessary to ensure that the maximum amount of power contained in the output signal from a sensor is conveyed to a display or recording instrument, so as to obtain a maximum deflection; it is then necessary to match (see section 1.4.3) the output impedance of the signal source to the input impedance of the instrument.

6.1 VOLTAGE SCALING

Voltage dividers are an important aspect of scaling and have been mentioned in connection with the range extension of voltmeters and for use with, and within, potentiometers and multimeters. Voltage dividing resistors are sometimes confusingly termed potentiometers as an abbreviation of the term potential or potentiometric divider.

6.1.1 Resistance Divider

Resistance chain

The resistance chain is the simplest form of divider, the voltage division being due to the total voltage drop across the chain in comparison with the volt drop across the end unit. The chain may be connected in series with a pointer instrument (see figure 2.7) when the resistance of the measuring instrument forms part of the chain, or the measuring instrument is connected across the low voltage end of the divider. If the latter method of operation is used it is extremely important that the input impedance of the measuring instrument should be very much greater than the chain resistor across which it is connected, or a large error in the measurement will result. Consequently, this form of divider should only be used with potentiometers or electronic voltmeters which have a high input impedance. A further alternative, commonly used in electronic (both analogue and digital) voltmeters is that shown in figure 2.18 where the input voltage is connected across the whole chain and the high input impedance measuring circuits are switched across an increasing number of sections of the resistance chain as the sensitivity is increased.

All these voltage dividers are of course suitable for d.c. use, but may be used on a.c. provided they are pure resistance (see section 7.2.2), that is, the impedance remains constant irrespective of frequency. The range of d.c. voltages over which this type of divider is used is limited by power dissipation and earth leakage path resistance.

Kelvin–Varley divider

The Kelvin–Varley divider was mentioned in chapter 3 in connection with its use in potentiometers. It is an inherently more precise method of voltage division than the simple resistance chain and finds extensive application in the standards laboratory. Considering the Kelvin–Varley divider in detail, it is seen to consist of several decades of resistors interconnected as in figure 6.1. Each voltage division decade is made up of 11 equal resistors, successive division decades having a total resistance equal to twice the value of a unit resistor in the previous decade. For example, if in a four-decade divider the first decade is constructed using 11 × 10 kΩ resistors, the second decade will have 11 × 2 kΩ resistors, the next decade 11 × 400 Ω resistors and the fourth decade or final division will have 10 × 80 Ω resistors. The use of 11 resistors to obtain a decade voltage division enables the Kelvin–Varley divider to have a constant input impedance (strictly with the output open circuited) irrespective of which switch positions are connected on the various decades. For example, decade 3 will have a constant impedance of

$$9 \times 400 + \frac{2 \times 400 \times 10 \times 80}{800 + 800} = 4 \text{ k}\Omega$$

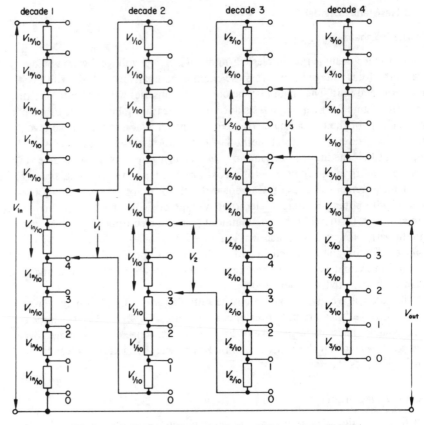

Figure 6.1. Kelvin–Varley resistive divider set to 0.4374

and decade 2 an impedance of

$$9 \times 2000 + \frac{2 \times 2000 \times 4000}{800} = 20 \text{ k}\Omega$$

and the input terminal impedance will be 100 kΩ irrespective of the decade switch positions (providing that the output current is small).

Another advantage of the Kelvin–Varley divider is the reduction of switch contact resistance effects due to the current sharing within the divider.[1] The drawbacks of the device are calibration (which can be simplified) and temperature distribution in the resistance chains (since all the resistors of a chain do not carry the same current they will not all operate at the same temperature). This latter effect can be reduced to negligible proportions by using resistors of low temperature coefficient, resulting in dividers with a total uncertainty of ± 1 part in 10^7.

6.1.2 Capacitive Divider

The voltage dividers so far described have been mainly applicable for d.c. and low frequency a.c. The capacitive divider is basically unsuitable for d.c. use, since voltage division would then rely on leakage current, but it may be used on a.c. from power frequencies to MHz. It consists of a chain (usually two in series) of capacitors, the voltage division being inversely proportional to the magnitudes

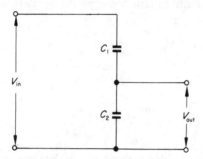

Figure 6.2. Capacitive divider

of capacitance. Figure 6.2 shows a capacitor divider consisting of a 100 pF capacitor in series with a 0.1 μF capacitor, the voltage ratio being

$$\frac{V_{out}}{V_{in}} = \frac{1}{1001} \qquad (6.1)$$

This form of divider is commonly used for high voltage applications when the small value capacitor is of the compressed gas type [2] and where the low voltage high value unit is a good quality mica capacitor. To obtain larger ratios a number of low value capacitors may be connected in series, hence increasing the impedance of the high voltage section. The frequency range and magnitude of voltage that can be scaled with such a divider will be limited by the leakage resistance of the capacitors and the errors introduced by stray capacitance. It cannot, of course, be used for direct voltages.

6.1.3 Resistance–Capacitance Divider

The high frequency limit of the resistance divider and the low frequency limit of the capacitive divider can be overcome by the combined R–C divider. The basic arrangement is shown in figure 6.3 the voltage ratio being

$$\frac{V_{out}}{V_{in}} = \frac{(R_2/j\omega C_2)/(R_2 + 1/j\omega C_2)}{\dfrac{R_2/j\omega C_2}{R_2 + (1/j\omega C_2)} + \dfrac{R_1/j\omega C_1}{R_1 + (1/j\omega C_1)}}$$

$$= \frac{R_2/(1 + j\omega R_2 C_2)}{\dfrac{R_2}{1 + j\omega R_2 C_2} + \dfrac{R_1}{1 + j\omega R_1 C_1}} \tag{6.2}$$

$R_1 C_1$ is the time constant of the R_1-C_1 combination and $R_2 C_2$ is the time constant of R_2-C_2 combination. If one component, say C_2, is adjusted, so that $R_1 C_1 = R_2 C_2 = T$ the uniform time constant can be rewritten as

$$\frac{V_{out}}{V_{in}} = \frac{R_2/(1 + j\omega T)}{\dfrac{R_2}{1 + j\omega T} + \dfrac{R_1}{1 + j\omega T}}$$

or

$$\frac{V_{out}}{V_{in}} = \frac{R_2}{R_1 + R_2} \tag{6.3}$$

showing that the voltage division is theoretically the same for all frequencies from zero to infinity. In practice the imperfections of components (see section 7.2) will commonly result in an upper frequency limit of several MHz.

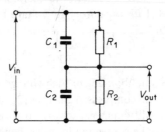

Figure 6.3. Resistance–capacitance divider

6.1.4 Inductive Divider

A ratio transformer or inductive divider provides a relatively inexpensive means of obtaining a division of alternating voltages with small uncertainties. The major application for such devices is in bridge circuits (see section 3.4.2) although their excellent performance has been used in other equipment requiring exact voltage ratios.

Principle of operation

The operation of a ratio transformer consists of obtaining a voltage division which is dependent on the number of turns in a tapped transformer winding, the transformer constructed so that its performance approaches that of an 'ideal' transformer (that is, no core loss, windings with perfect coupling and zero resistance). Then the voltage E appearing at the terminals of a transformer winding of N turns is

$$E = 4KN\Phi_m f \qquad (6.4)$$

where K is a constant depending on the waveform of the flux, which has a maximum value of Φ_m and f is the frequency of flux variations. Thus for given values of Φ_m, f and K

$$E = K'N \qquad (6.5)$$

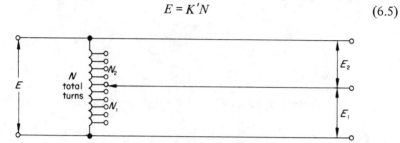

Figure 6.4. Tapped autotransformer

If the transformer in question is of the autotransformer type (figure 6.4), the division of the applied voltage E into E_1 and E_2 will be

$$E_1 = \frac{EN_1}{N} \quad \text{and} \quad E_2 = \frac{EN_2}{N}$$

assuming the transformer is ideal.

In practice the 'ideal' transformer cannot be constructed, but the ideals of perfect coupling, zero winding resistance and zero core loss can be approached. Consider the core loss: this may be reduced to negligible proportions by, firstly, selecting a core material which has the smallest magnetic hysteresis and eddy current losses possible at the intended frequency of operation, and second, constructing the core to have a minimum reluctance (that is absence of air gaps and use of the core material in its preferred grain direction, resulting in a toroidal clock spring core). To approach the ideal of perfect coupling requires that the magnetic flux produced by one turn should link all the others, that is a transformer with zero leakage flux. Fortunately a winding on a toroidal core has a very small leakage reactance, and this can be further reduced by using a high permeability core material and windings which take the form of a multiconductor rope (figure 6.5). If the multi-conductor rope has 10 wires, connecting successive sets of turns in series and taking a tapping from each joint to a terminal, a decade of voltage division is provided.

There remains only the problem of reducing the series resistance of the winding, the possibilities here are to use as large a copper cross-section as possible, and to use a core material such that the transformer has as high a Q as possible.

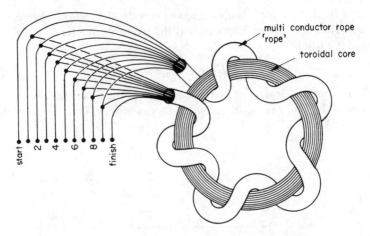

Figure 6.5. Tapped toroidal transformer winding

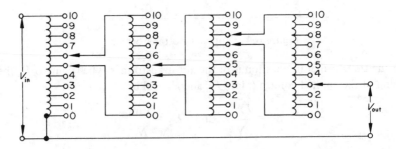

Figure 6.6. Four-decade ratio transformer, set to 0.5473

Using a series of autotransformers of this type, and interconnecting them using the Kelvin–Varley principle of voltage division (figure 6.6) an a.c. voltage divider[3] may be produced which has an accuracy of 1 part in 10^7 for considerably less cost than a resistance divider of the same accuracy of ratio. However, the maximum voltage that may be applied to an inductive divider is limited by the core cross-sectional area and is typically quoted as 200 V or 0.2 × frequency, whichever is the smaller.

6.1.5 Voltage Transformer

One of the commonest forms of voltage scaling used at power frequencies is the voltage transformer. This device is similar in construction (figure 6.7) to a power transformer (that is, concentric windings on a rectangular core), operating on a very light load. Its physical size is largely dependent on the insulation required to isolate the high voltage winding from the earthed core and the steel tank.

The voltage drop due to the secondary load (or burden) and the no load (or iron) losses both contribute to the errors in ratio and phase displacement which

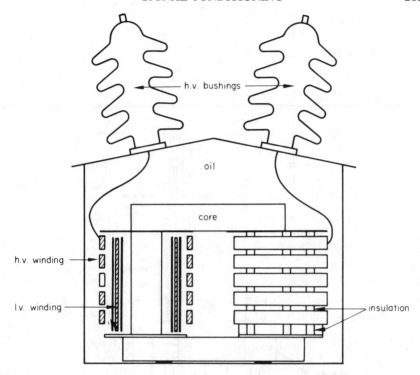

Figure 6.7. Outline drawing of a single phase double wound voltage transformer

exist between the primary (supply) and secondary (metering) terminals. One of the principle advantages of the voltage transformer (v.t.) is the electrical isolation of primary and secondary circuits allowing the high voltages of power circuits to be safely metered.

For very high voltages, 200 kV and above, the simple double wound v.t. is not a satisfactory arrangement due to the necessary physical size and cost of construction. The alternative arrangements are as follows.

(a) *The capacitor* v.t. (figure 6.8), which consists of a capacitance divider and a double wound step down v.t. that reduces the current taken by a meter circuit. The primary of the v.t. is in series with a reactor and connected across the low voltage capacitor. The values of inductance and capacitance of the various components are selected so that resonance occurs at the frequency of operation.

(b) *The cascade* v.t.[4] (figure 6.9), which breaks away from the two-winding principle in having the primary winding in several series connected sections stepping down the high voltage in stages thereby reducing the amount of insulation between the primary winding and the cores that are electrically connected to the primary winding at intervals down its length. The secondary winding is only wound on to the lowest potential core, but coupling

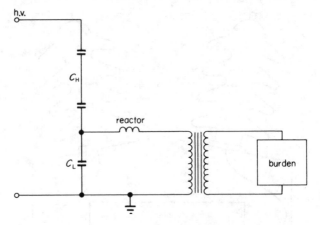

Figure 6.8. Capacitor voltage transformer

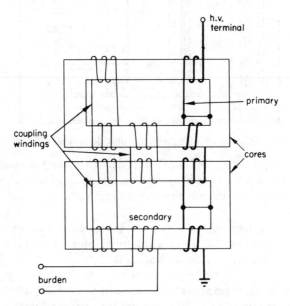

Figure 6.9. Principle of the cascade connected voltage transformer

windings must be incorporated between each limb of the core to ensure a balance of ampere turns in each stage when current is flowing in the meter or burden circuit. These coupling windings also assist in reducing leakage reactance between the primary and secondary circuit to a minimum. The complete cascade v.t. is built into a porcelain housing; a unit for operation with a primary voltage of 400 kV would have six stages.

It has been stated above that the secondary output voltage will be slightly different both in magnitude and phase from the desired or ideal value. This is of extreme importance in metering, for if the power supplied to a load is measured by a circuit incorporating a v.t., errors in it will affect the power meter readings and result in a consumer being incorrectly charged. Thus it is important to have a knowledge of these errors so that compensation or allowance may be made for them.

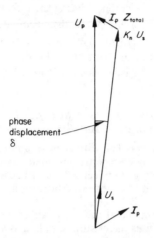

Figure 6.10. Simplified phasor diagram of a voltage transformer (not to scale)

Consider the simplified phasor diagram for a v.t. as shown in figure 6.10. The difference in magnitude between the primary voltage (U_p) and the rated transformation ratio (K_n) multiplied by the secondary voltage (U_s) depends on the primary current and the total effective winding impedance (Z_{total}) of the transformer. Thus it is desirable that these quantities are kept to a minimum.

The British Standard on voltage transformers (BS 3941: 1975) defines the voltage error (ratio error) as

$$\frac{(K_n U_s - U_p) \, 100}{U_p} \ \% \qquad (6.6)$$

where U_p is the actual primary voltage and U_s the actual secondary voltage when U_p is applied under the conditions of measurement.

Further inspection of figure 6.10 will show a small phase angle (δ) between U_p and U_s and in BS 3941 this is defined as the phase displacement which, by convention, is considered to be positive if the phasor (vector) of U_s leads the phasor (vector) of U_p. It is apparent also from the phasor diagram that the magnitude and the phase angle of the primary current I_p will affect both the ratio and phase angle errors.[5] Now I_p has two components, I_0 the no-load current of the transformer, and I_s' the referred secondary or load current; therefore, the load or burden connected to the secondary terminals will affect the v.t. errors. Thus a v.t. rating plate will stipulate primary and secondary voltages and the rated burden. This latter quantity will be in VA (that is, the product of secondary voltage and current) and indicate the output at rated voltage. The phase angle of the secondary load on a v.t. will normally be very small since a voltmeter or the voltage coil of a wattmeter is predominantly resistive. However, should an inductive load be applied to a v.t. the ratio error will be increased and the phase displacement, which is normally negative, may become positive.

Golding and Widdis[2] give graphs relating the effect of burden and applied voltage variations on ratio error and phase displacement, for a voltage transformer.

The determination of voltage (ratio) and phase errors may be performed either as an absolute measurement or in terms of the known errors of a high quality v.t. [2,5] The classification of v.t.s by their magnitude of error is stipulated in BS 3941 as shown in table 6.1.

Table 6.1. Extracted from BS 3941: 1975 Specification for voltage transformers (Reproduced by permission of the British Standards Institution)

Measuring voltage transformers. The voltage error and phase displacement, at rated frequency, of measuring voltage transformers shall not exceed the values given in the table at any voltage between 80% and 120% of rated voltage and with burdens of between 25% and 100% of rated burden, at a power factor of 0.8 lagging.

The errors shall be determined at the terminals of the transformer and shall include the effects of any fuses or resistors supplied as an integral part of the transformer.

Limits of voltage error and phase displacement for measuring voltage transformers

Accuracy class	Percentage voltage (ratio) error	Phase displacement	
		Minutes	Centiradians
0.1	± 0.1	± 5	± 0.15
0.2	± 0.2	± 10	± 0.3
0.5	± 0.5	± 20	± 0.6
1.0	± 1.0	± 40	± 1.2
3.0	± 3.0	not specified	not specified

Example

A single phase 11 000/110 V, 5 VA, 50 Hz transformer is to be used to monitor an appropriate voltage. If the input resistance of the voltmeter is 10 kΩ, what magnitude of resistor should be connected in parallel with the voltmeter so that the instrument transformer operates with its correct burden?

Required burden is 5 VA. Therefore

$$\text{resistance of load on secondary} = 110/(5/110) = 2420 \ \Omega$$

$$\text{magnitude of parallel resistance} = \frac{2420 \times 10\,000}{10\,000 - 2420} \ \Omega$$

$$= 3192.\,6 \ \Omega$$

6.2 CURRENT SCALING

The majority of current measuring instruments are only capable of measuring directly milliamperes or at the most a few amperes, the exceptions being some dynamometer ammeters and moving iron ammeters which are specially constructed to measure currents of the order of 100 A. Since currents of several thousands of amperes are used in many applications current scaling and voltage scaling are of equal importance.

6.2.1 Current Shunts

Current shunts have already been mentioned in connection with moving coil multi-meters (see section 2.1.2), and the use of a potentiometer, both of which with the aid of shunts may be used for measuring large direct currents. The use of current shunts is, however, not limited to d.c. provided that a shunt used for alternating current measurements is nonreactive. Its principal disadvantages are power consumption and the fact that the metering current must be operated at the same potential to earth as the current carrying line and therefore limits its use to low voltage applications.[6,7,8]

Four-terminal Shunts

A current shunt (figure 6.11) is in general a four-terminal resistance the current to be measured being connected to the current terminals. The potential terminals are arranged so that an accurately known resistance and voltage drop exists between them, and situated so that they are unaffected by any heating which may occur at the current terminals.

The application of current shunts lies in the extension of ammeter range (where the volt drop across the shunt drives a proportion of the current through the ammeter); measurement of current by potentiometer; recording of current wave-forms and the measurement of low voltage power. It should be appreciated that with the increasing use of electronic measuring instruments with a high input resistance, the measurement of current as a voltage drop across a known resistance is tending to become a much used method of measurement.

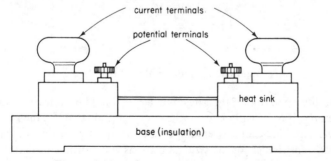

Figure 6.11. A four-terminal current shunt

Universal Shunt

This is a device that may be incorporated into a galvanometer as a sensitivity control and is very useful when such an instrument is used as a null detector. Probably a wider use is in providing current ranges in multi-meters (see section 2.1.2). Figure 6.12 shows the basic arrangement for a universal shunt of resistance R shunting a galvanometer of resistance R_g. With the switch on contact a, the galvanometer current

$$I_g = \frac{R_1}{R + R_g} I \qquad (6.7)$$

and if $R \gg R_g$

$$I_g = \frac{I}{1000}$$

Similarly with the switch at point b

$$I_g = \frac{I}{100}$$

at point c

$$I_g = \frac{I}{10}$$

and at point d

$$I_g = I$$

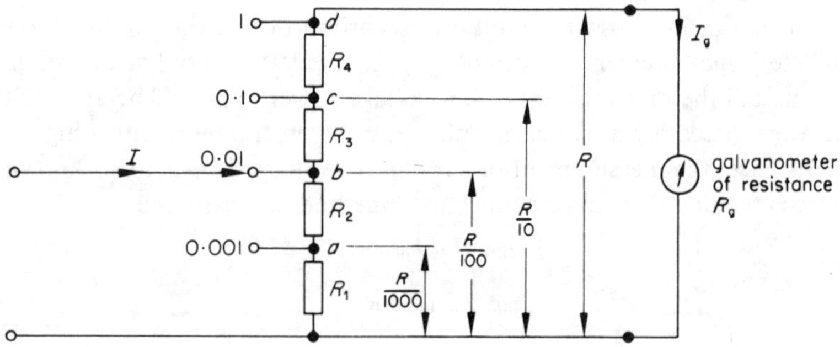

Figure 6.12. Universal shunt

For satisfactory operation of the galvanometer, R should be at least 10 times greater than R_g. If R is nearly equal or less in magnitude than R_g the galvanometer movement will become overdamped, but irrespective of this the ratio of galvanometer sensitivities for the switch positions will remain constant. Let $R_g = R$, then for position a

$$I_g = \frac{I}{2000}$$

for position b

$$I_g = \frac{I}{200}$$

for position c

$$I_g = \frac{I}{20}$$

for position d

$$I_g = \frac{I}{2}$$

Thus the universal shunt increases the versatility of a galvanometer and may also enable it to be used as a multi-range milliammeter. Its use is primarily for direct currents but, provided its resistance is nonreactive, it may be used for low frequency a.c.

Example

Determine the components of a universal shunt arrangement which would provide ranges of 1 mA, 500 μA, 200 μA and 100 μA when used with a moving coil microammeter that has a full scale deflection of 50 μA and a resistance of 10 kΩ.

The general circuit arrangement for the shunt in this example will be the same as that shown in figure 6.12 although the operating conditions, and therefore the ratios, will be different.

Firstly, consider the condition when the input is connected to terminal d. This will be the most sensitive range, so applying the *current division* principle

$$I_g = \frac{R}{R + R_g} I$$

or

$$50 = \frac{R}{R + 1000} 100$$

giving

$$R = 1000 \ \Omega$$

With the input connected to c

$$I_g = \frac{(R - R_4)}{R + R_g} I$$

$$50 = \frac{(1000 - R_4)}{2000} \; 200$$

Therefore

$$R_4 = 500 \; \Omega$$

With the input connected to b

$$50 = \frac{(1000 - 500 - R_3)}{2000} \; 500$$

so

$$R_3 = 300 \; \Omega$$

Similarly R_2 and R_1 are calculated giving a universal shunt made with the following resistance values

$$
\begin{aligned}
R_1 &= 100 \; \Omega \\
R_2 &= 100 \; \Omega \\
R_3 &= 300 \; \Omega \\
R_4 &= 500 \; \Omega
\end{aligned}
$$

6.2.2 Current Transformers

The current transformer (c.t.) overcomes the power loss and circuit isolation problems of the current shunt, but like the v.t. introduces ratio and phase displacement errors.

Alternating Current Transformers

The construction of a current transformer, figure 6.13, is different from that of a power transformer although the basic theory of all transformers is the same, that is (a) the voltage induced in a transformer winding is proportional to $N\Phi_m f$, where N is the number of turns in the winding, Φ_m is the flux in the core and f the frequency of operation, and (b) the ampere turns of the windings balance. It is the latter feature which is exploited in the design of a current transformer, where to ensure that the current ratio approaches the inverse of the turns ratio the no-load or magnetisation current is made as small as possible. This is attained by using a toroidal core wound from a continuous strip of high permeability steel. The primary winding is commonly a single turn (referred to as a bar primary) but may consist of a tapped winding to produce a multi-ratio c.t. The secondary winding, rated at either 1 or 5 A, will have many turns tightly wound on to the core.

To investigate the current error (ratio error) and phase displacement for a current transformer[2,5] consider the simplified phasor diagram in figure 6.14. It may be seen that the difference in magnitude between the primary current I_p

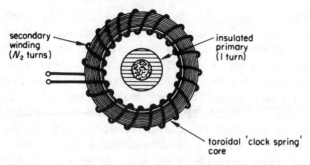

Figure 6.13. Current transformer with a 'bar' primary

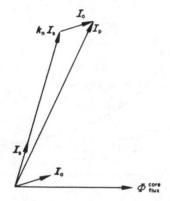

Figure 6.14. Simplified phasor diagram of a current transformer (not to scale)

and the secondary current multiplied by rated transformation ratio $(I_s K_n)$, is dependent on the amount of the primary current used to energise the core and this must therefore be kept to a minimum. It should be noted that a c.t. is operated with a load consisting of an ammeter which almost short circuits the secondary terminals; should this load be open circuited the whole of the current in the primary winding will become energising current, causing magnetic saturation of the core (which is detrimental to its magnetic properties), and causing a large peaky voltage to occur at the secondary terminals which may result in failure of the interturn insulation, apart from being dangerous to the operator. Thus it is important *never* to open circuit a.c.t.

The British Standard specification relating to current transformers (BS 3938: 1973) defines *current error (ratio error)* as

$$\frac{(K_n I_s - I_p)}{I_p} \times 100 \% \tag{6.8}$$

where K_n is the rated transformation ratio, I_s is the secondary current and I_p the primary current. *The phase displacement* is defined as the displacement in phase between the primary and secondary current vectors (phasors), the direction of the phasors being so chosen that the angle is zero for a perfect transformer. The phase displacement is said to be positive when the secondary current phasor leads the primary current phasor, and negative when it lags behind the primary current phasor; it is usually expressed in minutes or in centiradians.

A current transformer connected in the supply line to a power load will be required to operate over current values from no load ($I_p = 0$) to full load (I_p = rated value); it is therefore important to have some knowledge of how the variation of primary current will affect the current and phase displacement errors. Figure 6.15 indicates the characteristic shape of these variations, the increasing slope at low currents being due to the changes in permeability of the core material for very low flux densities.

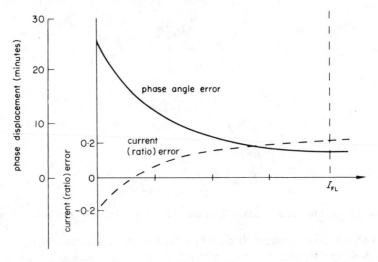

Figure 6.15. Typical error characteristics of a current transformer

The *burden* of a c.t. is the value of the impedance of the secondary circuit expressed in ohms (or in volt-amperes at the rated current) at the relevant power factor; a common value is 15 VA, which for a c.t. with a secondary rated at 5 A requires that the secondary terminal voltage is 3 V and the external impedance is 0.6 Ω, for operation at correct burden.

At very high voltages, the insulation of the current carrying conductor from the measuring circuits becomes an expensive problem. At 750 kV a successful solution has been the use of a cascade connected c.t. Alternatively a U.S. system uses a coaxial shunt to modulate an r.f. signal that is transmitted from the shunt (in the h.v. line) to receiving equipment on the ground, thus overcoming the insulation problems. This type of system has a severe limitation in its power output which must be amplified to operate relays, etc.

As with v.t.s the classification of c.t.s is decided by the magnitude of error and the extract from BS 3938 in table 6.2 shows the usage of c.t.s with various tolerances.

Table 6.2. Extracted from BS 3938: 1973 Specification for current transformers (Reproduced by permission of the British Standards Institution)

Class	± Percentage current (ratio) error at percentage of rated current shown below			± Phase displacement at percentage of rated current shown below (minutes)		
	10 up to but not incl 20	20 up to but not incl 100	100 up to 120	10 up to but not incl 20	20 up to but not incl 100	100 up to 120
0.1	0.25	0.2	0.1	10	8	5
0.2	0.5	0.35	0.2	20	15	10
0.5	1.0	0.75	0.5	60	45	30
1	2.0	1.5	1.0	120	90	60

Limits of error for accuracy Class 3 and Class 5

Class	± percentage current (ratio) error at percentage of rated current shown below	
	50	120
3	3	3
5	5	5

Note: Limits of phase displacement are not specified for Class 3 and Class 5.

Selection of class of accuracy of measuring current transformers

Application	Class of accuracy
(1) Precision testing, or as a standard for testing other current transformers	0.1
(2) Meters of precision grade in accordance with BS 37	0.2
(3) Meters of commercial grade in accordance with BS 37	0.5 or 1.0
(4) Precision measurement (indicating instruments and recorders)	0.1 or 0.2
(5) General industrial measurements (indicating instruments and recorders)	1 or 3
(6) Approximate measurements	5

Direct Current Transformers

A direct current transformer[9] would perhaps be more suitably named a direct current transducer as an alternating power supply is required for it to be able to function.

In its simplest form the direct current transformer consists of two identical saturable reactors with a common primary and secondary windings connected in series opposition, as shown in figure 6.16. As with conventional current transformers a bar primary is often used, the secondary or reactor windings being

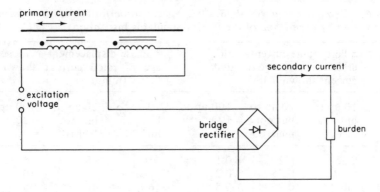

Figure 6.16. Basic direct current transformer circuit (after ref. 9)

toroidally wound on high permeability magnetic alloy. The presence of a direct current in the primary winding will cause the reactors to saturate and in consequence have a low impedance. The application of an alternating excitation voltage to the secondary circuit will alter the saturation level in the cores, and in a given half cycle one reactor will be forced further into saturation, its impedance thus remaining low. In the other reactor the magnetising forces will oppose, the core come out of saturation and the impedance of this reactor increases. During the other half cycle the roles of the reactors will be reversed. This action results in a secondary current which approaches a square waveform with an amplitude proportional to the direct primary current. After rectification a direct voltage wave with a characteristic 'notch' is obtained.

Under the above operating conditions the applied magnetising forces due to primary and secondary currents are in balance and

$$\text{primary ampere turns} = \text{secondary ampere turns}$$

That is

$$I_p N_p = I_s N_s$$

Assuming $N_p = 1$, $I_s = I_p/N_s$. So, as for the alternating current transformer, the current ratio is the reciprocal of the turns ratio.

Resin encapsulated units with primary current ratings between 50 and 10 kA are available from one manufacturer.[9]

6.3 ATTENUATORS

The term attenuator is often loosely used to denote a device which reduces the voltage and/or power conducted between the circuits connected to its input and output terminals; such an interpretation of the term may be applied to all the devices discussed so far in this chapter. A purer interpretation restricts the use of the term to apply only to those dividers which are constructed so that, as well as providing the reduction in voltage or power, the impedance of the divider is matched to the input and output circuits, and for a multi-ratio attenuator these impedances are constant irrespective of ratio setting.

It should be noted that the attenuation, A, is normally quoted as a power ratio in terms of decibels, that is

$$A = 10 \log_{10} \frac{P_s}{P_L} \text{ dB} \tag{6.9}$$

or

$$A = 20 \log_{10} \frac{V_{in}}{V_{out}} \text{ dB (provided } R_s = R_L) \tag{6.10}$$

Alternatively, the attenuation may be expressed in nepers (Np) when

$$A' = \log_e \frac{I_s}{I_L} \text{ Np} \tag{6.11}$$

This latter expression is commonly used in theoretical work. Now if $R_s = R_L$, then the attenuation in dB is

$$A = 20 \log_{10} \frac{I_s}{I_L} \text{ dB} = 8.686 \times \text{ attenuation in Np}$$

Conversely, attenuation in Np = 0.1151 × attenuation in dB.

6.3.1 Resistance Attenuators

Basic Attenuator Pad

Figure 6.17 shows a simple form of resistance attenuation pad for which $R_s = R_{in}$, $R_L = R_{out}$, V_{in} is the input voltage and V_{out} the output voltage. Let the attenuation be $20 \log_{10} k$, where

$$k = \left(\frac{P_s}{P_L} \right)^{\frac{1}{2}} = \left(\frac{I_s^2 R_s}{I_L^2 R_L} \right)^{\frac{1}{2}} \tag{6.12}$$

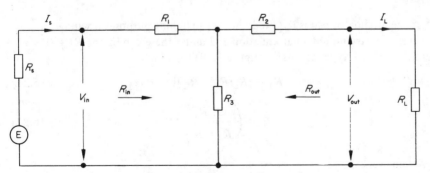

Figure 6.17. Resistance attenuator pad

Now the network equations are

$$R_{in} = R_s = R_1 + \frac{R_3 (R_2 + R_L)}{R_2 + R_3 + R_L} \qquad (6.13)$$

$$R_{out} = R_L = R_2 + \frac{R_3 (R_1 + R_s)}{R_1 + R_3 + R_s} \qquad (6.14)$$

$$\frac{I_s}{I_L} = \frac{R_2 + R_L + R_3}{R_3} \qquad (6.15)$$

From equations 6.12, 6.13, 6.14 and 6.15 it can be shown that

$$R_1 = R_s \left(\frac{k^2 + 1}{k^2 - 1} \right) - 2 (R_s R_L)^{\frac{1}{2}} \left(\frac{k}{k^2 - 1} \right) \qquad (6.16)$$

$$R_2 = R_L \left(\frac{k^2 + 1}{k^2 - 1} \right) - 2 (R_s R_L)^{\frac{1}{2}} \left(\frac{k}{k^2 - 1} \right) \qquad (6.17)$$

$$R_3 = 2 (R_s R_L)^{\frac{1}{2}} \left(\frac{k}{k^2 - 1} \right) \qquad (6.18)$$

See appendix III and reference 10.

Symmetrical T Attenuators

If the load and source impedance are equal the T attenuator will become symmetrical and

$$R_1 = R_2 = R_L \left(\frac{k - 1}{k + 1} \right) \qquad (6.19)$$

$$R_3 = \frac{2R_L k}{k^2 - 1} \qquad (6.20)$$

If the attenuator pad is required only for matching purposes it will be arranged to have minimum attenuation and under these conditions $R_2 = 0$ resulting in an L type attenuator (figure 6.18) for which

$$R_1 = [R_s (R_s - R_L)]^{\frac{1}{2}} \qquad (6.21)$$

$$R_3 = \left(\frac{R_s R_L}{R_s - R_L} \right) \qquad (6.22)$$

π Attenuators

Another common form of attenuator is the π type (figure 6.18) which, when used for matching, requires

$$R_1 = R_s \left[\frac{k^2 - 1}{k^2 - 2k \left(\frac{R_s}{R_L} \right)^{\frac{1}{2}} + 1} \right] \qquad (6.23)$$

$$R_2 = \frac{(R_s R_L)^{\frac{1}{2}}}{2} \left(\frac{k^2 - 1}{k} \right) \qquad (6.24)$$

$$R_3 = R_L \left[\frac{k^2 - 1}{k^2 - 2k \left(\frac{R_s}{R_L} \right)^{\frac{1}{2}} + 1} \right] \qquad (6.25)$$

and for attenuation alone, that is when $R_s = R_L$

$$R_1 = R_3 = R \left(\frac{k + 1}{k - 1} \right) \qquad (6.26)$$

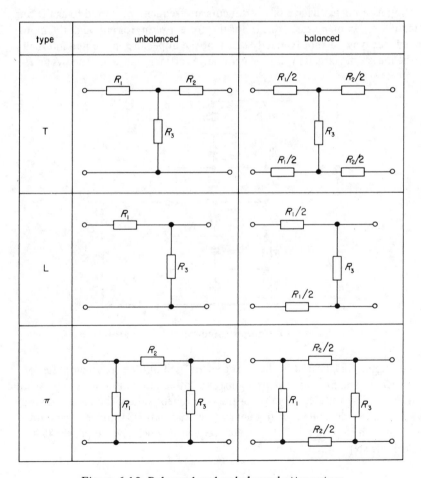

Figure 6.18. Balanced and unbalanced attenuators

and

$$R_2 = R \left(\frac{k^2 - 1}{2k} \right)$$ (6.27)

Balanced Attenuators

The above attenuators have all been unbalanced and in some applications it is desirable that the legs of the circuit should be balanced. This is simply arranged by dividing the series arm in half and placing the equal halves in each leg (see figure 6.18).

Resistance attenuators of this form may be used from d.c. to several hundreds of MHz. For higher frequencies wave guide devices are used.[11]

6.3.2 Instrument 'Input Attenuators'

The input or range dividers of instruments are frequently referred to as the 'input attenuators'. In many cases this is not the correct term, for although the input impedance may be approximately constant the impedance presented internally to the measuring circuits will vary with range setting. Figure 6.19 shows an R–C

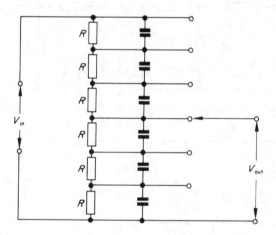

Figure 6.19. Compensated range 'attenuator'

'input attenuator', typical of the arrangement used in the vertical amplifier of oscilloscopes and in the sensitivity control of other alternating voltage measuring instruments. By suitable selection of the component values, the voltage division may be made independent of frequency (see section 6.1.3), and is commonly arranged with steps in a 1, 2, 5, 10, etc., sequence which gives approximately logarithmic steps in sensitivity.

6.4 FILTERS

A detailed description and analysis of filters is beyond the scope of this book, but H. Y-F. Lam[12] provides much useful information. Here we shall restrict ourselves to a general outline of the problems and terminology.

The term filter can be applied to any frequency selective device. In practice, however, it tends to be restricted in use to describe a system component, which permits the transmission of certain ranges of frequency while rejecting or preventing the transmission of others. The transmitted frequencies are termed 'pass bands' while the rejected ones are known as 'stop bands'.

Categories

The need to use filters in transmitting information may be illustrated by considering their origins in the evolution of electronic communications. Consider a radio receiver, which is required to discriminate in favour of just one of the many incoming signals picked up by its aerial. It does so on the basis of the different frequency bands of the various signals by using a highly selective or tuned filter. A filter processing continuous signals is generally referred to as an analogue filter, while the filters used on sampled data signals are generally known as digital filters and may be produced by using either programming (software) or electronic components (hardware).

Filters are further classified according to the frequency ranges that they transmit or reject. A 'low-pass' filter has a pass band in the low-frequency region, where as a 'high pass' filter permits only the transmission of high frequencies. 'Band-pass' and 'band-stop' filters are specified in terms of their ability to discriminate in favour of, or against, particular frequency bands. The actual frequency (or frequencies) at which the transition from pass band to stop band occurs varies from case to case, and is an important parameter in the design of a filter.

6.4.1 Passive Filters

Figure 6.20 shows the idealised responses of the various forms of analogue filters. However, the use of real components in practice will prevent the abrupt change from pass band to stop band. To appreciate why, let us first consider the behaviour of a capacitor subjected to a sudden, or step, change in the level of applied voltage. If the capacitor initially has zero charge, then on application of a voltage, current will flow into the capacitor, the magnitude of the current decreasing exponentially with time (figure 6.21a). During this charging time the voltage across the capacitor will increase until it is equal to the applied voltage (figure 6.21b). Should the charged capacitor be disconnected from the voltage source and then connected across a resistor of value R, the capacitor C will

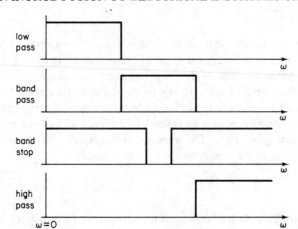

Figure 6.20. Idealised responses of analogue filters

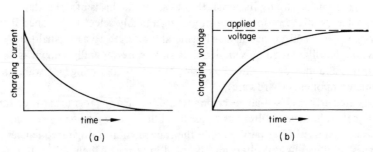

Figure 6.21a and b. Relationships of voltage and current with time when a voltage step is applied to an uncharged capacitor

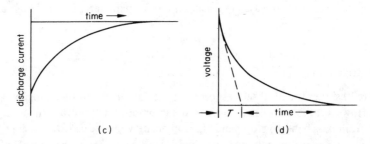

Figure 6.21c and d. Voltage and current characteristics of a discharging capacitor

discharge with characteristics of the form shown in figure 6.21c and d and time t constant T will be RC s.

For example, if $C = 1\ \mu F$ and $R = 100\ k\Omega$ then

$$T = RC = 100\,000 \times \frac{1}{1\,000\,000} = 100\ ms$$

The expression for the current at any instant, t, is

$$i = I_m \ e^{-t/RC} \tag{6.28}$$

so when $t = T = RC$

$$i = I_m \ e^{-1}$$

$$= 0.368 I_m$$

That is, i is 36.8 per cent of I_m, or has decayed by 63.2 per cent. If t is made equal to $5T$ then

$$i = I_m \ e^{-5}$$

$$= 0.00674 I_m$$

or i has reduced to 0.67 per cent of I_m. Hence, for the 1 μF 100 kΩ combination, 0.5 s is required for the current to decay to less than 1 per cent of its initial value. Similarly the same time is required for the voltage to rise to be within 1 per cent of its final value. Similar response characteristics are obtained when a step change in voltage is applied to an inductor, figure 6.22, it being noted that for the inductive case the time constant of the circuit is $T = L/R$.

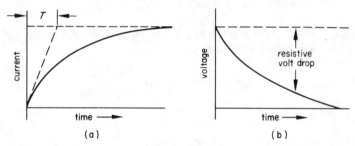

(a)   (b)

Figure 6.22. Transient response of an inductive circuit to a step function of voltage

Thus it will be apparent that any system for recording transients must contain a minimum of reactive impedance or distortion of the measurand will result. This property is made use of in filters, for the time constant of a circuit is directly related to the frequency response or bandwidth of a circuit (this is shown by the analysis that follows).

High Pass Filters

Consider the circuit in figure 6.23 which has open circuited output terminals (that is, $R_L = \infty$). Then

$$\frac{V_{out}}{V_s} = \frac{R}{R + \dfrac{1}{j\omega C}} = \frac{j\omega CR}{1 + j\omega CR}$$

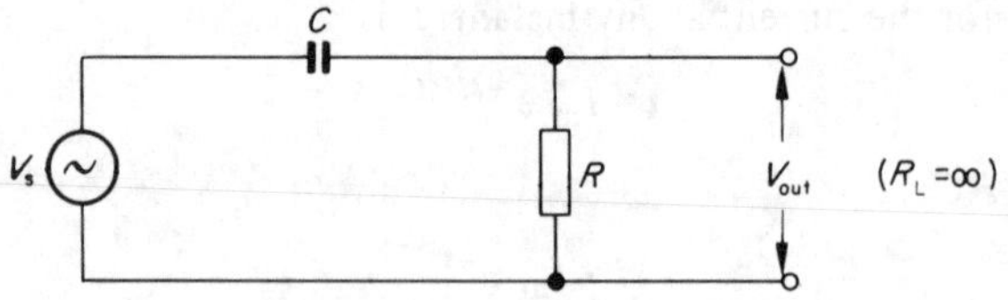

Figure 6.23. 'High pass' filter circuit

Now $CR = T$, the time constant, therefore

$$\frac{V_{out}}{V_s} = \frac{j\omega T}{1 + j\omega T}$$

or

$$\left|\frac{V_{out}}{V_s}\right| = \left[\frac{\omega^2 T^2}{1 + \omega^2 T^2}\right]^{\frac{1}{2}} \tag{6.29}$$

Now when $\omega = 1/T$

$$\left|\frac{V_{out}}{V_s}\right| = 0.707 \tag{6.30}$$

and this defines the -3 dB point, for by definition gain in dB $= 10 \log_{10} (P_{out}/P_{in})$ which by convention is taken as

$$\text{gain in dB} = 20 \log_{10} \frac{V_{out}}{V_s}$$

Therefore, if

$$\frac{V_{out}}{V_s} = 0.707$$

$$\text{gain} = 20 \log_{10} 0.707$$

$$= -3.01 \text{ dB}$$

The circuit in figure 6.23 will prevent the passage of direct and low frequency signals while allowing high frequency signals to flow. The frequency output characteristic of the circuit is shown in figure 6.24a and in figure 6.24b, a sketch of the phase angle against frequency characteristic is drawn and shows that at $\omega = 1/T$ there will be a 45° phase shift between V_s and V_{out}, that is

$$\text{phase angle } \phi = \tan^{-1} \frac{1}{\omega CR}$$

$$= \tan^{-1} \frac{1}{\omega T} \tag{6.31}$$

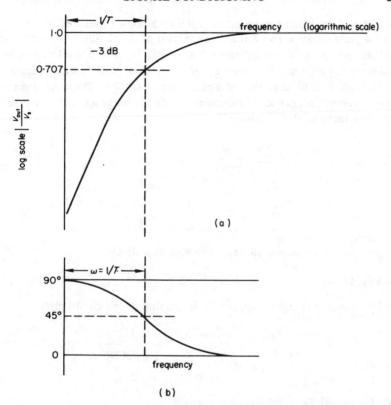

Figure 6.24. Characteristics of a high pass filter circuit: (a) response-frequency characteristic, (b) phase angle–frequency characteristic

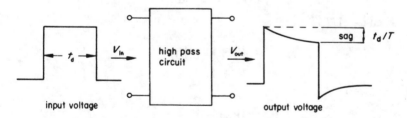

Figure 6.25. Distortion of a rectangular pulse through a high pass circuit

and if $\omega = 1/T$

$$\phi = \tan^{-1} 1 = 45°$$

Note: If $\omega \ll 1/T$ this circuit may be used as a differentiator.

The distorting effects of a high pass filter on a rectangular pulse are of interest, for the low frequency cut-off causes the top of the pulse to 'sag' as in figure 6.25, the fractional sag being approximately t_d/T for a single waveform, where t_d is the pulse duration and T the time constant of the circuit. It should be noted that this form of distortion will result if a rectangular wave is displayed on an oscilloscope by applying it to the a.c. input. A resistance–inductance combination (see figure 6.26), may also be used as a high pass filter. However, due to the size and inherent properties of inductors $R-L$ filters are generally less satisfactory than those using an $R-C$ combination.

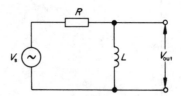

Figure 6.26. Inductive high pass circuit

Low Pass Filters

Consider now the circuit in figure 6.27. Inspection of this circuit gives

$$\frac{V_{out}}{V_s} = \frac{1/(j\omega C')}{R' + \frac{1}{j\omega C'}} = \frac{1}{1 + j\omega C'R'} \tag{6.32}$$

If the time constant of the circuit is T', then

$$\frac{V_{out}}{V_s} = \frac{1}{1 + j\omega T'}$$

and when $\omega = 1/T'$

$$\left|\frac{V_{out}}{V_s}\right| = 0.707$$

while at $\omega = 0$

$$\left|\frac{V_{out}}{V_s}\right| = 1$$

and at $\omega = \infty$

$$\left|\frac{V_{out}}{V_s}\right| = 0$$

This 'low pass' filter circuit will have characteristics of the form shown in figure 6.28, and if $\omega \gg 1/T'$ it may be used as an integrator.

The application of a rectangular pulse to a low pass circuit will produce the

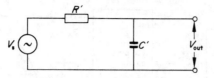

Figure 6.27. 'Low pass' filter circuit

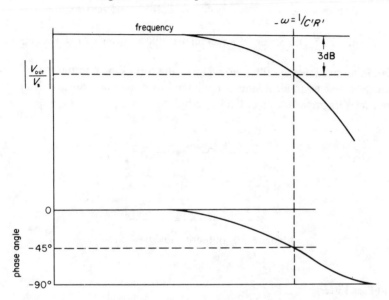

Figure 6.28. Characteristics of low pass filter circuit

type of distortion illustrated in figure 6.29, the rise time of the distorted wave being defined as the time interval from 10 per cent to 90 per cent of the maximum value. If $T = CR$ (or L/R) is the time constant of the circuit, v_1 the voltage of t_1, v_2 the voltage of t_2 and V_m the total or final voltage, then

$$v_1 = 0.1V_m = V_m \left(1 - e^{-t_1/T}\right) \tag{6.33}$$

$$v_2 = 0.9V_m = V_m \left(1 - e^{-t_2/T}\right) \tag{6.34}$$

from equations 6.33 and 6.34

$$0.9 = e^{-t_1/T} \quad \text{and} \quad 0.1 = e^{-t_2/T}$$

hence
$$0.1054 = \frac{-t_1}{T} \quad \text{and} \quad 2.303 = \frac{-t_2}{T}$$

Therefore

$$t_2 - t_1 = 2.197T \tag{6.35}$$

This rise time $t_r = (t_2 - t_1)$ is usually taken as $2.2T$.

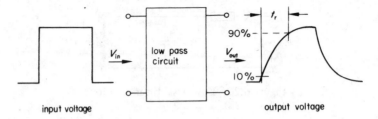

input voltage   output voltage

Figure 6.29. Distortion of a rectangular pulse through a low pass circuit

An inductive low pass filter would be of the form shown in figure 6.30 where at low frequencies an ideal inductor will tend to zero impedance, while at high frequencies its impedance will tend to infinity.

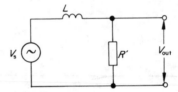

Figure 6.30. Inductive low pass circuit

Band Pass Filters

By combining high pass and low pass circuits a band pass filter may be produced, the conduction band of which will be the resultant of the characteristics of the high and low pass circuits (see figure 6.20).

6.4.2 Active Filters

The major limitation of passive filters is that when connected into a system the current drawn by the succeeding circuit will change the frequency characteristic of the filter. This problem can largely be overcome by using an operational amplifier[12,13] in the filter circuit as illustrated in figure 6.31, it being observed that by changing all resistors in figure 6.31a to capacitors and the capacitors to resistors, it changes the low pass to the high pass filter in figure 6.31b.

Band Pass Filter

As with the passive filter, a band pass filter can be produced by cascading high and low pass filters. An alternative and tidier technique is to use a twin T (see section 3.4.4) circuit in the feedback loop as shown in figure 6.32.

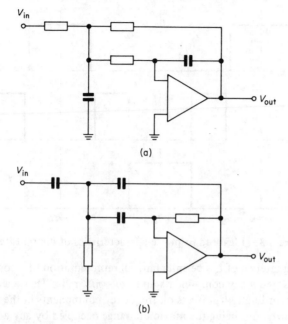

(a)

(b)

Figure 6.31. Active filters: (a) low pass, (b) high pass

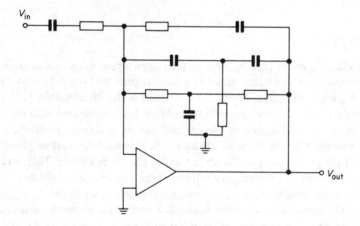

Figure 6.32. Active band pass filter

6.4.3 Digital Filters [12]

The frequency response of a linear sampled-data system is always a periodic function of ω, which repeats itself every $2\pi/t_s$ rad/s (t_s is the sampling interval). Thus for digital filters the terms low pass, high pass and band pass have to be interpreted differently.

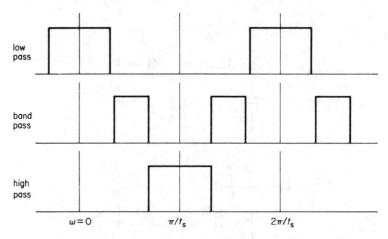

Figure 6.33. Idealised response characteristics of digital filters

A sampling interval of t_s s permits faithful representation of a continuous signal that has frequency components up to $\omega = \pi/t_s$ rad/s. Hence a digital filter is classified according to its effects on frequency components in the range $-\pi/t_s < \omega < \pi/t_s$, this being the maximum range occupied by any adequately sampled input frequency. The responses of idealised digital filters are shown in figure 6.33.

6.5 PROBES

The purpose of a probe is to connect an instrument, such as an oscilloscope or electronic voltmeter, to a test circuit in a manner such that the presence of the monitoring instrument does not affect the circuit under investigation.[14] In many applications the probe consists of a coaxial lead terminated with insulated 'prods'. A coaxial lead is used to prevent 'pick-up' distorting the signal that is being measured, the instrument having a high impedance so that any loading effects (of the instrument) on the circuit under test are negligible. This latter condition may not be satisfactorily fulfilled if the test circuit has either a very high impedance, or is operating at a very high frequency, when the capacitance of the coaxial connection will introduce a low impedance across the instrument's input impedance. A probe containing either an input 'attenuator' or a cathode follower must then be used to increase the impedance that the test circuit 'sees'.

6.5.1 Passive Probes

The input 'attenuator' type of probe will introduce a reduction in signal amplitude, but if the probe capacitor (C_1 in figure 6.34) is adjustable, compensation for stray capacitance may be made so that the signal presented to the instrument is not distorted, and the probe behaves as an R–C divider (see section 6.1.3). The

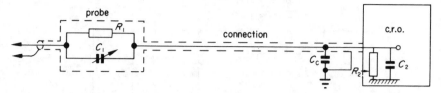

Figure 6.34. $R-C$ passive probe

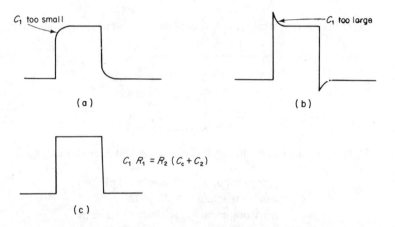

(a)

(b)

$$C_1 R_1 = R_2 (C_c + C_2)$$

(c)

Figure 6.35. Effects of probe adjustment on the displayed square wave: (a) mis-adjustment– high frequency attenuation, (b) misadjustment—accentuated high frequency response, (c) correct adjustment giving optimum high frequency response

adjustment of C_1 is normally provided by the longitudinal movement of one of a pair of concentric cylindrical conductors relative to the other. The effects of this adjustment are shown diagrammatically in figure 6.35. The reduction in signal level for passive probes, used between d.c. and 300 MHz is typically 1/10 from equation 6.3

$$\frac{V_{out}}{V_{in}} = \frac{R_2}{R_1 + R_2}$$

This signal reduction is commonly specified as a 10x attenuation.

Input Impedance Effects

The objective of using a probe is to reduce the loading of the instrument on the signal source. Consider, therefore, the effective input impedance of an oscilloscope connected to a signal via a probe as in figure 6.36

R_1 = probe resistance = 9 MΩ
R_2 = 'scope input resistance = 1 MΩ
C_1 = adjustable probe capacitance

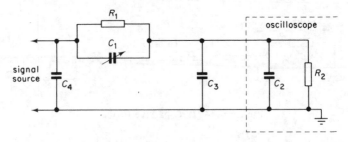

Figure 6.36. Equivalent circuit of oscilloscope and probe combination

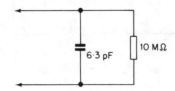

Figure 6.37. Effective circuit of oscilloscope and probe combination

C_2 = 'scope input capacitance $\approx$ 20 pF
C_3 = cable capacitance $\approx$ 23 pF/m
C_4 = environmental capacitance $\approx$ 1.5–2 pF

Assuming a 1 m cable is used, C_3 = 23 pF. For correct compensation

$$R_1 C_1 = R_2 (C_2 + C_3)$$

or

$$C_1 = 4.8 \text{ pF}$$

The effective input capacitance

$$C = C_4' + \frac{C_1 (C_2 + C_3)}{C_1 + C_2 + C_3}$$

$$= 6.3 \text{ pF}$$

and since the effective input resistance is $(1 + 9)$ MΩ the effective circuit becomes that shown by figure 6.37.

It should be observed that care must be taken to ensure that the probe impedance is compatible with the input impedance of the instrument it is to be used with.

Signal Response

The rise time (10 per cent to 90 per cent of final value) specified for a passive probe is commonly quoted for the situation in which the probe alone is connected to a matched 50 Ω source. Thus the instrument's response will depend

not only on the impedance of the probe and the instrument but also on the type
of signal and the impedance of the source.

Response to step function

In responding to a pulse or step function the parameters of importance are
amplitude, rise time, transient response and time distortion.

The output impedance of a signal source generally has a capacitive as well as a
resistive component, the magnitudes of which may typically range from 1 to
100 pF and a few mΩ to several kΩ respectively.

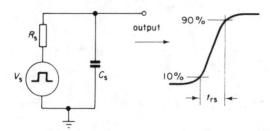

Figure 6.38. Equivalent circuit of pulse source

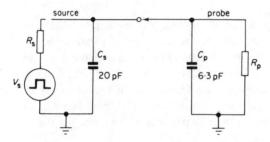

Figure 6.39. System equivalent circuit

Consider the source represented by figure 6.38 to be generating a squarewave,
if the source resistance, R_s, is 200 Ω and the source capacitance, C_s, 20 pF. The
rise time for the source alone, from equation 6.35 will be

$$t_{rs} = 2.2 R_s C_s = 8.8 \text{ ns}$$

Connecting the passive probe and oscilloscope combination, evaluated for figure
6.37, to this source gives a system circuit as shown in figure 6.39, in which since
$R_p > 10 R_s$, R_p may be neglected and the circuit reduced to that in figure 6.40,
which gives a system rise time of $2.2 \times 200 \times 26.3 = 11.6$ ns.

The loading effect of the probe and instrument on the signal source is the percentage change in the rise time

$$\frac{(11.6 - 8.8)}{8.8} \times 100 = 31.8\%$$

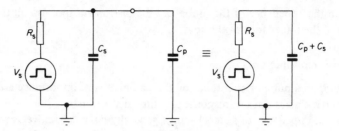

Figure 6.40. Reduced equivalent circuits of the system for rise time calculations

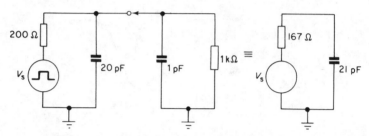

Figure 6.41. Circuit resulting from the connection of a low impedance probe to the source

Some passive probes have a relatively low resistance (1 kΩ) and a very low input capacitance ($<$ 1 pF). Connecting such a probe to the signal source under consideration would give the situation illustrated in figure 6.41 and the combined rise time becomes 7.7 ns with a loading effect of ($-$)12.5 per cent. This decrease in rise time is accompanied by signal amplitude reduction of 16.5 per cent.

It is apparent that the probe rise time is of importance and an accepted criteria is that it should be less than 20 per cent of the signal rise time.

Response to sinewave

In monitoring a sinewave the parameters of interest are amplitude and phase shift. Considering again the source shown in figure 6.38 but now supplying a sinusoidal signal, the output amplitude will have fallen by 3 dB when

$$\omega = \frac{1}{T} = \frac{1}{R_s C_s}$$

See equation 6.32 and figure 6.28. So for the source under consideration

$$\omega_{3\,dB} = \frac{10^{12}}{20 \times 200} \quad \text{or} \quad f_{3\,dB} = 39.8 \text{ MHz}$$

Additionally, since the source is equivalent to a low pass filter it will have a phase angle (shift) characteristic also as shown in figure 6.28. The magnitude of this phase shift at a frequency f is

$$\phi = \tan^{-1} 2\pi f C_s R_s \qquad (6.36)$$

Thus at a particular frequency (say 10 MHz) the amplitude of the output will be

$$V_{\text{out}} = V_s \frac{1}{1 + \omega T} = V_s \frac{X_s}{Z_s} \qquad (6.37)$$

Hence

$$V_{\text{out}} = \frac{796}{821} V_s \equiv 97\% \text{ of } V_s$$

The complete equivalent circuit of a typical probe is a complex arrangement, which is difficult to analyse satisfactorily. In consequence some manufacturers provide R_p and X_p against frequency characteristics of the form illustrated in figure 6.42, and at the frequency of 10 MHz, $X_p = 1.7 \text{ k}\Omega$ and $R_p = 40 \text{ k}\Omega$. Thus connecting the probe to the source that has been under consideration produces the situation represented by figure 6.43. Since $R_p \gg R_s$, R_p may be neglected and the total capacitive reactance of the equivalent circuit becomes

$$X_t = \frac{X_p X_s}{X_p + X_s} = \frac{1700 \times 796}{2496} = 542 \ \Omega$$

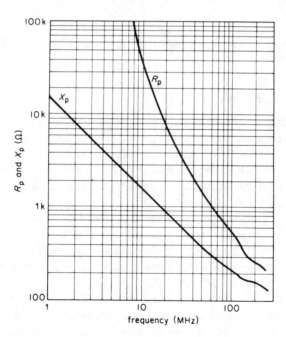

Figure 6.42. Typical reactance and resistance versus frequency curves for a probe and its cable (after reference 14)

Thus

$$V_{out} = V_s \frac{X_s}{Z_s} = V_s \frac{542}{(200^2 + 542^2)^{1/2}} = 93.8\% \text{ of } V_s$$

and

$$\text{phase shift} = \tan^{-1} \frac{200}{542}$$

$$= 20.25°$$

While the reduction in amplitude is relatively small the phase shift is appreciable, and to reduce the phase shift a low impedance probe may be used,[14] but such a procedure will result in considerable signal reduction.

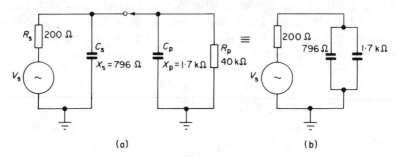

Figure 6.43. Probe connected to source: (a) values for $f = 10$ MHz, (b) reduced equivalent circuit of (a)

6.5.2 Active Voltage Probes

Although the passive probe is by far the most commonly used voltage probe, it is apparent from the previous section that low capacitive loading (and phase shift) can only be obtained at the expense of considerable attenuation. These problems can be overcome by using an active (FET) probe[15] which may have a loading effect as small as 10 MΩ in parallel with 2 pF, a bandwidth from d.c. to 500 MHz, and a ×1 attenuation.

Active voltage probes obtain the necessary power either from the designated source available on the front panel of the instrument or from a separate (probe accessory) power unit. To keep the probe small and easy to handle, and to meet the impedance requirements, a miniaturised amplifier, with an FET input stage is built into the tip of the probe.

Figure 6.44 is a simplified block diagram of an FET probe in which the alternating and direct voltage components are separated, amplified and then combined. This split-band amplification technique enables the optimum use of the device characteristics. To maintain a probe attenuation of ×1, the output signal is compared with the input signal via a feedback inverter and resistor R_2. If the

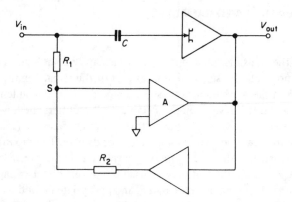

Figure 6.44. Simplified circuit diagram of an FET probe

inverter and the h.f. amplifier have the same gain, $R_2 = R_1$, so the difference between the input and output signals will appear at the summing point, S. This difference is amplified by the differential amplifier and fed to the output. The direct and low frequency components (blocked by C) appear as part of this difference signal and the result is a d.c. coupled h.f. amplifier.

6.5.3 Current Probes

To enable currents to be measured using instruments with high input impedances it is necessary to insert a known resistance in the circuit and measure the voltage across it. Apart from the isolation problems, such a process may, at the least, be inconvenient, and often impracticable. Oscilloscope current probes use the principles of current transformers to facilitate the measurement of the current in a conductor. The arrangements shown diagrammatically in figure 6.45 each have a core that may be slid open to allow the current carrying conductor to be inserted. The probe in figure 6.45a has typically a sensitivity of 1 mA/mV output over a bandwidth from 450 Hz to 60 MHz while the modified arrangement in figure 6.45b, incorporating a Hall effect device, has a frequency range from d.c. to 50 MHz.

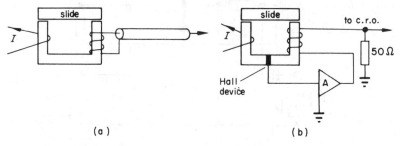

(a)   (b)

Figure 6.45. (a) a.c. oscilloscope current probe, (b) d.c. oscilloscope current
probe (courtesy of Tektronix Ltd)

6.6 MODULATION AND SAMPLING

Modulators

To assist in the transmission and storage or display of some signals it is advantageous to modulate the signal, that is, as part of the signal conditioning process
the signal from the measurand is varied, usually in a time dependent manner. For
example, prior to the development of stable d.c. amplifiers the low level d.c.
signal input to a sensitive electronic voltmeter was chopped up (modulated) into
quasi a.c., amplified, and then demodulated for display. The modulation methods
used in such instruments were commonly electromechanical or photoresistive
choppers. Another circuit that may be used to convert direct voltages to quasi-
alternating ones is shown in figure 6.46a, an appropriate demodulator being
illustrated in figure 6.46b. This latter circuit has a marked similarity to the phase
sensitive rectifier circuit discussed in chapter 2, a further application being the
circuit associated with the variable reluctance transducer.

The above form of modulation results in an output which has the form of a
chain of pulses the heights of which are dependent on the level of the input
signal, this form of modulation being termed pulse amplitude modulation

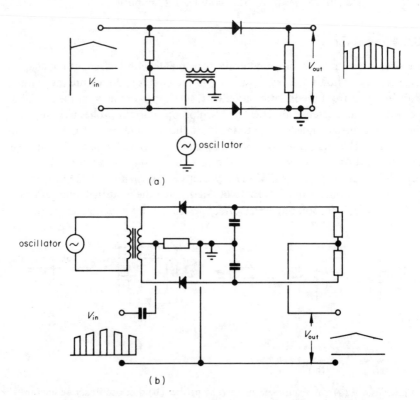

Figure 6.46. Pulse amplitude: (a) modulator circuit, (b) demodulator circuit

(p.a.m.). An alternative to this is a technique termed pulse duration (width) modulation (p.d.m.) or (p.w.m.), in which the leading edge of the pulse occurs at fixed time intervals; the time interval between it and the end of the pulse depends on the magnitude of the signal at the time of sampling. Pulse position modulation (p.p.m.) is derived from p.w.m. by differentiation and rectification; figure 6.47 shows the derivation of p.p.m. from p.w.m.

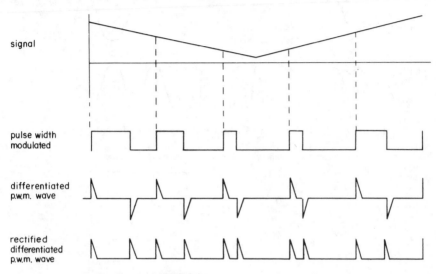

Figure 6.47. Derivation of p.w.m. and p.p.m. waveforms

Another modulation technique that may be applied to d.c. signals is that of converting the voltage magnitude to a frequency (this process is used in some digital voltmeters—see p. 208). It consists of applying the d.c. signal to a voltage controlled oscillator, the output frequency of which varies about a reference frequency by an amount dependent on the magnitude of the input signal.

In the above discussion the signal to be modulated has been assumed to be d.c. or to have only a slowly varying magnitude. However, for transmission purposes it is often necessary to modulate an a.c. signal; in such cases the methods used are as shown in figure 6.48, (a) being amplitude modulation (a.m.), (b) phase modulation (p.m.), and (c) frequency modulation (f.m.). The differences between these methods of modulation will perhaps be more easily understood if the general equation for an unmodulated waveform is considered as $V = V_m \sin(\omega t + \theta)$. Then the resultant modulated waveform may be obtained by modulating V_m (the amplitude), ω (the frequency), or θ (the phase of V with respect to a reference), it also being remembered that phase angle is equivalent to a time delay, so that phase modulation is equivalent to the variation of a time delay.[16,17]

An extensively used method of representing a signal by pulses is to use a pulse code, that is, a predetermined number of pulses represent discrete levels of signal;

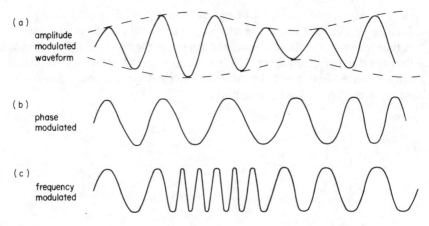

(a) amplitude modulated waveform

(b) phase modulated

(c) frequency modulated

Figure 6.48. Modulation of the waveform of an alternating signal

decimal	binary	waveform
O	0000	
I	0001	
2	0010	
3	0011	
4	0100	
5	0101	
6	0110	
7	0111	
8	1000	
9	1001	

Figure 6.49. Some waveforms of binary numbers

it is conventional to use a binary coding of the decimal equivalent. Figure 6.49 shows an example of pulse coding. The pulse code modulation (p.c.m.) methods have been found to be the most effective of the pulse modulation systems used in the transfer of data. In particular, the p.a.m. method suffers a loss of accuracy during transmission due to attenuation of the pulse height.

Sampling

When a continuous signal is to be represented by a set of samples, care must be taken to ensure that the scanning rate is sufficiently fast for all the variations in the measurand to be reconstructed from the record. The limiting requirement of sampling is that the frequency of sampling[17] shall be at least twice the highest frequency component of the signal being sampled in order that it may be reconstructed in its original form. An alternative method of looking at this is to consider a system which has a pass band of (say) d.c. to f Hz, then the sampling frequency must be at least $2f$. However, the sampling theory assumes the presence of signal reconstruction equipment and a more practical sampling rate for many instrumentation applications is six times the highest frequency component of the signal.

6.7 ANALOGUE PROCESSING

In many measuring situations the signal must be 'processed' in order to obtain a reading that is a meaningful representation of the measurand. The developments in digital electronics are continually extending the range of what it is possible to do in a digital instrument but for some situations analogue signal processing will remain the most satisfactory.

6.7.1 Amplification

The use of amplifiers in instrumentation is extensive, and in such an application they can be thought of as 'black boxes' or building bricks, their function being to operate in some manner on the signal from the measurand. This operation may simply be to increase the magnitude of the signal or it may be to perform a mathematical function on it, for example, to differentiate or integrate the signal; other possibilities are the summation of a number of signals, or the removal (filtering) of unwanted components. Figure 6.50 shows the accepted symbols for operational amplifiers which are known as (a) single-ended and (b) differential input amplifiers. The normal method of construction used for an operational amplifier is as an integrated circuit with a differential input, a single-ended amplifier being created by suitable connection of one input. In either case, as an operational amplifier, it will have a high gain, typically 10^6, it will invert (there will be a reversal of polarity between input and output), and it will have a large input impedance, typically 100 kΩ. It should also have a bandwidth which extends from d.c. upwards, together with low offset and drift properties. The symbol in figure 6.50c represents an operational amplifier with feedback.

The gain of an amplifier is the ratio V_{out}/V_{in}; thus, for an operational amplifier this should be a large negative number. However, conventionally the gain is considered as the modulus of the voltage ratio and is therefore positive, that is

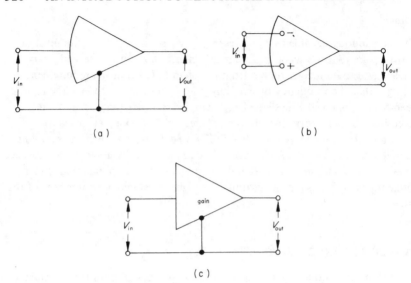

Figure 6.50. Operational amplifier symbols: (a) single-ended, (b) differential, (c) single-ended with incorporated feedback circuit

$$\text{gain} = \left| \frac{V_{\text{out}}}{V_{\text{in}}} \right| = A \tag{6.38}$$

To enhance the stability and the precision of the gain of an operational amplifier, whose nominal gain may have an appreciable specification tolerance, for example 20 per cent, lack linearity, and be temperature dependent, a proportion of the output is fed back to the input. To use an operational amplifier without feedback in an instrumentation chain would require continual recalibration of the system, but by using negative feedback on the amplifier the gain may be made largely dependent on stable passive components and independent of the gain of the operational amplifier. For the arrangement in figure 6.51 the gain is

$$\frac{V_{\text{out}}}{V_{\text{in}}} = \frac{AR_2}{AR_1 - R_1 + R_2}$$

and since $AR_1 \gg (R_2 - R_1)$

$$\text{gain} = \frac{R_2}{R_1} \tag{6.39}$$

The amplifier with feedback will have an input impedance of R_1 Ω, and an output impedance of a few mΩ, that is r_{out}/A at unity gain, r_{out} being the output impedance of the amplifier without feedback (typically 10 Ω to 1 kΩ). Another important effect of the use of feedback, in conjunction with the high gain of the operational amplifier, is that the input terminal is nominally maintained at earth potential, that is a few μV of input may result in the output reaching its maximum level, and so it is seen that the self-adjusting nature of negative feedback always holds the potential of the input terminal within a few microvolts of earth potential, no matter how the amplifier supply voltage or the values of R_1 and R_2 are varied, provided that (a) the output of the amplifier does not saturate, or (b) the upper frequency limit of the amplifier is not exceeded. This property of the input terminal being at zero potential is termed a virtual earth.

Attenuated feedback

A variation of the use of resistive feedback is illustrated in figure 6.52, where the 'attenuation' of feedback is a means of using low to medium value resistors while retaining a high stable gain, for example, a situation in which a gain of 1000 is desired with an input impedance greater than 5 kΩ. If the circuit in figure 6.51 were used, it would be necessary for R_2 to have a value of 5 MΩ, a value of

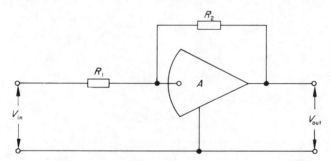

Figure 6.51. Operational amplifier with resistive feedback

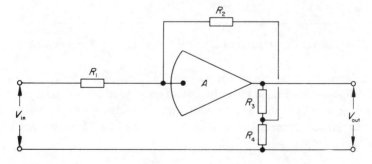

Figure 6.52. Operational amplifier with 'attenuated' feedback

resistance that is difficult to obtain with a tolerance of less than ± 5 per cent. However, using the circuit of figure 6.52 for which

$$\text{gain} \approx \frac{R_2}{R_1}\left(\frac{R_3 + R_4}{R_4}\right)$$

provided $R_3 \ll R_2$. Then with $R_2 = 100$ kΩ, $R_3 = 1$ kΩ and $R_1 = 5$ kΩ; $R_4 = 20.4$ Ω. These values of resistances are more likely to be stable than the 5 MΩ of the first arrangement. See also references, 18, 19 and 20.

Charge amplifier

Some other useful applications of the operational amplifier in instrumentation are those associated with transducers. It has been shown that piezoelectric trans-ducers have an output that is in the form of an electric charge proportional to the force on the crystal, that is, the transducer may in electrical terms be represented by a charged capacitor. If such a transducer is loaded solely with a circuit that resolves to a capacitance across the transducer output, the voltage developed at the transducer terminals is $V = Q/C_1$, where C_1 is the combined transducer and load capacitance. Connecting this combination across the input of an operational amplifier, with feedback capacitor C_2, as in figure 6.53, will result in an output voltage

$$V_{out} = \frac{C_1}{C_2} \times V_{in} = \frac{C_1}{C_2} \times \frac{Q}{C_1} = \frac{Q}{C_2} \qquad (6.40)$$

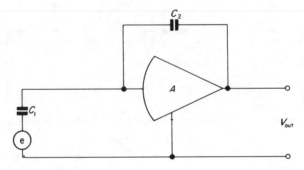

Figure 6.53. Operational amplifier used as a charge amplifier

The capacitor C_2 will normally be made equal in magnitude to C_1, the usefulness of this application being in the reduction of output impedance. Interposing the charge amplifier between the transducer and recording instrument enables instru-ments having low or medium input impedances to be used for recording the transducer's output.

Differential amplifier

The preceding applications have assumed that the operational amplifier was of the single-ended type. Very many of the operational amplifiers that are made are manufactured with differential inputs, and to use such a device as a single-ended amplifier simply requires the earthing of one of the input terminals via a resistance that has a magnitude equal to R_1 (if $R_2 \gg R_1$). The difference or

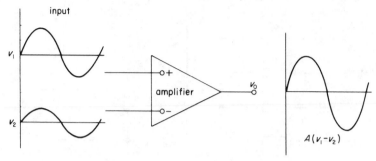

Figure 6.54. Difference of sinewaves

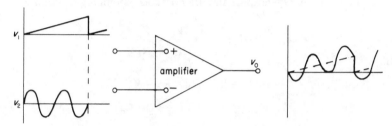

Figure 6.55. Result of applying dissimilar waveforms to a difference amplifier

differential amplifier may be used to amplify the difference between two signals. For example, figure 6.54 shows two voltage waveforms of equal frequency but unequal magnitude applied to the input of a differential amplifier. The result is an output that is an amplification of the difference between V_1 and V_2. A further illustration of the difference effect is shown in figure 6.55, where a ramp waveform is applied to one input and a sinusoidal voltage to the other.

One application of the differential amplifier is as the input amplifier of some oscilloscopes. This enables small voltage differences at a voltage to earth to be observed, and under these conditions it is desirable for the operational amplifier to have a high common mode rejection (see section 7.4).

6.7.2 Mathematical Functions

Using Operational Amplifiers

Further to the difference amplifier mentioned above, by incorporating suitable feedback arrangements, operational amplifiers may be used to perform various mathematical functions as follows.

Summing amplifier

The proximity of the input terminal to zero potential is termed a virtual earth and this facet is utilised when an operational amplifier is functioning as a summing amplifier. For the arrangement shown in figure 6.56

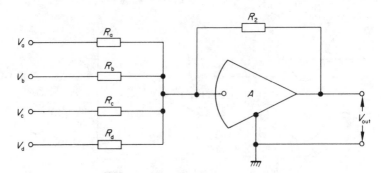

Figure 6.56. Operational amplifier used as a summing junction

$$V_{out} = -R_2 \left(\frac{V_a}{R_a} + \frac{V_b}{R_b} + \frac{V_c}{R_c} + \frac{V_d}{R_d} \right)$$

or if

$$R_2 = R_a = R_b = R_c = R_d$$

$$V_{out} = -(V_a + V_b + V_c + V_d) \qquad (6.41)$$

that is, the sum of the input voltages but with a reversal of polarity.

Computing amplifier

So far, apart from the charge amplifier, the feedback circuits considered have all been resistive; the introduction of reactance (normally capacitive) into the circuit enables other operations to be performed. Two such applications of major importance in the use of operational amplifiers are

(a)   as an integrator, figure 6.57a, where

$$V_{out} = \frac{1}{R_1 C} \int V_{in} \, dt \qquad (6.42)$$

The switch is included in the circuit to ensure that there is zero stored charge in the capacitor C at time $t = 0$. If R_1 is in Ω, C in F, and their product is 1 ΩF (1 s) then the circuit is termed a 'unity integrator'.

(b) as a differentiator, figure 6.57b, where

$$V_{out} = -R_2 C_1 \frac{dV_{in}}{dt} \qquad (6.43)$$

The resistor R_1 has to be included to decrease the amplification of unwanted noise, for the impedance of the capacitor will fall with increase of frequency and the system provides a high gain for high frequencies. The frequency limit for differentiation is

$$f = \frac{1}{2\pi R_1 C_1} \text{ Hz} \qquad (6.44)$$

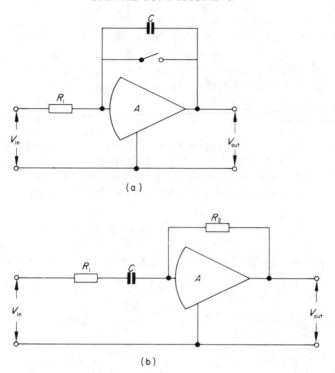

(a)

(b)

Figure 6.57. Feedback circuits to perform mathematical functions: (a) integrator, (b) differentiator

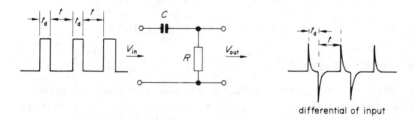

differential of input

Figure 6.58. Simple differentiation circuit

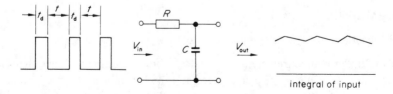

integral of input

Figure 6.59. Simple integration circuit

It should be noted that passive R–C circuits may be used to obtain these effects. For example in figure 6.58 if the CR product is less than $t/100$, satisfactory differentiation is produced, whereas by making $CR \gg t$ in figure 6.59 an integrator is produced. Both these arrangements have small output amplitudes and are affected by the impedance of the instrument connected to them.

Logarithmic converter

A further application of the single-ended operational amplifier is as a logarithmic converter (see figure 6.60). The feedback in this application is via a silicon diode, for these devices have a logarithmic relationship between voltage and current over several decades of current values. The output equation of this arrangement is

$$\log \frac{V_{in}}{R_1} = k \, (V_{out} - V') \qquad (6.45)$$

where k is a constant and V' an offset voltage, which must be allowed for in subsequent circuitry.

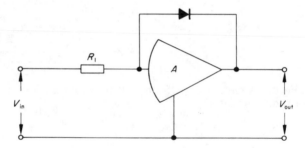

Figure 6.60. Logarithmic converter

Mean or average values

In a number of applications it is necessary to determine the mean or rectified value of a waveform. The forward voltage drop of diodes prevents the straight-forward use of these devices if the magnitude of the signal is small. However, if an operational amplifier is incorporated in the circuit as shown in figure 2.17, where the diodes are in the feedback loop, this problem is effectively overcome.

Using Multipliers

Multiplication

The multiplier is an extremely powerful device for processing analogue signals.[21] In its simplest form it may be considered as a three-terminal integrated circuit as shown in figure 6.61, the output being the product of two input signals divided by a fixed voltage (E_R), which can be considered as a dimensional constant.

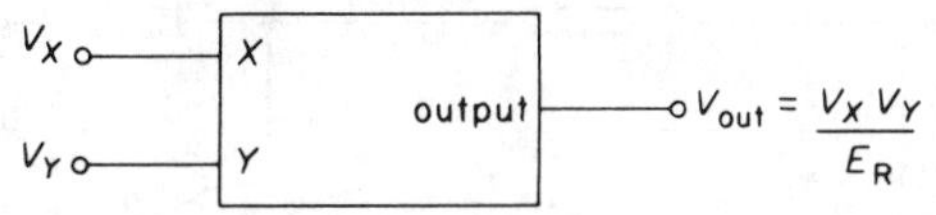

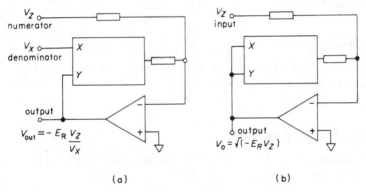

Figure 6.61. Basic multiplier configuration (E_R is a dimensional scale constant, usually 10 V)

Since squaring is simply the multiplication of a variable by itself, it follows that connecting the same signal to the X and Y inputs will result in a squared term (divided by E_R) at the output.

Division

By adding a feedback path containing an operational amplifier the multiplier can be used for division and determining square roots. The basic arrangements for both these functions are given in figure 6.62. In figure 6.62a the numerator V_z divided by the denominator V_x produces the answer at the Y terminal, and in figure 6.62b the square root is produced at the connection of the X and Y terminals. It should be noted that since most multiplier integrated circuits incorporate an operational amplifier in their output circuit, suitable external connection arrangements permit a single device to be used for all these basic functions.

Figure 6.62. Concepts of: (a) division, (b) square root using a multiplier

R.M.S. values

The determination of the r.m.s. value of a waveform has always been of importance. For many years the only satisfactory method of producing a direct voltage with a simple relationship to the r.m.s. value of an alternating wave was to use a thermocouple arrangement (see reference 17 of chapter 2). Developments have resulted in the production of a number of electronic alternatives (see reference 7 of chapter 2). Figure 6.63 shows the use of a multiplier circuit, which results in an error less than 0.1 per cent for signals having frequencies of up to 100 kHz

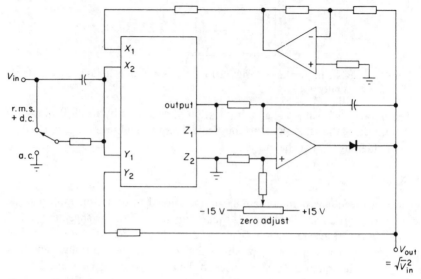

Figure 6.63. R.M.S. to d.c. converter using a multiplier (after reference 21)

and crest factors less than 10 (provided the peak input is not exceeded). The 100 kHz frequency band may be extended to 1 MHz if the allowable error limit is raised to 0.5 per cent.

6.7.3 Dependent Functions

There are many and various integrated circuits that can be used to produce a change in a signal. Some that are in common use in instrumentation systems are listed below.

Voltage to frequency converter

These are used in some A/D converters and in some test systems where stimulae of various frequencies are to be applied.

Linearisers

These are used to compensate for nonlinearities in the output of some trans-ducers and unbalanced bridges—another possible application of a multiplier.

Voltage to current amplifier

When signals have to be transmitted over considerable distances (for example, in a large chemical processing plant) it has become customary to transmit the signal as a variation in current level between 4 and 20 mA. The signal strength is then independent of variations in circuit resistance, a fault is normally apparent as a zero current condition and the signal simply reconverted to a voltage by passing the current through a known stable resistance.

6.8 DIGITAL-ANALOGUE CONVERSION

The use of digital displays has undisputed advantages of clarity, reduction of operator fatigue, etc., over an analogue display, and a number of analogue to digital conversion techniques are described in connection with the operation of digital voltmeters (see section 4.2.1). However, it is sometimes advantageous to convert digital signals to analogue ones for display purposes, for example, presenting computer output in graphical form. The process of digital to analogue (D/A) conversion is illustrated in principle in figure 6.64, where the summation properties of an operational amplifier are used to form an analogue voltage from digital

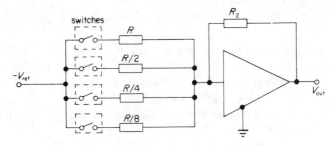

Figure 6.64. Digital to analogue converter

information. The summing resistors, R, have values in a binary progression and are connected to a fixed voltage source via switches (bistable circuits) which are controlled by the digital information. The voltage source must have a precisely known value, and the summing resistors must be stable. The scale of the output voltage will be dependent on the value of the feedback resistor R_2.

REFERENCES

1 Jan Slyper, Advanced d.c. calibration techniques, E.E.E. European Seminar (Fluke Manufacturing Co., Seattle, Wash., 1969)
2 E. W. Golding and F. C. Widdis, *Electrical Measurements and Measuring Instruments* (Pitman, London, 1963)
3 J. J. Hill and A. P. Miller, A seven decade adjustable ratio inductively coupled voltage divider with 0.1 ppm accuracy, *Proc. I.E.E.*, **109B** (1962) 157–62
4 Britain's first 400 kV cascade-voltage transformers, *Electronics Power,* **13** (1967) 470–1

5   B. D. Jenkins, *Introduction to Instrument Transformers* (Newnes, London, 1967)

6   F. E. Terman and J. M. Petit, *Electronic Measurements* (McGraw-Hill, New York, 1952)

7   F. K. Harris, *Electrical Measurements* (Wiley, New York, 1962)

8   J. H. Parks, Shunts and inductors for surge current measurements, *J. Res. natn. Bur. Stand.,* **39** (1947) 191

9   S. J. Turner, The operation and application of direct current transformers, *Electl Equip.,* **17** (1978) 71-6

10 *The Royal Signals Handbook of Line Communications*, Vol. 1 (H.M.S.O., 1947)

11 M. Sucher and J. Fox (ed.), *Handbook of Microwave Measurements* (Wiley, New York, 1965)

12 H. Y-F. Lam, *Analog and Digital Filters; Design and Realisation* (Prentice-Hall, Englewood Cliffs, N.J., 1979)

13 R. W. Henry, *Electronic Systems and Instrumentation* (Wiley, Chichester, 1978)

14 —, Probes, parts I and II, *Tekscope,* **6** No. 2, 8-11, No. 3, 10-14 (1974)

15 R. Lang, A new and low-cost 500 MHz probe, *Tekscope,* **8** (1976) 11-13

16 P. A. Lynn, *An Introduction to the Analysis and Processing of Signals* (Macmillan, London and Basingstoke, 1973)

17 S. Stein and J. Jay Jones, *Modern Communication Principles* (McGraw-Hill, New York, 1967)

18 R. Morrison, *D.C. Amplifiers in Instrumentation* (Wiley, New York, 1970)

19 G. B. Clayton, *Operational Amplifiers* (Butterworth, London, 1971)

20 R. J. Isaacs, Optimising op. amps, *Wireless Wld,* **79** (1973) 185-6

21 D. H. Sheingold (ed.), *Multiplier Application Guide* (Analog Devices Inc., New York, 1978)

7

Interference and Screening

In practical engineering the conduction of an electrical signal from the measurand to a measuring instrument can be affected by a number of forms of interference. These may, broadly speaking, be divided into

(a) the effects of the environment on the component parts of an instrument, or measurement system;
(b) impurities in individual components and their effects on the measuring system; and
(c) injection of unwanted signals from unrelated electrical circuits and fields into the measuring system.

7.1 ENVIRONMENTAL EFFECTS

The resultant effect of environmental interference is usually apparant as a gradual change, or drift, in the output from part of the measuring system when there is no change in the input.

7.1.1 Thermal Effects

These are undoubtedly the most common causes of drift and may be due to heating of components within an instrument, or due to changes in the ambient temperature.

Expansion coefficient

Temperature changes will cause dimension changes dependent on the thermal coefficient of expansion of the material from which components are constructed. This causes, for example, changes in the dimensions of inductors which in turn cause a change of magnitude. If a number of different materials, each with its own coefficient of expansion, are involved in the construction of a component, mechanical stresses will result and these can also cause a change in value particularly if semiconductor devices are involved.

Resistance coefficient

Conductive materials and those used in the construction of resistors have, in addition to the temperature coefficient of expansion, a temperature coefficient of resistance, that is, their resistance is temperature dependent. Hence in sensitive instrumentation systems it is essential for components with small temperature coefficients to be used in a constant temperature environment. This latter requirement explains why it is necessary to provide in the measurement uncertainty specification an allowance for the effects of temperature, should a particular instrument be operated outside a specified temperature range.

Thermoelectric generation

The production of voltage by this process has been described elsewhere (section 5.4.3) and since junctions between dissimilar materials are inevitable, for example, at the ends of a resistor, care may be necessary to ensure that components are arranged so that pairs of junctions are at the same temperature, that is, a resistor should be mounted horizontally rather than vertically; also it is necessary to ensure that excessive heating of components is avoided by arranging that they are operated well below their rated capacity.

7.1.2 Humidity Effects

The effects of the moisture content of air generally tend to be small although some materials used in the construction of components are hygroscopic and this will affect the value of the component when the humidity changes. This may be due to a variation in conduction or in the dielectric properties[1] of materials. Alternatively, it may be due to the absorption of moisture in materials (for example, wood) causing a dimensional change and a consequent change in component value, this latter effect being one reason for stipulating an allowable humidity band in the operation of a standards laboratory.[2]

The combination of high humidity, causing condensation, and dirt on surfaces may have two results, as follows.

Leakage resistance

The surface resistance between terminals of an instrument with a high (say 100 MΩ) input resistance, must be very much greater than the specified value. However, should the surface become contaminated with dirt and moisture, a reduction in the surface resistance will result, eventually leading to a situation in which the instrument's input resistance specification is no longer met. The same result can also be obtained by irresponsible use—do not handle surfaces that have to provide a large surface resistance, except in a clean room with recommended procedures and equipment.

Galvanic voltages

The use of electronic production techniques in instruments is now so extensive that it is evident that few, if any, contemporary sensitive instruments do not have a printed circuit in their construction. A problem that might arise from this situation, particularly after a repair or modification involving soldering, is that a condition may be created in which a copper strip is linked via a dried flux path to a soldered joint. If the flux is acid based and becomes damp, the constituent parts of a battery (copper plus acid plus zinc) are present and a galvanic voltage is produced which can add to (or subtract from) the measurand.

7.1.3 Pressure

The effects of environmental pressure changes are most likely to occur in the instances that involve the dielectric properties of air at atmospheric pressure. A situation where this is possible is one in which an air vane capacitor is in use, but fortunately the change in capacitance due to the small changes in dielectric will be very small and therefore normally negligible.

Of greater consequence is the effect of pressure in the method used for measuring a high voltage by the breakdown of an air gap between spheres. In setting a gap length for a particular voltage, an allowance must be made for any deviation from a pressure of 760 mm of mercury (see BS 358: 1960). Should relatively rapid changes in pressure occur due, say, to unsettled weather conditions, inconsistency in measurement will result.

7.1.4 Multiple Earths and Earth Loops

Ideally all the earth connections in a system are at the same (zero) potential but this can only be true if the earth path has zero resistance and inductance. This is not possible in a practical case, and any circuits which use the earth connections as a current return path will cause a voltage gradient to exist along the earth path. Two effects result from this. First, capacitive coupling between the earth path and the signal conductor may result in electrostatic interference being added to the signal. Secondly, if the return current is added to earth currents from shields and other circuits, these will appear to the measuring circuit as an increase in signal level.

To reduce this type of interference it is vital to avoid using the earth path as a signal return path, and also to make sure that a circuit is only earthed at one point—if more than one point is used and currents are flowing in the earth path,

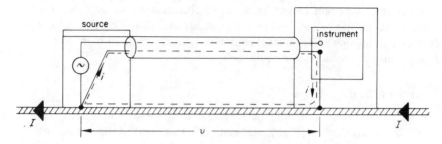

Figure 7.1. Earth loop and circulating current

a current i will circulate through the signal circuit (see figure 7.1), the magnitude of i depending on v, the volt drop between earth points and the lead resistances. [3,4] This circulatory path is termed an earth loop.

7.1.5 Inherent Noise

Some noise or unwanted signals that are present in a sensitive measuring system are generated within the components or parts of the system. One such source of electrical noise results from poor connections, which may be due to bad soldering or dirt on switch contacts. It is therefore vital when dealing with small signal levels that great care is taken in forming joints and contacts. Another source of noise (normally at twice power frequency) is that which results from insufficient smoothing of direct voltage supplies to such items as amplifiers.

Voltage and current noise also result from the energy fluctuations generated by the random movement of free electrons within a conductor (Brownian movement). The spectrum of this noise covers all frequencies and is the limiting level to which noise may be reduced in a sensitive measuring system. Its effect may only be limited by making the system bandwidth as narrow as is acceptable in relation to the bandwidth of the signal.

7.2 COMPONENT IMPURITIES

It is almost impossible to manufacture a component so that it has only one property: for example, a resistance will have an associated reactance, a capacitor will have a leakage resistance and an inductor will have a resistance per turn and an interturn capacitance. However, a particular quantity may be made dominant, and it is possible to design 'pure' components for specified limits of operation.

Under zero frequency conditions of operation the quantity most likely to cause interference is the leakage resistance of insulating materials, where conduction may be either through the material or across its surface. When components have, for isolation purposes, to be mounted on insulating supports, the insulation should be of good quality and have sufficient length so that the conduction paths between the terminals of the component and between the

component and earth are of negligible consequence. This is of particular impor
ance when high voltages are in use, or when high resolution measurements are
being made.

7.2.1 Frequency Effects

The effects of frequency on the permittivity and dielectric loss of an insulating
material are of consequence and figure 7.2 shows typical characteristics. These
variations are largely due to polarisation effects, of which there are two types—
dipole and interfacial. Dipole polarisation occurs in dielectrics having polar

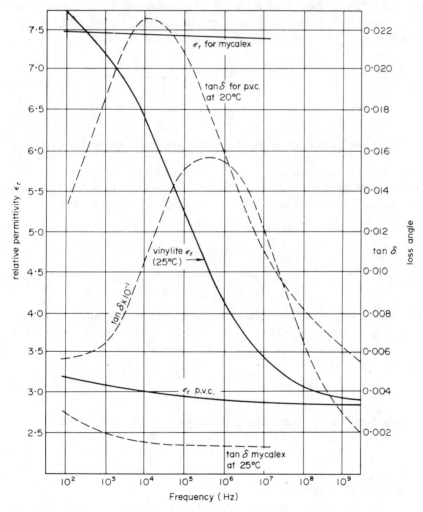

Figure 7.2. Frequency characteristics of some insulating materials (see
reference 7)

molecules, and causes the permittivity and loss angle to be appreciably affected by variations in both temperature and frequency. Interfacial polarisation (also known as dielectric absorption) occurs in composite dielectrics such as mica, but the effects of frequency on the permittivity and loss angle of this type of material are generally not as large as the effects on a dipole material.

7.2.2 Resistor Impurities

The use of resistors and resistive networks in instrumentation is extensive, and since many resistors are constructed by winding resistance wire on to bobbins, they will possess an amount of inductance. This inductive impurity of a resistor may be greatly reduced by using one of the various special noninductive forms of winding[5,6] (for example, bifilar, woven mat, Ayrton–Perry, etc.), but a

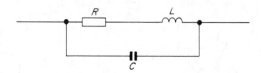

Figure 7.3. Equivalent circuit of a resistor at low and medium frequencies

small amount of inductance will remain together with a self capacitance. The resulting impedance, which is predominantly resistive, may be represented (at medium and low frequencies) by the circuit in figure 7.3 from which

$$Z = \frac{(1/j\omega C)(R + j\omega L)}{R + j\omega L + (1/j\omega C)} \tag{7.1}$$

$$= \frac{R + j\omega(L - \omega^2 L^2 C - CR^2)}{1 + \omega^2 C^2 R^2 - 2\omega^2 LC + \omega^4 L^2 C^2} \tag{7.2}$$

Now for a resistor that has been constructed so that its inductance and capacitance are small, $\omega^2 LC \ll 1$ and the $\omega^4 C^2 L^2$ term may be neglected as the square of a small number, so that equation 7.2 may be simplified to

$$Z = \frac{R + j\omega [L(1 - \omega^2 LC) - CR^2]}{1 + \omega^2 C(CR^2 - 2L)} \tag{7.3}$$

Splitting Z into the real and imaginary terms gives an effective resistance

$$R_{eff} = \frac{R}{1 + \omega^2 C(CR^2 - 2L)} \tag{7.4}$$

and an effective reactance

$$X_{eff} = \frac{\omega [L(1 - \omega^2 LC) - CR^2]}{1 + \omega^2 C(CR^2 - 2L)} \tag{7.5}$$

Now X_{eff} will be small and therefore the term $\omega^2 LC$ may be dropped from the numerator of equation 7.5; then

$$X_{eff} = \frac{\omega(L - CR^2)}{1 + \omega^2 C(CR^2 - 2L)} \qquad (7.6)$$

The phase angle of a resistor is often of importance. Let the phase angle be ϕ, then from equations 7.4 and 7.6

$$\tan \phi = \frac{X_{eff}}{R_{eff}} = \frac{\omega(L - CR^2)}{R} = \omega\left(\frac{L}{R} - CR\right) \qquad (7.7)$$

It is interesting to note that $(L/R - CR)$ is the time constant of the resistor.

From equation 7.4 it is apparent that if $CR^2 = 2L$ then $R_{eff} = R$ (the zero frequency resistance). Also from equation 7.7 it is desirable that $L = CR^2$ so that the resistor has zero time constant, reactance and phase angle. The term CR^2 cannot be equal to $2L$ and L simultaneously, it being more desirable in practice to make $L = CR^2$ to obtain zero time constant and accept the resulting small change in resistance value with frequency. Then

$$R_{eff} = \frac{R}{1 - \omega^2 CL} \qquad (7.8)$$

Note: Equation 7.8 is only valid if $L = CR^2$. If this condition is not met R_{eff} will behave according to equation 7.4 and will increase or decrease with increasing frequency depending on whether CR^2 is larger or smaller than $2L$.

At high frequencies the resistor must be represented by an equivalent circuit of distributed components (figure 7.4). This circuit is a simplification, for a complete analysis should include the effects of interturn capacitance, and mutual couplings between turns. The solution of this type of network is performed using the techniques found in transmission line theory.

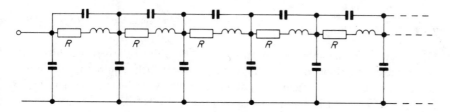

Figure 7.4. Equivalent circuit of a resistor for high frequency analysis

7.2.3 Inductor Properties

The equivalent circuit of an air-cored inductor may also be represented by that in figure 7.3, except that the relative magnitudes of the components will be different. Thus at low and medium frequencies the impedance of an inductor is obtained by using the same mathematical expression as for a resistor, that is, equation 7.2 which is

$$Z = \frac{R + j\omega\,[L(1 - \omega^2 LC) - CR^2]}{1 + \omega^2 C^2 R^2 - 2\omega^2 LC + \omega^4 L^2 C^2}$$

Now in the construction of such an inductor, the resistance and capacitance will be the components that are kept to a minimum, so that if in the above expression the products of small quantities are neglected (that is, the terms $\omega^2 C^2 R^2$ and CR^2)

$$Z = \frac{R + j\omega L(1 - \omega^2 CL)}{1 - 2\omega^2 LC + \omega^4 L^2 C^2} \tag{7.9}$$

giving an effective resistance

$$R_{\text{eff}} = \frac{R}{(1 - \omega^2 LC)^2} \tag{7.10}$$

Now, the effective reactance

$$X_{\text{eff}} = \frac{\omega L(1 - \omega^2 LC)}{(1 - \omega^2 LC)^2} \tag{7.11}$$

and the effective inductance

$$L_{\text{eff}} = \frac{L}{(1 - \omega^2 LC)} \tag{7.12}$$

thus showing that both the effective resistance and inductance of an inductor increase with frequency. As with the resistor this analysis is a simplification and can only be said to apply for an air-cored inductor at low and medium frequencies. At high frequencies the inductor should be treated as consisting of distributed parameters and resolved by using transmission line analysis techniques.

7.2.4 Capacitor Properties

The effects of frequency on a capacitor are two-fold. Firstly, there are the effects due to the connections to and within the capacitor, which require the inclusion in the equivalent circuit (figure 7.5) of a resistor and an inductance (R and L). The other effects of frequency on a capacitor are those effects of frequency already referred to in the behaviour of dielectrics (section 7.2.1). Thus the resistor R_1 representing the leakage resistance of the capacitor in the equivalent circuit will have a value that is a function of frequency. However, in the following analysis it is assumed that the capacitor is to be operated at a low or medium frequency such that R_1 may be considered as having constant magnitude. Then

$$Z = R + j\omega L + \frac{R_1/(j\omega C)}{R_1 + (1/j\omega C)}$$

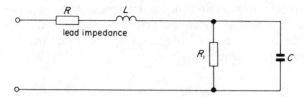

Figure 7.5. Equivalent circuit of a capacitor

$$Z = R + \frac{R_1}{1 + \omega^2 R_1^{\ 2} C^2} + j\omega \left(L - \frac{CR_1^{\ 2}}{1 + \omega^2 R_1^{\ 2} C^2} \right) \qquad (7.13)$$

Also

$$\text{effective reactance} = \frac{1}{j\omega C_{\text{eff}}}$$

$$\frac{1}{\omega C_{\text{eff}}} = -\omega L + \frac{\omega C R_1^{\ 2}}{1 + \omega^2 R_1^{\ 2} C^2}$$

or

$$\omega C_{\text{eff}} = \frac{1 + \omega^2 R_1^{\ 2} C^2}{\omega C R_1^{\ 2} - \omega L (1 + \omega^2 R_1^{\ 2} C^2)} \qquad (7.14)$$

and provided that $\omega^2 R_1^{\ 2} C^2$ is large compared with 1

$$\omega C_{\text{eff}} = \frac{\omega C}{1 - \omega^2 CL}$$

The effective capacitance (medium frequencies) is

$$C_{\text{eff}} \approx C(1 + \omega^2 CL) \qquad (7.15)$$

Note: At the frequency $\omega = 1/(LC)^{1/2}$ a resonant condition will be produced; it is therefore important that the inductance of leads is kept to a minimum so that the resonant frequency is high.

The effective series resistance (medium frequency) is

$$R_{\text{eff}} = R + \frac{R_1}{1 + \omega^2 R_1^{\ 2} C^2} \qquad (7.16)$$

The loss angle δ is obtained from

$$\tan \delta = \frac{1}{\omega C_{\text{eff}} R_{\text{eff}}} = \frac{(\omega C R_1^{\ 2} - \omega L - \omega^3 R_1^{\ 2} C^2 L)}{R + \omega^2 R_1^{\ 2} RC + R_1}$$

$$\approx \frac{1 - \omega^2 CL}{\omega R + (1/\omega C R_1)} \qquad (7.17)$$

At low frequencies the effects of the series inductance L and the series resistor R are negligible provided that external connections are kept as short as possible. Then from equations 7.14 and 7.16 it can be seen that the effective series resistance (low frequency) is

$$R_{eff} = \frac{R_1}{1 + \omega^2 C^2 R_1{}^2} \tag{7.18}$$

and the effective capacitance (low frequency) is

$$C_{eff} = C + \frac{1}{\omega^2 C R_1{}^2} \tag{7.19}$$

As the frequency applied to a capacitor is increased the values of capacitance and tan δ show a fall in magnitude until the effects of lead inductance become important, when an increase in loss angle and effective capacitance will occur.[6, 7,8,9] Figure 7.6 shows the form of characteristic to be expected from a capacitor with a mica dielectric. Mica (a composite dielectric) exhibits a small amount of dielectric absorption (interfacial polarisation) and is the most suitable dielectric for use in capacitors where a high degree of stability is required.

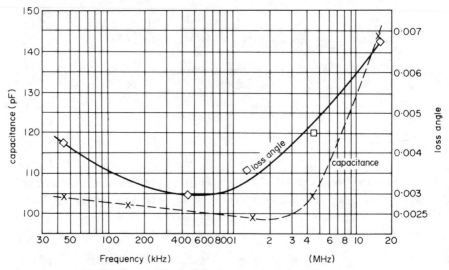

Figure 7.6. Frequency characteristics of a 100 pF mica dielectric capacitor measured using a Q meter

7.2.5 Component Impurity Effects on Signals

There is a tendency to think of instrument input impedances as purely resistive. From the above it is apparent that this is unlikely to be true, and the reactive component of an instrument's input impedance could introduce both a phase angle error and a frequency dependent error into the measurement. Although in general the phase angle error is of negligible consequence (the quantity of interest being the modulus of the measurand), the change with frequency occurring in the input impedance of an instrument cannot be neglected since an inductive component in a measuring circuit will cause the impedance to increase with frequency and a capacitive reactance results in a decreasing impedance with frequency. Both these effects are likely to vary with the instrument's sensitivity, while another effect may result if the measuring circuit contains both inductance and capacitance in series, for then at some frequency

$$f = \frac{1}{2\pi(LC)^{1/2}} \qquad (7.20)$$

there will be resonance.

Since the performance of a measuring circuit containing reactance will be affected by frequency, the effects of reactance in a measuring circuit will be of particular importance if transient phenomena are involved, for example, the monitoring of a pulse train. This situation is equivalent to a series of step changes and, should undesired parasitic reactances be present in the circuitry of an instrument, the signal will emerge distorted, for effectively it has been passed through filters (see section 6.4).

7.3 COUPLED INTERFERENCE

In section 1.6 the situations creating coupled interference voltages were described as resulting from electrostatic and electromagnetic fields.

7.3.1 Electrostatic Interference

This is due to the capacitive coupling that exists between conducting surfaces. To shield one conducting surface from the electrostatic field caused by the potential on another, an earth (or zero potential) screen must be positioned between them.

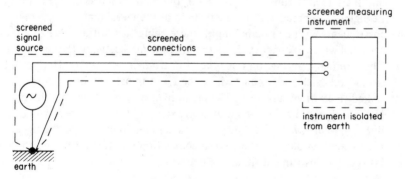

Figure 7.7. 'Ideal' screened measuring system

In a practical measuring system this principle must be extended so that both the connections between, and the component parts of, the system are contained within the shield (see figure 7.7). Such an arrangement is an ideal, being a simplification of the conditions that are probable in practice where, for example, both the source and the measuring instrument may have one terminal permanently connected to the power supply earth. In addition to this any practical screen will have a resistance and an inductance, and earth currents flowing through it will cause a potential gradient along the length of the screen. Since there will be a capacitive coupling between the screen and the screened conductor or components, a certain amount of interference may result. It is therefore necessary to consider the conditions that are likely to occur in practice, although it should be realised that there are an almost infinite number of combinations of connections, components and arrangements. It is therefore only possible to indicate general principles.

Instrument screen connections

It has been stated that a measuring instrument may in practice have a shielding arrangement different from that of the ideal shown in figure 7.7 and since the measuring instrument is likely to be the most expensive component of a measuring system, it is sensible to arrange the screening of the system based on the measuring instrument's earth. This 'earth' will be combined with the input terminals in one of the following ways.

(a) Instruments with two input terminals, one of which is connected to the power line earth. This type of arrangement, which is used on many popular instruments (for example, many general purpose oscilloscopes and valve voltmeters), means that only signals from sources isolated from earth (figure 7.8a) may be measured without introducing errors due to interference voltages. The alternative to this is that the instrument measures the signal plus any interference e.m.f.s, for example, those due to current circulating around the 'earth' loop formed between the earth connections and the screen (figure 7.8b). However, these interference voltages may be negligible compared with the magnitude of the measurand.

(b) Instruments with an isolated input, there being an additional 'earth' input terminal which is connected, via the instrument chassis, to the supply earth. The terminal markings on this type of instrument are usually Hi (high), Lo (low), and earth (or ground) where the Lo terminal may be a virtual earth or linked to earth via a resistor. The instrument may be fitted with an input lead which could either be a double coaxial lead (or a screened twin conductor), figures 7.8c and d being typical connections. Should the signal source have an output via a coaxial connection, the three conductor input leads of the instrument should be connected to it as shown in figures 7.8e or f.

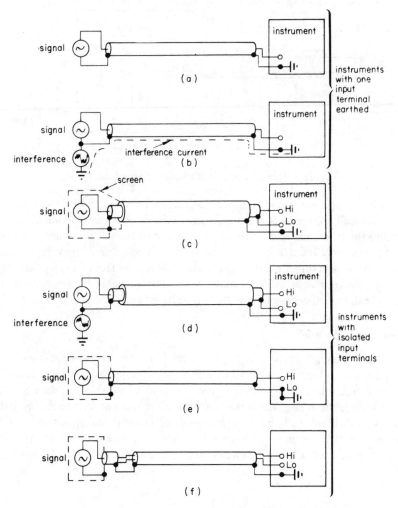

Figure 7.8. Practical screen connections for measurement systems

(c) The fulfilment of the ideal, where the only earth connection is on one side
     of the signal source, may only be obtained when instruments are used that
     have no connections with external supplies (for example, battery powered
     instruments), or are fitted with special guard circuits which isolate the
     instrument and its screen from the power supply earth, that is, power is fed
     into the instruments via a screened isolating transformer (figure 7.9). This
     sort of screening technique is expensive and is only normally resorted to in
     high calibre instruments (for example, in some sensitive digital voltmeters)
     which are termed *guarded instruments*.

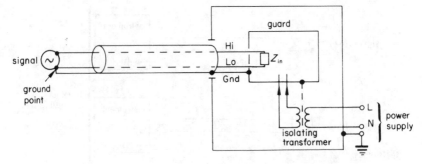

Figure 7.9. Instrument with isolated guard circuit

It will be apparent from the above that there are three common forms of electrostatically screened connection, namely the coaxial lead, the double coaxial lead and the twin conductor with screen. The last of these is sometimes termed microphone cable and is only suitable for zero and medium frequency applications, while the coaxial (single and double) are suitable for use from d.c. to gigahertz, although at high frequencies care may be necessary to match the impedance of the cable to that of connectors to avoid reflections and distortion of the signal.

Transformer screening

Signal conditioning circuits may require external power, for example when operational amplifiers are involved (see section 6.7.1); it may also be desirable to screen and isolate them from the power supply. A few remarks relating to the use of screened isolating transformers are therefore relevant. A screened isolating transformer will normally have either a single or a double screen and when constructed with the former it is usual to connect the screen either into the circuit (figure 7.10a), or to the mid-point of the secondary winding (figure 7.10b). [10]

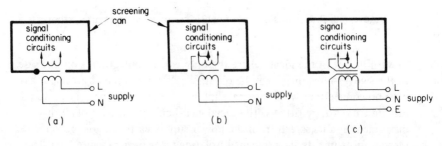

Figure 7.10. Isolating transformer screen connections

Neither of these arrangements removes all the interference, and while a single screen is satisfactory for some applications, the best results are obtained when a double screen is used and connected as shown in figure 7.10c.

Amplifier screening

The connection of guard or screen circuits to and around amplifiers is of considerable importance, for if interference voltages are applied to their input the magnitude of these unwanted signals will be increased along with the signal from the measurand. Consider first the use of a single-ended amplifier as part of a measurement system comprising of sensor, signal conditioning and display or recording instrument. If the transducer has a single coaxial lead output then the connection arrangement should be as in figure 7.11, but when the transducer has a 'twin plus earth' output the connections used are as shown in figure 7.12.

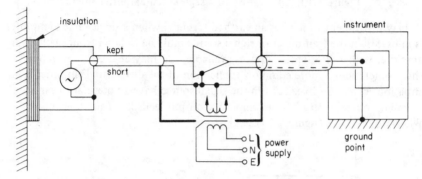

Figure 7.11. A practical shielding arrangement when the source has a single coaxial output connection

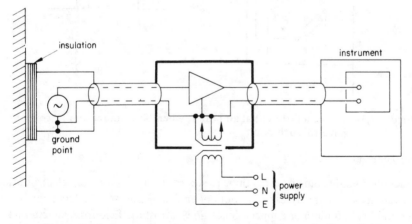

Figure 7.12. A superior arrangement to that shown in figure 7.11

Although both these arrangements reduce the interference from that which would exist if no shielding were used, a greater reduction still may be obtained by using segmented shielding, such as that shown in figure 7.13 where the amplifier shield is held at the same potential as the zero (low) potential input lead of the amplifier. It must, however, be appreciated that should it be desired to use a

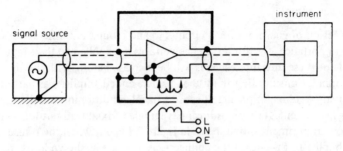

Figure 7.13. Application of a segmented amplifier shield

display instrument which has an earthed terminal when a single-ended amplifier is in use, then the transducer or signal source must be isolated from earth. If an amplifier with a differential input is available, this may be used to overcome the problem, but a more common application of the differential amplifier is in situations where both leads from the signal source have a potential to earth, or 'common mode' voltage, for example the output leads from an unbalanced Wheatstone bridge (figure 7.14).[11]

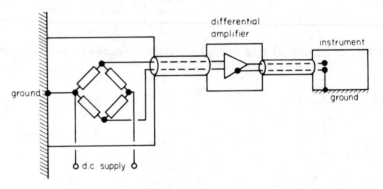

Figure 7.14. Use of a differential amplifier, when both source and instrument have an earth point

Faraday cage

A method used in some investigations to screen the apparatus from electrostatic interference is a 'Faraday cage'—a room or enclosure constructed from wire mesh (preferably aluminium or copper). Since no electrostatic field from an external source can exist within a metal container, the apparatus within the cage will only be subject to electrostatic fields produced within the cage, provided power supplies are conducted into it via screened isolating transformers. When using this technique to shield from electrostatic interference, moderately sized holes may be cut in the enclosing screen without impairing the effectiveness of the screen.

Guard rings

One further application of electrostatic screening that should be mentioned is
the use of guard rings in the control of the magnitude of a capacitance. Figure
7.15 illustrates that without the use of an earthed guard ring the value of capacitance between the plates A and B could only be calculated approximately.
Because of the unknown magnitude of the fringing effects, however, when an
earthed guard ring is added the field between A and B is more defined and agreement between calculated and measured values of capacitance will be much closer.
Possibly of greater value will be the fact that external fields and objects will have
very much less effect on the magnitude of the guarded capacitor than these
effects on an unguarded capacitor. Figure 7.16 is a diagrammatic section of a
high voltage capacitor, fitted with guard rings, and filled with gas at a pressure
above atmospheric. The connection of such a capacitor into a screened Schering
bridge circuit is given in figure 7.17 (see also section 3.4.1).

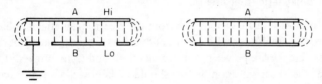

Figure 7.15. Circular parallel plate capacitor, with and without a guard ring

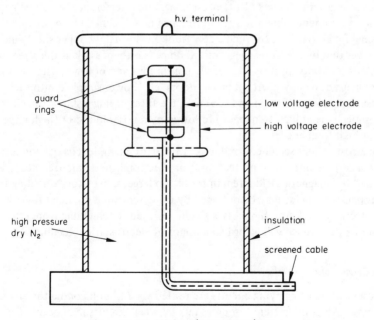

Figure 7.16. High voltage capacitor

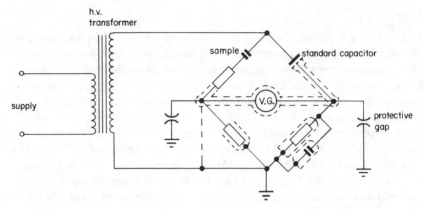

Figure 7.17. Shielding arrangement of a high voltage Schering bridge

7.3.2 Electromagnetic Interference

Since this form of interference results from the electromagnetic coupling of a current carrying conductor with other conductors, the most likely sources of this type of interference are power supply connections and transformers. It is evident that signal carrying conductors should be kept well clear of such items, and if necessary screened from them by using a shield made from a high permeability material.

To eliminate the effects of r.f. electromagnetic interference it may be necessary to place equipment subject to r.f. interference in a screened enclosure or room. The shield material used for such a construction is usually copper sheet, and since the prevention of electromagnetic interference is only possible if the screen is complete, all joints must be electrically continuous and of low resistance, that is, there must not be any open circuits at doors, etc. Power supplied into such an enclosure should be filtered and screened, the filter having a shunt capacitor (low impedance at high frequency) followed by a series inductor (high impedance at high frequency).

Electrostatically screened conductors[3,4] (for example, coaxial connections) afford a certain amount of protection from electromagnetic interference, and provided the magnetic field strength is not too large, satisfactory shielding from electromagnetic fields may be obtained by using screening intended for shielding from electrostatic fields. Similarly a shield designed for shielding from electromagnetic interference will afford an amount of electrostatic screening.

7.3.3 Cross Talk

When several signal carrying circuits are routed via a ribbon conductor or a multi-conductor cable, interference or cross talk between circuits may occur. The magnitude of this form of interference, which appears as a mixing of signals, is dependent on a combination of electrostatic and electromagnetic coupling and results from the size and spacing of conductors, the strength of the signals and the magnitudes of the impedances of the signal sources and the instrument or circuit receiving the signal. The effects of cross talk may be reduced to acceptable levels by increasing the spacing between conductors, screening the most affected circuits, or (if a ribbon conductor is used), interspersing signal carrying conductors with earthed conductors. Cross talk can also occur across switches (for example, where one from a number of inputs can be connected to the input of an amplifier) and between amplifiers that share, for example, a power supply. In some situations (decoupling) capacitors can advantageously be connected across the input of the instrument or circuit that is receiving the interference, but care must be taken in doing this or loading of the source and distortion of the signal may occur.

7.4 NOISE REJECTION SPECIFICATIONS

In a practical situation a signal source will be subject to some if not all the types of interference described above. So that the capabilities of instruments to reject noise may be specified, and compared, interference of all frequencies and from all sources is considered either as occurring within the signal source and referred to as *normal mode noise*, or to occur between the earth terminal of the instrument and the lower potential terminal of the measurand when it is termed *common mode noise*. The basic equivalent circuit for the combined situation is shown in figure 7.18.

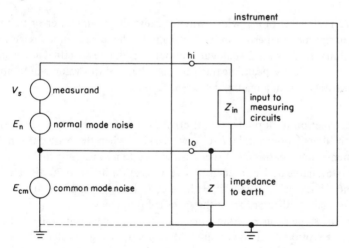

Figure 7.18. Simplified equivalent circuit for instrument connected to measurand subjected to interference

7.4.1 Normal Mode Noise

This is the blanket term applied to all direct and alternating interference voltages that appear to the instrument (or measuring circuit) as part of the measurand.
   If the measurand is effectively a direct voltage (that is, a slowly varying volt-

age level), interference voltages resulting from galvanic and thermoelectric effects within the signal source are, to the instrument, indistinguishable from the actual quantity it is desired to measure. It is therefore vital to ensure that the possibilities for their occurrence are kept to a minimum. Alternating normal mode interference can be caused by external electrostatic and electromagnetic fields coupling with the components and connections of the signal source or by inherent effects such as Brownian noise within components.

The ability of an instrument or system to reject an alternating signal superimposed on a direct voltage measured is termed its *normal mode rejection ratio* (N.M.R.R.) or *series mode rejection ratio* and is usually specified in one of two ways.

(a)   As the ratio of the peak of the normal mode interference voltage (E_n) to the peak of the error (E_e) it produces in a reading at a particular frequency. That is

$$\text{N.M.R.R.} = 20 \log_{10}\left(\frac{E_n \text{ (peak volts)}}{E_e \text{ (peak volts)}}\right) \text{dB at } f \text{ Hz} \qquad (7.21)$$

For example, the N.M.R.R. for a particular instrument could be specified as 60 dB at 50 Hz. *Note:* This ratio should apply to all signal levels from zero to full scale of all ranges.

(b)   As a peak value of E_n, which will not cause the voltmeter error to be greater than the specified error limit. For example, the normal mode rejection for a 100 mV f.s.d., class 2 analogue voltmeter, could be specified as a 50 Hz voltage of 200 V peak, meaning that a voltage of this value would not cause the total error in a reading to exceed 2 mV.

The reduction of normal mode alternating interference may be performed by rejection filters (for example, L–C, low pass) but when these are used in digital instruments, the measurement speed is reduced to allow a 'settling' time. Commercially available active filters may give a rejection of 30 to 70 dB at a specified frequency, but some of these filters have considerably less attenuation at frequencies only slightly different from the specified frequency.

The dual slope or integrating conversion technique used in some digital voltmeters (see section 4.2.1) owes much of its popularity to its characteristic interference rejection for frequencies that have a period which is a sub-multiple of the sampling interval, that is, if the sampling time were 40 ms, good rejection of 25, 50, 75, 100, 125, 150, 175, 200 Hz, etc., is obtained. Figure 7.19 shows the characteristic N.M.R.R./frequency curve for a digital voltmeter of this type. The slow response curve is the result of combining the effects of the digitising technique and a low pass rejection filter.

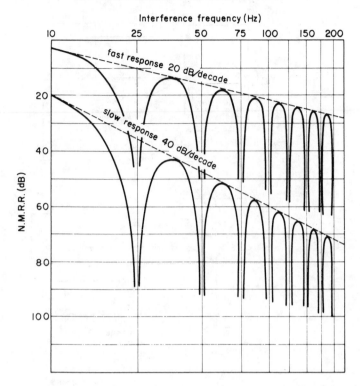

Figure 7.19. Variation in normal mode rejection ratio with frequency

7.4.2 Common Mode Noise

This is the term used to encompass all alternating and direct voltages that are present between the earth of the measuring instrument and the lower potential connection of the signal being measured. Hence common mode voltage may be a combination of

(a) the measurand being at some voltage level (or reference) to earth (figure 7.20a)
(b) the effects of earth loop currents (figures 7.1 and 7.20b), and
(c) the result of other sources of interference, for example, electrostatic and electromagnetic coupling (figure 7.20c).

Floating instruments

To facilitate the taking of measurements in the presence of common mode voltages, the measuring circuit of the instrument must be electrically isolated (insulated) from earth, a condition that is conventionally termed 'floating'. The effectiveness of this isolation is specified by the ability of an instrument to

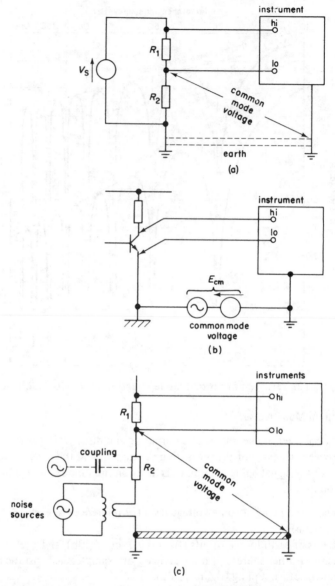

Figure 7.20. Common mode voltages produced by: (a) voltage across other components, (b) earth loop, (c) coupling

prevent common mode voltages introducing an error into a reading. Since common mode voltages may be alternating or direct, and the isolation between measuring circuits and earth will, effectively, be an impedance with resistive and reactive (capacitive) components, the magnitude of the common mode rejection ratio (C.M.R.R.) will be frequency dependent. Hence for direct voltages

$$C.M.R.R. = 20 \log_{10}\left(\frac{E_{cm}}{E_e}\right) \text{ dB} \qquad (7.22)$$

and for alternating voltages

$$C.M.R.R. = 20 \log_{10}\left(\frac{E_{cm} \text{ (peak)}}{E_e \text{ (peak)}}\right) \text{ dB at } f \text{ Hz} \qquad (7.23)$$

where f is a specified frequency.

Ideally the C.M.R.R. of any floating instrument should be infinite, and dia-grammatically the ideal case may be as shown in figure 7.21, where Z_2 and Z_3 are the isolation impedances between 'low' and earth and 'high' and earth respectively.

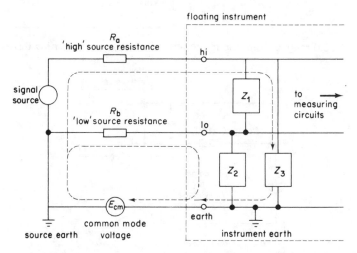

Figure 7.21. Ideal common mode rejection situation in floating instrument

If Z_3 and Z_2 are equal and much larger than R_a and R_b (the lead resistances), the common mode current will divide equally between the two loops shown in figure 7.21. Additionally, if $R_a = R_b$ the voltage drop across Z_3 applied to the top of Z_1 would equal the drop across Z_2 applied to the bottom of Z_1 and there would be no voltage difference across Z_1 due to the common mode current, that is, no error voltage due to the common mode voltage. Such a voltmeter is termed a 'balanced' floating voltmeter. If $R_a \neq R_b$ there will be a normal mode offset voltage proportional to the difference between R_a and R_b.

In most floating instruments Z_2 and Z_3 are far from equal, Z_3 being $\gg Z_2$ ($Z_3 \to$ O.C.). The instrument is then represented by the diagram in figure 7.22 and the common mode current flows through the parallel paths shown, develop-ing a voltage across R_b. The same voltage will be dropped across R_a in series with Z_1, the greater portion being across Z_1, which the measuring circuits will respond to. Now most of the common mode voltage dropped across R_b will become

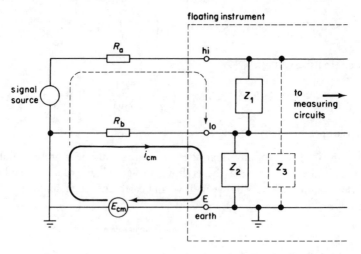

Figure 7.22. Practical common mode rejection situation in floating instrument

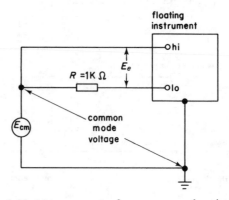

Figure 7.23. Measurement of common mode rejection

normal mode offset, so the common mode error depends almost entirely on the relationship between Z_2 and R_b. R_b is usually lead resistance and Z_2 the isolation impedance between two metallic chassis (10^8-10^{10} Ω) shunted by a capacitance of a few pF to fractions of a μF. At d.c. $Z_2 \gg R_b$ but as frequency rises Z_2 falls, giving poorer immunity to common mode signals at high frequencies. Z_2 is also very dependent on the environment, high humidity and dust causing a decrease in its value.

For conformity of specifications, instrument manufacturers have agréed that C.M.R.R. should normally be specified with an unbalance of 1 kΩ in source resistance (for example R_b = 1 kΩ, R_a = 0). An arrangement suitable for measuring the C.M.R.R. of an instrument with a floating input is shown in figure 7.23. For the conditions in that diagram, E_{cm} is the applied common mode voltage (alternating or direct as appropriate) and E_e is the error it causes in the voltage reading on the instrument.

Example

For a particular digital voltmeter, when subjected to the situation illustrated in figure 7.23, a voltage reading of 15 mV was observed when the applied common mode direct voltage was 100 V. What is the C.M.R.R. of the voltmeter?

$$\text{C.M.R.R.} = 20 \log_{10} \left(\frac{100}{0.015} \right) \text{dB}$$

$$= 76.5 \text{ dB}$$

In a practical measurement situation the imbalance between R_a and R_b will not always be 1 kΩ, but since it has been shown that the C.M.R.R. is really dependent on R_b and Z_2, to a close approximation

$$\text{C.M.R.R.} = 20 \log_{10} \left(\frac{i_{cm} Z_2}{i_{cm} R_b} \right) \text{dB}$$

or

$$\text{C.M.R.R.} = 20 \log_{10} \left(\frac{Z_2}{R_b} \right) \text{dB} \qquad (7.24)$$

and an estimate of the magnitude of Z_2 can be made enabling the error effect of R_b and the common mode voltage to be apparent as

$$E_e = \frac{R_b E_{cm}}{Z_2}$$

Example

A digital voltmeter is specified as having a direct voltage C.M.R.R. of 100 dB with a source unbalance of 1 kΩ. Determine the maximum error voltage that a 20 V common mode voltage would give in reading a signal from a source that has a 600 Ω unbalance.

$$\text{C.M.R.R.} = 20 \log_{10} \left(\frac{Z_2}{1000} \right) \text{dB}$$

Therefore

$$Z_2 = 10^8 \ \Omega$$

and

$$E_e = \frac{600 \times 20}{10^8} = 120 \ \mu\text{V}$$

'Floating' instruments usually have a C.M.R.R. of 80 to 120 dB for direct voltages and 60 to 100 dB at line frequency. These levels are sufficient for analogue and three-digit instruments, but for high resolution sensitive voltmeters they will not be adequate and the 'guard' technique must be used.

Guarded voltmeter

This type of voltmeter has an additional shield between the low and ground, effectively increasing the low to ground leakage impedance—this shield or guard is normally connected into the circuit via the guard terminal. The extra shield divides the low to ground impedance into series impedances Z_2 and Z_3 (figure 7.24), increasing the leakage resistance and decreasing the capacitance. This

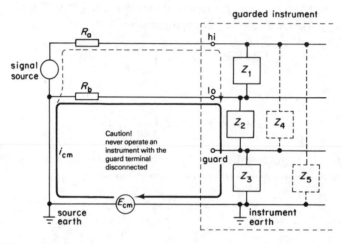

Figure 7.24. Common mode current paths in a guarded voltmeter

improves the C.M.R.R. but the greatest advantage is obtained when the guard is properly connected into the circuit being investigated. If the guard is not connected, the arrangement is theoretically as before but with a slight improvement due to the increase in the impedance of the common mode current path. However, such an attitude is bad practice[12] for it can cause reading errors due to currents through the stray capacitances between Lo, guard and earth. Also if the common mode voltage is large, the voltage stored on the Lo to guard capacitance may exceed the 100 V maximum that is usually allowed between these points. Hence, proper connection of the guard is important. If the guard terminal is not being used, it should be connected to the Lo terminal, such a situation being acceptable when

(a) no common mode voltage exists
(b) making low accuracy measurements
(c) making insensitive measurement (resolution above 10 μV)
(d) using short signal leads.

Connection of the guard terminal is required when

(a) common mode voltages exist
(b) making accurate measurements
(c) required resolution is below $10 \ \mu V$
(d) using long signal leads.

By correctly connecting the guard, the common mode current is shunted away from the source resistance and virtually removes the effects of R_a and R_b from the common mode circuit. That is, since the common mode current through R_b tends to zero, the error caused by the common mode voltage tends to zero.

To obtain the best results in connecting the guard the following rules should be applied.

(a) Connect the guard so that it and the low terminal have as small a voltage difference between them as possible.
(b) The guard should be connected so that no common mode current or guard current flows through any resistance associated with the input voltage.

The application of these rules to three situations is illustrated in figure 7.25. In figure 7.25a the output from a 'floating' signal source is shown and by connecting the low of the source to the guard of the voltmeter, these points are maintained at the same voltage and no common mode current will pass through R_b. The arrangement in figure 7.25b represents the measurement of the output voltage from a transducer, and while currents due to earth loop and interference common mode voltages are shunted away from the source resistances, there is still a voltage between the low and the guard of the voltmeter. The situation in/ figure 7.25b can be improved on by using the technique shown in figure 7.25c which is known as a *driven guard*. The magnitudes of R_5 and R_6 should be such that their sum is less than one-tenth of the resistance through the bridge [$(R_1 + R_3)$ in parallel with $(R_2 + R_4)$] and the ratio of R_5 to R_6 making E_{guard} approximately equal to E_{low}. If these requirements are met then nearly all of the common mode current will flow through the guard

7.4.3 Signal-to-noise Ratio

There will be internally generated noise in all electronic instruments, and if high gain amplifiers are used in making measurements on small signals, a criterion is required by which the effect of this internally generated noise can be judged. The signal-to-noise ratio is used for this purpose and is defined as the ratio of signal level to noise level. Although it is a power ratio it is usually determined as the ratio of r.m.s. voltages. It is commonly expressed in decibels, that is

$$ S/N = 20 \log_{10} \left(\frac{V_s}{V_n} \right) dB \qquad (7.25) $$

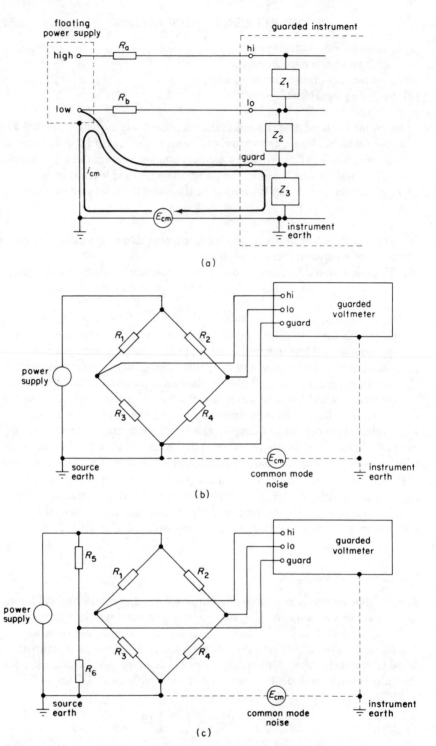

Figure 7.25. Examples of guard connections: (a) floating power supply, (b) output from a bridge circuit, (c) driven guard for a bridge circuit

A method of determining this ratio is to measure, with a suitable r.m.s. responding instrument, the value of the signal plus the noise giving

$$V_{total}^2 = V_{signal}^2 + V_{noise}^2$$

then measuring the noise alone, so that the signal can be evaluated.

REFERENCES

1 N. Channon, The design and analysis of a novel dielectric paste and its use in a thick film humidity transducer (PhD Thesis, Brighton Polytechnic. 1977)

2 British Calibration Service, *General Criteria for Laboratory Approval* (London, 1967)

3 B. A. Gregory, An experiment in shielding and screening, *Int. J. electl engng Educ.*, **9** (1971) 31–5

4 B. A. Gregory, Interference, A teaching package (Brighton Polytechnic, 1979)

5 B. Hauge and T. R. Foord, *A. C. Bridge Methods*, 6th Ed. (Pitman, London, 1971)

6 F. E. Terman and J. M. Pettit, *Electronic Measurements* (McGraw-Hill, New York, 1952)

7 A. R. Von Hippel (ed.), *Dielectric Materials and Applications* (M.I.T. Press, Cambridge, Mass., 1954)

8 J. V. L. Parry, E.R.A. Technical Reports L/T 275 and 325 (Leatherhead, Surrey)

9 H. Fröhlich, *Theory of Dielectrics*, 2nd Ed. (Clarendon, Oxford, 1958)

10 R. Morrison, *Grounding and Shielding Techniques in Instrumentation* (Wiley, New York, 1967)

11 Floating measurements and guarding, Hewlett-Packard Application Note 123 (1970)

12 Calibration-philosophy in practice, *Guarding of Digital Voltmeters, Application Bulletin 20* (John Fluke Manufacturing Co., Seattle, Wash. 1977)

8

Instrument Selection and Specification Analysis

The considerations for selecting an instrument may be regarded as falling into two categories: either an engineer is selecting the most suitable instrument from those within a department or establishment to perform a particular measurement, or he is undertaking the purchase of a new instrument to perform a particular measurement and possibly at the same time extend the measurement capabilities of the department or establishment in which he works. Many of the criteria in selecting an instrument are the same, whether the engineer is selecting an instrument off the shelf or purchasing new equipment. In either case a major pitfall is to 'acquire' the newest and most sophisticated pieces of equipment in the department, or on the market, simply as a prestige exercise. This is of little value if within a week, justifiable pressure is brought to bear by one's colleagues and the prestige instrumentation system is reduced to its minimum requirements—which could be two suspect multimeters and the oldest oscilloscope in the department!

8.1 INSTRUMENT SELECTION

The general criteria for selecting an instrument may be summarised by the following check list, which although it may be more suitable when considering a moderately sophisticated instrument, could prove valuable as a guide in selecting the 'right' instrument on every occasion.

Ranges

(a) What are the maximum and minimum magnitudes of the values to be measured?
(b) Will a single range, or multi-range instrument be the most suitable?

Accuracy

(a) What is the maximum tolerance acceptable?
(b) Is the resolution of the instrument consistent with its specified errors?

Response Characteristics

(a) What is the acceptable response time/bandwidth?
(b) Are frequency compensating probes required?
(c) For autorange (for example, d.v.m.) instruments, must (a) include the time for range and polarity changes, or 'switch on' time?
(d) For a.c. instruments is it desired to sense mean, peak, or r.m.s. values?

Input Characteristics

(a) What are the allowable limits of instrument input impedance?
(b) Can calculations be made to correct for the instrument loading on the measurand?
(c) Is the instrument input impedance constant for all ranges? If not are the variations in magnitude acceptable?
(d) Are there any source impedance restrictions? If so will they affect the operation of the instrument?

Output Characteristics

(a) What form of display is required? For example, graphical, digital, etc.
(b) Is an electrical output required to operate in conjunction with other equipment? If so, what signal levels are required, and what codes are used?

Stability

(a) What is the maximum acceptable time between calibrations?
(b) Is the instrument to be operated unattended for long periods?
(c) Is there a 'built-in' calibration system?

Environment

(a) Over what range of temperature, humidity, line voltage variations, etc., will the instrument be required to operate, and how do these factors affect the errors?
(b) Will the instrument be subjected to mechanical shock or vibration? If so, what will the fundamental frequency be?
(c) Are there any size limitations?
(d) If the instrument is to be permanently installed will access be required for maintenance?

Isolation and Screening

(a) Will the instrument be subjected to stray electromagnetic or electrostatic fields?
(b) Is the measurand 'floating' or has it one side earthed?
(c) Is battery operation or 'guarding' required to ensure adequate performance?
(d) What is the rejection of d.c. and a.c. common mode voltages?

Operation

(a) Is remote control required?
(b) Is automatic or programmed operation required?
(c) What are the effects of intermittent energisation?
(d) Will multi-function operation be advantageous?
(e) Will operator fatigue cause reading interpretation problems?
(f) What power supplies will be required?

Reliability

(a) What is the specified operational life?
(b) What will the consequences of failure be?
(c) Is duplication or standby instrumentation required?
(d) Will special spares and maintenance equipment be required?
(e) Does the instrument incorporate any limit detection or alarm facilities? If so, must a 'fail safe' arrangement be incorporated?

On completion of the above check list for a particular application, the derived specification for the desired instrument may not be possible in practical terms, and a compromise between that which is available within an organisation, or can be afforded, will have to be adopted.

If a new instrument is to be purchased it is essential to ensure that the 'right' instrument is being purchased. This is particularly relevant if the instrument is for a permanent installation although it may be considered as 'good practice' to purchase to a slightly higher specification if the proposed instrument is for use in a laboratory where the measurement requirements may change with experience and time. The problem here, of course, is over-specification resulting in the purchase of an instrument that is much more sophisticated (and expensive) than is really necessary.

The following list is a rough guide to the factors that will increase the cost of an instrument.

(a) reduction of error magnitudes
(b) increasing the speed of reading
(c) increasing the sensitivity
(d) improving the stability
(e) improvement of isolation/guarding (except for battery operation)
(f) the addition of input/output facilities
(g) the addition of programmable capabilities
(h) the extension of operating conditions.

Thus having decided on the requirements of the instrument it is desirable to purchase, it is necessary to study manufacturers' literature and decide on a 'best buy'.

8.2 SPECIFICATION ANALYSIS

Many instruments are manufactured to meet the requirements of national or international standards. To exist in a competitive industry manufacturers will either meet the standard and compete to produce the lowest cost unit or, as is more frequent, endeavour to produce an instrument which they feel has a superior performance to that required by the standard and thereby provide a more satisfactory purchase for the customer. The pressure of sales, and in many cases the lack of an agreed standard, result in manufacturers writing specification or data sheets for each instrument so as to emphasise what they consider the merits of a particular unit while sometimes omitting its less desirable features. These result in different manufacturers emphasising different features of what should be comparative units. It is therefore necessary to extract from the specification sheets the data relevant to one's specific requirements and reduce this to a common level for comparison purposes.

Probably one of the greatest uses of 'spec-manship' is in the specification of the errors of digital voltmeters, which are normally quoted in two parts, for example

(a) 0.01 per cent of reading ± 0.01 per cent of full scale; or
(b) 0.01 per cent of input ± 1 least significant digit (ℓ.s.d.).

Taking these two forms of specification (and there are others), let us compare the maximum uncertainty in instrument reading that is possible if the two forms of specification are applied firstly to an instrument that has a full scale of 9999, and secondly to an instrument that has a full scale of 4999.

For the 9999 full scale instrument, when reading full scale, the maximum possible uncertainty in reading is 0.01 per cent + 0.01 per cent = 0.02 per cent of reading, and over a range will vary as shown in table 8.1. Since 1 ℓ.s.d. = 100

Table 8.1.

Reading	% f.s.	Quoted % uncertainty in reading	Uncertainty quoted as + a % of f.s. as a % of reading	=	Total uncertainty as a % of reading
9999	100	0.01	$\left\{\dfrac{0.01}{100} \times \dfrac{9999}{9999} \times 100 = 0.01\right\}$		0.02
5000	50	0.01	$\left\{\dfrac{0.01}{100} \times \dfrac{9999}{5000} \times 100 = 0.02\right\}$		0.03
2000	20	0.01	$\left\{\dfrac{0.01}{100} \times \dfrac{9999}{2000} \times 100 = 0.05\right\}$		0.06
1000	10	0.01	$\left\{\dfrac{0.01}{100} \times \dfrac{9999}{1000} \times 100 = 0.10\right\}$		0.11

× 1/9999 = 0.01 per cent of full scale the two forms of specification are equivalent for this instrument.

Consider now the 4999 digital voltmeter. Here 1 ℓ.s.d. = 100 × 1/4999 = 0.02 per cent of full scale and an accuracy quoted as ± 0.01 per cent of reading ± 0.01 per cent of range would be incompatible with the resolution of the instrument, for there will always be an uncertainty of at least ± 1 ℓ.s.d. in the display of a digital instrument. Thus the error specification for the 4999 d.v.m. must be of the form ± (0.01 per cent of input + 1 ℓ.s.d.) and the maximum possible uncertainty in the reading over a range may be tabulated in table 8.2.

Table 8.2.

Reading	% f.s.	Quoted % uncertainty + in reading	Uncertainty quoted as 1 l.s.d., as a % of = reading	Total uncertainty as a % of reading
4999	100	0.01	$\dfrac{1}{4999} \times 100 = 0.02$	0.03
2000	40	0.01	$\dfrac{1}{2000} \times 100 = 0.05$	0.06
1000	20	0.01	$\dfrac{1}{1000} \times 100 = 0.10$	0.11
500	10	0.01	$\dfrac{1}{500} \times 100 = 0.20$	0.21

The values of uncertainty tabulated above may, for comparison purposes, be presented in graphical form. By using horizontal axes of (a) percentage of full scale, and (b) reading in volts, two different pictures are presented (see figures 8.1 and 8.2). The latter graph shows that in measuring voltages between 1.000 and 5.000 there is no difference in the magnitude of the uncertainty in the reading when measured by either instrument, whereas this is not at all apparent from the curve in figure 8.1.

The question of digital voltmeter error specification may be further obscured by the influence of temperature. For example the above form of error specification may apply for a range of temperatures from 15 to 40 °C for a particular instrument, whereas other instruments of the same type may have temperature coefficients which affect the accuracy specification. A typical method of specifying this effect is to quote an uncertainty allowance for temperature effects as a percentage of reading plus a percentage of range. For example, ± (0.005 per cent of reading + 0.002 per cent of range) per °C and such effects must be taken into account when the errors of two or more instruments are being compared. As an example, let us reconsider the 9999 d.v.m. and 4999 d.v.m. compared above, assuming that the full error specification of the 9999 instrument is

± (0.01 per cent of reading + 0.01 per cent of range) at 23 °C ± 2 °C

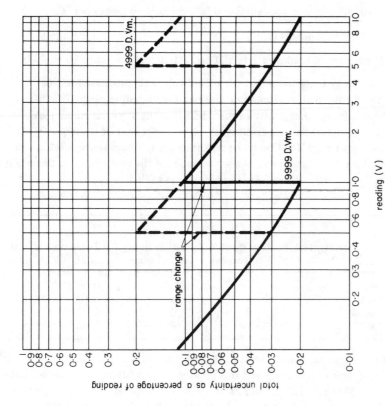

Figure 8.2. Limit of error plotted against reading

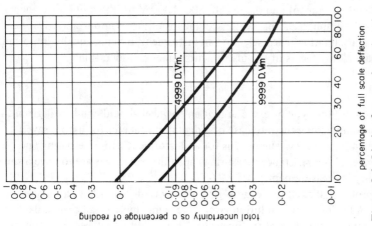

Figure 8.1. Limit of error plotted against percentage of full scale

$\pm$ (0.005 per cent of reading + 0.002 per cent of range) per $^{\circ}$C

and for the 4999 instrument is

$\pm$ (0.01 per cent of reading + 1 ℓ.s.d.) over a temperature range 10 to 40 $^{\circ}$C

Let it further be considered that the digital voltmeter purchased will be required to operate in an environment that has a temperature range from 20 to 35 $^{\circ}$C. The maximum uncertainty in the reading on the 4999 instrument will be as calculated before but an uncertainty of + (0.005 per cent of reading + 0.002 per cent of range) $\times$ 10 $^{\circ}$C/$^{\circ}$C must be added to the values previously tabulated for the 9999 d.v.m. so that an allowance is made for the worst possible uncertainty, that is, that which will occur at 35 $^{\circ}$C, as shown in table 8.3.

Table 8.3.

| | | Effect of temperature allowance | | |
Reading	% uncertainty at 23 $^{\circ}$C	Portion quoted as % of reading	Portion quoted as % of range	Total uncertainty at 30 $^{\circ}$C
9999	0.02	0.05	0.02	0.09
5000	0.03	0.05	0.04	0.12
2000	0.06	0.05	0.10	0.21
1000	0.11	0.05	0.20	0.36

Thus the error comparison curves for our hypothetical digital voltmeters at 35 $^{\circ}$C are as shown in figure 8.3 and this presents a very different picture to that indicated by figure 8.1. This should illustrate that considerable thought must be given before arriving at a decision on the most suitable of a number of instruments, particularly if the ranges are overlapping, for example, 1, 10, 100, 1000 V for the 9999 instrument and 0.5, 5, 50, 500, 1000 V for the 4999 instrument.

It must be emphasised that while accuracy is of major importance, it is not the only consideration when selecting an instrument, it being equally important to compare all the facets of the instruments under consideration.

Example

Let us consider the type of exercise that an engineer should conduct if given the task of recommending the purchase of a digital multimeter for use in, say, a development laboratory. The need is for an instrument with alternating and direct ranges plus a resistance measuring capability; all ranges are to have a small uncertainty in measurement.

This problem, like all real engineering problems, does not have a unique solution. Additionally the solution given here is incomplete—all the similar units on the market at the time of the investigation should be analysed. For convenience and reasons of reducing the amount of information to be detailed, only three instruments (selected at random), have been considered. Further to this the requirements for the instrument are vague and this is a problem common in

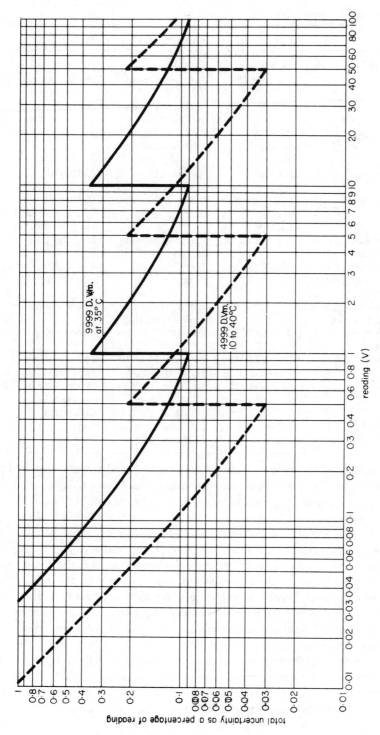

Figure 8.3. Limit of error comparison at 35 °C for the hypothetical d.v.m.s

Table 8.4. General data

	Datron 1057	Fluke 8800A	Solartron 7051
Maximum display	199999	199999	109999
Type	not specified	Seven-segement 0.3 in. L.E.D. automatic decimal location	Seven-segment L.E.D.
Function selection	By front panel push button	By front panel push button	By front panel switch
Range selection	Manual	Manual or automatic	Automatic
Over range	100 % on all except 1000 V	Nil	10% on all ranges except 750 V alternating and 1000 V direct
Overload indication	Not supplied	Flashing display of 188888	Flashing 1
Maximum common mode voltage	500 V pk	1000 V d.c. or peak a.c.	400 V direct or pk alternating
Maximum Lo to guard voltage	250 V pk	100 V direct or peak alternating	100 V maximum
Operating temp range	0 to 50 °C	0 to 50 °C	0 to 45 °C
Supply	105–127 V or 205–255 V at 48 to 440 Hz, 12 VA	110/230 V ± 10 per cent; 50 or 60 Hz, 8 W	115/230 V (+ 10 per cent–15 per cent) Freq. 50 or 60 Hz ± 1 per cent Consumption 12 VA
Price July 1979	£650	£699	£650
Options		BCD output	

a development laboratory situation when frequently what will be required from a general purpose instrument tomorrow will not be known today. A tendency therefore exists to purchase the unit with the greatest capability to the limit of the funds available at the time.

The details contained in tables 8.4 to 8.8 are those extracted from the sales data sheets supplied by the three companies[1,2,3] and where comparative details are omitted from a data sheet this is denoted in the tables as *not specified* although such information is normally readily available from the manufacturer by means of a telephone call. The tables and graphs that have been drawn up are a suitable first step in the selection process after a general decision has been made on the type of instrument that should be purchased. However, note that in the data sheets all the manufacturers quote an allowance, to be added to the limits of error, for the effects of temperature. In tables 8.4 to 8.8 and figures 8.4 to 8.7 this has been omitted to remove some of the complexity. Should it be intended to operate the instrument outside the 18 to 28 °C temperature band, all the error limit curves should be redrawn to include a suitable allowance.

Table 8.5. *Direct voltage*

	Datron 1057	Fluke 8800A	Solartron 7051
Ranges and Limits of error in reading	6 months, 18 to 28 °C 100 mV; ±(0.015% of input + 10 ℓ.s.d.) 1 V; 10 V; 100 V; ±(0.015% of input + 2 ℓ.s.d.) + 1 µV 1000 V; as above plus 0.15 p.p.m./V above 300 V	90 days, 18 to 28 °C 200 mV; ±(0.01% of input + 10 ℓ.s.d.) 2 V; 20 V; 200 V; ±(0.01% of input + 3 ℓ.s.d.) 1200 V; ±(0.1% of input + 6 ℓ.s.d.)	6 months, 18 to 28 °C 100 mV; ±(0.012% of input + 4 ℓ.s.d.) 1 V; 10 V; 100 V; ±(0.006% of input + 4 ℓ.s.d.) 1000 V; ±(0.01% of input + 6 ℓ.s.d.)
Resolution	1 µV on 100 mV range	1 µV on 200 mV range	1 µV on 100 mV range
Polarity	Automatic bipolar display	Automatic bipolar display	Automatic bipolar display
Input resistance	100 mV range; 1 V range; 10 V range } 10 GΩ 100 V range; 1 kV range } 10 MΩ	200 mV range; 2 V range; 20 V range } >1 GΩ 200 V range; 1200 V range } 10 MΩ	100 mV range > 100 MΩ; 1 V range; 10 V range } >1 GΩ 100 V range; 1 kV range } > 10.1 MΩ
Common mode rejection	120 dB d.c.; 140 dB 50 Hz } with 1 kΩ unbalance	120 dB d.c. to 60 Hz with 1 kΩ unbalance	120 dB d.c.; 120 dB 50 Hz } with 1 kΩ unbalance
Normal mode rejection	80 dB at 50 Hz	60 dB at 50 Hz and 60 Hz	40 dB at 50 Hz and 60 Hz
Response time	2½ bipolar readings/s	1 s maximum to within rated accuracy	1 s to within rated accuracy (10 s on 100 mV range)

Table 8.6. Resistance Measurement

	Datron 1057	Fluke 8800A	Solartron 7051
Ranges and Limits of error in measurement	6 months, 18 to 28 °C 1 kΩ;} ±(0.01% of input + 4 ℓ.s.d.) 10 kΩ;} +100 mΩ) 100 kΩ;} (can be zeroed) 1 MΩ; ±(0.03% of input + 4 ℓ.s.d.) 10 MΩ; ±(0.5% of input + 4 ℓ.s.d.)	90 days, 18 to 28 °C 200 Ω; ±(0.02% of input + 10 ℓ.s.d.) 2 kΩ } 20 kΩ } ±(0.01% of input + 3 ℓ.s.d.) 200 kΩ } 2 MΩ; ±(0.05% of input + 3 ℓ.s.d.) 20 MΩ; ±(0.2% of input + 3 ℓ.s.d.)	6 months, 18 to 28 °C 10 kΩ; ±(0.015% of input + 5 ℓ.s.d.) 100 kΩ; ±(0.015% of input + 4 ℓ.s.d.) 1 MΩ; ±(0.025% of input + 5 ℓ.s.d.) 10 MΩ; ±(0.05% of input + 5 ℓ.s.d.)
Resolution	10 mΩ on 1 kΩ range	1 mΩ on 200 Ω range	100 mΩ on 10 kΩ range
Configuration	2 terminal	2 or 4 terminal	2 terminal
Overload immunity	250 V direct or r.m.s. alternating	250 V direct or r.m.s. alternating	200 V peak
Response	2½ reading/s	1 s; 200 Ω to 200 kΩ 3 s; 2 MΩ and 20 MΩ	1 s; 10 kΩ and 100 kΩ range 2 s; 1 MΩ range 5 s; 10 MΩ range
Maximum current through unknown	not specified	1 mA; 200 Ω and 2 kΩ 250 μA; 20 kΩ 25 μA; 200 kΩ 2.5 μA; 2 MΩ 0.25 μA; 20 MΩ	100 μA; 10 kΩ and 100 kΩ 1 μA; 1 MΩ and 10 MΩ

Table 8.7. Direct current

	Datron 1057	Fluke 8800A	Solartron 7051
Ranges and error limit	Nil–currents measured as voltage drop across known resistance	Nil–currents measured as voltage drop across known resistance	6 months, 18 to 28 °C 100 μA ± (0.04% of input + 5 ℓ.s.d.) 1 mA ± (0.04% of input + 5 ℓ.s.d.) 100 mA ± (0.05% of input + 50 ℓ.s.d.) 1 A ± (0.05% of input + 5 ℓ.s.d.)

Input resistance	As used	As used	100 μA⎫
			  1 mA⎭ < 5 Ω
			100 mA⎫
			  1 A⎭ < 2 Ω

Resolution	1 μV on 100 mV range	1 μV on 200 mV range	1 nA on 100 μA range

It must also be remembered that the error curves for the three instruments are not strictly comparable. The Fluke error limit specification is for any time up to 90 days after calibration, while the specifications for the Datron and Solartron instruments are for 6 months.

General data

The general properties of the instruments have been summarised in table 8.4. All instruments have a display of seven-segment numerals. The maximum indications of the Datron and Fluke instruments are 199999, while the Solartron instrument has a maximum of 109999.

The Datron unit has a purely manual range selection, the Solartron has only an automatic range selection while the Fluke instrument can be operated in either mode.

The Fluke unit can sustain the largest common mode voltage (1000 V) whereas the Datron instrument is capable of coping with a Lo to guard voltage very much greater than either of the others.

The only unit capable of being fitted with an output would appear to be the Fluke 8800A.

Direct voltage measurement

Table 8.5 shows a comparison between the direct voltage measuring capabilities of the three instruments. The accuracy specifications (or limits of error in reading) have been modified from the data sheets to a common form in an attempt to ease the comparison. This is further assisted by the curves in figure 8.4. All the instruments have five ranges and a resolution of 1 μV on the most sensitive

Table 8.8. Alternating voltage measurement

	Datron 1057	Fluke 8800A	Solartron 7051
	Senses r.m.s. (crest factor 5:1)	Senses mean value	Senses mean value
Ranges	1 V, 10 V, 100 V, 700 V	2 V, 20 V, 200 V, 1200 V	1 V, 10 V, 100 V, 750 V
Resolution	10 μV on 1 V range	10 μV on 2 V range	10 μV on 1 V range
Limits of error in measurement	All ranges: 6 months, 18 to 28°C 40 Hz–3 kHz; ±(0.1% of input + 100 ℓ.s.d.) 3 kHz–30 kHz; ±(0.2% of input + 200 ℓ.s.d.) 700 V range: to the above specification add 0.2 p.p.m./V above 300 V	2 V to 200 V: 90 days, 18 to 28°C 30 Hz–50 Hz; ±(1.0% of input + 60 ℓ.s.d.) 50 Hz–100 Hz; ±(0.25% of input + 20 ℓ.s.d.) 100 Hz–10 kHz; ±(0.1% of input + 10 ℓ.s.d.) 10 kHz–20 kHz; ±(0.25% of input + 20 ℓ.s.d.) 20 kHz–100 kHz; ±(1.0% of input + 60 ℓ.s.d.) 1200 V range: 90 days, 18 to 28°C 30 Hz–100 Hz; ±(0.5% of input + 40 ℓ.s.d.) 100 Hz–10 kHz; ±(0.3% of input + 20 ℓ.s.d.) 10 kHz–20 kHz; ±(0.5% of input + 40 ℓ.s.d.)	1 V range: 6 months, 18 to 28°C 40 Hz–20 kHz; ±(0.1% of input + 30 ℓ.s.d.) 10 V to 750 V: 6 months, 18 to 28°C 40 Hz–20 kHz; ±(0.2% of input + 30 ℓ.s.d.)
Input impedance	1 V range: 1 GΩ shunted by 150 pF; 10 V to 700 V ranges; 10 MΩ	All ranges: 2 MΩ shunted by 100 pF	All ranges: 1 MΩ shunted by 100 pF
Common mode rejection	d.c. to 60 Hz; 1 kΩ unbalance signal Lo, 60 dB signal Hi, 100 dB	not specified	d.c. > 120 dB 50 Hz > 40 dB 60 Hz > 40 dB
Response	1 s	1.5 s to within rated accuracy	3 s to within rated accuracy

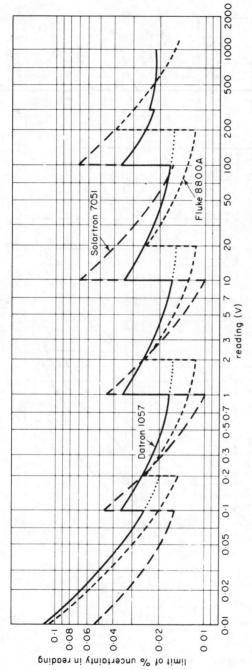

Figure 8.4. Limit of error curves for the direct voltage ranges when operating between 18 and 28 °C. (*Note*: The Fluke 8800A curve is for a 90-day specification while the Datron 1057 and Solartron 7051 curves are for 6-month specifications)

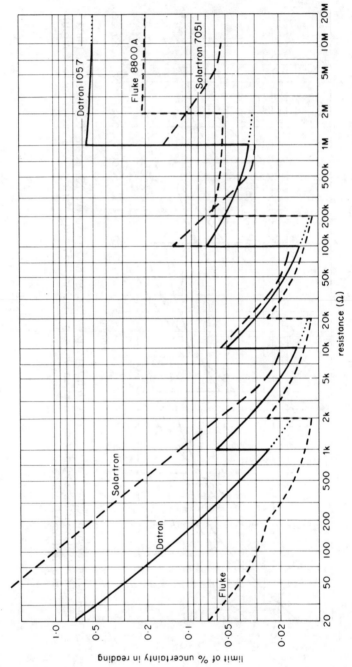

Figure 8.5. Limit of error curves for the resistance ranges when operating between 18 and 28 °C. (*Note*: The Fluke 8800A curve is for a 90-day specification, the others are for 6-month specifications)

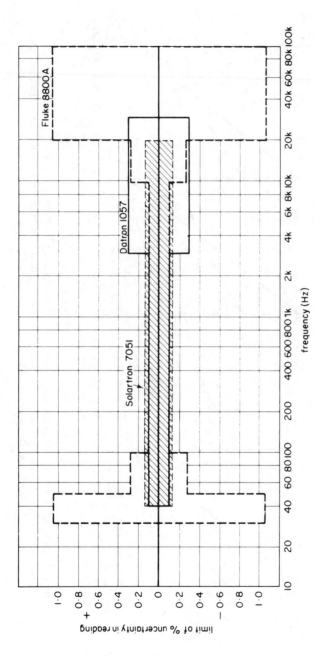

Figure 8.6. Specified limits of error plotted against frequency, for measuring 1 V

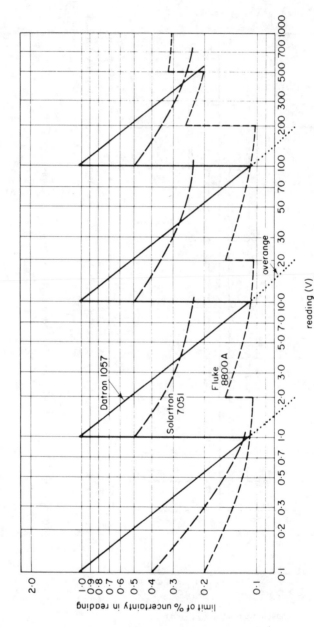

Figure 8.7. Limit of error curves for the three instruments for frequencies between 100 Hz and 3 kHz when operating between 18 and 28 °C. (*Note:* The Fluke 8800A curve is for a 90-day specification, the others are for 6-month specifications)

range. The 8800A is capable of measuring the highest voltage (1200 V). The curves show that it is not true to say that one instrument has smaller errors than the others; for example, the Solartron 7051 has the least uncertainty for voltages below 100 mV but the largest limit of error between 10 V and 200 V. So unless it is known that the purpose of the exercise is to purchase an instrument for use at a particular level of voltage, the uncertainty in measuring direct voltages cannot be used as a means of deciding on the most desirable instrument.

The Datron 1057 has the highest input resistance on the low voltage ranges and has the highest normal mode rejection figure both of which are points in its favour.

Resistance measurement

Perusal of table 8.6 shows that the Fluke 8800A has six resistance ranges as opposed to the five of the Datron and four of the Solartron instrument. Figure 8.5 indicates that below 200 kΩ the Fluke multimeter has the smallest uncertainty in measurement (if calibrated twice as often as the others); it is also the only instrument capable of being used to make four terminal resistance measurements—an essential property when measuring resistances with a 1 mΩ resolution! The specification of the possible current through the unknown is useful information and indicates another plus for the Fluke 8800A.

Current measurement

The Solartron 7051 is the only instrument of the three compared that has internal current ranges and this is therefore a feature in its favour. To measure currents using either of the other instruments, a resistor with a very small tolerance (± 0.01 per cent or less) must be used and the unknown current measured as a voltage drop.

Alternating voltage measurement

Table 8.8 indicates that each of the instruments has four ranges, the maximum resolution in each case being 10 μV. However, the maximum voltages measurable vary, 700 V on the Datron, 750 V on the Solartron and 1200 V on the Fluke instrument. The Datron is the only r.m.s. sensing instrument, although all three are calibrated in terms of r.m.s. values.

In an attempt to compare the frequency ranges of the three instruments, figure 8.6 has been drawn, and this shows that (in measuring 1 V) the 8800A has the widest frequency range and the 7051 the narrowest frequency range.

Figure 8.7 shows the limit of error curves for the three instruments for frequencies between 100 Hz and 3 kHz, it being apparent that except for operating the Datron 1057 in an overrange condition, the Fluke 8800A gives the smallest uncertainty of measurement. As on the direct voltage ranges the Datron instrument has the highest input impedance. The a.c. common mode rejection of this instrument is better than the Solartron although the d.c. common mode rejection is poorer; somewhat surprisingly the C.M.R. figures are not specified for the Fluke instrument.

Best buy decision

Before reaching a decision on which of these instruments would be the 'best buy', two further procedures would be necessary. Firstly, an attempt should be made to reassess the requirements of the proposed use of the instrument, paying particular attention to such aspects as the likely operational common mode voltages, the frequency range necessary and the requirements for current and resistance measurements. After establishing these needs the second step would be to request from each manufacturer a demonstration of their instrument. At the demonstration particular performance aspects and omissions from the data sheet can be clarified, for example

(a) Are the quoted response times of the Datron instrument to within rated accuracy?
(b) What is the C.M.R. of the Fluke instrument on the alternating voltage ranges?
(c) Is it possible for the Solartron instrument to be supplied with an output?

On completion of such procedures for all the instruments available a decision can be made.

Note: The above comparison was drawn up in the summer of 1979. The rate of electronic development is such that by the date of publication of this book these instruments may well have been superseded. The reader should realise that the above exercise is an example of procedure and not intended as a 'state of the art' comparison.

REFERENCES

1 *1057 Multimeter Data Sheet* (Datron Electronics Ltd., Norwich, 1979)
2 *Fluke 8800A Digital Multimeter* (John Fluke Manufacturing Co., Seattle, Wash.)
3 *Digital Voltmeter 7051* (Solartron Ltd, Farnborough, Hants, 1979)

9

Instrumentation Systems

Definition

Instrument systems refine, extend, or supplement human facilities and abilities to sense, perceive, communicate, remember, calculate or reason.[1] To relate this definition to practical terms means that any use of instruments constitutes an instrumentation system, since a suitable instrument or chain of instruments will always convert an unknown quantity into a record or display which human faculties can interpret.

9.1 SYSTEM DESIGN

In creating an instrumentation system one of the first requirements is to decide exactly what the purposes of the measurement are, that is, to create a realistic specification of the quantitites it is necessary to measure, the tolerance allowable on the measurements, and what will actually be done with the data collected. The answers to these questions should define the type of system necessary to provide an acceptable solution to the problem.

Type of System

The basic form of an instrumentation system consists of the measurand, a transducer or sensor, signal conditioning equipment, and the display or recording instrument (see figure 9.1). Such a system simply converts the measurand into a record or display so that an operator may observe the variations in, or magnitude of, an unknown. This type of system becomes more complex as sophisticated automatic recording is added, enabling an increase in the number of measurands

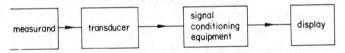

Figure 9.1. Basic open loop instrumentation system

that may be observed and recorded by a single operator. The addition of such equipment may also enable computations to be performed on the quantities measured.

If an open loop instrumentation system is used in a manufacturing process it will require the continual vigilance of an operator to maintain the measurand (for example, the temperature of a furnace) at a predetermined level. However, by adding a reference, some form of comparator and a feedback path to the basic system, a closed loop system is formed (see figure 9.2). This type of system is finding an ever-increasing number of applications in manufacturing industries where automation increases the speed of production and reduces the wages bill. It is also the basis of control engineering, which is a continually developing branch of engineering.[2]

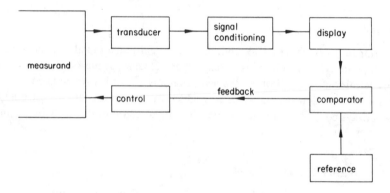

Figure 9.2. Closed loop instrumentation and control system

Among the many difficult decisions that will have to be made is the one concerning the use of analogue or digital instruments, and careful use of the selection procedures listed in chapter 8 will assist in the solution of this problem, although in an increasing number of applications a combination of digital and analogue techniques will provide the most satisfactory solution.

It must be appreciated that the solution to any instrumentation problem is unlikely to be unique, there being as many satisfactory solutions (all affected by the experiences of the individuals) as people solving it.

9.2 ANALOGUE SYSTEMS

From the descriptions of various instruments in the previous chapters it should be apparent that the advantage of an analogue system is that variables are continuously monitored and/or recorded, while a major disadvantage is the restriction on performing calculations, within the instrument, on the readings made.

To illustrate this category of system, the following possible outline solutions to some instrumentation problems are given.

9.2.1 Open Loop Systems

Since this type of system does not exert any control, it merely monitors, or may-be records, the events as they occur. There are very many applications for which an open loop system is suitable. The following are but two examples, for which possible outline solutions are given; the detailed solution requires an appraisal of the manufacturers' literature on instruments that are currently available.

Problem 1

To facilitate an investigation of the magnitude and waveform of the in-rush current, when a 500 VA, 240/20 V, single phase, 50 Hz transformer is connec-ted to both a 240 V, 50 Hz supply, and loads of various magnitudes and phase angles.

An outline solution

Perusal of appropriate books and literature will show that, depending on the design, the construction, the magnetised state of the transformer core and the instant in the cycle of the closure of the switch connecting the transformer to the supply, a transient current wave having peaks of decaying amplitude in alternate half cycles will occur. It will therefore seem reasonable to record

(a) the supply voltage
(b) the voltage across the 240 V winding of the transformer
(c) the current through the 240 V winding, and possibly
(d) the voltage produced at the 20 V terminals
(e) the current to the load on the 20 V winding.

As possibly five waveforms are to be recorded simultaneously the use of a u.v. recorder seems appropriate with suitable matching circuits connecting the measurands to galvanometers of sufficient sensitivity and frequency response. The use of scaling circuits or signal conditioning amplifiers should be investigated from an impedance loading point of view. The final decision on the use of the latter may depend on the availability of funds (that is, can the extra expense be justified as essential to the operation of the system).

Figure 9.3 shows the general arrangement of a suitable system that would permit the peak values and wave shapes of in-rush currents to be investigated for various conditions from no load to full load.

The instrument requirements for the system are

(a) a u.v. recorder, with a minimum capability of six channels
(b) six galvanometers (one spare) with a flat frequency response from d.c. to at least 550 Hz as this caters for the eleventh harmonic (this will require fluid damped galvanometers)
(c) recording paper
(d) two nonreactive current shunts, rated at 25 A

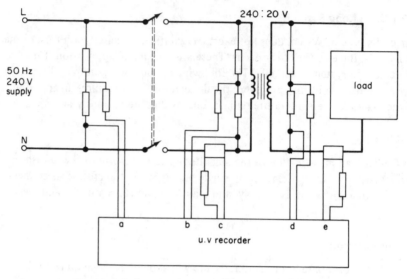

Figure 9.3. System for recording in-rush values

(e) nonreactive resistors for the divider networks and/or signal conditioning amplifiers
(f) calibration source and instruments—so that the system may be calibrated as a whole.

The next stage must be a careful analysis of manufacturers' literature (or the handbooks of instruments previously purchased) to establish the most suitable equipment for the system bearing in mind the criteria laid down in chapter 8. Resulting from the searches of data sheets the details of the system are resolved, for example, whether or not signal conditioning amplifiers are essential, the cost of the system, uncertainty of measurement, calibration requirements, etc. Another point that should perhaps be considered is that in the system as outlined, the closure of the switch will occur at random instances on the supply waveform. Many recordings would therefore be required to provide a satisfactory analysis of the effect of the instant of switch closure. Hence a useful addition to the system would be a 'point on wave' selector so that the transformer could be connected to the supply at predetermined instances of the supply waveform.

Problem 2

To produce in graphical form the gain frequency response curve for an audio amplifier which has the following specification

    voltage gain: 100
    input signal: 100 mV pk
    bandwidth (3 dB): 30 Hz to 10 kHz
    load impedance: 50 Ω
    input impedance: 1 kΩ

An outline solution

A possible system is shown in figure 9.4, the requirements for the component parts being

(a) a voltage controlled oscillator, having a constant voltage output over a frequency range from 20 Hz to 20 kHz, a logarithmic change in frequency occurring with a linear change in applied voltage
(b) a ramp generator, compatible in voltage levels with (a) and producing a linear ramp over, say, a 30 s time interval
(c) a terminating or load resistor of more than adequate power capacity (so that it remains at constant temperature during the test)
(d) an a.c. to d.c. converter—this must have linear voltage and frequency characteristics
(e) an X-Y recorder with input sensitivities compatible with the outputs of (b) and (d).

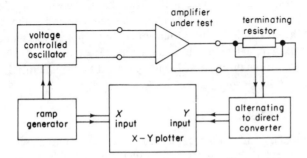

Figure 9.4. Schematic diagram of system for recording amplifier characteristics

If items (a) to (e) are the main blocks of the system a search of manufacturers' literature will reveal the availability and cost of the most suitable units. It could well be that items (a) (b) and (d) are each available as individual integrated circuits, and the 'in house' manufacture of a special piece of test equipment is a practical alternative to the purchase of production pieces of equipment. It also should be observed that most manufacturers market an X-Y recorder that can be mounted into customer-designed equipment. Such items are usually termed O.E.M. (operator's equipment mounting).

9.2.2 Closed Loop Systems

In this type of system the signal from the measurand is compared with a reference and if necessary an appropriate adjustment is initiated to the condition of the measurand, this action forming a control or feedback loop. In the simplest case the monitoring or recording instrument will simply be fitted with limit switches so that if a preset level is exceeded an alarm is sounded and possibly some action taken, for example, the supply to a heater switched off. In such a system, for example, a heating process, the temperature may be controlled by a thermostat

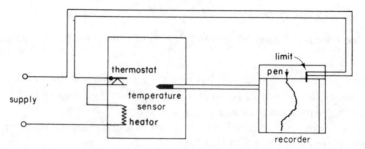

Figure 9.5. System with limit control provided by the instrumentation

and the monitoring instrumentation limits provided as a safety back-up (see figure 9.5). *Note:* Care must be taken so that the switching capabilities of the limit switches are *not* exceeded.

If an additional switch is added to the recorder, the energy supply to, say, the heater of a vat may be both controlled and monitored by the recorder. If a number of switches were used it could be arranged that if the vat were a long way below the desired temperature a lot of heat was supplied and as the temperature approached the correct level the amount of energy supplied was reduced. The use of a number of switched circuits in this way creates a number of maintenance problems so electronic proportional control is used to provide this desirable situation.

9.3 DIGITAL SYSTEMS

Digital instruments can, of course, be used in both open and closed systems. The considerable calculating capability now available by using digital systems means that problems of greater complexity can be solved within the instrument.

9.3.1 Data Loggers

In many practical situations the requirement is for a system that can monitor a large number of measurands which under normal conditions have relatively constant values, which for record purposes need only be noted from time to time. Additionally, should an abnormal condition occur the results should be noted and if they approach a hazardous condition alarms should be activated.

It was not long after digital voltmeters appeared that the first data loggers were created by using a scanning switch or multiplexer to sequentially connect the measurands to the d.v.m., the output of the voltmeter being connected to some form of printer. The operation of the data logger was controlled by a clock, as in figure 9.6. To this basic system were then added limit detectors, alarms and linearising circuits so that the printed output could be in engineering units and indicate if preset limits were exceeded.

Hardwired, rackmounted data loggers with a 20 to 100 channel capacity were evolved and used in many development laboratory applications. Their major

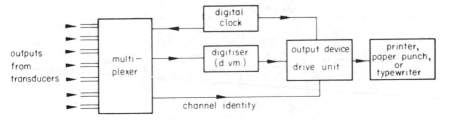

Figure 9.6. Block diagram of the basic data logger

limitations were speed of operation, a certain susceptibility to noise, their size, weight and lack of any calculation capability.

To overcome some of these problems[3] and be of greater use in a permanent installation, systems linked to a central computer were developed, control of the system being organised within the capability of the large machine to handle other functions simultaneously, for example, payroll and stock inventory (figure 9.7). The cost of transmitting lines for the data in such a system was high, and analogue signals sent over considerable distances are very susceptible to the effects of interference and a computer failure and 'down time' could have unfortunate consequences.

The development of minicomputers provided a means of returning data acquisition and logging into the laboratory or point of manufacture—a desirable step in decentralising data collection and control. The minis worked well, but it was found that the closer the processor was put to the sensors the more could be measured. Minis were, however, too expensive to distribute, but with the evolution of the microcomputer it became possible to distribute low cost processing power to a number of sensors, thus enabling data acquisition, collection, storage and some data reduction to be performed at the measurement source. A number

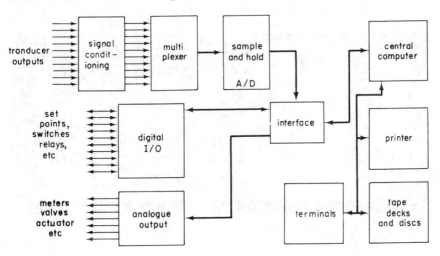

Figure 9.7. Data logging (acquisition) system under central computer control

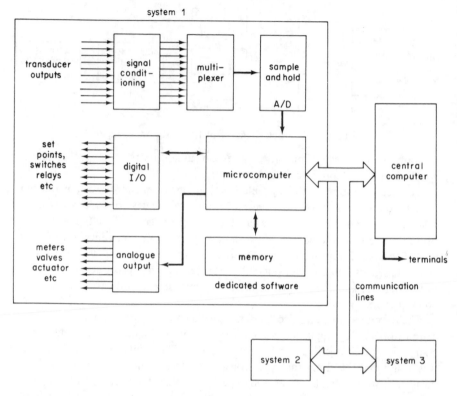

Figure 9.8. Distributed data acquisition system incorporating microcomputers linked to central computer

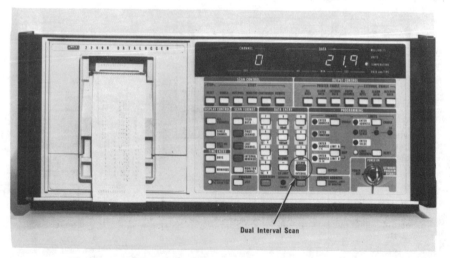

Figure 9.9. Programmable datalogger (courtesy of John Fluke Manufacturing Co.)

of microcomputer controlled stations, or process loops are then linked via a serial communications line to a central management computer, which oversees the total system (figure 9.8).

Such an arrangement is suitable for a large installation such as a chemical process plant or a ship. On a smaller scale such as that encountered in most research investigation, the use of microprocessors[4,5] has resulted in self-contained data loggers with fairly extensive programmable and preprogrammed capabilities. For example, the instrument illustrated in figure 9.9 has a 1000 channel capability, an interactive keyboard programming capability for range, function, skip and limits selection for each channel, signal conditioning for the standard thermocouple types, a reading resolution of 1 μV or 0.1 °C, selectable scan rates, a clock to monitor real or elapsed time in days, hours, minutes and seconds, an internal printer to record the data and, if required, a printout of the complete program.

9.3.2 Bus-connected Systems

The possibilities of programmably controlling instruments and printing or graphically presenting the results of measurements are very desirable features in any measurement system. The cost of producing a single instrument capable of satisfying every requirement for all measurement situations would be so high that few, if any, organisations would be able to justify the purchase. In the mid to late 1960s a number of manufacturers began producing modular instruments so that customers could select suitable units and plug them into a main frame to form a system tailored to their particular requirements. The limitations of compatibility between manufacturers resulted in the CAMAC (computer automated measurement and control) system of standard instrumentation interface[6]. This is an arrangement that provides for the use of units from different manufacturers within a common main frame.

At much the same time discussions took place in Europe and the United States on the feasibility of a standard interface between complete instruments, so that instrumentation systems could be designed and assembled using several separate instruments of different manufacture. The interface concepts then under development by Hewlett-Packard were selected as a model, and have resulted in the arrangement known variously as the IEC BUS, IEEE Standard 488-1975, HP-IB, GBIB, Plus Bus and ANSI std MC1-1 (see reference 7, 8, 9 and 10).

Both the CAMAC and HP-IB systems have their applications (although the latter seems to be gaining greater acceptance) and were evolved in response to the rising need to minimise the resources repeatedly expended on unique solutions to the problem of interconnection of system components. Prior to their adoption, system design engineers were tending to select interface methods to satisfy specific and immediate needs. The development costs were high, each solution being a somewhat unique selection of codes, logic sense, levels and timing protocols for each application.

System structure or architecture

A bus–line system is a special interface system in which all the instruments are connected in parallel to a number of communication lines as illustrated in principle by figure 9.10. The advantage of such a system is that interconnecting cable problems have effectively been eliminated and that additional units can easily be added. However, complications have been created: for example, if it is required to transfer information from instrument A to instrument C, a number of arrangements must be made.

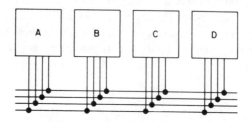

Figure 9.10. Four line interconnecting bus

(a) Intrument A must be set ready to supply the data to the line *it must be addressed as a 'talker'*.
(b) Instrument C must be set ready to receive the data—*it must be addressed as a 'listener'*.
(c) All other instruments must be set passive.
(d) If a series of data has to be transferred, steps must be taken to ensure that no new data is supplied by the talker before the current set has been completely accepted by the 'listener'. *This is taken care of by the 'handshake' or data-byte transfer control procedure*.
(e) All instruments must understand a number of general statements and commands such as 'message starts' 'message ends' and 'attention please'.

To oversee such an arrangement it is apparent that some kind of controller is required to regulate the traffic between the various instruments via the bus.

The IEC Bus

This is a system with 16 parallel lines, which are divided into three groups according to function as shown in figure 9.11. Eight of the lines form the 'data bus' which is used for transferring measuring data, addresses and programming data. Three lines are used for direct communication between a 'talker' and 'listeners', a process correctly termed the 'data-byte transfer control' but more commonly referred to as the 'handshake' function. The remaining five lines are used for general 'interface management' messages, that is, communication between the controller and the controlled.

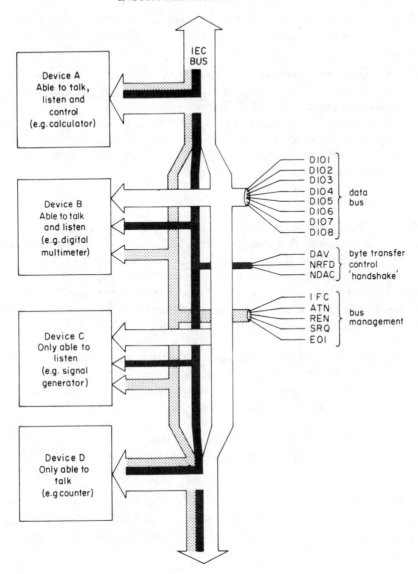

Figure 9.11. IEC BUS system for interconnecting instruments

The data bus

As indicated, the data bus consists of eight data lines, thus a data item can contain a maximum of eight bits in parallel or one 'byte'. If, as is generally the case, one byte is insufficient to convey the whole message, a series of bytes will have to be transferred. The message code generally used is the international seven-bit

ISO code, which covers nearly all the figures, letters and signs required in practice.

The type of information transferred via the data bus can be subdivided as follows.

(a) Addresses, that is, information offered by the controller to all the instruments in parallel. Each compares the address on the data bus with its own address and the one that identifies itself reacts.

(b) Data—this may be programming or measurement data communicated by the instrument addressed as a talker and received by those addressed as listeners. For example, the selection of a voltmeter range and the magnitude of the reading respectively.

The 'handshake' function

When a multiple-byte message has to be transferred from one instrument to another, it is apparent that an organisation structure is required to ensure that the talker does not talk if the listener is not listening, and that the talker does not operate for a shorter time than the slowest listener can accept the information. These requirements are met with the aid of the data-byte transfer control or 'handshake' function embodied in the three lines set aside for the purpose. Each of the lines has its own specific function as follows.

> DAV (Data valid): a 'low' signal from the talker on this line indicates that the data on the data lines is correct and suitable for acceptance.
> NRFD (not ready for data): the listeners indicate via this line if they are ready to listen to (new) information—'High' if ready, 'Low' if not ready for data.
> NDAC (Data not accepted): the listeners indicate their acceptance of the message via this line, a 'high' indicating acceptance and a 'low' being not accepted.

Both the NRFD and NDAC lines are 'wired-OR' that is these lines can only be 'high' if all instruments programmed as listeners have a 'high' output. This ensures that the line is only 'high' when all the listeners, (including the slowest) are ready for new data or have accepted the data.

The sequence of operations on the handshake lines, when involved in transferring each data byte across the interface, can be represented by the timing diagram in figure 9.12, as follows.

> T.1: initial conditions are set up in all the talkers and listeners
> the DAVline is set high
> the NRFDline is set low, and
> the NDACline is set low.
> T.2: The talker checks the line conditions, and puts a data byte on the lines.

T.3: Listeners are ready to accept data, so the NRFD line goes high—note that this cannot happen before all listeners are ready.

T.4: When a talker senses that the NRFD is high, it sets the DAV low to indicate that the data are valid.

T.5: the fastest listener sets NRFD to low and accepts the data. In doing so it will be in the 'longer ready' state. The other listeners follow at their own speeds.

T.6: the first listener to finish sets NDAC to high thereby indicating it has accepted the data.

T.7: when all the listeners have indicated that the data has been accepted NDAC goes high.

T.8: the talker senses NDAC is high and sets DAV high to indicate that the data are no longer valid.

T.9: the talker removes the data from the line.

T.10: the listeners, sensing DAV is high, set NDAC low in preparation for the next cycle.

T.11: the cycle is complete and all three lines have returned to their initial state.

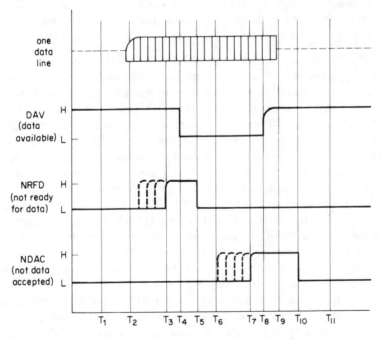

Figure 9.12. Timing diagram for the 'handshake' process

General interface management

This is organised by the third section of the bus in which there are five lines each with a specific function. All the commands on this group of lines are of a general nature, being for communication between the controller and the other devices. The use and identification of these lines are as follows.

ATN (Attention): used by the controller to indicate that it has a message such as an address, an unlisten command or a polling command (see below) for all instruments in the system.

IFC (Interface clear): used by the controller to set all instruments in the system to a known quiescent state (that is, no device is addressed), thus providing a uniform starting point for any operation.

REN (Remote enable): used to switch instruments (of suitable capability) from front panel to remote control. To perform such an operation, the controller activates REN + ATN and gives the address of the instrument to be set to remote control. The instrument will stay in remain under remote control as long as REN is activated.

EOI (End of output/identify): used by a talker to indicate the end of a multiple-byte transfer squence.

SRQ (Service request): used by a device to indicate the need for attention from the control element and to request the interruption of the current sequence of events. The service request signal can be used by any instrument to ask for new instructions from the controller, even when the data bus lines are occupied by messages between other instruments.

Some of the operations performed by individual instruments in a system (for example, measurements of very low frequencies) may take a long time (of the order of tens of seconds). In such cases it is not sensible to block the whole system until such a measurement is complete—it is better to continue with other activities and interrupt these when the lengthy measurement is over. The SRQ can be used for such a purpose, since if it is set true by one of the devices, the controller can interrupt all other activities and pay attention to the device emitting the SRQ signal. However, before it can do this it must detect which instrument produced the SRQ. It may be arranged that either the parallel-poll or the serial-poll mode is adopted for doing this. In the parallel-poll mode, each instrument has a specific data line as its identification tag and the controller can identify the instrument asking for service by seeing which data line carries the signal. The controller makes the management lines ATN and EOI true and reads the response given by the instrument via the data bus. It is evident that the parallel-poll mode can only be used to identify up to eight instruments.

In the serial-poll mode, all instruments are asked individually if they called for service. To do this the controller first gives a general unlisten command followed by a general command via the data bus to put the interface into the serial-poll mode; it then transmits the individual talker addresses of the devices in turn until one of them responds positively. Having detected which instrument requested service, the controller removes the interface from the serial-poll mode and gives the required service.

Addressing an instrument

An address is a code which identifies a particular instrument; it is also used in assigning the role of talker or listener to an instrument, and should it be capable of both, a separate address is needed for each function.

The address of an instrument (consisting of seven-bit codes) is set using jumpers or multi-position switches in the bus–line interface. To call an instrument, the controller puts the appropriate address on the data line and makes the ATN line true (low). All instruments react with the normal handshake procedure and compare the address on the line with their own, the one identifying itself then assuming the function of talker or listener. Talkers have to be addressed in turn and to avoid the possibility of talkers operating in parallel, each time a talker is addressed, all other instruments are automatically set to 'untalk'.

Listeners, however, can operate in parallel and to address more than one listener the addresses can be given one after the other, an 'unlisten' command being given to reset a listener to the inactive state. As the addressing of a new talker automatically resets any other talker, while several listeners can be addressed consecutively it is necessary to have a difference between talker and listener addresses. By convention 01XXXXX is used for listener addresses and 10XXXXX is used for talkers, so in decoding the first two bits as 1 and 0 the current talker will be switched to 'untalk' and a new talker will be addressed.

Operating arrangements

The organisation within a system interconnected using an IEC BUS has been likened to a repertory company, [11] wherein each device may take more than one role, and to a well organised meeting[12] where, directed by the chairman, people talk one at a time while the rest listen to what is of interest to them. While both of these similies have merit, the imperfections and *laissez-faire* that exist of necessity in practice in both such organisations could not be tolerated in a bus interconnected system, the rigidity of command of a military situation perhaps being more appropriate.

Whatever the analogy, a control element or controller is required to command the sequence of operation of the instruments in the system. In a simple system, such as a voltmeter–printer combination, the control element could be built into one of the instruments, but in most cases a special control unit is required. The controller may be a programmable calculator, microcomputer or minicomputer, which in general can offer not only control as such but a supply of programming data, data processing I/O facilities and software providing a simplification of system programming.[13] A system may contain more than one device capable of exercising control but only one can be active at any one time, and the currently active controller can pass control to one of the other capable devices. Only the device designated as system controller can assume control.

The number of instruments that may be interconnected using the bus system

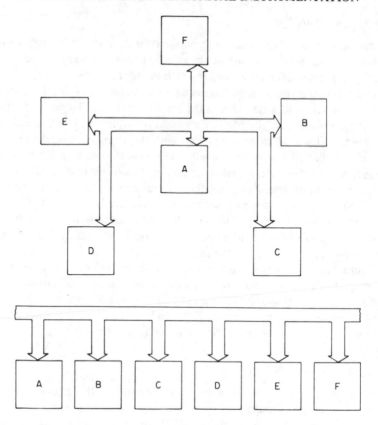

Figure 9.13. Bus interconnection methods

is a maximum of 15 either in a star or linear network (figure 9.13). The specified cable connector has both male and female terminations so plugs may be stacked as in figures 9.14, 9.16 and 9.17.

The data transmission rate is specified as 1 megabyte/s over limited distances but 25 to 50 per cent of this figure would seem to be more realistic over the full path length, which should not exceed 20 m. The distance between devices should in general be less than 2 m. [11] This last statement is correct for a single location but by using an extender[14] the bus system may be operated over distances far greater than the permitted cabling lengths. Figure 9.15 shows a possible extended system which retains all the normal functions except parallel poll and pass control. The data transmission rate is also slowed down.

Applications

The possible applications of the IEC BUS are almost limitless. The following are but two examples in which there are a number of common instruments so that one system could readily be converted to the other.

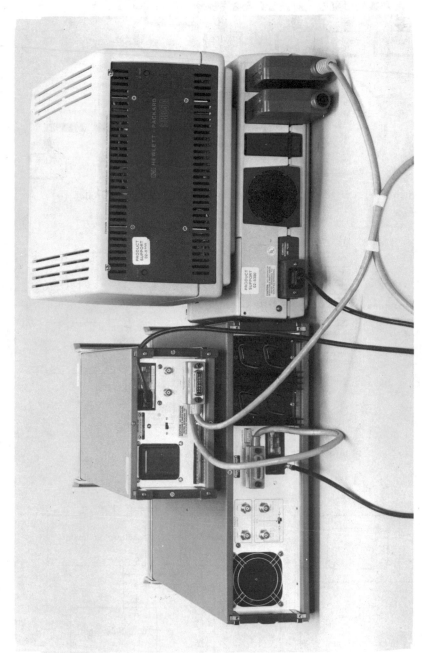

Figure 9.14. Interconnection of bus-compatible instruments (courtesy of Hewlett Packard Ltd)

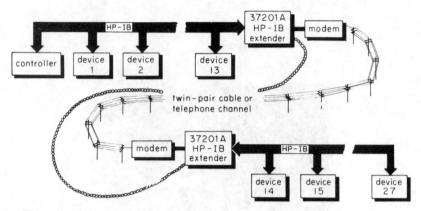

Figure 9.15. Extended bus interconnected system (after reference 14)

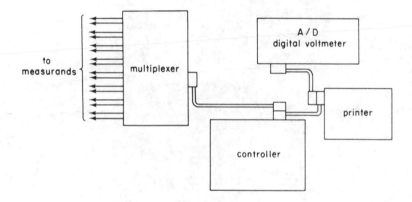

Figure 9.16. Bus-connected data logging system

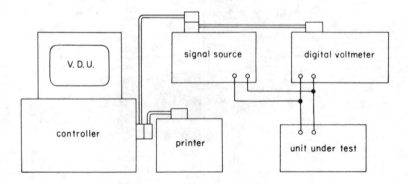

Figure 9.17. Bus-connected calibration system

Data logging

The purpose-built data logger may have programming capabilities but these are frequently limited to such applications as thermocouple linearisation and simple arithmetic functions. By assembling a data logger from individual instruments using the IEC BUS, a system with a much greater calculation capability will result, and this will provide such functions as Fourier analysis. A bus connected data logging system is shown in figure 9.16; should the controller not contain a clock it would be necessary to add one. The limit, linearisation and other functions would all occur as controller software.

Calibration system

A system using a controller with a V.D.U. can be compiled so that instructions to an operator of limited skill may be used for checking the calibration of quite complex instruments. A possible system arrangement is shown in figure 9.17, and the controller would be programmed so that the operator would be led through a sequence of operations and checks.

REFERENCES

1   *Encyclopedia of Science and Technology* (McGraw-Hill, New York, 1971)
2   B. Jones, *Instrumentation, Measurement and Feedback* (McGraw-Hill, Maidenhead, 1977)
3   F. Molinari and A. Fishman, Yesterday, today and tomorrow, the evaluation of data acquisition, *Mini-micro Syst.*, **9** (1976) 32, 34, 38
4   S. C. Blachford, Computerised data loggers, *New Electronics*, **24** (1975) 124-7
5   Programmable data logger, Technical Data, Hewlett-Packard.
6   *CAMAC Instrumentation and Interface Standards* (IEEE, New York, 1976)
7   M. Richter, Get on the IEC Bus, *Electron Des.*, **24** (1976) 76-80
8   J. McDermott, The IEEE 488 bus plays a major role in programmable instrumentation, *Electron. Des.*, **24** (1976)
9   D. C. Loughry, The Hewlett-Packard Interface Bus: current perspective, *HP Jl*, **26** (1975) 2-4
10 D. C. Loughry, IEEE Standard 488 and microprocessor synergism, *Proc. I.E.E.E.*, **66** (1978) 162-72
11 J. Kimball, The IEEE 488 Bus–going your way?, *Tekscope*, **10** (1978) 3-10
12 H. G. Onstee, The IEC Bus, T & M News Supplement, General Series No. 3, (N. V. Philips Gloeilampenfabrieken, Eindhoven, The Netherlands)
13 D. W. Ricci and P. S. Stone, Putting together instrumentation systems at minimum cost, *H.P. Jl*, **26** (1975) 5-11
14 HPIB Extender, *Hewlett-Packard Electronic Instrument and Systems Catalogue* (1980) p. 32

Problems and Exercises

10.1 PRINCIPLES

1. Discuss the differences between
(a) substitution and null methods of measurement
(b) analogue and digital instruments.

2. Write brief notes explaining
(a) the methods used to reduce the possibility of parallax error in reading an analogue instrument
(b) the techniques used to produce alpha-numeric displays.

3. A resistor was measured, using a Wheatstone bridge as having a value of 1243 Ω ± 0.1%. The same resistor was remeasured, under identical environmental conditions using a digital multimeter and purported to have a value of 1244.5 Ω ± (0.05% of reading + 2 ℓ.s.d.). Postulate a value for the resistance and a tolerance within which the actual value must lie.

4. A resistance box has the following components and tolerances
   10 resistors each of 100 kΩ ± 0.05%
   10 resistors each of 10 kΩ ± 0.05%
   10 resistors each of 1 kΩ ± 0.05%
   10 resistors each of 100 Ω ± 0.1%
   10 resistors each of 10 Ω ± 0.5%
Determine, both in ohms and as a percentage, the limit of uncertainty in a setting of 453.72 kΩ.

5. The value of a capacitor was to be evaluated using a circuit which resolved to the expression

$$C_x = \frac{2}{\omega^2 R^2 C_1}$$

Given that $\omega = 10^4 \pm 0.01\%$, $R = 100$ k$\Omega \pm 0.05\%$ and $C_1 = 500$ pF ± 1 pF, determine the value of C_x and the limit of uncertainty in the measurement.

6. A class 0.5 ammeter (fiducial value 1 A), and a class 0.2 voltmeter (fiducial value 10 V) were used to determine the value of a resistor. If the readings on the instruments were 0.72 A and 9.5 V respectively, calculate the value of the resistor and the limit of uncertainty in the measurement. (Neglect the impedance effects of the instruments.)

7. A $3\frac{1}{2}$-digit panel meter has a full scale indication of 1.999 V. Draw a limit of error curve from 0.1 to 2 V, given that the accuracy specification is $\pm$ (0.05% of reading + 1 l.s.d.) when the instrument is operated between 10 and 35 °C.

8. A multimeter was used to measure the current in a circuit. When the 300 μA range was used a reading 90 μA was observed, however on changing to the 100 μA range the reading became 60 μA. Given that the voltage drop across the meter is 500 mV when full scale is indicated on either of these ranges, calculate the effective series resistance of the circuit under investigation.

9. A direct voltage source that has an ouput resistance of 125 Ω is connected to a circuit that has an input resistance of 3000 Ω. If the magnitude of the input voltage to the circuit is set at 10 V using a voltmeter that has a full scale of 10 V and an internal resistance of 500 Ω/V, calculate the magnitude of the voltage that will be applied to the circuit when the voltmeter is removed.

10. A resistor is connected in series with a 10 mA full scale ammeter across a variable direct voltage supply that has an internal resistance of R_s Ω. When a 10 V full scale voltmeter (internal resistance 1000 Ω/V) is connected across the terminals of the supply, which is then adjusted so that the voltmeter indicates 10 V, the current through the ammeter is 9.80 mA. On reconnecting the circuit so that the voltmeter is connected across the unknown resistor only, and the supply adjusted so that the milliammeter indicates full scale, the reading on the voltmeter is 5.05 V. Calculate the value of the unknown resistor and the resistance of the milliammeter.

11. In measuring the magnitude of a 2 kHz signal a reading on a mean sensing (but r.m.s. calibrated) voltmeter was 7.5 V, while on a r.m.s. sensing instrument the indication was 7.8 V. Determine the form factor of the signal and the contribution of the distorted waveform to the error in measurement that would be present when using the mean sensing instrument.

12. Evaluate the mean, peak and r.m.s. values of the waveform $v = 5 + 3 \sin \theta$.

10.2 ANALOGUE INSTRUMENTS

1. List the characteristic properties of a moving coil instrument. A moving coil microammeter has a full scale, or range value, of 100 μA and an internal resistance of 750 Ω. Calculate

(a) the value of shunt resistance required for its conversion into an ammeter with a range value of 20 mA

(b) the series resistance that is required to convert the microammeter into a voltmeter having a full scale indication when 30 V is applied to the combination

(c) the value of the adjustment resistor necessary for the conversion of the moving coil instrument into an 'ohm-meter' assuming a 1.5 V battery to be used.

2. Discuss the methods used in moving coil pen recorders to improve the linearity of recording. A moving coil pen recorder operates with its pen moving in a circular arc on an 80 mm long radial arm (r) giving a deflection $y = r \sin \theta$. Calculate the percentage error in the actual deflection due to linearity effects at a deflection angle (θ) of 20°.

3. A transducer, using four 120 Ω strain gauges for the sensing element, was supplied from a direct voltage source of negligible internal resistance. When the transducer was subjected to its working load and the output measured on the 300 μA current range of a multimeter a reading of 120 μA was obtained. The specified voltage drop at full scale on the 300 μA range was 400 mV. Calculate the magnitude of deflection that could be expected if the multimeter were replaced by a galvanometer having a resistance of 500 Ω and a sensitivity of 12 μA/mm.

4. Explain why u.v. recorder galvanometers should be operated at 0.64 of critical damping.

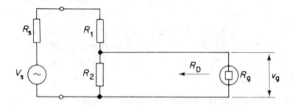

Figure 10.1.

Derive expressions for R_1 and R_2 of figure 10.1, and hence determine suitable values for the components of that circuit, given that V_s is a 20 Hz, 0.2 V r.m.s. signal from a source of resistance (R_s) equal to 100 Ω. It is required to obtain a record of the signal waveform with a peak-to-peak amplitude of 100 mm using an electromagnetically damped galvanometer that has the following specification

Sensitivity: 20 μA/mm
Terminal resistance (R_g): 25 Ω
Damping resistance for 0.64 of critical damping (R_D): 250 Ω

5. Sketch the characteristic curves of u.v. recorder galvanometer performance against frequency and comment on the desirability of using 0.64 of critical damping for such galvanometers.

It is required to record the voltage waveform of an 11 kV, single-phase power line during a switching operation. An 11 000/110 V, 5 VA voltage transformer is available, together with a u.v. recorder fitted with galvanometers that have the following specification
Resonant frequency: 600 Hz
Sensitivity: 100 μA/mm
Terminal resistance (R_g): 75 Ω
Damping resistance for 0.64 of critical damping (R_D): 150 Ω
Devise a matching circuit that would result in a 100 mm peak-to-peak record of the 11 kV r.m.s. line voltage. (Assume that the effective output resistance of the voltage transformer is negligible.) Describe the precautions and procedures that should be followed before taking readings.

6. Explain how an electrodynamometer instrument functions and how it may be used as a voltmeter, an ammeter and a wattmeter.

An electrodynamometer instrument, with a scale of 150 divisions, has a moving coil whose impedance is 35 Ω and 25 mH and fixed coils with a total series resistance of 50 Ω and inductance of 20 mH. The current rating of each of the coils is 30 mA but by the addition of suitable 'pure' resistors the instrument has been adapted for use as a 30 V, 1 A, 30 W wattmeter. If the added resistor magnitudes are such that full scale deflection is correct for a direct voltage and current calibration, calculate the instrument reading that will be obtained when it is supplied with 30 V, 50 Hz in phase with 1 A.

7. The power dissipated in a 33.5 Ω resistive load connected to a 100 V, 50 Hz, single-phase supply of negligible impedance is to be measured using a wattmeter that has a 100 V voltage coil (resistance 5 kΩ) and a 5 A current coil (impedance $0.4 + j\,0.3$ Ω at 50 Hz). Calculate
(a) the wattmeter reading for the two methods of connecting the voltage coil
(b) the corrections in watts which should be applied to the appropriate readings
(c) the power actually dissipated in the load in each case.

8. Show that two wattmeters may be used to measure the power consumed by a three-wire three-phase load. Two wattmeters are used to measure the power taken by a three-phase, 5 kW, 400 V, delta connected motor. If readings of 2235 W and −209 W were observed when the line currents were all equal and 5 A, evaluate the power consumed by the motor and the power factor under these load conditions.

9. Describe the construction of attraction and repulsion types of moving iron ammeters.

The coil of a moving iron instrument (f.s.d. 100 mA at 50 Hz) has a resistance of 40 Ω and an inductance of 60 mH. Calculate the value of a pure resistance shunt which when connected across the coil will result in full scale deflection occurring when 10 A, 50 Hz is applied to the combination. If the shunted meter is inadvertently used to measure a 100 Hz current, determine the total current flowing when the moving iron instrument indicates 100 mA. If such a method of measurement is unavoidable, describe the form the shunt should take and calculate its component values.

10. An unknown capacitor (C_x) was investigated using a Q meter. Resonance with a 10 mH inductor was found to occur under the following conditions

	Capacitor dial setting (pF)	Resonant frequency (kHz)	Q value
Case 1 (C_x absent)	500	44.8	250
Case 2 (C_x absent)	120	89.6	250
Case 3 (C_x present)	115	44.8	130

Calculate the capacitance of C_x and its leakage resistance deriving any formulae used.

11. Outline the operation of a Q meter and show how such an instrument may be used to determine the effective value of an inductance as opposed to the apparent or indicated inductance of an inductor. Resonance was found to occur under the following conditions

	Capacitor dial setting (pF)	Resonant frequency (kHz)	Q value
Case 1	500	44.7	320
Case 2	120	89.4	—

Determine the indicated inductance, the self capacitance, the effective series resistance and the effective inductance of the coil at frequency f_1, deriving any formulae used.

12. The sets of readings given below were obtained when an inductor that has a ferrite core was connected to a Q meter.

	Capacitor dial setting (pF)	Resonant frequency (kHz)	Q value
Measurement 1	500	20.7	220
Measurement 2	350	23.9	180
Measurement 3	300	25.4	160
Measurement 4	200	29.4	137
Measurement 5	60	41.4	51

Calculate the effective resistance and effective inductance of the coil and show graphically the variation of these quantities with frequency. Hence determine the true inductance of the coil.

Explain why the graph of effective resistance against frequency does not conform to the expression

$$R_{eff} = \frac{R}{(1 - \omega^2 LC)^2} \qquad (7.10)$$

13. Describe the operation of a cathode ray oscilloscope, with particular reference to the timebase, the vertical amplifiers, the deflection system, and the triggering of the trace.

The input 'attenuator' of an oscilloscope is set to 100 mV/div. If a sinusoidal trace has a peak-to-peak amplitude of 6.4 div. what is its r.m.s. value? For the same waveform the horizontal distance between identical points is four divisions when the timebase is set to a speed of 0.1 ms/div. Evaluate the frequency of the signal.

The above signal is the voltage across a capacitive impedance Z. A second waveform (the voltage drop across a pure 10 Ω resistor in series with Z) has a peak-to-peak amplitude of 4.8 div. (vertical amplifier sensitivity 1 mV/div.) and is displaced from the first wave by 0.8 div. What are the magnitudes of the series components of Z?

14. Describe methods by which a c.r.o. may be used to measure
(a) the r.m.s. value of a sinewave
(b) the frequency of a sinewave.

For the trace in figure 10.2a deduce an expression for the phase angle between the sinusoids that result in such a display and hence determine the phase angle for the given display.

Describe the procedure by which a trace of the type shown in figure 10.2b is obtained and then calculate the rise time of the voltage step shown in figure 10.2b given that the oscilloscope timebase when this display was obtained was set to 1 μs/div. and the $\times$ 5 condition had been applied.

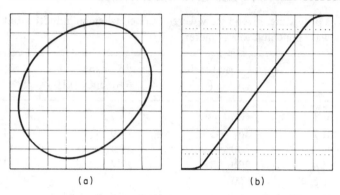

(a)   (b)

Figure 10.2.

10.3 NULL OR COMPARISON MEASUREMENTS

1. A d.c. potentiometer is used to compare the voltage drop across an unknown resistance with that across a 1000 Ω ± 0.01% resistor. Given that the following readings were taken at the same temperature, calculate a value for the unknown and a tolerance in ohms on the measured value.

	Forward current	Reversed current
Voltage across 1 kΩ resistor (V)	0.9325	0.9400
Voltage across unknown resistor (V)	1.5672	1.5678

Assume a tolerance of ± 0.2 mV on each potentiometer reading.

2. Discuss the use of the potentiometric principle in pen recorders and indicate the types of application appropriate to the various forms (flat-bed, circular, etc.) of recorder.

An *X-Y* recorder has a specified slewing speed of 1.8 m/s and equal *X* and *Y* maximum velocities. If its maximum *Y* acceleration from rest is 40 m/s² determine the peak amplitudes possible for the display of 3 Hz and 8 Hz waveforms.

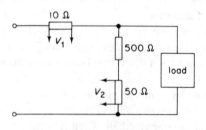

Figure 10.3.

3. For the circuit in figure 10.3 determine the magnitudes of the impedance components and the power dissipated in the load. V_1 and V_2 were measured at 50 Hz by an a.c. potentiometer as $1.15 - j0.34$ V and $1.63 + j0.175$ V respectively.

4. Show how the multi-range commercially available Wheatstone bridge has developed from the basic circuit; also comment on modifications necessary to the basic circuit for the satisfactory measurement of resistances having values of less than one ohm.

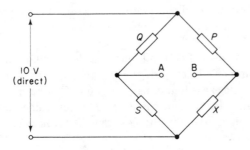

Figure 10.4.

A Wheatstone bridge as depicted by figure 10.4 has resistance arms of $X = 615\ \Omega$; $P = 1010\ \Omega$ and $Q = 975\ \Omega$; find the value for S that will give a balance. Assuming P, Q and S then remain constant, find the open circuit voltage between A and B when X is increased by 5%.

5. Comment on the advantages of the Kelvin double bridge for the measurement of low value resistances.

Show that the balance equation for the bridge circuit in figure 10.5 is

$$X = \frac{Q}{M} S + \frac{mr}{m + q + r}\left(\frac{Q}{M} - \frac{q}{m}\right)$$

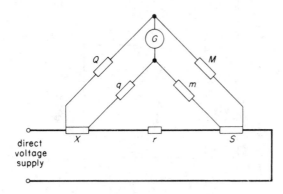

Figure 10.5.

and explain why in practice this expression is usually simplified to $X = QS/M$.

In operating this bridge, balance was obtained with $Q = q = 1025\ \Omega$, $S = 0.010\ \Omega$, $r = 0.001\ \Omega$, $M = 1000\ \Omega$ and, by accident, $m = 100\ \Omega$. If the operator used the simplified expression for X, determine the percentage error in his result.

6. Briefly describe two methods that are used for the measurement of high resistances at zero frequency.

A 100 V direct voltage supply is connected across a series combination of a 1 MΩ and an unknown resistance. If the voltage across the known resistor was measured as 542 mV with a digital voltmeter that has an input resistance of 10 MΩ, calculate the magnitude of the unknown resistance.

7. Discuss the advantages of two and four-variable arm unbalanced bridges over a single variable arm unbalanced bridge.

A Wheatstone bridge has four arms each of 600 Ω at balance. If two diametrically opposite arms are both increased by 30 Ω, determine the output resistance and the open circuit voltage if the bridge is supplied from a 15 V source of negligible internal resistance.

Comment on the above values compared with those obtained from a two-variable arm arrangement in which one arm is increased by 30 Ω while an adjacent arm is decreased by 30 Ω.

8. Explain why a double-ratio transformer bridge may be used to measure the characteristics of any two or three terminal network.

Determine the series components of an unknown impedance if the displayed values for bridge balance were 5.32 mS and −2.67 nF at a frequency of 5 kHz.

9. For the bridge circuit in figure 10.6 show that, provided $R \gg 2z$

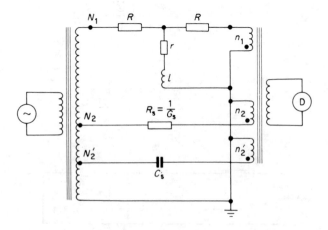

Figure 10.6.

$$\dot{z} = r + j\omega\ell = \frac{R^2}{N_1 n_1}(N_2 n_2 G_s + j\omega N_2' n_2' C_s)$$

If, for this arrangement, at a frequency of 2 kHz, balance is obtained when: $R = 1000 \ \Omega \pm 0.02\%$, $C_s = 532.0 \ \text{nF} \pm 0.02\%$, $G_s = 73.60 \ \mu\text{S} \pm 0.05\%$, $N_2/N_1 = N_2'/N_1 = 0.1$ and $n_2/n_1 = n_2'/n_1 = 0.01$, each of the ratios having an uncertainty of less than ± 1 part in 10^5, determine
(a) the magnitudes of r and l
(b) the uncertainties in each of these quantities
(c) the Q of the unknown inductor at the measurement frequency.

10. Explain the difference in principle between the simple ratio and the double-ratio transformer bridges shown in figures 10.7a and b respectively, and deduce the balance equation for the determination of C_x from each circuit.

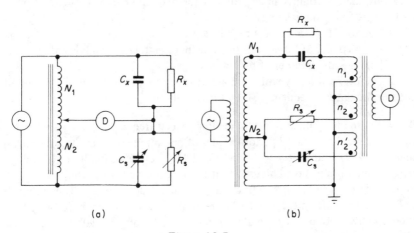

(a)   (b)

Figure 10.7.

An unknown capacitor was measured by each of these methods. The results and the details of the components of the bridges were as follows.
Simple transformer bridge
    Unknown capacitor (C_x): 135.60 nF
    Leakage resistance (R_x): 95.30 kΩ
    Measurement frequency: 10 kHz $\pm 0.01\%$
    Tolerances: ratio of transformer ± 1 part in 10^4
        standard capacitor (C_s): $\pm 0.02\%$
        standard resistor (R_s): $\pm 0.05\%$
Double-ratio transformer bridge
    Unknown capacitor (C_x): 135.70 nF
    Leakage resistance (R_x): 95.20 kΩ
    Measurement frequency: 10 kHz $\pm 0.01\%$

Tolerances: ratios of voltage and current transformers
$\pm$ 5 parts in 10^5
standard capacitor (C_s): $\pm 0.05\%$
standard resistor (R_s): $\pm 0.07\%$

Assuming that in each case the determination errors could be neglected, postulate magnitudes and tolerances for the unknown capacitor and its leakage resistance.

10.4 DIGITAL INSTRUMENTS

1. Discuss briefly the advantages and disadvantages of using a counter-timer to measure frequencies in the 2 to 9 kHz band: (a) by frequency measurement; and (b) by multi-period measurement. Given that the timebase oscillator in a counter-timer is known to have an uncertainty in value of less than 5 p.p.m., evaluate the total possible uncertainty in determining the magnitude of a frequency from each of the following readings

(i)   07.3560 kHz (using a 10 s time interval)
(ii) 135.943 μs for 1000 periods (assume that the trigger error is less than $0.3/n$, where n is the number of periods averaged).

Describe a method by which a counter-timer could be used to determine the drift in the output frequency of a 4 kHz oscillator.

2. Sketch the total uncertainty in reading against frequency characteristics for the 'frequency' and 'multi-period' modes of operation for a counter-timer. A six-digit (999999) counter-timer which has a 1 MHz reference oscillator (stability better than 9 p.p.m.) is to be used to measure a sinewave frequency of approximately 11 kHz. In the frequency mode of operation gate time intervals of 1 ms, 10 ms, 100 ms, 1 s and 10 s are available while in the multi-period mode, where 1 count = 1 μs, and n values of 1, 10, 10^2, . . ., 10^6 are possible. Determine the measurement method and range that will result in a minimum of uncertainty in the measurement of the unknown frequency. Assume that the reading determination error = 1 ℓ.s.d., an eight-digit calculator is available, and for a sinewave the trigger error = $0.3\%/n$. Briefly describe a method of checking that the sensitivity of a counter timer is within its specification.

3. Describe in outline the dual-slope conversion technique used in digital voltmeters and comment on the ability of this technique to provide rejection of supply frequency interference.

A dual-slope $3\frac{1}{2}$-digit voltmeter has an accuracy specification on its 20 mV range of $\pm$ (0.05% of reading + 0.05% of range) at 23 °C, a temperature allowance of $\pm$ (0.01% of reading + 5 μV) per °C and a d.c. common-mode rejection ratio of 120 dB. Calculate the total possible uncertainty in reading the voltage drop across R_1 in figure 10.8 at 20 °C, given that R_1 = 1 kΩ, R_2 = 10 MΩ and V_s = 100 V.

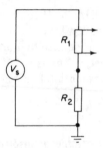

Figure 10.8.

Describe briefly how the C.M.R.R. specification of a digital voltmeter could be checked and why a different value would be obtained if the unbalance resistor were changed from the Lo to the Hi input terminal.

4. (a) The 2 kΩ resistance range of a $5\frac{1}{2}$-digit (199999) multimeter has the following specification

$\pm$ (0.008% of input + 0.001% of range) at $18\,^\circ$C $\pm$ (0.001% of input + 0.0003% of range) per $^\circ$C

If a reading of the value of a resistor at $22\,^\circ$C was 1353.52 Ω calculate the tolerance, in ohms, that is present in this measurement.

(b) The same resistor was remeasured at $22\,^\circ$C by comparing V_x, the voltage across it, with V_s, the voltage across a standard resistor which had a value of 1000.01 $\Omega \pm$ 0.005 Ω at $22\,^\circ$C. The voltage readings for one direction of current were

$$V_x = 1.5561 \text{ V} \quad \text{and} \quad V_s = 1.1495 \text{ V}$$

while for the reverse current direction values of

$$V_x = 1.5565 \text{ V} \quad \text{and} \quad V_s = 1.1496 \text{ V}$$

were obtained. Calculate the value of the resistance and its tolerance in ohms as measured by this method if the uncertainty in each voltage reading is $\pm$ 0.1 mV.
(c) By combining the results of the above measurements postulate a realistic value and tolerance for the resistor.

5. Draw accuracy curves for the frequency and multi-period methods of measurement over the frequency range 10 Hz to 10 MHz, for a 6 month old counter-timer that has the specification given below. Hence determine which bands of frequency should be measured by each method to obtain the least uncertainty in reading. Assume trigger error to be $\pm$ (0.3/n)%.
Extract from specification of counter-timer
    Display: 6 digit
    Gate times: 100 μs to 10 s in decade steps
    Divider, n: 1 to 10^5 in decade steps

Timebase: frequency—5 MHz (1 MHz output); accuracy—determined at any given time by the deviation from the initial setting caused by ageing and environmental effects as defined by the specified stability; stability/ ambient temperature effect, ± 3 parts in 10^6 between 20 and 40°C; ageing, ± 1 part in 10^6 per month (after 3 months).

10.5 TRANSDUCERS

1. The output signal from a potentiometric displacement transducer is to be recorded using a fluid damped galvanometer in a u.v. recorder. The transducer, which has an output resistance that may be varied from 0 to 1000 Ω, is supplied with direct current from a 20 mA constant current source. If the galvanometer has a terminal resistance of 26 Ω, a sensitivity of 90 μA/mm and requires a damping resistance of between 50 Ω and 2 kΩ for operation at 0.64 of critical damping, calculate the value of resistance that must be placed in series with the galvanometer so that the maximum deflection is limited to 50 mm. Assuming that the constant current source has an infinite output impedance draw a graph relating displacement as a percentage of that possible at the transducer with deflection of the recorder trace.

How could the linearity be improved?

2. Show how resistance strain gauges may be incorporated in transducers to measure force, acceleration, pressure, temperature and humidity.

Discuss the use of unbalanced bridges in such devices and describe suitable methods of recording steady state and transient changes in the measurand.

Four strain gauges each having a resistance of 125 Ω are connected to form a Wheatstone bridge, so that adjacent arms have a resistance change of opposite sense (that is, increase and decrease). If this resistance change has a maximum value of 5 Ω, calculate the peak open circuit output voltage from the bridge when it is supplied from a 10 V direct source of negligible internal resistance.

If two galvanometers A and B are available for measuring the strain gauge bridge output, determine which should be used to obtain the largest deflection given that galvanometer A has a sensitivity of 10 μA/mm and terminal resistance of 500 Ω, and that galvanometer B has a sensitivity of 15 μA/mm and terminal resistance of 200 Ω.

3. Explain why initial balancing circuits are necessary when using strain gauges in bridge circuits.

A recorder galvanometer with the specification given below is to be used to measure the output from the strain gauge bridge arrangement shown in figure 10.9. Find

(a) The value of R_p that provides the galvanometer with the damping resistance for optimum performance.

(b) The peak open circuit value of V_{out} which, if the bridge were connected to

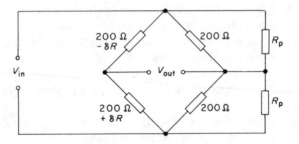

Figure 10.9.

the galvanometer, would cause a 50 mm deflection of the trace.

(c) The magnitude of V_{in} that is required to produce this 50 mm deflection, if δR has a maximum value of 2 Ω.

(d) The peak-to-peak trace amplitudes that would be obtained at frequencies of 85 Hz and 170 Hz.

Galvanometer specification

   Sensitivity: 1.2 $\mu A/mm$
   Terminal resistance: 20 Ω
   Damping resistance (for 0.64 of critical damping): 180 Ω
   Resonant frequency: 150 Hz

4. Outline the basic operational details of the various types of capacitance transducer and indicate how these devices may be arranged to measure displacement, pressure and temperature.

A particular capacitance transducer may be varied in value from 10 pF to 100 pF. Determine the ratio required on an ideal ratio transformer so that a variable capacitor, which has a residual capacitance of 98 pF and a dial calibrated from 0 to 1000 pF, may be used to evaluate the transducer capacitance value.

Derive any expressions used and find the value of the transducer capacitance when the dial setting is 450 pF. How could the impurities in either the transducer or the measuring capacitor be compensated?

10.6 SIGNAL CONDITIONING

1. Draw a four-decade Kelvin–Varley divider with the switch positions set so that the output voltage is 0.5463 of the input voltage. Assuming that the output is connected to a high resistance instrument, calculate the resistance values of the components in each decade if the input resistance of the Kelvin–Varley divider is 200 kΩ.

2. Explain the meaning of the term 'burden' when applied to instrument transformers.

A 5 VA, 11000/110 V, 50 Hz voltage transformer is to be used with a digital panel meter to monitor the 11 kV line voltage. Devise a suitable scaling and matching circuit to interface the voltage transformer to the panel meter which has for an alternating input, a resistance of 100 kΩ and a full scale of 19.99 V (neglect the output impedance of the V.T.).

3. Define the terms 'current error' ('ratio error') and 'phase displacement' as applied to a current transformer.

   Explain why the secondary winding of a current transformer should not be open circuited while the primary is carrying current.

   A current transformer has a phase displacement of +20' and ratio error of −4% at its rated burden of 15 VA. If the voltage across the secondary terminal is 2.37 + j1.84 V, calculate the current (referred to the same reference) in the primary winding. The rated transformation ratio of the C.T. is 25/5 A.

4. Discuss the use and properties of the following forms of voltage divider:
(a) resistance chain
(b) inductive divider (ratio transformer)
(c) capacitive divider.

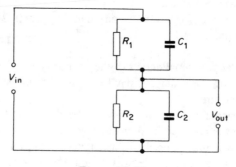

Figure 10.10.

   For a resistance–capacitance divider of the type shown in figure 10.10 show that

$$\frac{V_{out}}{V_{in}} = \frac{R_2}{R_1 + R_2} \quad \text{provided} \quad R_1 C_1 = R_2 C_2$$

   A voltage divider of this type has a ratio of 10:1 and a d.c. input resistance of 1 MΩ. Determine the magnitudes of all the components if the 3 dB point for each of the sections occurs at 0.5 MHz. Comment on the advantages of this form of divider over the others referred to in this question.

5. Show why it is not practical to match via a π or T resistive attenuator a 20 W, 600 Ω oscillator to a 0.5 W, 50 Ω load. Calculate the component values of an L attenuator suitable for matching such a source and load.

6. Comment on the advantages of connecting a signal to a c.r.o. via a passive probe.

An R–C passive probe provides a 10:1 signal reduction when used with an oscilloscope that has an input impedance of 20 pF in parallel with a 1 MΩ resistance. Given that the connection between the probe and the oscilloscope is 1 m long and has a capacitance of 2.5 pF per 100 mm, calculate the approximate values of the components in the probe that give correct compensation.

If the environmental capacitance effects can be neglected, what is the effective input impedance of the oscilloscope and probe combination?

What is the fastest signal rise time that can be measured in a system consisting of the above probe, oscilloscope and a signal source that has an output imped-ance of a 100 Ω resistance shunted by a 10 pF capacitor?

10.7 INTERFERENCE

1. A resistor has at zero frequency a value of 5000 Ω. If its self-inductance is 20 μH and its self-capacitance 0.1 pF, determine its effective resistance at 159.15 kHz
(a) as it is
(b) if a capacitance is added to make its phase angle zero and
(c) if its total self-capacitance is made 5 pF.

2. At 2 kHz an air-cored inductor has an effective resistance of 2.1 Ω and an effective inductance of 9 mH. If its self-capacitance is 10 pF, what are its effective resistance and inductance at 500 kHz?

3. By using a Q meter the following sets of readings were obtained for a mica capacitor

(a) With a 1 mH standard inductor (self-capacitance 10 pF)

	Calibrated capacitor (pF)	Q value	Frequency (kHz)
Standard inductor and	500	172	223
Standard inductor, unknown and	381	168	223

(b) With a 0.2 μH standard inductor (self-capacitance 9 pF)

	Calibrated capacitor (pF)	Q value	Frequency (MHz)
Standard inductor and	500	128	15.2
Standard inductor, unknown and	376	117	15.2

Calculate the value of the unknown capacitor and its leakage resistance for each set of readings. Explain the difference in the values obtained.

4. Explain the difference between electrostatic and electromagnetic interference and describe how the effects of each may be reduced.

Show by means of diagrams how a source which has one side earthed should be connected to an instrument which has terminals labelled 'high', 'low' and 'earth'.

Explain why a guarded instrument has a higher common mode rejection capability than a floating instrument.

5. Calculate the direct voltage common mode rejection ratio for an instrument in which a common mode voltage of 100 V produces an error in reading of 5 mV.

6. A digital voltmeter is specified as having a direct common mode rejection ratio of 140 dB with a source unbalance of 1 kΩ.

Calculate the possible error introduced into the measurement of a signal that is at a direct common mode voltage of 100 V if the source has an unbalance of (a) 1 kΩ, (b) 600 Ω, and (c) 10 kΩ.

7. A digital voltmeter was used to measure the voltage across a resistor which was simultaneously supplied with a direct voltage of 100 mV and an alternating voltage of 0.707 V r.m.s. Varying the frequency of the alternating voltage gave the following readings

Frequency (Hz)	Reading (mV)
43	102.3
47	101.5
50	100.2
53	101.6
57	102.5

Plot a curve of normal mode rejection ratio against frequency for the digital voltmeter used.

8. List the causes of normal mode interference and describe the techniques that may be used to reduce its effect in measurement circuits.

Given below is an extract from the specification of a digital multi-function meter. Determine the total percentage uncertainty in a direct voltage reading of 123.5 mV measured across a 1 kΩ resistor in the presence of a common mode direct voltage of 20 V and a 50 Hz normal mode voltage of 0.707 V r.m.s. at 27 °C.

Extract from specification
  Display: $3\frac{1}{2}$ digit (1999 max.)
  Ranges: 200 mV, 2 V, 20 V, 200 V
  Accuracy: 18 to 23 °C ± (0.05% of input + 1 ℓ.s.d.)
  Temperature effect: ± (0.005% of input + 0.001% of range + 25 μV) per°C
  Direct voltage common mode rejection ratio: 90 dB (1 kΩ unbalance)
  Alternating voltage normal mode rejection ratio: 60 dB at 50 Hz (1 kΩ
    unbalance)

9. Explain the differences between a 'floating' and a 'guarded' instrument and comment on the necessity for the latter type of instrument.

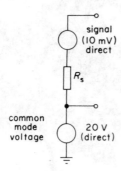

Figure 10.11.

If the circuit in figure 10.11 is considered as a source with a 1 kΩ unbalance, show how (a) a floating instrument and (b) a guarded instrument should be connected to it.

Determine the possible errors, due to common mode voltage, for the two instruments if the direct voltage voltage common mode rejections are 100 dB and 120 dB respectively.

Finally, explain why a common mode voltage may be considered as appearing to an instrument as a series mode signal.

10.8 SELECTION

1. In order that amplitude and phase measurements may be performed, describe in outline suitable instruments and measurement techniques which may be used to obtain permanent records of waveforms for *each* of the following separate situations.
(a) Two signals each of approximately 1 V peak and 0.1 Hz.
(b) Six signals that have amplitudes between 1 and 10 V r.m.s. and are at a frequency of 100 Hz.
(c) Three signals, each at a frequency of 5 kHz, and an amplitude of approximately 2 V r.m.s.

Figure 10.12. Digital multimeters: (a) AVO Model DA116 (courtesy of AVO Ltd), (b) Keithley Model 169 (courtesy of Keithley Instruments Ltd)

(d) The effect of an impact and the resulting vibration at a single point on a simple structure.

2. An oscillographic recorder has a specification that is summarised below. Assuming that a wide range of equipment is available (for example, as in well-equipped teaching laboratories), describe a series of tests that should be conducted, on receipt of such a recorder, to establish that it conforms to the manufacturer's specification.

Extracts from the specification of an ink-writing oscillographic recorder

    Number of channels: two

    Chart description: 50 mm wide per channel (50 div. full scale)

    Chart speeds: 1, 5, 25, 125 mm/s

    Chart speed accuracy: ± 0.05%

    Zero: adjustable by ± 30 divisions either side of chart centre

    Ranges: 1, 2, 5, 10, 20, 50, 100, 200, 500 μV/div., 1, 2, 5, 10, 20, 50, 100, 200, 500 mV/div., 1, 2, 5 V/div., with a continuously variable vernier between ranges

    Accuracy (including linearity and dead band): ± 1% of full scale, ± 0.2% of reading

    Input resistance: 1 MΩ (minimum)

    Common mode rejection: 150 dB d.c. and 140 dB at 50 Hz with 1 kΩ source unbalance

    Maximum allowable common mode voltage: 200 V d.c. peak

    Frequency response: −3 dB for 50 division deflection at 50 Hz

    Rise time: 7.5 ms (10 to 90% of full scale deflection)

3. Using the data sheet details given below, draw up a comparison table and brief so that you can recommend the purchase of ten of one of the digital multimeters (see figure 10.12) as an instrument suitable for service/installation technicians of process control equipment.

Specification: Keithley Instruments Ltd Model 169

D.C. Voltage

Range	Resolution	Accuracy (1 year)
200 mV	100 μV	
2 V	1 mV	
20 V	10 mV	± (0.25% of reading + 1 digit)
200 V	100 mV	
1000 V	1 V	

Maximum allowable input: 1000 V d.c., 1400 V peak a.c.
Input resistance: 10 MΩ
Normal mode rejection ratio: > 50 dB at 50 Hz, 60 Hz
Common mode rejection ratio: > 100 dB at d.c. 50 Hz, and 60 Hz (1 kΩ
   unbalance, 500 V)

A.C. Voltage

| Range | Resolution | Accuracy (1 year) 18–28 °C | |
		45 Hz–1 kHz	1 kHz–5 kHz
200 mV	100 μV		
2 V	1 mV		
20 V	10 mV	± (0.75% rdg + 5 digits)	± (5% rdg + 7 digits)
200 V	100 mV		
1000 V	1 V		

Maximum allowable input: 1000 V r.m.s., 1400 V peak, 10^6 V Hz contin-
   uous except 200 mV range: 350 V continuous, 15 s max above 350 V
Input impedance: 10 MΩ shunted by < 100 pF
Response: average responding, calibrated in r.m.s. of a sinewave

Resistance

Range	Resolution	Accuracy (1 year) 18–28 °C	Full scale voltage
200 Ω	100 mΩ	± (0.3% rdg + 3d)	< 0.5 V
2 kΩ	1 Ω	± (0.2% rdg + 1d)	< 0.5 V
20 kΩ	10 Ω	± (0.2% rdg + 1d)	> 0.7 V
200 kΩ	100 Ω	± (0.2% rdg + 1d)	> 0.7 V
2000 kΩ	1 kΩ	± (0.2% rdg + 1d)	> 0.7 V
20 MΩ	10 kΩ	± (2.0% rdg + 1d)	> 0.7 V

Maximum open circuit voltage: 1.5 V except 200 Ω range: 3.5 V
Maximum allowable input: 300 V d.c. or r.m.s.

D.C. Current

Range	Resolution	Accuracy (1 year) 18–28 °C	Maximum voltage burden
200 μA	100 nA		0.25 V
2 mA	1 μA		0.25 V
20 mA	10 μA	± (0.75% rdg + 1 digit)	0.25 V
200 mA	100 μA		0.3 V
2000 mA	1 mA		0.7 V

Overload protection: 2 A fuse (250 V), externally accessible

A.C. Current

Range	Resolution	Accuracy (1 year) 18-28 °C, 45 Hz-1 kHz	Maximum voltage burden
200 μA	100 nA		0.25 V r.m.s.
2 mA	1 μA		0.25 V r.m.s.
20 mA	10 μA	$\pm$ (1.5% rdg + 5 digits)	0.25 V r.m.s.
200 mA	100 μA		0.3 V r.m.s.
2000 mA	1 mA		0.7 V r.m.s.

Overload protection: 2 A fuse (250 V) externally accessible

General

Display: $3\frac{1}{2}$-digit LCD, 0.6 in. numeral height, with polarity, range and function indicators

Over-range indication: 3 least significant digits blanked

Maximum common mode voltage: 1400 V peak

Operating environment: 0 to 50 °C; < 80% RH up to 35 °C, < 70% RH from 35 to 50 °C

Storage environment: −35 to 60 °C

Temperature coefficient (0-18 °C and 28-50 °C): < 0.1 × applicable accuracy specification per °C

Power: six 1.5 V 'C' cells

Battery life: 1000 h typical with carbon–zinc cells, 2000 h with alkaline cells

Battery indicator: display indicates 'BAT' when < 5% of life remains

Dimensions, weight: 85 mm high × 235 mm wide × 275 mm deep; net weight 1.4 kg

Accessories available: 1691 general purpose test lead set; 1699 spare parts kit to maintain ten 169s for one year; 1600 high voltage probe; 1651 50 A shunt; 1681 clip-on test lead set; 1682 r.f. probe; 1683 universal test lead kit; 1684 hard shell carrying case; 1685 clamp-on current probe

Price (1979): £99 excluding VAT

Specification: AVO Ltd Model DA116

Ranges

d.c. and a.c. voltage: 200 mV, 2 V, 20 V, 200 V, 1000 V

d.c. and a.c. current: 200 μA, 2 mA, 20 mA, 200 mA, 2000 mA, 10 A

resistance: 200 Ω, 2 kΩ, 20 kΩ, 200 kΩ, 2000 kΩ, 20 MΩ

High-speed ohms: 2 kΩ

Junction test: 0–2000 mV at nominal test current of 0.5 mA

Accuracy (20 °C)

d.c. voltage ranges 200 mV, 2 V: ± 0.2% of reading ± 1 digit; other ranges ± 0.5% of reading ± 1 digit

a.c. voltage ranges 200 mV: ± 1% of reading ± 4 digits; other ranges ± 1% of reading ± 2 digits

d.c. current ranges: ± 1% of reading ± 1 digit

a.c. current ranges: ± 3% of reading ± 4 digits

resistance ranges 20 MΩ, high-speed ohms: ± 3% of reading ± 1 digit; other ranges ± 1% of reading ± 1 digit

temperature effect: d.c. ranges ± 0.03%/°C; a.c. ranges ± 0.05%/°C; resistance ranges ± 0.05%/°C

frequency effect: for operation at frequencies other than 50 Hz or 60 Hz an additional error of ± 1% of reading must be allowed between 40 Hz and 5 kHz (200 V range and below)

Input Characteristics

voltage ranges: 10 MΩ in shunt with not more than 100 pF

current ranges: voltage drop of 200 mV nominal for full range, plus the voltage drop across the fuse

resistance ranges: 150 mV nominal voltage on 200 Ω range, 1.5 V–3 V nominal voltage on other ranges

Temperature Range

0 to 40 °C

Long-term Stability

Not normally expected to require recalibration over extended periods. Good stability is assured in the design and only two adjustments are provided for internal references. For critical requirements confirmation of accuracy is recommended annually.

Input Overload Ratings

a.c. and d.c. voltage ranges: 200 mV 2 V·500 V r.m.s. or d.c.; other ranges 1500 V peak or d.c.

a.c. and d.c. current ranges: 10 A range not protected; other ranges 2 A (250 V) fuse protected

resistance ranges: 350 V peak or d.c.

junction test range: 250 V a.c. r.m.s.

Series Mode Noise Rejection

Greater than 40 dB at 50 Hz and 60 Hz

Display

$3\frac{1}{2}$-digit liquid crystal display, autopolarity. Over-range and battery low
indications. Characters 13 mm high

Batteries

type: four 1.5 V cells, IEC R14, 'C' size (SP11, HP11, 214, 114C, U11MJ);
batteries not supplied with instrument
life: 500 h approx.

Fuse

20 × 5 mm ceramic cartridge
2 A 250 V. IEC 127/1

Dimensions

instrument only: 185 × 147 × 87 mm
with protective cover: 185 × 150 × 106 mm

Weight

1.0 kg (approx.)

Accessories

Supplied with instrument: Lead, prods and insulated clips, instruction
booklet, Top cover with lead compartment, Battery divider, Key to
remove fuse, Two spare fuses

Accessories

Available at extra cost: Multi-range current transformer (Part No.) 6330-
259, 30 kV d.c. probe 6310-525, r.f. probe 6310-531, lightweight lead
set, (max. 50 V) 6320-134, carrying case—ever-ready leather 6320-136

Price (1979)

£106.90

10.9 SYSTEMS

1. Describe a measurement system that could be used to investigate and record
the relevant parameters during the 2 s following the connection of a 400 V supply
to a 10 kVA, three-phase, 400/50 V, star–delta transformer. Your solution should
contain a list of the parameters it is desirable to measure, a diagram of the
proposed system and brief notes on the relevance and operation of each of the

component parts. (Assume that the star point connection may be made by external connections.)

2. Describe and explain, with the aid of a schematic diagram, the technique used in *one* form of automatic digital impedance (L.C.R.) meter currently available.

Discuss the benefits (to an employer) of such instruments relative to the manually operated bridge techniques they supersede.

3. (a) Explain, with the aid of diagrams, the function of the IEC BUS.
(b) Describe the operation of a data logging system produced by using such a bus to interconnect suitable equipment.
(c) Comment on the versatility of the bus interconnected system compared with a traditional purely hardware data logging system.

4. By using data sheets of currently available equipment write a report in the form of a recommendation to a senior executive on *one* of the following topics. (*Note:* The report should include an analysis of the cost of purchase and operation, your reasoning for the selection of particular instruments and an analysis of the accuracy and reliability of the results that it will produce.)
(a) Devise an instrumentation/recording system to monitor the vibration and stresses in the chassis of a lorry when it is driven over rough ground at 65 km/h.
(b) Devise an automated test and record system to quality check audio amplifiers on a production line. The amplifier specification is
  Voltage gain: 40 dB
  3 dB bandwidth: 0 to 100 kHz
  Supply voltage: -12 V, 0, $+12$ V
  Output current: 3 A continuous; 4 A maximum
(c) Devise an instrumentation system to record over an extended period (at least 1 year) the variables associated with and within a small tidal river at a point approximately 0.5 km from the shore line. Assume that a single phase 240 V power supply and suitable buildings to house equipment are available 25 m from the river bank. For one possible solution see figure 10.13!

10.10 ANSWERS

10.10.1 Principles

3. 1243.96 Ω ± 0.283 Ω or ±0.023%.   **4.** ± 227.3 Ω, ± 0.05(01)%.   **5.** 4.0 nF ± 0.32%.   **6.** 13.19(5) Ω ± 0.120 Ω or ± 0.90(5)%.   **7.** 1.999 V ± 0.1%, 1.000 V ± 0.15%, 0.500 V ± 0.25%, 0.200 V ± 0.55%, 0.100 V ± 1.05%.   **8.** 5000 Ω.
9. 10.24 V.   **10.** 531.9 Ω, 488.5 Ω.   **11.** 1.154, -4%.   **12.** 5 V, 8 V, 5.43 V.

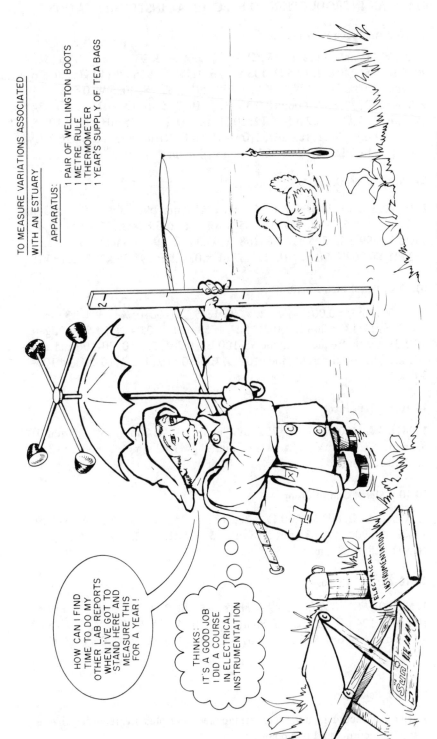

Figure 10.13. An anonymously suggested solution to the problem 4(c) of section 10.9.

10.10.2 Analogue Instruments

1. 3.769 Ω, 299.25 kΩ, 14.25 kΩ.   **2**.)2.06%.   **3**. 23.4 mm.   **4**. 157 Ω, 9016 Ω.   **5**. 2404 Ω, 17.5 Ω, 133 Ω.   **6**. 1.546 Ω, 965 Ω, 147.9(5) divisions. **7**. 295 W, 293.3 W, 3.5 W, 2 W, 291.5 W, 291.4 W.   **8**. 2026 W, 0.585. **9**. 0.4463 Ω, 12.42 A, 606 μH, 0.404 Ω.   **10**. 385 pF, 1.9 MΩ.   **11**. 25.34 mH, 6.67 pF, 21.7 Ω, 25.02 mH.   **12**. 100.8 mH, 51 Ω; 101.5 mH, 68 Ω; 101.5 mH, 79 Ω; 102 mH, 96 Ω; 102 mH, 210 Ω; 100 mH, ferrite core.   **13**. 226.7 mV, 2.5 kHz; 414.5 Ω, 49.9 nF.   **14**. 72° 36′, 0.96 μs.

10.10.3 Null Methods

1. 1674.23 Ω ± 0.74 Ω.   **2**. 67.5 mm pk, 15.8 mm pk.   **3**. 171.5 Ω, 323 mH, 1.41 W.   **4**. 593.69 Ω, 115 mV.   **5**. + 8%.   **6**. 166.8 MΩ.   **7**. 614.6 Ω, 366 mV; 599.6 Ω, 375 mV   **8**. 188 Ω, 94.3 μH.   **9**. 73.6 mΩ ± 0.092%; 532 μH ± 0.062%; 90.8.   **10**. 135.63 nF ± 0.012 nF; 95.26 kΩ ± 0.018 kΩ.

10.10.4 Digital Instruments

1. ± 0.00186%, ± 0.00154%.   **2**. ± 0.00181%, ± 0.00105%.   **3**. ± 1.33% **4**. 0.2064 Ω, 1353.848 Ω ± 0.2115 Ω, 1353.68 Ω ± 0.047 Ω.   **5**. See figure 4.12. Hence by frequency mode 35–100 Hz, 0.3–1, 2.2–10, 30–100 and above 300 kHz; by multi-period mode 10–35, 100–300 Hz, 1–2.2, 10–30 and 100– 300 kHz.

10.10.5 Transducers

1. 3418.4 Ω; 100%, 50 mm; 75%, 39.7 mm; 50%, 28.2 mm; 25%, 15 mm; 10%, 6.3 mm.   **2**. 400 mV pk, A gives 64 mm, B gives 82 mm.   **3**. 800 Ω; 12 mV; 2.4 V; 100.7 mm, 67.6 mm.   **4**. 10, 45 pF.

10.10.6 Signal Conditioning

1. 20 kΩ, 4 kΩ, 800 Ω, 160 Ω.   **2**. 2.18 kΩ, 243 Ω.   **3**. 26.04 A $\angle$37° 29′. **4**. 100 kΩ, 900 kΩ, 0.35 pF, 3.18 pF.   **5**. 575 Ω, 55 Ω.   **6**. 9 MΩ, 5 pF; 10 MΩ, 4.5 pF; 3.2 ns.

10.10.7 Interferences

1. 5000.019 Ω, 5000.08 Ω, 4997.88 Ω.   **2**. 168.2 Ω, 80.5 mH.   **3**. 119 pF, 10.1 MΩ; 124 pF, 28 kΩ.   **5**. 86 dB.   **6**. 10 μV, 6 μV, 100 μV.   **7**. −53 dB, −56.5 dB, −74 dB, −55.9 dB, −52 dB.   **8**. ± 1.56%.   **9**. 200 μV, 20 μV.

10.10.8 Selection

1. Two pen recorders, u.v. recorder, tape recorder plus u.v. recorder, digital transient recorder and pen recorder.

Appendix I

UNITS, SYMBOLS AND CONVERSION FACTORS

The international system of units (Système International d'Unités – SI) has been established by international agreement to provide a logical and interconnected framework for all measurements in science and industry. It is based on six units: the metre (length), the second (time), the kilogram (mass), the ampere (electric current), the kelvin (temperature) and the candela (luminous intensity). The majority of the world's population already use the SI system of units and it is possible that by 1985 the only major countries who have not changed will be Canada and the U.S.A.

In addition to the defining of the six basic units the SI establishes a set of factors that should be applied to all quantities so that their magnitude may always be written with less than four numerals before the decimal point, thus removing some of the difficulties associated with manipulating very large and very small numbers (see table A.1). Table A.2 lists the units in the SI system.

Table A.1 Multiples

Prefix	Symbol	Factor by which the unit is to be multiplied
tera	T	10^{12}
giga	G	10^{9}
mega	M	10^{6}
kilo	k	10^{3}
milli	m	10^{-3}
micro	μ	10^{-6}
nano	n	10^{-9}
pico	p	10^{-12}
femto	f	10^{-15}
atto	a	10^{-18}

Table A.2. Units

Quantity	SI Units	Standard – definition	Equivalents Imperial	Equivalents M.K.S.	Conversion factor
Mass	kilogram (kg)	mass of a platinum-iridium cylinder kept at Sèvres, France	pound (lb)	(kg)	1 lb = 0.454 kg 1 cwt = 50.8 kg 1 ton = 1016 kg
Length	metre (m)	distance between two engraved lines on a platinum-iridium bar kept at Sèvres, France – also as 1 650 763.73 wavelengths in vacuo of the orange line (spectroscopic designation $2 p_{10} 5 d_5$) emitted by the krypton-86 atom	foot (ft)	(m)	1 in = 0.0254 m 1 ft = 0.3048 m 1 yd = 0.9144 m 1 mile = 1.61 km
Time	second (s)	the fraction 1/31 556 925.975 of the tropical year for 1900 Jan. 0. Also as the interval occupied by 9 192 631 770 cycles of the radiation corresponding to the transition between the two hyperfine levels of the ground state of caesium 133	(s)	(s)	
Temperature (absolute)	kelvin (K)	the degree interval on the thermodynamic scale on which the temperature of the triple point of water is 273.16 K	degree fahrenheit (°F)	degree centigrade (°C)	
(interval)	Celsius (°C)	temperature difference in degrees Celsius ($\equiv$ Centigrade) is the same as in Kelvins	(°F)	(°C)	1 °F = 5/9 °C
(scale)	Celsius (°C)	temperature scale in degrees Celsius is the scale value in Kelvin minus 273.15	(°F)	(°C)	0 °C = 273.15 K

Quantity	SI unit	Definition	Other units	Conversions
Electric current	ampere	the current that if flowing in two infinitely long parallel wires spaced 1 m apart in vacuo, would produce a force of 2×10^{-7} N per metre of length between the wires	A	
Force	newton (N) $N = kg\ m/s^2$ $N = J/m$	that force which, when acting on a mass of 1 kg gives it an acceleration of $1\ m/s^2$	pound (lbf) kilogram (kgf)	1 kgf = 9.8066 N 1 lbf = 4.4482 N
Work, energy, quantity of heat	joule (J) $J = N\ m$ $J = W\ s$	the work done by a force of 1 N when its point of application is moved through a distance of 1 m in the direction of the force. This unit is used for every kind of energy including heat	ft lbf m kgf	1 ft lbf = 1.3558 J 1 m kgf = 9.8066 J 1 eV $= 1.6021 \times 10^{-19}$ J 1 cal = 4.1868 J 1 Btu = 1055.06 J
Power	watt (W) $W = J/s = N\ m/s$	1 J/s	watt (W)	1 hp = 745.7 W
Electric charge	coulomb (C) $C = A\ s$	the quantity of electricity transported in 1 s by a current of 1 A	coulomb (C)	
Electric potential	volt (V) $V = W/A$	the difference of potential between two points of a conducting wire which carries a constant current of 1 A when the power dissipated between these two points is 1 W, or 1 J/s	volt (V)	
Electric capacitance	farad (F) $F = A\ s/V$ $F = C/V$	a capacitance is 1 F if a difference of potential of 1 V appears between the plates of a capacitor when it is charged with 1 C of electricity	farad (F)	

Table A.2 (cont.)

Quantity	SI Units	Standard – definition	Equivalents Imperial	M.K.S.	Conversion factor
Electric resistance	ohm (Ω) $\Omega = V/A$	the resistance between two points of a conductor when a constant difference of potential of 1 V applied between these two points produces a current of 1 A in the conductor. The conductor must not be the source of any electro-motive force at that time	ohm (Ω)		
Magnetic flux	weber (Wb) $Wb = Vs$	the flux which, when linking a circuit of one turn, and being reduced to zero at a uniform rate in one second produces in the circuit an electromotive force of 1 V	weber (Wb)		
Magnetic flux density	tesla (T) $T = Wb/m^2$	Magnetic flux per square metre		Wb/m^2	$1 \text{ gauss} = 10^{-4} \text{ T}$
Electric inductance	henry (H) $H = Vs/A$ $H = Wb/A$	the henry is the inductance of a closed circuit in which an electro-motive force of 1 V is produced when the electric current in the circuit varies uniformly at the rate of 1 A/s		henry (H)	
Electric conductance	siemens (S) $S = A/V$ $S = 1/\Omega$	reciprocal of resistance	mho ($\mho$)		
frequency	hertz (Hz) $Hz = 1/s$	number of complete periods of oscillation per second	cycles per second (c/s)		

For fuller details see:

1. *Symbols and Abbreviations for use in Electrical and Electronic Engineering Courses* (Institution of Electrical Engineers, London, 1979)
2. BS 1991, *Letter Symbols, Signs and Abbreviations*
3. BS 3763: 1970 *International System (SI) Units*
4. PD 5686, The Use of SI Units (British Standards Institution, London, 1972)

DYNAMIC BEHAVIOUR OF MOVING COIL SYSTEMS

a. Equation of motion; damping magnitude

It is indicated in chapter 1 that a number of factors affect the movement of the coil of an instrument, these being:

- (a) the moment of inertia J
- (b) the damping constant D
- (c) the control constant or spring stiffness C

These factors may be equated with the deflecting torque (GI) to form the equation of motion

$$J \frac{d^2\theta}{dt^2} + D \frac{d\theta}{dt} + C\theta = GI \qquad (II.1)$$

To obtain the transient solution of this equation consider the deflecting torque (GI) to be removed; the moving coil then twisted through an angle and released. The equation of motion then becomes:

$$J \frac{d^2\theta}{dt^2} + D \frac{d\theta}{dt} + C\theta = 0 \qquad (II.2)$$

This equation is satisfied by a solution of the form

$$\theta = k_1 e^{\lambda t} \qquad (II.3)$$

differentiating equation II.3 gives

$$\frac{d\theta}{dt} = k_1 \lambda e^{\lambda t} \quad \text{and} \quad \frac{d^2\theta}{dt^2} = k_1 \lambda^2 e^{\lambda t}$$

Substituting in equation (II.2) gives

$$J\lambda^2 e^{\lambda t} + D\lambda e^{\lambda t} + C e^{\lambda t} = 0 \qquad (II.4)$$

or $\qquad J\lambda^2 + D\lambda + C = 0 \qquad (II.5)$

if λ_1 and λ_2 are the two roots of this equation

$$\lambda_1 = \frac{-D + (D^2 - 4CJ)^{\frac{1}{2}}}{2J}$$

and $\quad \lambda_2 = \dfrac{-D - (D^2 - 4CJ)^{\frac{1}{2}}}{2J}$

As two arbitary constants are required in the solution of a second order differential equation, the complete solution of (II.2) is

$$\theta = Ae^{\lambda_1 t} + Be^{\lambda_2 t} \tag{II.6}$$

where A and B are the arbitary constants, the values of which may be obtained from the conditions of motion.

It is necessary to consider three cases:

(1) *Overdamped*

$D^2 > 4CJ$ — the roots are real and unequal, the solution taking the form of the sum of two quantities both of which diminish exponentially.

that is $\quad \theta = \dfrac{\theta_0}{\lambda_2 - \lambda_1} \left\{ \lambda_2 e^{\lambda_1 t} - \lambda_1 e^{\lambda_2 t} \right\} \tag{II.7}$

being the curve (*a*) in figure A.1.

(2) *Critically damped*

$D^2 = 4CJ$ — the roots being equal and real. The curve (*b*) in figure A.1 is computed from the equation

$$\theta = \theta_0 \cdot \left(1 + \frac{D}{2J} \times t \right) e^{\lambda t} \tag{II.8}$$

(where $\lambda = -D/2J$). This is a special case, being termed critical damping, and is the condition in which an instrument coil will change from one position to another in a minimum of time without overshoot.

(3) *Underdamped*

$D^2 < 4CJ$ — the roots becoming conjugate — complex

$$\lambda_1 = -\alpha + j\omega \quad \text{and} \quad \lambda_2 = -\alpha - j\omega$$

$$\alpha = \frac{D}{2J} \quad \text{and} \quad \omega = \left(\frac{C}{J} - \alpha^2 \right)^{\frac{1}{2}}$$

Substituting these values of λ_1 and λ_2 in II.6 gives

$$\theta = e^{-\alpha t} \left\{ A e^{j\omega t} + B e^{-j\omega t} \right\}$$

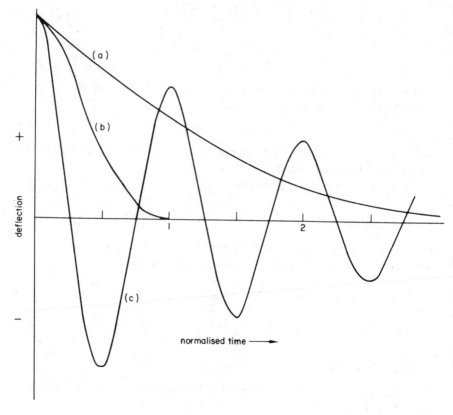

(a)

(b)

(c)

deflection

+

−

1

2

normalised time ⟶

Figure A.1. Dynamic behaviour of a moving coil instrument

Since $e^{\pm j\omega t}$ is complex and θ must be real as it represents a physical quantity, it follows that A and B must be complex.

Let $A = a + jb$ and $B = c + jd$, then if $e^{\pm j\omega t} = \cos \omega t \pm j \sin \omega t$

$$\theta = e^{-\alpha t} \left\{ (a + jb) \left[\cos \omega t + j \sin \omega t \right] + (c + d) \left[\cos \omega t - j \sin \omega t \right] \right\}$$

and since the imaginary part must be zero for all values of t

$$(b + d) \cos \omega t + (a - c) \sin \omega t = 0$$

now $a = c$ and $b = -d$ hence A and B must be complex conjugates. The real part of θ which remains is

$$\theta = 2e^{-\alpha t} (c \cos \omega t + d \sin \omega t) \tag{II.9}$$

which may be expressed as a single trigonometric function as

$$\theta = U e^{-\alpha t} \sin (\omega t + \phi)$$

where $U = 2(c^2 + d^2)^{\frac{1}{2}}$ and $\phi = \tan^{-1} \dfrac{c}{d}$

Showing that the transient is a damped sinusoid, of angular frequency

$$\omega = \left[\frac{C}{J} - \left(\frac{D}{2J} \right)^2 \right]^{\frac{1}{2}}$$

as shown by curve (c) in figure A.1.

If the instrument coil has only a small amount of damping so that $D^2/4J^2$ may be neglected in comparison with C/J

$$\omega_0 = \left(\frac{C}{J} \right)^{\frac{1}{2}} \qquad (\text{II}.10)$$

giving the natural frequency of oscillation of the instrument coil as

$$f_0 = \frac{1}{2\pi} \left(\frac{C}{J} \right)^{\frac{1}{2}} \qquad (\text{II}.11)$$

b. Deflection amplitude of vibration galvanometer

The vibration galvanometer (see chapter 2) has a narrow air cored coil of low inertia, and a stiff suspension (large control constant). If the current in such a coil is $i = I_m \sin \omega t$ the equation of motion is

$$J \frac{d^2\theta}{dt^2} + D \frac{d\theta}{dt} + C\theta = GI_m \sin \omega t \qquad (\text{II}.12)$$

In this case the transient solution is not of practical importance but the steady state solution will be and is obtained from the particular integral which is of the form

$$\theta = A \sin (\omega t - \phi) \qquad (\text{II}.13)$$

where A and ϕ are constants.

Now $\qquad \dfrac{d\theta}{dt} = A\omega \cos (\omega t - \phi) \qquad (\text{II}.14)$

and $\qquad \dfrac{d^2\theta}{dt^2} = -A\omega^2 \sin (\omega t - \phi) \qquad (\text{II}.15)$

Substituting (II.13, II.14 and II.15) in II.12 gives

$$-AJ\omega^2 \sin (\omega t - \phi) + A D\omega \cos (\omega t - \phi) + AC \sin (\omega t - \phi) = GI_m \sin \omega t$$

$$(\text{II}.16)$$

This expression must be true for all values of t and when $\omega t = \phi$

$$A D\omega = GI_m \sin \phi \qquad (\text{II}.17)$$

and when $(\omega t - \phi) = \pi/2$

$$-AJ\omega^2 + AC = GI_m \cos \phi \qquad \text{(II.18)}$$

As the phase angle ϕ is of no practical significance — the amplitude of movement being the important quality when considering a vibration galvanometer, ϕ may be eliminated by squaring and adding equations II.17 and II.18.
Hence

$$A^2 D^2 \omega^2 + A^2 (C - J\omega^2)^2 = G^2 I_m^2$$

or
$$A = \frac{GI_m}{[D^2 \omega^2 + (C - J\omega^2)^2]^{\frac{1}{2}}} \qquad \text{(II.19)}$$

A being the amplitude of the oscillation resulting from the application to the coil of an alternating current having a peak value of I_m.

Now for a given frequency ω, amplitude will be a maximum if $\omega = (C/J)^{\frac{1}{2}}$ which is also the angular frequency of undamped oscillation of the moving coil (equation II.11). Thus a vibration galvanometer should be 'tuned' so that the frequency of its undamped oscillations is equal to the system frequency, the amplitude of oscillations for other frequencies being calculated using equation II.19.

c. Amplitude and phase distortion of a u.v. recorder galvanometer

Consider a current $I_m \sin \omega t$ applied to a recorder galvanometer. Since the construction of a recorder galvanometer (see page 86) is similar to that of a vibration galvanometer in that it has low inertia, is air cored, and has a moderately stiff suspension the amplitude of vibrations will be described by the equation II.19, namely

$$A = \frac{GI_m}{[D^2 \omega^2 + (C - J\omega^2)^2]^{\frac{1}{2}}}$$

Now an 'ideal' recorder galvanometer would have zero damping and inertia effects, that is it would respond exactly to any current variations whatever the frequency. In such a case the amplitude A_i (ideal) would be GI_m/C (for $D = 0$ and $J = 0$). Now in the u.v. recorder, resonance effects and troubles due to transients are reduced by damping of the galvanometer. Critical damping would lead to a certain amount of distortion but by using less than critical damping an optimum of performance may be obtained (see chapter 2).

If a damping (d) is used such that $d = \zeta D$ [D being critical damping $= (4CJ)^{\frac{1}{2}}$]

The amplitude A_a (actual) $= \dfrac{GI_m}{[d^2 \omega^2 + (C - J\omega^2)^2]^{\frac{1}{2}}}$ \qquad \text{(II.20)}

$$= \frac{GI_m}{(\zeta^2 D^2 \omega^2 + C^2 - 2J\omega^2 + J^2 \omega^4)^{\frac{1}{2}}}$$

now $\qquad D = (4CJ)^{\frac{1}{2}}; \quad$ and $\quad \dfrac{J}{C} = \dfrac{1}{\omega_0^2}$

$$A_a = \frac{GI_m}{C\left(\zeta^2 \, 4 \dfrac{\omega^2}{\omega_0^2} + 1 - 2\dfrac{\omega^2}{\omega_0^2} + \dfrac{\omega^4}{\omega_0^4}\right)^{\frac{1}{2}}}$$

putting $\omega_r = \omega/\omega_0$

$$A_a = \frac{GI_m}{C(1 - 2\omega_r^2 + \omega_r^2 + 4\zeta^2 \omega_r^2)^{\frac{1}{2}}}$$

or $\qquad A_a = \dfrac{GI_m}{C\,[(1 - \omega_r^2)^2 + (2\zeta\omega_r)^2\,]^{\frac{1}{2}}} \qquad$ (II.21)

$\therefore$ Relative amplitude of A_a to A_i is

$$\frac{A_a}{A_i} = \frac{1}{[(1 - \omega_r^2)^2 + (2\zeta\omega_r)^2\,]^{\frac{1}{2}}} \qquad (II.22)$$

Now $\omega_r = \omega/\omega_0 = f/f_0 = f_r$ the ratio of the frequency of the signal to the resonant frequency of the galvanometer.

$$\therefore \quad \frac{A_a}{A_i} = \frac{1}{[(1 - f_r^2)^2 + (2\zeta f_r)^2\,]^{\frac{1}{2}}} \qquad (II.23)$$

To estimate the amplitude distortion in any recorded wave it is necessary to calculate A_a/A_i for the fundamental and for each harmonic.

To assess the possible phase distortion of harmonics or the time displacement error between channels using different galvanometers it is necessary to reconsider equations II.17 and II.18 from which:

$$\tan \phi = \frac{G \cdot I_m \, \sin \phi}{G \cdot I_m \, \cos \phi}$$

$$= \frac{A \, d\omega}{AC - AJ\omega^2}$$

$$= \frac{\zeta \, (4CJ)^{\frac{1}{2}} \, \omega}{C - J\omega^2}$$

$$= \frac{2\zeta\omega}{\left(\dfrac{C}{J}\right)^{\frac{1}{2}} - \left(\dfrac{J}{C}\right)^{\frac{1}{2}} \omega} = \frac{2\zeta}{\dfrac{\omega_0}{\omega} - \dfrac{\omega}{\omega_0}}$$

$$\therefore \quad \tan \phi = \frac{2\zeta}{\dfrac{1}{f_r} - f_r} = \frac{2\zeta f_r}{1 - f_r^2} \qquad (II.24)$$

Note. This expression gives the phase displacement of the recorded frequency with respect to its true position, *measured on its own time scale* of angular frequency. To estimate the distortion produced in a recorded wave it is necessary to calculate the phase displacement of the fundamental and each harmonic, and to allow for the different angular frequency scales of the various harmonics. For example a 25° displacement of a 5th harmonic on its own time scale represents 5° displacement on the angular frequency scale of the fundamental or vice versa.

For further analytical work see:

E. Frank, *Electrical Measurement Analysis* (McGraw-Hill, New York, 1959)

EQUATIONS TO DETERMINE THE COMPONENTS OF A RESISTIVE 'T' ATTENUATOR PAD

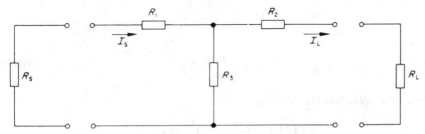

Figure A.2. Resistive attenuator pad

Consider the resistive attenuator pad shown in figure A.2 for which

$$\frac{I_s}{I_L} = \frac{R_3 + R_2 + R_L}{R_3} = K \qquad \text{(III.1)}$$

For correct matching (see p. 39)

$$R_s = R_1 + \frac{R_3 (R_2 + R_L)}{R_2 + R_3 + R_L} \qquad \text{(III.2)}$$

and

$$R_L = R_2 + \frac{R_3 (R_1 + R_s)}{R_1 + R_3 + R_s} \qquad \text{(III.3)}$$

From equation III.1

$$\frac{R_2 + R_L}{R_3} = K - 1$$

or

$$R_2 + R_L = R_3 (K - 1) \qquad \text{(III.4)}$$

now from equations III.1 and III.2

$$R_1 + \frac{(R_2 + R_L)}{K} = R_s \qquad \text{(III.5)}$$

Substituting equation III.4 in III.5 gives:

$$R_1 + \frac{R_3 (K - 1)}{K} = R_s$$

or
$$R_1 = \frac{R_3 (1 - K)}{K} + R_s \tag{III.6}$$

Now substituting equations III.4 and III.6 in III.3 gives:

$$2R_L = R_3 \left\{ (K - 1) + \frac{R_3 \left(\dfrac{1}{K} - 1 \right) + 2R_s}{R_3 \left(\dfrac{1}{K} - 1 \right) + 2R_s + R_3} \right\}$$

or
$$R_L = \frac{K^2 R_3 R_s}{R_3 + 2K R_s}$$

and
$$R_3 = \frac{2K R_s R_L}{K^2 R_s - R_L} \tag{III.7}$$

Now from equations III.1 and 6.12

$$k = \left(\frac{P_s}{P_L} \right)^{\frac{1}{2}} = \left(\frac{I_s^2 R_s}{I_L^2 R_L} \right)^{\frac{1}{2}} = K \left(\frac{R_s}{R_L} \right)^{\frac{1}{2}}$$

or
$$K = \frac{k (R_L R_s)^{\frac{1}{2}}}{R_s} \tag{III.8}$$

Substituting equation III.8 in III.7 gives

$$R_3 = \frac{2k (R_s R_L)^{\frac{1}{2}}}{k^2 - 1} \tag{III.9}$$

Substituting equations III.8 and III.9 in III.4 gives

$$R_2 = R_L \left[\frac{k^2 + 1}{k^2 - 1} \right] - \frac{2k (R_s R_L)^{\frac{1}{2}}}{k^2 - 1} \tag{III.10}$$

and substituting equations III.8 and III.9 in III.6 gives

$$R_1 = R_s \left[\frac{k^2 + 1}{k^2 - 1} \right] - \frac{2k (R_s R_L)^{\frac{1}{2}}}{k^2 - 1} \tag{III.11}$$

Note. $k = (P_s/P_L)^{\frac{1}{2}}$; and attenuation, $A = 10 \log_{10} (P_s/P_L)$ dB

Hence $k = 10^{A/20}$ or $e^{0.11513A}$ where A is in dB.

accelerometer 235
acceptable values 24
accuracy 22
accuracy class 34
acquisition of data 385
active filters 306
active voltage probe 314
actuating mechanisms 239
addressing (instruments) 393
admittance, measurement of 177
ageing of equipment 27
air flow measurement 253
air vane damping 55, 97
airborne data recorder 134, 140
alternate mode 122
alternating current, measurement of, by
    c.r.o. 124
            by multimeter 65, 213
alternating current bridges 166
alternating current carrier system 247
alternating current potentiometer 155
alternating current to d.c. converter 73, 74,
    106, 327
alternating current transformer 290
alternating voltage, measurement 66, 71,
    213, 377
ammeter 61, 66, 69, 99, 104
ampere 35, 427
amplifier, configurations 78
        gain 320
        galvanometer 56
        screening 345
        signal processing 319 ff.
        strain gauge 247
        vertical 119
amplitude, deflection error 89
        recorder galvanometer 87
analogue, display 17
        instruments 2, 54 ff.
        signal processing 319
        system 380

analogue to digital conversion 205
analysers, data 228
analysis, of attenuators 437
        of errors 25
        of moving coil instrument 4, 430
        of specifications 363
AND gate 11
AND network 191
anemometer, hot wire 253
angular deflection 2, 53
angular measurement 266
apparent inductance 108
apparent strain 245
approximation errors 26
architecture 217, 388
asynchronous counter 187
attenuated feedback 321
attenuators 294 ff.
        analysis of 437
atto 425
autocorrelation function 230
automated instrumentation system 5
automatic calibration 218
autotransformer 174, 281

band diagram 23
band pass filter 306
bandwidth 303
        of instrument 48
best buy 378
bias 46
binary bit 9
binary coding 9, 14
binary to decimal 189
bistable 14, 187
bistable storage 130
bit rate 10
Boolean algebra 11
bridge, a.c. 166 ff.
        d.c. 7, 156 ff.
        double ratio transformer 174 ff.

bridge, (*cont.*)
    output   161, 164
    strain gauge   246
    Wheatstone   8, 156, 161
British Calibration Service   36
Brownian movement   334
burden   285, 292
bus connected system   387

cable capacitance   310
calculation errors   26
calibration   36, 96
calibration systems   396
calibrator   37, 122
cameras   123
capacitance   427
    effective   339·
    measurement, by Q meter   111
        by Schering bridge   167
        by transformer bridge   173, 178
capacitive divider   279
capacitive transducer   255
capacitor, compressed gas   347
    frequency characteristics of   340
    high voltage   347
    properties   338
capacitor voltage transformer   283
carrier frequency   136, 247
cascade voltage transformer   283
cathode ray oscilloscope   115 ff.
cathode ray tube   21, 115
Celsius   426
central processing unit (CPU)   15
charge, electric   427
charge amplifier   322
chopped mode   122
circular chart recorder   151
classification, of current transformers   293
    of instruments   18, 34
    of transducers   237
    of voltage transformers   286
clock spring suspension   54
closed loop system   383
codes, digital   14, 189, 318
common mode rejection   351, *see also*
  sample specifications
comparators   175
comparison (null) methods   5, 146
compensated wattmeter   102
compensating thermocouple   269
compensation, of lead resistance   248
    of strain gauge   245
component impurities   334 ff.
    measurements of   108, 177, 221
computer controlled system   15, 385
computing amplifier   324
conductance   176
conducting shield   50

connection errors   27
connections, screened   341 ff.
constructional errors   26
control torque   2, 54
controller   15, 388
conventional true value   25
conversion, A to D   205
    D to A   329
coordinate potentiometer   155
correlator   229
coulomb   427
counters, digital   186 ff.
coupled interference   49, 341
crest factor   45, 213
critical damping   5, 87
cross-correlation function   229
cross talk   348
current error (ratio error)   291
current measurement, by c.r.o.   124
    by d.c. potentiometer   148
    by digital multimeter   377
    by electrodynamometer   99
    by electronic multimeter   69
    by moving coil multimeter   60
current probe   315
current shunts   40, 287
current transformer   66, 290

D to A converter   329
damping   4, 55, 86, 97, 235
damping resistance   92
damping torque   4, 86
data analysers   228
data bus   389
data logger   384, 396
data transmission   9, 316, 384, 394
dead resistance   242
decade resistance box, errors   30 ff.
deflection plates   117
deflection torque   2, 54, 97
demodulator   316
dependent functions   328
De Sauty bridge   167
detectors, null a.c.   59, 167
    d.c.   56
        phase sensitive   59
determination error   26
deviation, standard   33
dielectric loss   335
differential amplifier   320
differentiator   303, 324
diffraction (optical) grating   273
digital counter   186 ff.
    displays   20
    encoder   273
    filter   307
    instruments   2, 8, 186 ff.
    multimeter   210 ff.

digital counter (*cont.*)
    recorders 224
    systems 384
    tape recording 142
    techniques 8, 74
    transducers 272
    wattmeter 224
direct acting galvanometer 56
    multimeter 66
    recorder 76
direct current transformer 293
direct recording 136
displacement transducers 240
display, choice 22
    digital 20
    distortion 91, 120, 142, 305
    divider (decade) 193, 277 ff.
    methods 16
    multiple trace 122
    stored 20
    X–Y 120, 125
drift 143
drivenguard 357
dropouts 137
dual beam oscilloscope 122
dual slope d.v.m. 209
dummy strain gauge 245
dynamic behaviour, of moving coil system
    5, 430
dynamic skew 143
dynamometer *see* electrodynamometer

earphones 167
earth connections 341
earth loop 333
eddy current damping 4, 54
effective capacitance 339
effective inductance 338
effective range 18
effective resistance 336
electric capacitance 427
electric charge 427
electric current 427
electric potential 427
electrodynamometer 97
electromagnetic damping 86, 92
electromagnetic interference 50, 348
electromagnetic transducer 265
electrometer valve 70, 160
electron gun 117, 122
electronic galvanometer 56
electronic instruments 107
electronic multimeter 69
electronic pen recorder 78
electronic signal conditioning 94
electrostatic instruments 107
electrostatic interference 49, 341

electrostatic stylus 80
encoder, digital 273
energy 427
energy meters 113
environmental errors 26
environmental interference 49, 331
equalisation 135
equation of motion 4, 430
equivalent circuit capacitance 339
equivalent circuit resistance 336
errors, analysis of 25 ff.
    correction (wattmeter) 99
    current (ratio) 291
    digital multimeter 34, 363 ff.
    linearity 77
    phase 88
    pointer instruments 34
    random 32
    timing 143
    voltage ratio 285
expansion coefficient 331

farad 35
Faraday cage 346
femto 425
fibre optic 132
fiducial value 18
filter 299 ff.
firmware 16
five terminal resistance measurement 215
fixed reference transducer 234
flat bed recorder 153
flip-flop 14
floating instruments 351
fluid damped galvanometer 92
fluid damping 86
flutter 143
flyback 117
foil strain gauge 244
force 427
force measurement 251
form factor 44
four-terminal resistance measurement 215
frequency characteristics, of capacitor 340
    of insulating materials 335
    of multimeters 375
    of recorder galvanometers 87
    of strain gauges 244
    of transducers 236
frequency effects 335
frequency equalisation 135
frequency measurement, by counter 196,
    203
    by c.r.o. 125
frequency-modulated recording 137
frequency selective detector 167
frequency standard 426
front gap 134

functional amplifiers 323
functional programs 218

gain, amplifier 320
galvanic voltages 333
galvanometer 56 ff.
galvanometer matching 93
gas discharge (display) 21
gauge factor 243
gaussian distribution 32
giga 425
graphical instruments 19
grid lines 83
guard circuits 356
guard ring 347
guarded instruments 343, 356

handshake 388
hardware 15
harmonics 47
heads, record and reproduce 134
heated stylus recorder 80
Heaviside bridge 167
henry 428
hertz 428
hexadecimal code 14
high pass filter 301
high resistance measurement 159
high voltage capacitor 347
high voltage current transformer 283
histogram 33
hot wire ammeter 104
hot wire anemometer 253
humidity gauge 254
hybrid instruments 2, 221

ideal rectifier 72
ideal transformer 281
IEC bus 155, 388
impedance, effects of
    input 27, 37
    measurement of 156
    Thévenin 162
impedance matching 39
impurities, component 334
'in situ' measurement 180
inductance, effective 338
    indicated 110
    measurement of, by a.c. bridge 168
        by Q meter 110
        by transformer bridge 178
inductance change transducers 258
inductive divider 280
inductor properties 110
inherent noise 334
input attenuator 298
input characteristics 37
input circuitry 194

input device 15
insertion errors 27
instrument system 379
instrumentation tape recorders 134
instruments, analogue 17, 53 ff.
    controller 15
    digital 20, 186, 366 ff.
    electronic 69
    hybrid 221
    screening 342
    selection of 1, 51, 360
integrators 304, 324
intelligent instruments 215
interconnection methods 394
interface 391
interference 49, 331
internal oscillator 192
I/O 15, 393
isolating transformer 344

joule 427

kelvin 426
Kelvin-Varley divider 277
Kelvin double bridge 26, 158
kilo 425

L attenuator 296
large scale integration (LSI) 15
LCR meter 222
lead resistance, compensation of 157, 247
lead resistance strain gauge 248
lead twisting 51
leakage resistance 332
length 426
light emitting diode 21
light spot galvanometer 57, 82
limits 219
linear display 115, 155
linear velocity transducer 265
lineariser 220, 328
liquid crystal displays 21
Lissajous' figures 126
listener 388
load cells 251
logarithmic converter 326
logic 11, 191
logic analyser 227
long scale instrument 55
loss angle 113
low impedance measurement 179
low pass filter 304
low resistance measurement 158, 172
LVDT 260

magnetic heads 140
magnetic recording 134
magnetic shield 50

magnetic tape 134
magnetostriction transducers 272
main gate 193
mass 426
mass spring transducer 235
matching impedances 39, 295
matching transformer 40
matching u.v. galvanometers 93
material standards 425
maximum power transfer 41
Maxwell bridge 167
mean value 42
measurand 2
measurement criteria 1
measurement methods 2
mega 425
memories 14
mesh storage 131
metre 425
micro 425
microprocessor 15
microstrain 242
milli 425
minicomputer 385
minimum impurity (of resistance) 336
modulator 316
Moiré pattern 273
MOSFET 71
moving coil instrument 55 ff.
moving coil recorder 76 ff.
moving iron instrument 104
multi-channel recorder 79, 82, 134, 152
multi-function d.v.m. 205
multimeter, electronic 69
        moving coil 60
multiple earths 333
multiple period measurement 197
multiple trace displays 122
multiples 425
multiplexer 140, 385
multiplication 219, 326
multiplier 326
multipoint recorder 152
multitrack heads 142

NAND 13
nano 425
national standards 35, 426
nepers 294
network characteristics 181
newton 427
noise, electrical 334
        rejection 349
nominal value 23
nonlinearity 77
nonvolatile memory 15
NOR 13
normal distribution 32

normal mode noise 349
normal mode rejection 208, 350
null detector 56
null methods 6, 146

OEM 383
offset 219
ohm 35
open loop system 381
operational amplifiers 320
operator costs 5
optical grating 273
optimum performance (galvanometer) 88
OR 12
oscilloscope 115 ff.
output characteristics 164, 361
overdamping, analysis of 4, 430
overflow 200
overshoot 90, 127
Owen bridge 167

parallax error 17
parallel data transmission 9
passive filters 299
passive probes 308
peak acceleration 235
peak responding voltmeter 73
pen recorders 76, 150 ff.
pencil galvanometers 84
period measurement 197
permanent display 20
permanising 83
phase angle measurement, by c.r.o. 124
        by u.v. recorder 97
phase angle of a resistor 337
phase displacement 285, 291
phase error 89
phase modulation 317
phase relationships 45
phosphors (c.r.t.) 121, 130
photodevelopment 83
photodiodes 264
phototransistors 264
pi (π) attenuator 296
pico 425
piezoelectric transducer 267
platinum resistance thermometer 252
playback 135
plotters, X–Y 154
pneumatic damping 4
pointer instrument 17, 34
Poisson strain 243
polarisation of dielectric 335
potentiometer, d.c. 6, 146
potentiometric recorder 150
potentiometric transducer 238
power 45
power density spectrum 232

power measurement, by a.c. potentiometer 156, *see also* wattmeter
    three phase 102
practical sampling rate 319
probes 122, 308
process temperature recording 151
processing u.v. sensitive paper 83
programmed instrumentation 5, 225, 385
programming 16
PROM 15
pulse height analysers 228
pulse modulation 138, 316
pyrometer 271

Q meter 108 ff.

RAM 15
ramp d.v.m. 206
random errors 32
range attenuators 298
raster (display) 133
rated transformation ratio 285, 291
ratio errors 285, 291
ratio measurement, frequency 203
    voltage 219, 278
ratio transformer 174
reactance, effective 336, 338
recorder amplifier configurations 78
recorder galvanometers 86 ff.
recorders, circular chart 151
    digital 224
    electronic 78
    flat bed 153
    light spot 82
    moving coil 76
    multipoint 152
    potentiometric 150
    programmable 225
    rectilinear 80
    tape 134
    temperature 151
    ultraviolet 82
recording head 134
rectifier, ideal 72
    characteristic 65
reference oscillator 192
reference voltage 7
rejection filter 183
reliability 362
reproduce head 135
resistance, attenuator 295
    chain 277
    damping 92
    dead 242
    effective 336
    four terminal 215
    high, measurement of 159

leakage 332
measurement of, by ammeter and voltmeter 29
    by d.c. potentiometer 150
    by Kelvin double bridge 158
    by multimeter 63, 71, 215, 221, 377
    by substitution 6
    by transformer bridge 174
    by Wheatstone bridge 156
resistance–capacitance divider 279
resistance change transducers 238
resistance dividers 276
resistance strain gauge 241 ff.
resistance thermometer 252
resistor impurities 336
resolution 17
resonant frequency 87, 108, 300
response characteristics 311
ribbon suspension 54
rise time 48, 127, 311
r.m.s. values 43, 74, 327
ROM 15
rotary speed 266

sag 303
sample specifications (1979), counter timer 199
    digital multimeter 210, 213, 368, 417
    driver amplifier 94
    electronic galvanometer 58
    electronic multimeter 74
    flat bed recorder 153
    LCR meter 223
    moving coil multimeter 67
    oscilloscope 128
    pen recorder 81
    recorder galvanometers 95
    transformer bridge 181
sampling of data 8, 319
sampling oscilloscope 120
sampling theory 319
saw tooth waveform 118
scales 17
scaling 37, 92, 97, 276 ff.
Schering bridge 167, 348
screen phosphors 121
screened isolating transformer 345
screening 341
second 426
Seebeck 268
segmented display 20
seismic transducer 235
selection 1, 51, 91
self-balancing bridges 183
self-capacitance 111

self-generating transducers 264
semiconductor transducers 261
sensitivity 37
serial data transmission 9
series mode noise 350
series resistance of an inductor 111, 336
shaft position encoder 274
shield 50
shunt 287
     universal 288
SI units 425
siemen 428
signal conditioning 93, 276 ff.
signal response 311
signal to noise ratio 357
simple transformer bridge 171
sinewave 42
skew 143
slewing speed 155
software 16
solid state display 20, 115
sources of error 25
specification analysis 33, 363
specifications see sample specifications
spectrum analyser 226
standard cell 7, 146
standard deviation 33
standard of temperature 252, 426
standardisation 146
standards 6, 35, 426
state analysers 228
statistical analyser 228
statistics 220
storage oscilloscope 130
strain gauge 241
     attachment of 249
     bridge 164, 245
     semiconductor 263
     transducer 250
strain sensitivity 242
strays and residuals 27
stretching (tape) 143
substitution measurements 6, 108
successive approximation d.v.m. 205
summation of errors 28
summing amplifier 323
suspension 54
sweep delay 118
symbols 13, 425
synchro 261
synchronous counter 187
system bandwidth 48
system instrumentation 379
system operation 16

T attenuator 296
tachometer 267

talker 388
tan δ (loss angle) 113
tape recorders 134
tape transport 142
temperature 426
temperature effects in strain gauges 245
temperature measurement 252, 268
temperature recorder 150
tera 425
thermal effects 331
thermal e.m.f. 332
thermistors 262
thermocouple 268
thermocouple instrument 74, 105
thermometer, platinum resistance 252
thermopile 271
Thévenin impedance 162
three dB point 302
time 426
time constant 300, 305
time interval measurement 204
time shift 89
timebase (c.r.o.) 117
timers (counters) 186 ff.
timing analyser 227
timing bus system 390
timing lines 83
tolerance 23
tooth rotor tachometer 266
toroidal core 282
torsion measurement 252
totalising 195
trace identification 83
transducers, capacitive 255
     classification of 237
     digital 273
     electromagnetic 265
     fixed reference 234
     inductive 258
     linear velocity 265
     magnetostriction 272
     mass–spring 235
     piezoelectric 266
     potentiometric 238
     resistance change 238
     resistance strain gauge 241
     seismic 235
     semiconductor 261
     thermoelectric 268
     ultrasonic 272
transfer instrument 155
transformation ratio 285, 291
transformer bridge 171
transient distortion 91
transient response 90, 301
transient solution (moving coil instrument)
    4, 430

trigger, counter 194
    c.r.o. 117
true value 23, 25
tuned amplifier detector 167
twin T network 182
twisting of leads 51
two wattmeter power measurement 103

ultrasonic transducer 272
ultraviolet recorder 82 ff.
unbalanced bridge 161
unbalanced resistor 354
unbonded strain gauge 250
uncertainty in reading 34
uncertainty (tolerance) 23, 218
underdamping 5, 431
units 425
universal shunt 61, 288

velocity transducer 265
vertical amplifier (c.r.o.) 119
vibration galvanometer 56
vibration transducer 265
visual display unit (VDU) 15, 22
volatile memory 15
volt 427
voltage divider 276
voltage measurement, by c.r.o. 124
        by d.c. potentiometer 148
        by digital voltmeter 210

by electrodynamometer 99
by electronic instrument 70
by multimeter 62, 210, 217, 371,
    377
voltage scaling 276
voltage standard 427
voltage to current converter 328
voltage to frequency converter 208, 328
voltage ratio error 291
voltage transformer 67, 282
voltmeter see voltage measurement

watt 427
wattmeter, electrodynamometer 100
        digital 224
waveform 11, 41, 47, 317, 318
weber 428
Wien bridge 167
Wheatstone bridge 8, 156, 161
work 427
wow 143
writing speed 117, 155
writing systems 79

X–Y display 120, 125
X–Y plotter 154

Y (vertical) amplifier 119

Z modulator 120